Journey To Cumorah

A Book of Mormon Commentary

Volume Three

Helaman thru Moroni

Philip M. Hudson

"I hid up in the hill Cumorah all the records which had been entrusted to me by the hand of the Lord." (Mormon 6:6).

"I will proceed to do a marvellous work among this people, even a marvellous work and a wonder: for the wisdom of their wise men shall perish, and the understanding of their prudent men shall be hid."
(Isaiah 29:14).

Copyright 2023 by Philip M. Hudson.
Published 2023.
Printed in the United States of America.
All rights reserved.

No portion of this book may be reproduced,
stored in a retrieval system, or transmitted
in any form or by any means, mechanical,
electronic, photocopy, recording, scanning,
or other, except for brief quotations in
critical reviews or articles, without
the prior written permission
of the author.

ISBN 978-1-957077-55-0

Illustrations - Google Images.
This book may be ordered from
online bookstores.

Publishing Services
by BookCrafters, Parker, Colorado.
www.bookcrafters.net

The prophet Joseph Smith "has translated the book, even that part which I have commanded him, and as your Lord and your God liveth, it is true." (D&C 17:6).

"And I saw another angel fly in the midst of heaven, having the everlasting gospel to preach unto them that dwell on the earth, and to every nation, and kindred, and tongue, and people." (Revelation 14:6).

Under the best of circumstances, both in and out of the Church, "we talk of Christ, we rejoice in Christ, we preach of Christ, we prophesy of Christ, and we write according to our prophecies, that our children may know to what source they may look for a remission of their sins." (2 Nephi 25:26).

"And if ye shall
believe in Christ ye will believe in
these words, for they are the words of
Christ, and he hath given them unto me;
and they teach all men that they should do
good. And if they are not the words of Christ,
judge ye - for Christ will show unto you, with
power and great glory, that they are his words,
at the last day; and you and I shall stand
face to face before his bar; and ye shall
know that I have been commanded
of him to write these things."
(2 Nephi 33:10-11).

"Take thee one stick,
and write upon it, for Judah, and for the
children of Israel his companions: then take
another stick, and write upon it, For Joseph,
the stick of Ephraim, and for all the house
of Israel his companions. And join them
one to another into one stick; and they
shall become one in thine hand."
(Ezekiel 37:16-17).

Table of Contents

"Scripture consists not in what we read, but in what we understand."
(St. Hilary).

Acknowledgements

Acknowledgements...1

Preface

Preface...3

Introduction

Introduction..5

The Book of Helaman
52 B.C. – 1 B.C.

Chapter 1..17
Chapter 2..21
Chapter 3..23
Chapter 4..27
Chapter 5..31
Chapter 6..35
Chapter 7..41
Chapter 8..47
Chapter 9..51
Chapter 10..55
Chapter 11..59
Chapter 12..61
Chapter 13..65
Chapter 14..69
Chapter 15..73
Chapter 16..77

Third Nephi

The Book of Nephi, The Son of Nephi, Who Was The Son of Helaman

Around 1-4 A.D. - 34-35 A.D.

Chapter 1	81
Chapter 2	85
Chapter 3	87
Chapter 4	89
Chapter 5	91
Chapter 6	95
Chapter 7	99
Chapter 8	103
Chapter 9	105
Chapter 10	107
Chapter 11	109
Chapter 12	115
Chapter 13	121
Chapter 14	125
Chapter 15	131
Chapter 16	135
Chapter 17	139
Chapter 18	141
Chapter 19	145
Chapter 20	149
Chapter 21	153
Chapter 22	155
Chapter 23	159
Chapter 24	161
Chapter 25	165
Chapter 26	169
Chapter 27	173
Chapter 28	179
Chapter 29	183
Chapter 30	185

Fourth Nephi

The Book of Nephi, Who is the Son of Nephi, One of The Disciples of Jesus Christ

About 35 A.D. – 321 A.D.

Chapter 1 189

The Book of Mormon

321-326 A.D. – 401-421 A.D.

Chapter 1 195
Chapter 2 199
Chapter 3 201
Chapter 4 203
Chapter 5 205
Chapter 6 207
Chapter 7 209
Chapter 8 211
Chapter 9 219

The Book of Ether
The record of the Jaredites, taken from the twenty-four plates found by the people of Limhi in the days of King Mosiah.
2,200 B.C. to 261 - 121 B.C.

Chapter 1	223
Chapter 2	227
Chapter 3	231
Chapter 4	237
Chapter 5	241
Chapter 6	243
Chapter 7	247
Chapter 8	249
Chapter 9	253
Chapter 10	255
Chapter 11	257
Chapter 12	259
Chapter 13	265
Chapter 14	269
Chapter 15	271

The Book of Moroni
400 A.D. - 421 A.D.

Chapter 1	273
Chapter 2	275
Chapter 3	277
Chapter 4	279
Chapter 5	281

Chapter 6..283
Chapter 7..289
Chapter 8..295
Chapter 9..299
Chapter 10..301

Observations..305

Authors Note..453

Addendum
A Sampling of Scriptures
(Helaman – Moroni)

A sampling of scriptures (Helaman – Moroni) 481

Commentary and Compendium Index

Commentary and Compendium Index 553

If
our hearts
are hardened
against The Book
of Mormon, it will be
as though our portion has
been diminished further and
further, until the point is reached
that our natural defenses against
the aggressive tactics of the Devil
crumble, and we find ourselves
left to fight our battles all
by ourselves.

Acknowledgements

The creation of my Commentary would have been impossible without stability and support on the home front. In the early years of its genesis, my children Tara, Joanna, Christopher, Patrick, Elizabeth, Kathryn, and Andrew tolerated the late hours when their sleep must have been interrupted many times by the incessant tapping on my keyboard. Later, when I was preoccupied with endless revisions, their insight and suggestions helped to define and refine the work. I will always remember the conversations we had concerning the lessons we learned from the scriptures. Often, listening to their perspective propelled me in new directions that expanded my appreciation of themes that I would have otherwise only narrowly or superficially addressed. Their example always gave me courage and the inspiration to make the study of The Book of Mormon relevant to our family's circumstances.

Throughout the process, my wife Jan has stood by my side and put up with my fixation on this project in countless ways. Without her constant support, my efforts would have fallen far short of my envisioned goal. She became the rudder of my ship, guiding me past unseen rocks and reefs. She has been my helm, holding steady when winds of adversity blew, and has been my telltale, who always alerted me to threatening squalls. She has been my keel, who helped me to move against the current and the wind, and my mainsheet, who held firm with just enough pressure to prevent me from capsizing when I was dangerously heeled over. She has been my safety-line, providing security when my footing was unsure and the foaming sea was streaming across my deck. She has been my compass, showing me the way, especially when the course was unclear, my chart, warning me of hidden dangers, and my barometer, cautioning me to take heed of impending storms. She has always been my lookout, standing as my faithful sentinel whenever I became distracted by trivial concerns. It was she who held the line that trailed in my wake, offering the promise of safety whenever I slipped and fell overboard. She has been and ever will be the wind that fills my sails. Jan and I may be partners in this great adventure, but she is my better half.

The Book
of Mormon
teaches use that
the consequences of
sin are inevitable and
inescapable, except for the
intercession by our faith in
the Atonement of Christ. The
Maker and the Fashioner of the
universe, Who is both the Author
and Administrator of The Plan
of Salvation, must intervene by
engaging laws that will restore
equilibrium, or all is lost. It
is in the heavens, after all,
that we will experience
a better spirit and a
more enduring
substance.

Preface

I have always wanted to write a Commentary on The Book of Mormon. In 1981, when the New English Language Edition of the Standard Works was published, I began to comprehensively organize my card files and correlate them with the marginal notations that I had made over the years in my copies of the scriptures. These references became the foundation of my written impressions in this Commentary.

Collating my source material was daunting, especially before the age of word processing began in earnest, with the introduction of personal computers in the early 1980s.

I have attributed quotations to original authors whenever possible, as well as when I have editorialized the thoughts expressed by others. In many cases, however, the language in my Commentary will naturally reflect the teachings of leaders in The Church of Jesus Christ of Latter-day Saints. Of course, I alone am responsible for the content of these volumes. I hope my interpretation of the teachings of The Book of Mormon will cultivate your interest to dig deeper into the themes woven into its tapestry. My only goal is to help you to expand your insights into the foundation truths, core doctrines, and eternal principles that are the celestial guideposts embedded within its verses.

Hugh Nibley observed: "Men fool themselves, when they think for a moment that they can read scripture without ever adding something to the text or omitting something from it". Therein lies the power inherent in its study. We glean insight and understanding every time we investigate the word of God. I have learned to love the scriptures, and I often think of St. Hilary, who wrote: "Scripture consists not in what we read, but in what we understand". In my Commentary, I have consistently tried to anchor to the scriptures the ideas swirling around in my head.

Utilization of a Commentary does not replace personal scripture study. The spiritual awakening that accompanies prayerful efforts to understand the mysteries of God through the study of His word cannot be achieved through another person's interpretation. Perhaps, though, my own perspectives on the eternal themes expressed within The Book of Mormon will be helpful to you as you read and seek your own guidance. It is my hope that you will use this Commentary only to assist you in your own personal journey to Christ.

Our challenge is to enlist the aid of the Holy Ghost as we process the world around us. Many years ago, Dallin Oaks said: "Latter-day Saints know that learned or authoritative commentaries can help us with scriptural interpretation, but we maintain that they must be used with caution. Commentaries are not a substitute for the scriptures any more than a good cookbook is a substitute for food. When I refer to "commentaries", I mean everything that interprets scripture, from the comprehensive book-length commentary to the brief interpretation embodied in a lesson or an article, such as this one".

"One trouble with commentaries", he continued, "is that their authors sometimes focus on only one meaning to the exclusion of others. As a result, commentaries, if not used with great care, may illuminate the author's chosen and correct meaning but close our eyes and restrict our horizons to other possible meanings. Sometimes, those other less obvious meanings can be the ones most valuable and useful to us as we seek to obtain answers to our own questions. This is why the teaching of the Holy Ghost is a better guide to scriptural interpretation than is even the best commentary".

I could not agree more heartily with these wise words of counsel from President Oaks. As a matter of fact, every time I proofed a chapter (and I did this many times) I found myself scribbling additional notes in the margins and thinking to myself, "Why didn't I see that before?". That is precisely what I hope will be the experience of everyone who takes the time to read my Commentary. I trust the process will motivate you to search the scriptures more carefully and to be instructed by the Spirit, as you do so, that you might be led in directions that will prove to be personally illuminating.

I would expect that my older grandchildren who read this Commentary will be impacted in ways that are different from my adult children or my contemporaries. I hope that my observations will touch you differently each time you read them. When I am long-gone, perhaps the considerable thought that went into its production will generate a palpable bond that will span the years separating us. Maybe, the gulf that then divides us will not be as great, and our shared energies will pave the way to an eventual joyous reunion.

Know that I have been exhilarated when I have found wisdom and great treasures of knowledge, even hidden treasures, in the scriptures. These doctrinal themes have become pearls that I might have overlooked had I taken only a cursory glance. I hope that I am planting seeds so that you might harvest greater understanding, as well.

I had the opportunity to visit the Holy Land many years ago. We stopped, too briefly, at Qumran. The Dead Sea Covenantors lived there, and in the ruins of their library, I was able to pause and reflect upon their Eleventh Hymn that had been recovered from parchments hidden within caves high above their community. The translation reads, in part: "Behold, for mine own part I have reached the intervision, and through the spirit thou hast placed within me, come to know Thee, my God". In similar fashion, Moses wrote: "But now, mine own eyes have beheld God; but not my natural, but my spiritual eyes, for my natural eyes could not have beheld; for I should have withered and died in his presence; but his glory was upon me; and I beheld his face". (Moses 1:11)

I am continually reminded of Nephi's counsel to press forward with complete dedication and steadfastness, or confidence and a firm determination in Christ, having a perfect brightness of hope, or perfect faith, and charity, or a love of God and of all men. If we do this, he promised, feasting upon the word of Christ, or receiving strength and nourishment from the scriptures, and endure to the end in righteousness, we shall have eternal life, that is the greatest gift God can bestow upon His children. (See 2 Nephi 31:20). It is with love that I extend to you the invitation to enjoy my Commentary.

Introduction

Cicero wrote: "The first law for the historian is that he shall never dare utter an untruth. The second is that he shall suppress nothing that is true. Moreover, there shall be no suspicion of partiality or of malice in his writing". The accounts in The Book of Mormon abridged by the prophet-historian Mormon were true to the mandate given by Cicero. Although, as Washington Irving brooded: "It is the rule that history fades into fable; fact becomes clouded with doubt and controversy; the inscription moulders, and columns, arches, and pyramids are but heaps of sand, and their epitaphs, nothing but characters written in the dust", yet The Book of Mormon stands as a shining example of the divine model.

The Book of Mormon "is the witness that testifies to the passing of time. It illuminates reality, vitalizes memory, provides guidance in daily life, and brings us tidings of antiquity". It is the "evidence of time, the light of truth, the life of memory, the directress of life, committed to immortality". (Cicero, "De Oratore", ii, 36). In its pages, "the centuries roll back to the ancient age of gold". (Horace, "Odes", IV, ii, 39).

Those who read The Book of Mormon undertake an incredible journey through thousands of years of history as the pages of a profound text unfold before the panorama of great civilizations. Within its pages lies the intrigue of ancient Asia, as warlords battle for supremacy, the tension in Jerusalem mounts as rival empires of the Near East struggle for power, and the faithful prepare for a journey to a land of promise beyond the horizon of their vision.

The Book of Mormon may be devoured as if it were literally the bread of life, and those who read it feast upon the word of God and feel exhilaration as prophets counsel us from the dust. We seek, and yearn, and strive, and wrestle for our blessing, realizing that "unto some it is given by the Holy Ghost to know that Jesus Christ is the Son of God, and that he was crucified for the sins of the world", while "to others it is given … the word of knowledge". (D&C 46:13 & 18).

The Book of Mormon makes the bold claim that its pages contain "the fulness of the Gospel". (D&C 42:12). Even members of The Church of Jesus Christ of Latter-day Saints sometimes misinterpret this to mean that there will be found within its pages detailed instructions regarding every doctrinal principle that governs our lives in the last days, and that the Nephite Saints participated in every ordinance of the Gospel as we know it. But it is we, and not they, who live in the Dispensation of The Fulness of Times, when the knowledge of the ages is being revealed. The Book of Mormon Saints only received "the fulness of the Gospel", in the sense that they were given instruction for their own needs, and sufficient for their own salvation.

The Title Page of The Book of Mormon is an overview of its history, and was written by the Prophet Mormon who inserted it into the last leaf of the collection of plates. (See H.C., 1:71). It was translated by Joseph Smith and moved by him to the beginning of the book. It forthrightly explains that the book was written for doubters, "to the convincing of the Jew and Gentile" that Jesus is The Christ. But it also makes the astounding acknowledgement that it might contain mistakes. This admission, however, refer to faults other than theology. Joseph Smith assured the Saints that "The Book of Mormon (is) the most correct of any book on earth, and the keystone of our religion, and a man (will) get nearer to God by abiding by its precepts, than by any other book". (H.C., 4:461).

Most evidence suggests that he and Oliver Cowdery "began their work of translation" in April 1829, beginning with The Book of Mosiah, and that during the month of May they translated to the end of The Book of Moroni. They then translated the Title Page, and finally The Small Plates of Nephi and The Words of Mormon before the end of June. The text of the Title Page was used as the book's description on the copyright form filed on June 11, 1829. (See "Encyclopedia of Mormonism", V. 1, Book of Mormon Translation by Joseph Smith, John Welch).

The translation was unlike that of any other text, inasmuch as it was accomplished "through the mercy (and) power of God". (D&C 1:29). This is as specific an explanation as is found regarding just how Joseph created an evenly flowing and coherent narrative spanning a thousand years of history, that stands revealed today without the benefit of subsequent editorial revision. During his lifetime, he tended to let the record speak for itself. With an understanding of the revelatory process, we are drawn to the book itself rather than to the specific means of translation, and without distraction we focus on the challenge left by Moroni: "And when ye shall receive these things, I would exhort you that ye would ask God, the eternal Father, in the name of Christ, if these things are not true; and if ye shall ask with a sincere heart, with real intent, having faith in Christ, he will manifest the truth of it unto you, by the power of the Holy Ghost". (Moroni 10:4, see verse 5).

Jesus Christ Himself testified of the book's historical and doctrinal accuracy. Joseph Smith "translated the book, even that part which I have commanded him, and as your Lord and your God liveth, it is true". (D&C 17:6, see D&C 19:26). For emphasis, the Savior used an ancient Hebrew oath in His witness. "Because he could swear by no greater, he sware by himself". (Hebrews 6:13).

Sometimes, those who are learning about the Restoration of the Gospel ask why the Church does not still possess the plates from which the Nephite history was translated. But as Hugh Nibley pointed out: "The presence of the plates would only prove that there are plates, and no more. It would not prove that Nephites wrote them, or that an angel brought them, or that they had been translated by the gift and power of God. A far more impressive claim is put forth when the whole work is given to the world as a divinely inspired translation". (Hugh Nibley, "An Approach to The Book of Mormon", p. 17-18).

Thus, The Book of Mormon stands on its own merits, in sharp contrast to the confusion surrounding most biblical scholarship. For example, "there are so many Greek New Testament manuscripts (over 5,000) that effective management and citation in a critical text amount to highly selective and careful genealogical classification into families, so that over 150,000 alternative readings can be grouped and profiled in a useful way. Also, the American Bible Society has counted over 24,000 differences among only six separate pre-1830 editions of the 1611 King James Version of the Bible". (FARMS Report).

No wonder that, in the Sacred Grove, Joseph Smith learned of the sects of Christendom that "they were all wrong" and that "all their creeds were an abomination". (J.S.H. 1:19). Organizations or teachings that do not lead us clearly and unambiguously toward salvation and exaltation in the Celestial Kingdom are abominable in the sight of God because they thwart the stated purpose of The Plan of Salvation, which is to guide us unerringly and bring to pass our immortality and eternal life. (See Moses 1:39). It was such confusion, in Joseph Smith's mind, that led to his Theophany and introduced the world to the Dispensation of The Fulness of Times.

Today, there is remarkable harmony within the Church regarding the dogma embedded within The Book of Mormon. Every day throughout the world, millions of Latter-day Saints open their translations of this scripture and are exposed to the same identical doctrinal themes. Contrast this unity of the faith with the thousands of denominations that interpret, with significant differences and sometimes-heated discussions, hundreds of variants of single biblical verses of scripture. It is far better that the Church proclaims that The Book of Mormon has been translated by the gift and power of God through the Prophet Joseph Smith. This leaves little room for conflicting doctrinal interpretation either within or outside the Church.

So important is The Book of Mormon, that right after its publication on March 26, 1830, the faithful met in Fayette, New York, and officially organized The Church of Jesus Christ of Latter-day Saints on April 6, 1830. Fully ten years earlier, Joseph Smith had communed with The Father and The Son in the Sacred Grove. Three years after that theophany, he received several documented visits from the Angel Moroni. Between 1823 and 1830, he became personally acquainted with all of the important characters in The Book of Mormon and enjoyed additional visits from Moroni. Still, the Church could not be organized until the Nephite scriptures that had been miraculously handed down to us were ready for publication.

Joseph Smith is listed in that first edition as the books' "author and proprietor". Thus, enemies of the Church have claimed that he wrote it, but the truth is simply that in accordance with the copyright laws of the State of New York at the time, someone had to be listed as author and proprietor of a text, and Joseph Smith was the logical choice.

In the past, paragraph two in the Introduction invited misunderstanding, because Lamanites were identified therein as the "principal" ancestors of the American Indians. (This introduction was written by Bruce R. McConkie in 1981, and was not part of the original translation of the text). Archaeological, anthropological, and genetic research suggests that the civilizations whose histories are recorded in The Book of Mormon lived in rather narrowly defined geographical areas in Meso-America. Certainly, there are many Native Americans today whose lineage may be traced to peoples other than Nephites and Lamanites who co-inhabited the Americas two thousand years ago. In any event, the 2007 change of one word in the Introduction, eliminating the word "principal" from the phrase "the principal ancestors of the American Indians…" and rendering it "among the ancestors of the American Indians…" invites a clearer understanding of the intent of the Introduction that was originally written by McConkie.

In their written testimony found at the beginning of the text, three witnesses accorded honor to the "Father, and to the Son, and to the Holy Ghost, which is one God". Better than other Christians, Latter-day Saints understand the nature of the Godhead. They recognize the individuality of each member of the Holy Trinity, while acknowledging the spiritual rapport between the Father, Son, and Holy Ghost, and between Them and true believers who enjoy a Holy Communion as they have become "one" in a spiritual sense.

Eight additional witnesses saw and handled the plates and described them as "having the appearance of gold". (See J.S.H. 1:34). We really do not know how many of the plates were actually made of gold. The 24 Gold Plates of Ether are the only ones that are identified in the text of The Book of Mormon as having been made of gold. (See Mosiah 8:9). We do know, however, that they were heavy. These witnesses "hefted" the bound plates that are estimated to have weighed in the neighborhood of 36 kilograms. The plates from which Joseph translated The Book of Mormon may have been thin sheets of gold, (see "Testimony of Joseph Smith", J.S.H., 1:34) but the text itself suggests that, in general, the Nephite prophets engraved their records on a variety of metals.

The Three Witnesses to The Book of Mormon wrote only that they had "seen the plates which contain this record" without reference to the specific composition of the metal, although they went into great detail to describe the engravings themselves and their purpose to benefit humanity. Various record-keepers referred to "plates of ore". (See

1 Nephi 19:1, Mosiah 21:27, and Mormon 8:5). When the prophets referred to a specific material, it was generally to "brass". (See 1 Nephi 3:3, 3:12, 3:24, 4:16, 4:24, 4:28, 5:10, 5:14, 5:18-19, 13:23, 19:21-22, 22:1, 22:30, 2 Nephi 4:2, 4:5, 5:12, Omni 1:14, Mosiah 1:3, 1:16, 10:16, 28:11, 28:20, Alma 37:3, 3 Nephi 1:2 & 10:17). "Plates of gold" are mentioned only in Mosiah 8:9 and 28:11, where they specifically refer to the 24 Gold Plates of Ether. Mormon, who had access to all the records and who abridged many of them, never referred to plates of gold.

His son Moroni twice referred to the plates, but only in reference to hiding them in the earth. (See Ether 15:11 & Mormon 8:4). Likewise, "Ammaron, being constrained by the Holy Ghost, did hide up the records which were sacred, yea, even all the sacred records which had been handed down from generation to generation, which were sacred". (4 Nephi 1:48-49). It may simply be that the custodians of the record were more focused on the message than on the material.

Because gold itself was much more plentiful in the Lands of The Book of Mormon, it many have not mattered to them of what material the plates were crafted. Jacob reported that his people, who still had an "Old World" mindset, had "begun to search for gold, and for silver, and for all manner of precious ores". Note that Jacob qualified as "precious" the ore his people sought. "In the which," or in these precious materials, he continued, "this land ... doth abound most plentifully". (Jacob 2:12). In the same vein, Mormon reported: "Both the Lamanites and the Nephites ... did have an exceeding plenty of gold, and of silver, and of all manner of precious metals". (Helaman 6:9). As had Jacob before him, Mormon characterized the hoarded materials as "precious metals".

We do know that the Eight Witnesses to The Book of Mormon testified that the plates they were shown and "hefted" had "the appearance of gold" and that Joseph Smith wrote in his History that Moroni told him that the book that was hidden in the Hill Cumorah was "written upon gold plates". (J.S.H. 1:34). But The Book of Mormon record itself does not corroborate Moroni's characterization of the gold composition of the plates. In the Church, however, it is commonly accepted that the records, other than The Plates of Brass, were "gold plates". Gold has always denoted value, and at the very least, the precious gift of The Book of Mormon is equivalent to the gifts of gold, frankincense, and myrrh, traditionally bestowed by the Wise Men of the East upon the Christ child in Bethlehem.

Interestingly, however, none of The Book of Mormon chroniclers describe their records as "gold plates," with the prominent exception of the Plates of Ether, that are specifically characterized as being of "pure gold". (Mosiah 8:9). Nephi's record was engraven upon "plates of ore". (1 Nephi 19:1). It was the record upon these plates that was pleasing to Mormon, and not the plates themselves. (The Words of Mormon, 1:4). As a matter of fact, when occasion arose, the various record keepers in The Book of Mormon almost pointedly described only the intrinsic quality of the plates entrusted to their care, while pointedly and characteristically ignoring the temporal value of the metals upon which the records were engraven.

The Testimony of the Prophet Joseph Smith is also interesting because his account of the initial appearance of the angel who delivered the plates is unique. (See J.S.H. 1:29-43). Joseph wrote that late one evening a light started to appear in his bedchamber and grew brighter and brighter until it was lighter than at noonday. Suddenly the Angel Moroni appeared before him, standing in the air. Clearly, Moroni came from another realm or dimension. He did not come through the door to enter the room. Rather, he just "appeared".

After he had delivered a detailed message, the light began to gather up around Moroni, and he ascended in a conduit right into heaven. This remarkable description is alien to our experience. None of us has ever seen light gather around an individual in this manner, presumably leaving the rest of the room in enveloping darkness, and none of us has ever seen such a light surround an individual who is then sucked up into the heavens as though the ceiling of the room were non-existent. The events of that evening are more remarkable when we realize that they were repeated, for emphasis, two more times.

On the following day, and in broad daylight, Moroni again appeared to Joseph in a field near his home. Once more, this resurrected being was described as being surrounded by an unearthly light that transcended the brilliance of the sun itself.

Just how important is it for us to read, understand, and apply the principles contained in this book that was heralded by this heavenly angel? Joseph Fielding Smith, Jr. stated: "No member of this Church can stand approved in the presence of God who has not seriously and carefully read The Book of Mormon". (C.R., 10/1961). The witness of the divinity of Jesus Christ gained through study of The Book of Mormon is an invaluable aid for those who desire to be valiant in the testimony of Jesus. Often, we marvel at the care with which the foundation was laid for the Restoration of the Gospel and the translation and publication of The Book of Mormon. Sometimes, however, we are guilty of carelessness in the diligence with which we actually study its pages. President Smith's statement is a reminder that we all need to sharpen our scholarship to a fine point.

Moroni's challenge, therefore, should be thoughtfully pondered. Every day, in fact, thousands put his promise to the test. When Heavenly Father placed His spirit children on the earth, he anticipated their initial ignorance of the saving principles of the Gospel. But His nurture of our spirits in the pre-earth existence had endowed each of us with a solid understanding of Gospel principles. It was only when we could learn no more in that setting, that we welcomed the opportunity to come to the earth to continue our education. (See Abraham 3:26, & Titus 1:2). We left our heavenly home with the assurance from our Father that, while on earth, we would have the Light of Christ and the influence of the Holy Ghost, and that heavenly power would help us to recognize the truth when we heard it. (See D&C 84:46, & 93:2). As Brigham Young declared: "Every Gospel principle carries within it a witness that it is true". In fact, Joseph Fielding Smith, Jr. who, like President Young, was a prophet, seer, and revelator, said that the witness of the Holy Ghost is more powerful than a vision or even the manifestation of heavenly messengers.

This concept is one of the beautiful simplicities of the Gospel. The Plan allows all of us to enjoy the same access to the simplest, and yet most powerful, witness to the truth. In an inarticulate voice softer than the faintest whisper of sweet breath on the cheek, the Holy Ghost gently testifies, or bears witness, of truth. As Moroni 10:5 teaches (in a verse that is often overlooked, in favor of the previous verse): "By the power of the Holy Ghost ye may know the truth of all things".

The Holy Ghost has revealed all that is true, and has illuminated every eternal principle that has guided the minds of men and women since the dawn of history. We constantly benefit from that which He reveals. In the Last Days, when the Spirit is "poured out upon all flesh, and when "young men see visions, and old men dream dreams", it will be the Holy Ghost Who provides the creative drive. (Joel 2:28). The irony is that many will fail to recognize the source of their inspiration. Job did not. He wrote: "For God speaketh once, yea twice, yet man perceiveth it not. In a dream, in a vision of the night, when deep sleep falleth upon men, in slumberings upon the bed; then he openeth the ears of men, and sealeth their instruction." (Job 33:14-16). We cannot help but think of the experience of Joseph Smith in his bedchamber, when we read Job's description of how Heavenly Father communicates with His children.

Of course, Jesus Christ wants us to have a testimony of the divine authenticity of The Book of Mormon. It has come to us through thousands of years of effort on the part of ancient prophets and after the personal sacrifice of countless individuals who have passed through the refiner's fire. The prophet Isaiah foresaw a "marvelous work and a wonder" that would not come to pass for another 2,700 years (Isaiah 29:14), and in the apocalyptic vision of John, another angel was seen "in the midst of heaven, having the everlasting Gospel to preach unto them that dwell on the earth, and to every nation, and kindred, and tongue, and people". (Revelation 14:6).

Precisely because The Book of Mormon is another testament, or second witness, of Jesus Christ, missionaries use it to great effect as a principal tool of conversion. The organization of the book is divinely inspired to assist Heavenly Father in His work to bring to pass our immortality and eternal life, by teaching us the principles of faith, repentance, baptism, and the ordinances of the priesthood. (See Moses 1:39).

All who desire to have a sure personal witnesses must carefully and prayerfully read The Book of Mormon, and then ask in faith if what they have studied is true. They will then receive the testimony of the Holy Ghost to motivate them to seek out the Priesthood and to enter into sacred covenants with God. It will be as it was on the Day of Pentecost, when Peter and others were preaching to a multitude whose hearts and minds were open and receptive to the truth. The words of the Apostles carried the weight of authority, and penetrated the hearts of their listeners to the end that they asked: "Men and brethren, what shall we do? Then Peter said unto them, Repent, and be baptized every one of you in the name of Jesus Christ for the remission of sins, and ye shall receive the gift of the Holy Ghost". (Acts 2:37-38). On that day, there were about 3,000 souls added to the kingdom of God on earth. (See Commentary Reference to 3 Nephi 15:21-24).

A similar scenario exists today. Since the Restoration of the Gospel, there has been a Pentecostal outpouring of the Spirit, and those with a sincere desire to understand the will of God bring the same humble petition to the doorstep of the missionaries: "Now that we have heard your message, have put it to the test of prayerful inquiry, and have received a witness of the Spirit, what shall we do?" The response of the servants of the Lord is unequivocal: "You must exercise saving faith that leads to the waters of baptism and to continuing commitment, dedicated discipleship, selfless service, and sustained spirituality".

Members of the Church believe they "must be called of God, by prophecy, and by the laying on of hands, by those who are in authority, to preach the Gospel, and to administer the ordinances thereof". (5th Article of Faith). The first ordinance of the Gospel following baptism is confirmation as a member of the Church together with the bestowal of the Holy Ghost. Even though many individuals receive their testimony of The Book of Mormon before becoming members of the Church, their expanding understanding will be further enhanced following their baptism as the Spirit unfolds to them the mysteries of the kingdom. As Joseph Smith wrote of his own experience almost two years after the organization of the Church: "By the power of the Spirit our eyes were opened and our understandings were enlightened, so as to see and understand the things of God". (D&C 76:12).

Critical to comprehension of the monumental themes contained within The Book of Mormon is familiarity with the underlying structure of the text. It is not too difficult to understand, as long as we remember that Mormon was the prophet who gathered all the records together and who then abridged certain of these into The Plates of Mormon. (See Mormon 1:1). This is the main reason why the text is called The Book of Mormon. In a larger sense, though, it is not really his book, alone.

The scope of its 531 pages is far-reaching, and its literary style was intentionally designed to focus on the core material rather than on its various authors. It is remarkable, however, that 15 major writing styles and personalities survived both abridgment and translation. The working vocabulary of 1 Nephi alone has 23% more words than comparable Old Testament sections, and although there are only 2,696 root words in the entire book, or only 10% of Shakespeare's working vocabulary, its depth is breathtaking. Sometimes, less is more.

Mormon said that he could not write "the hundredth part of the things of (his) people". (Words of Mormon 1:5, see Jacob 3:13, & Helaman 3:14). Even though Joseph Smith wrote in his history that the plates at the Hill Cumorah were deposited in the earth in a box fashioned out of stone, other sources indicate that there were many more plates in the collection at that site. (See Helaman 3:15). Brigham Young said that there was a whole room, with plates stacked high against the walls. Together, he said that they would comprise several wagon loads.

What we do have, swells in significance when we realize that the body of the records included in The Book of Mormon is a condensation of that which had been considered to be of most importance in the eyes of a long line of Nephite prophet-historians. High Nibley rightly called the book "a blueprint for survival in the Last Days". As such, it is a detailed and accurate representation of a much larger structure. He said: "The events and situations that not many years ago seemed to some as wildly improbable and greatly overdrawn, have suddenly become the story of our times, and we see and shall see the words of the prophets who speak to us from the dust fearfully and wonderfully vindicated". ("The World and The Prophets", p. 196).

Nephi only started writing 30 years after leaving Jerusalem, which might give solace to those of us who have trouble maintaining the continuity of our own personal journals. He had plenty of time, beforehand, to distill in his mind just what he would include and how he would do it. Writing from the perspective of middle age might also have been an advantage, for hindsight always seems to be 20 / 20, and maturity often gives us a mentally, emotionally, and spiritually stable perspective that is too frequently lacking in youth.

First, he abridged the writings of his father that were collectively called The Book of Lehi, and then he made his own carefully constructed record. It took Nephi 10 years just to write the first 25 chapters, possibly because he wrote in a very stylized Hebraic pattern, the first nine chapters of 1 Nephi comprising a complex chiasm. Then, in chapters 10-22 he worked out a second, parallel chiasm. Note that Chapter 9 and Chapter 22 each end with a formal "Amen", signifying the end of that distinctive Hebraic literary device.

The Small Plates of Nephi in their entirety include the First and Second Books of Nephi, the Books of Jacob, Enos, Jarom, and Omni, and the Words of Mormon. These plates were placed in the repository at Cumorah for a reason that was unclear to Mormon. The Small Plates included a duplication of The Book of Lehi, an abridgement of which was written on The Large Plates of Nephi. The reason for their preservation became obvious only when Martin Harris lost the initial 116 pages of manuscript translation, forcing Joseph Smith to turn to The Small Plates of Nephi in order to translate a parallel history of the early Nephite record to be used as a substitute for the missing and potentially corrupted text.

The Small Plates of Nephi are always called "these plates". They were translated in the first-person tense, inasmuch as they came, not from an abridgement, but directly from the record of Nephi and his descendants, up to and including Omni. The period of history covered by these plates is slightly less than half of the Nephite history, or 470 out of a total of 1,021 years.

The Words of Mormon that follows Omni is an editorial insert written by Mormon in 385 A.D. and inserted by him in the record, to bridge the gap between The Small Plates of Nephi and The Plates of Mormon (his abridgement of the balance of The Large Plates of Nephi) that follow.

The literary labor of Mormon, called The Plates of Mormon, comprises The Books of Mosiah, Alma, Helaman, Third Nephi - The Book of Nephi, Fourth Nephi - The Book of Nephi, and The Book of Mormon chapters 1-7. When reading from the translation of The Plates of Mormon, the text is generally in the third person tense, inasmuch as it is an abridgement from The Large Plates of Nephi. When Mormon inserted editorial comments throughout his abridgement, it was written in the first-person tense., often accompanied by the phrase "and thus we see." When reading 1 Nephi through Omni, "those plates" means The Large Plates of Nephi that follow The Words of Mormon in the format of The Book of Mormon. The Plates of Mormon also included writings of Mormon's son Moroni. These are found in The Book of Mormon Chapters 8 & 9, and in The Book of Moroni.

The Book of Ether is an abridgment from an ancient record that was written upon 24 gold plates found by the people of King Limhi in the days of King Mosiah. At least a portion of these plates was abridged by Moroni, either from Mosiah's earlier translation or directly from The Plates of Ether. Moroni inserted editorial comments of his own, and included this record in a general history under the title "The Book of Ether". (See Ether 1:1-2).

At great expense and personal risk, Lehi's sons retrieved The Plates of Brass from Jerusalem. They contained "the five books of Moses (or the first five books of the Old Testament), and also a record of the Jews from the beginning down to the commencement of the reign of Zedekiah, king of Judah; and also, the prophecies of the holy prophets". (1 Nephi 5:11-13). Consequently, many of the writings of the prophet Isaiah are prominently found upon The Plates of Brass.

"The version of Isaiah in the Nephite scripture hews an independent course for itself, as might be expected of a truly ancient and authentic record. It makes additions to the present text in certain places, omits material in others, transposes, makes grammatical changes, finds support at times for its unusual readings in the ancient Greek, Syriac, and Latin Versions, and at other times no support at all. In general, it presents phenomena of great interest to the student of Isaiah". (Sydney B. Sperry, "Book of Mormon Compendium", p. 512).

"The text of Isaiah in The Book of Mormon is not word for word the same as that of the King James Translation. Of 433 verses of Isaiah in the Nephite record, Joseph Smith modified 234. Some of the changes were slight, while others were radical. However, 199 verses are word for word the same as the K.J.T. We, therefore, freely admit that Joseph Smith may have used the K.J.T. when he came to the text of Isaiah on the plates. As long as the K.J.T. agreed substantially with the text on the plates, he let it pass; when it differed significantly, he translated the Nephite version and dictated the necessary changes". (Sydney B. Sperry, "Book of Mormon Compendium", p. 507-508).

As Hugh Nibley has pointed out: "Resemblances between the Bible and The Book of Mormon are not hard to explain and are confirmation of authenticity. If The Book of Mormon is what it says it is, we should expect to find within its pages a strong biblical influence. Its prophets sound like those of the Old Testament because they studied and consciously quoted the words of those prophets, and all prophets moreover are programmed to sound alike, being called for the same purpose, under much the same conditions". ("Churches in The Wilderness").

The Plates of Brass were the Nephite scriptures, and included therein was the written record of their family histories and genealogies. They were revered by the Nephites, as evidenced by frequent quotations from and references to them throughout The Book of Mormon. As Nephi explained: "And I did read many things unto them which were written in the books of Moses; but that I might more fully persuade them to believe in the Lord their Redeemer I did read unto them that which was written by the prophet Isaiah; for I did liken all scriptures unto us, that it might be for our profit and learning". (1 Nephi 1:23).

The "books of Moses" to which Nephi referred concern the Pentateuch, Torah, or The Law. These are not to be confused with The Book of Moses in The Pearl of Great Price. Nephi's books of Moses were, in fact, the principal scriptures of the Jews. From these books of The Law, there sprang up an encyclopedic interpretation by the Jews at Jerusalem called The Talmud.

Readers of The Book of Mormon will repeatedly encounter direct references to Isaiah in its text. As a matter of fact, 32% of The Book of Isaiah is quoted in The Book of Mormon, while 3% is paraphrased. Following the pattern established earlier in The Book of Mormon, in the New Testament there are more quotations attributable to Isaiah than to all other Old Testament prophets combined. It is little wonder that The Book of Mormon should rely so heavily on Isaiah, however, since his prophecies not only reflect Old World religious philosophy, but also a latter-day world view and testament of Jesus Christ.

Nephi delighted in the words of Isaiah, and recorded 2 Nephi Chapters 12-24 in an effort to prove the truth of Christ's coming, and that save He should come, we must perish. Isaiah was what we call a "Messianic Prophet" whose principal mission was to point us toward the Savior, to His teachings, and to salvation through obedience to the principles of His Gospel.

During the ministry of Isaiah, the Ten Tribes were taken captive and later fled to the north where they were swallowed up and lost to history. But they carried with them the words of Isaiah, just as Lehi did in his journey to the Promised Land. (See D&C 133:26 & 2 Nephi 29:13-14). The Jews also retained Isaiah's words, and today, Covenant Israel, or the Church, has them. His is a very diversified audience.

Nephi knew that the words of Isaiah would be as a pearl of great price in the Last Days, and to those who would suppose that they are not, he said "I (will) speak particularly, and confine the words unto mine own people; for I know that they shall be of great worth unto them in the last days; for in that day shall they understand them; wherefore, for their good have I written them". (2 Nephi 25:8). Nephi considered the writings of Isaiah, who had lived just over a century earlier, to be scripture. Clearly, he understood that whatsoever the prophets speak when moved upon by the Spirit, "shall be the will of the Lord, shall be the mind of the Lord, shall be the word of the Lord, shall be the voice of the Lord, and the power of God unto salvation". (D&C 68:4).

Today, it is the clear responsibility of members of the Church to carefully and prayerfully study the prophecies of Isaiah, for they were meant for our generation. His language might be veiled in symbolism and shadows of meaning with which we are not superficially familiar. Nevertheless, we have been commanded by the Savior Himself: "Seek ye out of the best books words of wisdom; seek learning, even by study and also by faith" (D&C 88:118) and "live by every word that proceedeth forth from the mouth of God". (D&C 84:44).

Nephi recognized Isaiah's witness of the Lord Jesus Christ as pre-eminent among the testimonies of the prophets. It should be no surprise that the Savior declared to the Nephite Saints: "And now, behold, I say unto you, that ye ought to search (his teachings). Yea, a commandment I give unto you that ye search these things diligently; for great are the words of Isaiah". (3 Nephi 23:1). The main reason for the scriptures, after all, is to persuade us to believe in Christ. This is why the prophets all seem to sound alike. They all draw upon the same eternal truths to prove their points. Theirs is not vain repetition, but rather theatrical encore. "The prophets do have much the same message, and the now recognized practice by the prophets of giving out the words of their predecessors as their own receives its first clear statement and justification in The Book of Mormon". (Hugh Nibley, "Since Cumorah", p. 40-41).

Shakespeare wrote: "The past is prologue". ("The Tempest", Act 2, scene 1, 245-254). The phrase was intended to imply that our past is merely a prologue, or an introduction, to the great adventure upon which we will embark if we follow through on our plans. This original interpretation teaches that what has come before on our journey through life doesn't matter in the grand scheme of things, because a new future lies before us, subject to the choices we will yet make. The human condition does not change much over time, which is one reason why the Lord has revealed The Book of Mormon in the Last Days, so that we might profit from the experiences of the Nephites who are distant from us in time and yet are so like us.

Hugh Nibley observed: "The tragedy of the Nephites, who brought destruction by war upon their own heads, was not what became of them, but rather what they themselves became". ("Since Cumorah", p. 425). "A man's character is his fate", wrote the Greek philosopher Heraclitus. The Nephite scriptures are a study in human frailties, and the epic drama that unfolds before our minds' eye strengthens and clarifies our moral and ethical values.

In The Book of Mormon, "we are not laying down ground rules for taste, or saying that it is good because some people like it, or bad because others do not. What we are saying is that whatever one may think of it, is one of the great realities of our time, and that what makes it so is that millions of people believe it. Its literary or artistic qualities do not enter into the discussion. It was written to be believed. It's one and only merit is truth. Without that merit, it is all that non-believers say it is. With it, it is all that believers say it is". (Hugh Nibley, "Of All Things", p. 93). With this historical perspective, an abiding testimony in the divinity of the work, and an anticipation of enlightenment throughout the journey, let us commit and re-commit ourselves to a lifetime study of this keystone text.

Whenever our holy
vestments have become soiled by
the stains of sin, without repentance,
our spiritual death will forever alienate
us from heaven. The Book of Mormon
anticipated that mortality would be
a preparatory state, to permit us to
embrace the behavioral lifestyle
of the Saints of God, that we
might, in a coming day,
return to His presence
with our garments
washed clean and
without spot.

Sooner or later, every member of the Church will encounter a line drawn in the sand. Those who have the faith to endure unto the end, and to embrace The Book of Mormon as they conduct their lives in harmony with the principles of The Plan, "the same shall be saved." (Matthew 24:13).

The Book of Helaman
52 B.C. - 1 B.C.

Helaman
Chapter 1

The Book of Helaman is much smaller than The Book of Alma, with one-quarter as many pages and chapters. Its brevity gives the impression that events are speeding up, when actually they are not. Each book takes about half of the century preceding Christ's birth. Alma spans 90 B.C. - 51 B.C., and Helaman 52 B.C. - 1 B.C.

The Book of Helaman is mainly a historical text, and Mormon had quite an array of records from which to select the material for his abridgment. It contains narratives, discourses, communion with God, prophecies, prayers, commentaries, and editorial reflections.

We do not know why Mormon condensed his abridgment of Helaman so much more than that of Alma, but in doing so he created an interesting effect, compressing the last half-century before the Savior's birth into just a few pages of text. In a brief narrative, he illustrated the main themes of the entire history of the Nephites, including the one that he returned to again and again: "Serve God or perish."

The moral decay and spiritual decline of the Nephite nation that are reflected in this book provide insights and a warning about our own times and how to avoid destruction. The Book of Helaman is a micro-study of the forces that shape all of history. It contrasts what happens when people reject God and His prophets, with what happens when they humble themselves before Him. A careful study of these principles will make the later themes of The Book of Mormon more applicable to our circumstances.

The Elder Alma had been consecrated by Mosiah as first Chief Judge of the people. Also, he was given charge of all the affairs of the Church and of the records engraven upon The Large Plates of Nephi. His son Alma was later entrusted with these responsibilities, as was his grandson Helaman. (See Alma 44:24). For a time, Helaman's brother Shiblon kept the records, and finally Helaman's son by the same name did so. (See Alma 63:1 & 11). It is this Helaman, the great-grandson of the Elder Alma, for whom The Book of Helaman was named. (See Mormon's Superscription to The Book of Helaman).

Alma the Younger, Nephihah, and his son Pahoran had served as Chief Judges in Zarahemla from 92 B.C. to 52 B.C. During that time, there had been many internal and external threats challenging the Nephite lifestyle. Now, according to Mormon, there began to be an even more "serious difficulty among the people of the Nephites." (V. 1).

Pahoran had died, and there was contention among three of his sons "concerning who should have the judgment-seat." (V. 2). The tendency to appoint sons of former judges was a weakness in the Nephite system of government, because it introduced competition and outright fratricidal conflict in the society at times of governmental transition when power was already delicately balanced.

Pahoran, who was likely the eldest son of Pahoran, was "appointed by the voice of the people to be chief judge and a governor over the people of Nephi." (V. 5, see Mosiah 29:39). In other words, he was democratically elected by the people, as Mosiah had wisely foreseen should be done in most circumstances. (See Mosiah 29:25-27). His brother Pacumeni was gracious in defeat, and "he did unite with the voice of the people." (V. 6). That is to say, he threw his support and that of his followers behind the newly and freely elected Chief Judge.

But the third son, named Paanchi, entered into a conspiracy against his brethren. (V. 7). His contention is a good example of what can happen when the voice of the people in a democracy is unacceptable to even a few. In this case, it helped set the stage for much evil culminating in the eventual downfall of the Nephite nation itself. (See V. 18).

According to the law of the land, Paanchi was arrested, tried for treason, and condemned to death. (V. 8). In response, his supporters boldly "sent forth one Kishkumen, even to the judgment-seat of Pahoran, and murdered (him) as he sat upon the judgment-seat." (V. 9).

These conspirators then "entered into a covenant, yea, swearing by their everlasting Maker, that they would tell no man that Kishkumen had murdered Pahoran." (V. 11). In a twisted and perverted way, these Nephites justified the blood on their hands and actually viewed themselves as the saviors of society. As Hugh Nibley observed: "When men depart from God's way and substitute their own ways in its place, they usually do not admit that is what they are doing. On the contrary, they easily and largely convince themselves that their way is God's way." ("Beyond Politics," p. 288).

The children of men do not hearken to the counsels of God or His prophets. Instead, when things are going reasonably well, they say: "Behold, we are the sons of God; have we not taken unto ourselves the daughters of men? And are we not eating and drinking, and marrying and giving in marriage? And our wives bear unto us children, and the same are mighty men, which are like unto men of old, men of great renown." (Moses 8:21). But their actions are all form and no substance; the sizzle without the steak. They reveal their true character, when "every man (is) lifted up in the imagination of the thoughts of his heart, being only evil continually." (Moses 8:22).

In Zarahemla, the conspirators blended in with the people and mingled with their society, affording them the protection of anonymity. Whenever they could be identified, however, the authorities condemned them to death according to the laws of the land. (V. 12-13).

Mormon wrote: "Pacumeni was appointed, according to the voice of the people, to be a chief judge and a governor over the people, to reign in the stead of his brother Pahoran; and it was according to his right." (V. 13, see Commentary Reference to Mosiah 29:44, & to Helaman 3:37).

Now there loomed an even greater threat to the government. As a predator senses weakness in its prey, the Lamanites "came down again that they might pitch battle against the Nephites." (V. 15). They were always waiting in the wings to vex the Nephite nation as soon as it strayed from strict obedience to the commandments.

Even more worrisome, the Lamanites were no longer at a military disadvantage to the Nephites. Ever since Captain Moroni had commanded the Nephite armies, they had enjoyed strategic superiority over their adversaries. Moroni may have been introduced to these new tactics when he studied Mosiah's translation of the 24 Gold Plates of Ether that contained an account of the wars of the Jaredites. (See Alma 37:23-28, & Alma 50:14). If so, this may have given him access to innovative ideas that the Lamanites did not have, inasmuch as they did not enjoy access to the records of Ether. (See Mosiah 28:12). Now, however, the Lamanites were armed "with swords, and with cimiters and with bows, and with arrows, and with head-plates, and with breastplates, and with all manner of shields of every kind." (V. 14). Clearly, a significant military build-up and arms race had been rapidly progressing.

The leader of the Lamanite army was of the most dangerous sort, for he was "a dissenter from among the Nephites." (V. 15). "And thus, we can plainly discern," as Mormon had observed, "that after a people have been once enlightened by the Spirit of God, and have had great knowledge of things pertaining to righteousness, and then have fallen away unto sin and transgression, they become more hardened, and thus their state becomes worse than though they had never known these things." (Alma 24:30).

This man's "name was Coriantumr, and he was a descendant of Zarahemla." (V. 15). That his was a Jaredite name is not surprising, since the Jaredite and Mulekite cultures overlapped by at least 9 months, and perhaps for a much greater period of time. (See Omni 1:21). "At any rate, we have proof that the Jaredites made a permanent cultural impression on the Nephites through Mulek, for after the destruction of the Jaredite nation, we find a Nephite bearing the name of Coriantumr, and learn that this man was a descendant of Zarahemla, the illustrious leader of the Mulekites. This demonstrates that the Jaredite influence reached the Nephites through Mulekite channels, which is exactly what one would expect." (Hugh Nibley, "The World of The Jaredites," p. 244-245. See Ether 10:33).

The king of the Lamanites was named "Tubaloth, who was the son of Ammoron." (V. 16). Ammoron was the brother of Amalekiah, who had given Moroni so much trouble 15 years earlier. (See Alma 52:3). Tubaloth had been raised to hate everything about the Nephites. With their government in disarray, he was quick to "gather together his armies, and he did appoint Coriantumr to be their leader, and did cause that they should march down to the land of Zarahemla to battle against the Nephites." (V. 17).

In a blitzkrieg of lightning quickness, the Lamanites ruthlessly slew the guards at the city gates of Zarahemla, and dealt similarly with everyone else who subsequently stood in their way. When Pacumeni attempted to escape, he was captured and summarily executed. (V. 19-21).

Coriantumr was encouraged that the renowned city of Zarahemla, of such great reputation, had fallen so easily. Consequently, he took his army into the heart of Nephite territories, toward the city of Bountiful, thinking to divide and conquer with one bold stroke. (V. 22-24).

Moronihah, the son of Moroni who had previously distinguished himself against the Lamanites, again responded decisively to their threat. (V. 25-32, see Alma 62:43). Great numbers of the Lamanites were slain in battle, the City of Zarahemla was recovered, and in characteristic fashion, continuing the policy of forgiveness instituted by his father, Moronihah "caused that the Lamanites who had been taken prisoner should depart out of the land in peace." (V. 33, see Alma 62:17). There were no reprisals against an army that had seized the capital city, killed many of its inhabitants, and devastated the land without mercy. What would these Nephites think after learning of the conduct of our present-day wars? What lessons can we learn from considering the examples of Moroni and Moronihah?

"And so great was the prosperity
of the church, and so many the blessings
which were poured out upon the people, that even
the high priests and the teachers were themselves astonished
beyond measure. And it came to pass that the work of the Lord
did prosper unto the baptizing and uniting to the church of God,
many souls, yea, even tens of thousands. Thus, we may see that
the Lord is merciful unto all who will, in the sincerity of their
hearts, call upon his holy name. Yea, thus we see that the
gate of heaven is open unto all, even to those who will
believe on the name of Jesus Christ, who is the
Son of God. (Helaman 3:25-28).

Helaman
Chapter 2

The sickness among the Nephites was unrighteousness, whose signs and symptoms were sinful practices. The treatment protocol or vehicle for redemption was the Church, with its programs designed to help individuals. The medication was the Gospel of Jesus Christ. The cure was predicated upon proper attitude and self-mastery, through activity, good works, and the grace of God. The first six chapters of the Book of Helaman deal with all aspects of this condition.

"After Moronihah had established again peace between the Nephites and the Lamanites," the vacancy in the judgment seat remained. This is understandable, in light of what had happened to Pahoran and Pacumeni, the two previous Chief Judges. (V. 1, see Helaman 1:19-21). No-one was rushing forward to throw their hat in the ring. Only two family lines had filled the position of Chief Judge since its inception. These were those of Alma, and Nephihah. Precedent had been established, and the Nephites turned once again to the family of Alma for leadership.

"Helaman, who was the son of Helaman, was appointed to fill the judgment-seat, by the voice of the people." (V. 2). Even though the democratic process had once again prevailed, this was a brave act on the part of Helaman, for "Kishkumen, who had murdered Pahoran, did lay (in) wait to destroy Helaman also." (V. 3). He had organized a band, first called the band of Kishkumen. It was later called the band of Gadianton, named after its leader, "who was exceedingly expert in many words, and also in his craft, to carry on the secret work of murder and of robbery." (V. 4, see Helaman 3:23, & 6:18). Kishkumen was a professional hit man and the leader of a ruthless terrorist organization whose name would come to be synonymous with savagery.

Because this organization stole the Nephites' safety and security as well as their prosperity and freedom, this band came to be known as "Gadianton's robbers and murderers." (Helaman 6:18). Gadianton flattered his band, promising that they would "be placed in power and authority among the people" if Helaman could be destroyed and Gadianton put in the judgment-seat in his stead. (V. 5). Surely, he was a servant of the devil, who was a liar from the very beginning, for Gadianton could not hope to deliver on his promise.

Authority as defined by the world's standard is a poor substitute for leadership, and is antithetical to power, especially when it is exercised and sustained through the use of violent means. Power and violence are mutually exclusive; where one is present the other is absent. (See Commentary Reference to Mosiah 21:3).

In our day, the oath of the National Socialist (Fascist) Party of Germany was similar to that likely uttered by the members of the band of Kishkumen: "In the presence of the Almighty God," it read, "and on the sacred blood of the

Volk, I swear that my higher authority will find me obediently faithful and eager to obey in secret any command given me. I shall fight constantly for the victory of National Socialism. If I advance, follow me! If I retreat, shoot me! If I die, avenge me! So help me God!" (James Michener, "The Covenant," p. 713).

Fortunately, one of the servants of Helaman obtained "a knowledge of those plans which had been laid by this band to destroy Helaman." (V. 6). Specifically, their "secret plan and their combination" was "to murder, and to rob, and to gain power." (V. 8)

One can only imagine the intrigue and the danger involved in the process of discovering the secrets of what was surely a close-knit terrorist cell. It was brave of Helaman's servant to enter this shadowy world as a double agent. That he had gained the trust of Kishkumen is evident by the record, which states that, without the foreknowledge that his plan had been compromised, Kishkumen boldly approached Helaman as he sat upon the judgment-seat, with the intent to assassinate him. Instead, in a swift reversal of fortunes, the servant loyal to Helaman killed Kishkumen. (V. 9). The perfect crime and act of terrorism turned into a catastrophe for the would-be murderers.

Unfortunately, the band of Gadianton was able to avoid the authorities sent to arrest them as co-conspirators, and they fled into the wilderness following Kishkumen's death. One wonders whether the apostates who so characteristically "fled into the wilderness" ever recognized the symbolic significance of their action. Leaving the safety and security of religious orthodoxy for the dangerous wilderness of spiritual darkness always leaves casualties strewn along its path.

Mormon added an editorial comment that "in the end of this book ye shall see that this Gadianton did prove the overthrow, yea, almost the entire destruction of the people of Nephi." (V. 13, see Ether 8:21). He clarified his meaning in the following verse, writing: "Behold, I do not mean the end of the book of Helaman, but I mean the end of the book of Nephi, from which I have taken all the account which I have written." (V. 14). This is another example of the difficulty of engraving upon plates. Once the words are recorded, they become part of the permanent record. Clarification, when necessary, must follow in subsequent verses. (See Commentary Reference to Alma 24:19).

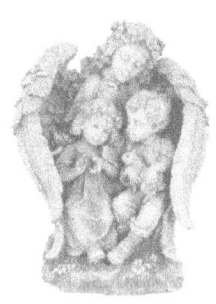

Helaman
Chapter 3

For three years, the Nephites prospered, and then contention and dissension again fragmented the nation. (V. 1-3). In those troubled times, many of the inhabitants of Zarahemla migrated northward into the land that had earlier been inhabited by the Jaredites. (V. 3-5, see Alma 50:29).

"And it came to pass that they did multiply and spread, and did go forth from the land southward to the land northward, and did spread insomuch that they began to cover the face of the whole earth, from the sea south to the sea north, from the sea west to the sea east." (V. 8). Just how far these emigrants traveled, or in which lands they ultimately settled, no-one knows. This verse that is a companion to Alma 22:27 that provides another geographical reference to the lands bordering the seas. "And it came to pass that the king (of the Lamanites in the Land of Nephi) sent a proclamation throughout all the land … which was bordering even to the sea, on the east and on the west, and which was divided from the land of Zarahemla by a narrow strip of wilderness, which ran from the sea east even to the sea west, and round about on the borders of the seashore, and the borders of the wilderness which was on the north by the land of Zarahemla, through the borders of Manti, by the head of the river Sidon, running from the east to the west." (Alma 22:27).

The Book of Mormon was written to be believed on its own merits, and so it is decidedly not a geographical primer. Such references are usually incidental remarks connecting the doctrinal and historical material. However, when they do appear, they provide interesting insight into the physical characteristics of the lands of The Book of Mormon.

We know that "timber was exceedingly scarce in the land northward." (V. 10). Consequently, the people there built houses of cement, protecting and conserving what trees there were. (V. 9). Also, as commerce was re-initiated with the Nephites back in the Land of Zarahemla, shipping lanes supplying much needed timber were established. (V. 10-11).

As he sifted through the records in his possession and pondered which of them he should abridge, Mormon must have been nearly overwhelmed by the sheer magnitude of the accounts contained on the plates, for he inserted into his narrative an editorial aside in verses 14-16. "There are many books and many records of every kind," he wrote, "and they have been kept chiefly by the Nephites." (V. 15, see Mormon 6:6). Other records were kept by the Jaredites, People of Zarahemla (Mulekites), and Lamanites. The Plates of Brass were also in the collection, but this verse leaves open the possibility that Mormon might have had at his disposal yet other records, kept by non-Nephite people.

Jacob had indicated: "A hundredth part of the proceedings of this people cannot be written upon (The Small) plates." (Jacob 3:13). He might have meant that there were so many proceedings that they could not be contained in one book. Or he might have meant that only one percent of the history of his people was religious in nature, and properly belonged on The Small Plates of Nephi. Support for the latter interpretation is found in Jacob's explanation that "many of their proceedings are written upon the larger plates, and their wars, and their contentions, and the reigns of their kings." (Jacob 3:13). It might also be that room for engraving was running out on The Small Plates of Nephi, which he had called "the plates of Jacob, made by the hand of Nephi." (Jacob 3:13).

Mormon had written essentially the same thing in his transitional book entitled The Words of Mormon that he inserted at the end of The Small Plates of Nephi. He explained: "I choose these things to finish my record upon them, which remainder of my record I shall take from the plates of Nephi; and I cannot write the hundredth part of the things of my people." (Words of Mormon 1:5).

Mormon expounded at great length on his responsibilities as a record-keeper. When only ten years of age, he had been charged by Ammaron: "Remember the things that ye have observed concerning this people." (Mormon 1:3). He wrote: "And there had many things transpired which, in the eyes of some, would be great and marvelous; nevertheless, they cannot all be written in this book; yea, this book cannot contain even a hundredth part of what was done among so many people in the space of twenty and five years. But behold there are records which do contain all the proceedings of this people; and a shorter but true account was given by Nephi." (V. 13-16, see 2 Nephi 25:17, 27:26, 3 Nephi 5:8 & 21:9, Moroni 10:3, D&C 4:1, & Isaiah 29:14).

Mormon said that these greater accounts dealt with "the Lamanites and the Nephites, and their wars, and contentions, and dissensions, and their preaching, and their prophecies, and their shipping and their building of ships, and their building of temples, and of synagogues and their sanctuaries, and their righteousness, and their wickedness, and their murders, and their robbings, and their plundering, and all manner of abominations and whoredoms, (which) cannot be contained in this work." (V. 14).

One reason we do not have these greater accounts today might be because they were "handed down from one generation to another by the Nephites, even until they have fallen into transgression and have been mixed with the Lamanites until they are no more called the Nephites, becoming wicked, and wild, and ferocious, yea, even becoming Lamanites." (V. 16). Mormon himself had been commanded to prevent the records in his possession from falling into the hands of the Lamanites for the very reason that "the Lamanites would destroy them." (Mormon 6:6, see 2 Nephi 26:17, & Enos 1:14).

He returned to his narrative in verse 17, and related that three years filled with contention had passed. In spite of this, "Helaman did fill the judgment-seat with justice and equity; yea, he did observe to keep the statutes, and the judgments, and the commandments of God; and he did do that which was right in the sight of God continually; and he did walk after the ways of his father." (V. 20). What a remarkable tribute, that is all the more inspiring when we recognize the challenging state of affairs then existing in Nephite society.

Mormon must have reported with satisfaction that Helaman "had two sons. He gave unto the eldest the name of Nephi, and unto the youngest, the name of Lehi. And they began to grow up unto the Lord." (V. 21). Certainly, both Mormon and Helaman felt that there was great motivating power in familiar names, having themselves been named after their own righteous fathers. (See Helaman 2:2, & Mormon 1:5).

Mormon had already abridged the record of Alma, and reported the activities of Moroni, who was "chief captain over the armies of the Nephites." (Alma 43:17). So impressed was he with Moroni, that Mormon named his own son after him. He had been moved to write of Captain Moroni: "Yea, verily, verily, I say unto you, if all men had been, and were, and ever would be, like unto Moroni, behold, the very powers of hell would have been shaken forever; yea, the devil would never have power over the hearts of the children of men." (Alma 48:17). Certainly, Mormon had the same high hopes and aspirations for his own son named Moroni.

Of himself, he recorded: "And behold, I am called Mormon, being called after the land of Mormon, the land in which Alma did establish the church among the people, yea, the first church which was established among them after their transgression." (3 Nephi 5:12, see Mormon 1:5). Obviously, then, Mormon also ascribed great power to names, and was particularly pleased with those Helaman had given his sons.

For a season, then, the Nephites enjoyed relative peace and prosperity. However, the "secret combinations which Gadianton the robber had established in the more settled parts of the land" continued to vex both the people and the authorities. (V. 22-23). They appear to have become urban guerillas, blending in with society, but rising up to wreak havoc at every opportunity.

Nevertheless, a great missionary harvest now took place with tens of thousands of people joining the Church, that moved Mormon to editorialize: "The Lord is merciful unto all who will, in the sincerity of their hearts, call upon his holy name," and "the gate of heaven is open unto all, even to those who will believe on the name of Jesus Christ, who is the Son of God." (V. 26-27).

Mormon knew from experience, and from studying the missionary efforts of Alma, that the word would "lead the man of Christ" through the valley of the shadow of death to "the right hand of God in the kingdom of heaven." (V. 29). He hoped that the examples of Lehi and Nephi, the sons of Helaman, would stand in stark contrast to those of Kishkumen and Gadianton, and would provide positive role models for readers living in strikingly similar circumstances in the Last Days.

After two years of peace and prosperity in Zarahemla, Mormon recorded that pride again "began to enter into the church - not into the church of God, but into the hearts of the people who professed to belong to the church of God." (V. 33). Again, we encounter the difficulty of engraving with accuracy on plates. It was required that Mormon correct himself through clarifications on the plates themselves, which were then faithfully preserved in Joseph Smith's translation. (See Commentary Reference to Alma 24:19).

The activity of these apostates "was a great evil, which did cause the more humble part of the people to suffer great persecutions, and to wade through much affliction." (V. 34). But it also helped them to exercise their faith and strengthen their bond to Heavenly Father. As they fasted and prayed, their humility increased, and they were "firmer and firmer in the faith of Christ." (V. 35). Finally, as they yielded their hearts to God, they experienced sanctification by the Holy Ghost. (See 2 Nephi 27:20, 31:17, Alma 13:11-12, & Moroni 6:4).

Mormon again drew a contrast by highlighting the concurrent but contrasting experiences of the apostates. Those qualities that marked them as disciples of the devil "did grow upon them from day to day." (V. 36). In our own environment, where the status of the heart and mind will determine outcomes, conditions in the world continue to deteriorate. Blessings that follow obedience do not have a monetary cost, but a performance cost. The Lord said: "He that receiveth my law, and doeth it, the same is my disciple." (D&C 41:5).

Eighteen years after his father's death, after keeping the records for fourteen years, and filling the judgment-seat through eleven difficult years, Helaman died. Mormon's editorial comments in this chapter paid indirect tribute to

Helaman by emphasizing the qualities of righteousness that, in the midst of external adversity, brought inner peace to the Saints in Zarahemla.

Helaman's "eldest son Nephi began to reign in his stead." (V. 37). Once again, the office of Chief Judge passed to a member of the family line of Alma, and the people intuitively regarded him almost as a monarch. (See Commentary References to Mosiah 23:6-7, 29:44, Alma 50:39, & to Helaman 1:13).

Helaman
Chapter 4

After a season of stability, internal contention created new problems in the Nephite nation. Dissenters were "driven out of the land, and they did go unto the king of the Lamanites." (V. 2). Once again, apostate Nephites drifted from Zarahemla through the dark jungle and spiritual wilderness to the Land of Nephi, and in a process of metamorphosis they evolved into cultural Lamanites. There they became the catalysts that drove the engine of hatred and aggression directed toward their former brethren. (V. 4).

As a result, the Lamanites "did commence the work of death" in Zarahemla, resulting in the loss of "all the possession of the Nephites which was in the land southward." (V. 5 & 8). "The Nephites and the armies of Moronihah were driven even into the land of Bountiful." (V. 6). There, they fortified "against the Lamanites, from the west sea, even unto the east; it being a day's journey for a Nephite on the line which they had fortified." (V. 6, see Commentary Reference to Alma 22:32). This was the "narrow neck of land" that separated the land of Bountiful from the land northward that was called Desolation. (Alma 63:5, see Alma 50:34, 52:9, Mormon 2:29 & 3:5, & Ether 10:20).

The fortunes of war swung as a pendulum, and the following year Moronihah's armies "succeeded in regaining even the half of all their possessions." (V. 10). But the rest of their land was lost forever. "Moronihah could obtain no more possessions over the Lamanites. Therefore, they did abandon their design to obtain the remainder of their lands, for so numerous were the Lamanites that it became impossible for the Nephites to obtain more power over them; therefore, Moronihah did employ all his armies in maintaining those parts which he had taken." (V. 18-19). In resignation, he instead adopted a long-term strategy of Lamanite containment. (See Helaman 5:17-18, & 50-52).

There is a great lesson to be learned here. Mormon made an observation as relevant today as it was 2,000 years ago: "This great loss of the Nephites, and the great slaughter which was among them, would not have happened had it not been for their wickedness and their abomination which was among them; yea, and it was among those also who professed to belong to the church of God." (V. 11).

So would it be in the Last Days, when "with the sword and by bloodshed the inhabitants of the earth shall mourn; and with famine, and plague, and earthquake, and the thunder of heaven, and the fierce and vivid lightning also, shall the inhabitants of the earth be made to fee the wrath, and indignation, and chastening hand of an Almighty God, until the consumption decreed hath made a full end of all nations." (D&C 87:6). In the judgments that precede the Millennium, all earthly kingdoms will come to an end, and the Kingdom of God will triumph and become the one political power during a thousand years of peace and righteousness. Before that glorious millennial day, there shall be "a day of wrath, a day of burning, a day of desolation, of weeping, of mourning, and of lamentation, and as a whirlwind it shall come upon all the face of the earth, saith the Lord." (D&C 112:24).

The cleansing will start with the Latter-day Saints: "And upon my house shall it begin, and from my house shall it go forth, saith the Lord." (D&C 112:25). "And it shall come to pass among the wicked that every man that will not take his sword against his neighbor must needs flee unto Zion for safety." (D&C 45:68). Holy places, typified by Zion, have more to do with how we live than where we live. If we enjoy the companionship of the Holy Ghost, then we surely stand in holy places where we enjoy the Spirit and Presence of Divinity.

Those of whom Mormon wrote only pretended to belong to the Church, having but temporary membership and influence in that body. They were "professors" of religion. (See J.S.H. 1:19). Insult is added to injury, when hypocrisy compounds the damage caused by adherence to humanized, impotent creeds, and when people do not really believe, but are only professors of religion. When the membership rolls are finalized and the accounting is made, their names will not be found on the records of the Church.

Mormon catalogued a number of reasons why these individuals had disqualified themselves for the blessings associated with Church membership, but chief among them was pride. (V. 11-12). Pride is enmity toward man and God and leads to all other transgressions. Ezra Taft Benson called pride "the universal sin that limits or stops progression and adversely affects all of our relationships." (C.R., 4/1989).

Because of their pride, the "exceeding riches of the people" proved to be a curse rather than a blessing. (V. 12). It is the Lord's will to bless His people in material as well as in spiritual ways. (See Malachi 3:8-10, Luke 12:15-21, 2 Nephi 9:30, Helaman 12:1, & Mormon 8:37 & 39). But inordinate desire for wealth divisively influences our relationship with God. (See Alma 34:40, D&C 38:17, 20, 24-27, 30, 42:54, & 136:27). The real lesson to be learned is how to use wealth, rather than to be used by it. It can be a tool to stay close to God, or it can dominate our lives and dictate inappropriate and self-destructive behavior.

It was pride that caused the Nephites to oppress the poor. They had a distorted sense of self-importance, that was unjustified, unsupportable, completely inaccurate, and unacceptable. Pride blinded them to a realization of their complete dependence upon God, of the ultimate equality of all of His children, and of their responsibility to act as His stewards in the service of their fellowmen.

Pride fostered a distorted sense of self-importance, a selfish power struggle for worldly supremacy, and a secular pseudo-sophistication that led to spiritual sclerosis and a stagnation of sensitivity. In their rigidity, the people made "a mock of that which was sacred; denying the spirit of prophecy and of revelation." (V. 12). They could not relate to things that they did not directly and physically experience, and so they were dead as to the workings of the Spirit. Consequently, they lashed out at whatever they could not understand, including the humble followers of Christ. It is ever so. (See Alma 5:30).

Their pride was "much more than an ordinary problem, because it activated all the cardinal sins. It was the detonator in the breaking of the Ten Commandments. These selfish Nephites thus sought to please not God, but themselves. They even broke their covenants in order to satisfy their appetites." (Neal Maxwell, C.R., 10/1990).

"Only by pride cometh contention," (Proverbs 13:10), that "results from a power struggle when we pit ourselves, our possessions, or our intellect, against others. The proud are easily offended, hold grudges, withhold forgiveness, and will not receive counsel or correction. All these internal traits become a fertile seedbed for the external manifestations of contention." (Robert L. Millet, "Doctrinal Commentary on The Book of Mormon," p. 348).

The people boasted in their own strength. This manifestation of pride is such a common sin that it is almost overlooked. (See Alma 31:25-28). Amulek encouraged the Zoramites: "Pour out your souls in your closets, and your secret places, and in your wilderness. Yea, and when you do not cry unto the Lord, let your hearts be full, drawn out in prayer continually." (Alma 34:26-27). We would do well to follow his counsel, for when we pray to the Father continually, we are not likely to lose sight of our utter dependence upon Him for both our temporal and spiritual welfare, nor will we soon forget from Whom both talents and blessings flow.

Every time the Nephites apprehensively turned to the arm of flesh for security, they did not prosper. (V. 13). But when Moronihah, Lehi, and Nephi exhorted them to turn to God, and "they did repent, they did begin to prosper. (V. 14-15). It was only in these circumstances that the Nephites were able to regain half of their lands. Nevertheless, "because of the greatness of the number of the Lamanites, the Nephites were in great fear, lest they should be overpowered, and trodden down, and slain, and destroyed." (V. 20).

"No matter how wicked and ferocious and depraved the Lamanites might be," observed Hugh Nibley, "no matter how much they outnumbered the Nephites, darkly closing in on all sides, no matter how insidiously they spied and intrigued and infiltrated and hatched their diabolical plots and breathed their bloody threats and pushed their formidable preparations for all out war, they were not the Nephite problem. They were merely kept there to remind the Nephites of their real problem, which was the difficulty with which they managed to walk uprightly before the Lord." ("Since Cumorah," p. 376).

"Because of their iniquity, the church had begun to dwindle." (V. 23). As the Spirit withdrew from the people, they no longer enjoyed the fruits of faith and gifts of the Holy Ghost. They were like a ship without a rudder, for they were left without guidance or direction from Heavenly Father; left to face their adversaries alone and to fight their own battles without His divine assistance. Consequently, "the judgments of God did stare them in the face." (V. 23).

"They saw that they had become weak, like unto their brethren, the Lamanites, and that the Spirit of the Lord did no more preserve them; yea, it had withdrawn from them because the Spirit of the Lord doth not dwell in unholy temples. Therefore, the Lord did cease to preserve them by his miraculous and matchless power, for they had fallen into a state of unbelief and awful wickedness." (V. 24-25).

Mormon's observation is more than an editorial comment. It is a clarion call to those living in the Last Days to learn from the mistakes of the Nephites, and to turn to the Lord for the protection so vital in our own perilous times. The past is prologue. (See Commentary Reference to Alma 43:1).

This is no mere recitation of history, no detached chronicle of a people distant from our time and circumstances. It is critical that we understand the forces that have always acted upon societies and will forever do so. Every prophet in former and latter times has stressed the same message: "If ye keep (the) commandments, ye shall prosper in the land, but if ye keep not (the) commandments, ye shall be cut off from His presence." (Alma 37:13, see 1 Nephi 2:20, 2 Nephi 1:9, Mosiah 1:7, & Helaman 12:1).

"This great loss of the Nephites, and the great slaughter which was among them, would not have happened had it not been for their wickedness and their abomination which was among them; yea, and it was among those also who professed to belong to the church of God. And it was because of the pride of their hearts, because of their exceeding riches, yea, it was because of their oppression to the poor, withholding their food from the hungry, withholding their clothing from the naked … making a mock of that which was sacred, denying the spirit of prophecy and of revelation … and because of this their great wickedness, and their boastings in their own strength, they were left in their own strength; therefore, they did not prosper, but were afflicted and smitten." (Helaman 4:11-13).

Helaman
Chapter 5

Thirty years before the birth of Christ, "Nephi delivered up the judgment-seat to a man whose name was Cezoram." (V. 1). He did this because the laws and government of the Nephites "were established by the voice of the people, and they who chose evil were more numerous than they who chose good, therefore they were ripening for destruction, for the laws had become corrupted." (V. 2).

The Lord warned Joseph Smith: "When the wicked rule, the people mourn. Wherefore, honest men and wise men should be sought for diligently, and good men and wise men ye should observe to uphold; otherwise, whatsoever is less than these cometh of evil." (D&C 98:9-10). The graduate school of hard knocks will always reinforce what spiritual kindergarten has taught: that "wickedness never was happiness." (Alma 41:10). Heavenly Father has devised a perfect Plan, and as we strive to abide by its principles, we should not try to re-invent the wheel, rely on the arm of flesh, or trade telestial toys for celestial sureties.

Perhaps the people in Zarahemla would no longer sustain a righteous individual like Nephi in his position, because the scriptures reveal that he "yielded up the judgment-seat." (V. 4). On the other hand, Nephi might have been following the example of his great grandfather Alma the Younger, who had retired from government service 53 years earlier in Zarahemla, in order to initiate a religious reformation movement among the Nephites. (See Alma 4:20). That effort had also resulted in the conversion of the poorer members of the Zoramite people. Now, the further fruits of Alma's labors so many years earlier would blossom in the Land of Nephi through the efforts of his descendant Nephi. (See Commentary Reference to V. 41). Once again, we see evidence of The Butterfly Effect.

It was probably a blessing in disguise for Nephi that he did yield up the office of Chief Judge, because Cezoram ruled for only five years before he "was murdered by an unknown hand as he sat upon the judgment-seat." (Helaman 6:15). Then, Cezoram's son, who was appointed by the people in his stead, was also murdered. In these times of apostasy, when the protecting hand of the Lord had been withdrawn from the people, it was hazardous to accept positions of responsibility within the Nephite government. The Band of Gadianton was gaining strength by the day, and engaging in increasingly bold acts of terrorism.

In response to escalating wickedness in the Land of Zarahemla, Nephi "took it upon himself to preach the word of God all the remainder of his days, and his brother Lehi also, all the remainder of his days." (V. 4). The ministry of Nephi and Lehi was destined to be one of the most powerful in the history of the Nephites. Their experiences reflect their understanding that the Lord's servants do not preach and teach only to make people's lives better. They baptize people in order to bring them into the fold and save their souls in the Celestial Kingdom of God.

Also, the conduct of their lives illustrated the principle that individual spiritual growth precedes collective numerical growth. Nephi and Lehi were prepared to teach the Gospel with power and authority, and when they did so, multitudes were converted. In the family line of virtually every member, there is a missionary instrumental in the conversion of that member's first ancestor to join the Church. In the case of Nephi and Lehi, that missionary was Abinadi, who had brought the Gospel message to their great-great grandfather Alma. (See Mosiah 17:2, & Commentary Reference to verses 48-49).

The brothers also "remembered the words which their father Helaman spake unto them." (V. 5, see Enos 1:3). He had taught that although they had been given powerful names, righteousness, and not lineage, is important to the Lord. As a matter of fact, "the Lord esteemeth all flesh in one, (and) he that is righteous is favored of God." (1 Nephi 17:33-35, see 2 Nephi 30:2).

Helaman had exhorted his sons "that it is upon the rock of our Redeemer, who is Christ, the Son of God, that ye must build your foundation." (V. 12). If they would follow His counsel, they would not be dragged down to misery and a gulf of endless wo by the "mighty winds" of the devil, that represent the sectarian philosophies and false ideologies of men that are continually raging on the earth.

"So much depends upon our willingness to make up our minds," Spencer W. Kimball said, "collectively and individually, that present levels of performance are not acceptable, either to ourselves or to the Lord. In saying that, I am not calling for flashy, temporary differences in our performance levels, but for a quiet resolve to lengthen our stride." ("Church News," 3/22/1975).

When President Kimball urged members of the Church to lengthen their stride, he knew that the exertion would cause discomfort, as it tested their limits of endurance. But in doing so, they would build spiritual muscle. Christ urged those in bondage to do the same thing, to go the second mile, doubling their stride. "The second mile is a gift of spiritual independence that removes the veil of insensitivity from a destiny." (Richard L. Gunn, "A Search for Sensitivity and Spirit," p. 197).

A young man was in the habit of running several miles every morning in order to maintain physical health and endurance. One day, after four miles of steady running, but yet one mile short of his intended goal, he had an almost overpowering urge to stop. Runners tend to develop a certain mental toughness to combat physical pain, and yet he was experiencing a battle within his body as his cortex fought against his aching muscles, burning lungs, and pounding heart. At the very moment when he had resigned himself to throw in the towel and slow to a "survival shuffle," he chanced to look up. Through perspiration-soaked eyes, he was shocked to see directly before him a flashing red neon sign, associated with a traffic signal, that urged "DON'T WALK!" He completed the last mile at his normal pace and crossed the finish line with an imaginary ribbon streaming across his chest!

The real tragedy in life is not that we set our sights too high, and then fail to achieve our goals. Rather, it is that we aim too low, too easily reaching our objectives while accomplishing little, having nothing to show for our consistently timid efforts.

Helaman had taught his sons never to accept mediocrity in their lives. "And they did remember his words; and therefore, they went forth, keeping the commandments of God, to teach the word of God among all the people of Nephi, beginning at the city Bountiful." (V. 14). They went throughout all the land southward, "and from thence into the land of Zarahemla, among the Lamanites" who had entrenched themselves in part of that land. (V. 16, see Helaman 4:18-19). They preached with such power that many of the dissenters who had gone over from the Nephites were baptized, as were "eight thousand of the Lamanites who were in the land of Zarahemla." (V. 17-18).

It was reminiscent of the days of the Prophet Elijah, who cried to the Lord: "The children of Israel have forsaken thy covenant, thrown down thine altars, and slain thy prophets with the sword; and I, even I only, am left; and they seek my life, to take it away." Then the Lord answered, saying: "Yet I have left me seven thousand in Israel, all the knees which have not bowed unto Baal." (1 Kings 19:14 & 18). The Lord numbers His children only by their willingness to accept His covenants. (See Commentary Reference to 2 Nephi 30:3, & Deuteronomy 32:8).

The missionary effort of members of the Church in the conversion process is actually quite simple. Just find those who are the elect, and teach by the Spirit. "Ye are called to bring to pass the gathering of mine elect," commanded the Lord, "for mine elect hear my voice and harden not their hearts." (D&C 29:7). In order to find the elect, Nephi and Lehi even went into the Land of Nephi, where Ammon had taught the Gospel in 121 B.C. (See Mosiah Chapters 7-8). To their credit, they preached so powerfully that the wicked inhabitants of that land were thoroughly intimidated by the strength of their testimony, and the missionaries were thrown into prison in a futile attempt to still their voices. But even in these circumstances, they were protected so completely that they "were encircled about as if by fire, even insomuch that (their captors, who were Lamanites and Nephite dissenters) durst not lay their hands upon them for fear lest they should be burned." (V. 23).

Accompanying this matchless spiritual manifestation, a voice from heaven declared: "Repent ye, repent ye, and seek no more to destroy my servants whom I have sent unto you to declare good tidings." (V. 29). Now this voice "was not a voice of thunder, neither was it a voice of a great tumultuous noise, but behold, it was a still voice of perfect mildness, as if it had been a whisper, and it did pierce even to the very soul." (V. 30, see v. 31-32). This episode was reminiscent of Paul's conversion experience while he was on the road to Damascus, where he intended to persecute the Saints. "Saul, Saul, why persecutest thou me?" a voice had asked. "And the men which journeyed with him stood speechless, hearing a voice, but seeing no man." (Acts 9:4 & 7).

Again, the voice came, "and did speak unto (Nephi and Lehi) marvelous words which cannot be uttered by man." (V. 33, see 3 Nephi 26:8-12). Joseph Smith taught: "The word of Jehovah has such an influence over the human mind that it is convincing without other testimony. Faith cometh by hearing." ("Joseph Smith Diary", by Willard Richards, 8/6/1843). So completely thrilled were those who heard the voice, and so penetrating was the message, that words could not be articulated to convey the impressions the people had received. As Hugh B. Brown revealed: "Sometimes during solitude, I hear truth spoken with clarity and freshness; uncolored and untranslated, it speaks from within myself in a language original but inarticulate, heard only with the soul." ("Hugh B. Brown Quotes").

Among those who shared this experience was a dissenter from among the Nephites by the name of Aminadab. (V. 39). The name easily translates as "my divine kinsman is noble." This was certainly an appropriate name for one who heard the voice of God, and saw how the faces of Nephi and Lehi "did shine exceedingly, even as the faces of angels." (V. 36). Aminadab exhorted his kinsmen within the walls of the prison: "Repent, and cry unto the voice, even until ye shall have faith in Christ." (V. 41). Some of these "Lamanites" were really apostate Nephites or Zoramites, because in this verse Aminadab reminded his brethren: Christ has been "taught unto you by Alma and Amulek, and Zeezrom" who must have gone to these same people in the Land of Antionum 44 years earlier! (See Alma Chapters 31-35).

It had taken almost half a century for them to come to their spiritual senses. Probably Alma and his brethren had thought the Zoramites beyond redemption and their own missionary efforts among them fruitless. But sometimes, when the seeds are planted, it is left to others to reap the harvest. In these special circumstances in the Land of Nephi around 30 B.C., these individuals finally chose to follow the counsel of Alma, Amulek, Zeezrom, and Aminadab. (See Alma 31: 3-7).

A most remarkable thing then happened to this repentant multitude. "They saw that they were encircled about, yea every soul, by a pillar of fire. And Nephi and Lehi were in the midst of them; yea, they were encircled about; yea, they were as if in the midst of a flaming fire, yet it did harm them not, neither did it take hold upon the walls of the prison; and they were filled with that joy which is unspeakable and full of glory. And behold, the Holy Spirit of God did come down from heaven, and did enter into their hearts, and they were filled as if with fire, and they could speak forth marvelous words." (V. 43-45).

Fire and smoke are frequently cited in the scriptures to depict the glory of God. In the language of Joseph Smith: "God Almighty Himself dwells in eternal fire; flesh and blood cannot go there, for all corruption is devoured by that fire. Our God is a consuming fire. Immortality dwells in everlasting burnings." ("Teachings," p. 367, see Deuteronomy 4:24, & Hebrews 12:29).

Again, the voice came unto them, "yea, a pleasant voice, as if it were a whisper, saying: Peace, peace be unto you, because of your faith in my Well Beloved, who was from the foundation of the world." (V. 46-47). Then, "they saw the heavens open; and angels came down out of heaven and ministered unto them. And there were about three hundred souls who saw and heard these things." (V. 48-49). They had been invited to enjoy a refuge from the cares of the world and the consequences of sin, that is born of a settled conviction of the truth. (See Commentary Reference to Alma 16:17).

Among the greatest miracles that faithful members of the Church are privileged to witness is the healing of the spiritually sick. The Plan of Salvation truly is the Plan of Redemption for those who are suffering in the bondage of sin. (See Commentary Reference to Alma 12:25-26). These three hundred who had come back from the dead may have formed the core of converted Lamanites from whom Samuel the Lamanite, who appears later in the record, might have come. (See Helaman Chapters 13-15). For "they did go forth, and did minister unto the people, declaring throughout all the regions round about all the things which they had heard and seen, insomuch that the more part of the Lamanites were convinced of them, because of the greatness of the evidences which they had received. And as many as were convinced did lay down their weapons of war, and also their hatred and the tradition of their fathers. And it came to pass that they did yield up unto the Nephites the lands of their possession." (V. 50-52, see Helaman 4:18-19).

These verses suggest that this missionary force of recent converts had the authority of the priesthood to administer the affairs of the kingdom on behalf of their brethren, and that they had the power to drive that effort. (See Commentary Reference to Helaman 6:5). Whether they received their commission from Nephi and Lehi, or from the angels who had administered to them, the scriptures just cited testify of the success of their efforts.

Once again, the actions of an inspired Chief Judge were vindicated by the subsequent harvest of souls. Nephi and Lehi understood that knowledge of the Gospel does not come automatically as a fringe benefit of maintaining body temperature. They had instead followed the uncomfortable road to which the Savior beckoned them, knowing that it might take then to their personal Gethsemane, where they would yield their agency to the Savior on the altar of faith, but the inevitable result of their efforts would be a magnificent and sustaining outpouring of the Spirit.

Bruce R. McConkie declared in his last General Conference address before his death in 1979: "In a coming day I shall feel the nail marks in His hands and in His feet and shall wet His feet with my tears. But I shall not know any better then, than I know now, that He is God's Almighty Son, that He is our Savior and Redeemer, and that Salvation comes in and through His atoning blood and in no other way." (C.R., 4/1985). Because of the efforts of Nephi and Lehi, the sons of Helaman, many formerly wicked Lamanites could now say the same thing.

Helaman
Chapter 6

Incredibly, a majority of the Lamanites were converted to the Gospel, "insomuch that their righteousness did exceed that of the Nephites, because of their firmness and their steadiness in the faith." (V. 1). In a reversal of fortunes, they even became missionaries to the Nephites, coming down into the Land of Zarahemla to "exhort them to faith and repentance." (V. 4). Perhaps Samuel the Lamanite was among those numbers, for "many did preach with exceedingly great power and authority." (V. 5, see Commentary Reference to Helaman 5:48-49, & Helaman Chapters 13-15).

"They did fellowship one with another," and went "whithersoever they would … among the Lamanites or among the Nephites." (V. 3 & 8). They had "an exceeding plenty of gold, and of silver, and of all manner of precious metals." (V. 9, see V. 11). It seems that it was important for Mormon to stress their temporal as well as their spiritual prosperity. Their abundance of "precious" things might typify their conversion, and that they were no longer a "lazy and idolatrous people." (Mosiah 9:12). The "filthiness" so long associated with them had been washed away in the waters of baptism.

In this chapter is another of the widely scattered geographical footnotes in The Book of Mormon, that, pieced together, form a tapestry of relatively coherent design. (V. 10). This one identifies where two prominent groups of Book of Mormon peoples made their first New World landfall, and states that the land south of the narrow neck was called Lehi, and that the land to the north of the narrow neck was called Mulek.

Further, we learn that Father Lehi was led to the land south, and that Mulek, who was "the son of Zedekiah," was led to the land north. (See Commentary Reference to Alma 22:30-31). The land north was the place of Mulek's landfall, but was not the more southerly location of their ultimate settlement that they called Zarahemla. (V. 10, see Helaman 8:21, & Omni 1:13-16).

About 590 B.C., the Babylonians "slew the sons of Zedekiah before his eyes." (2 Kings 25:7). Obviously, the biblical account failed to mention the son named Mulek who escaped with faithful retainers, and who was carried across the oceans to settle in the New World. (See Helaman 8:21, Commentary Reference to Omni 1:16, & Ezekiel 17:22-24). The descendants of these people and those of Lehi, who joined them in Zarahemla between 279 B.C. and 130 B.C., continued to define riches in terms of silver and gold, even though these metals were plentiful in their adoptive lands. (V. 11, see Omni 1:12-13). Their abundant crops were more important in their agricultural society that supported a large population. (V. 12).

Book of Mormon accounts frequently speak of the ebb and flow of large groups of people across the panorama of the promised land. Specific numbers are not mentioned to avoid hyperbole, but those who recorded these events were not simply taking poetic license. The fact is that the people "did multiply and wax exceedingly strong in the land." (V. 12).

The scriptures plainly teach that the spirits of mankind are known and numbered unto God before their earthly advent. "Remember the days of old, consider the years of many generations: ask thy father, and he will shew thee; thy elders, and they will tell thee. When the most High divided to the nations their inheritance, when he separated the sons of Adam, he set the bounds of the people according to the number of the children of Israel." (Deuteronomy 32:7-8). "The number or extent of the temporal creations of God is not left to chance. (See Moses 3:4-7). The population of the Earth is fixed according to the number of spirits appointed to take tabernacles of flesh upon this planet; when these have all come forth in the order and time appointed, then, and not until then, shall the end come." (James E. Talmage, "The Articles of Faith," p. 193-194).

Two people multiplying arithmetically could result in a population in the 25th generation of 33,554,432. Given 20 years per generation, such a population would be possible in just 500 years. The total number of people born during that time span resulting from the union of the initial couple would be 67,108,862. No-one would suggest that the number of Book of Mormon peoples was anything near that number, and yet the record tells us that by 322 A.D., "the whole face of the land had become covered with buildings, and the people were as numerous almost, as it were the sand of the sea." (Mormon 1:7).

In 28 B.C., the society was already well developed, insomuch that Mormon reported: "Their women did toil and spin, and did make all manner of cloth, (and) fine-twined linen." (V. 13). What "fine-twined linen" was, we do not know. But the Hebrew background of the Nephites is reflected in their use of this term that appears 6 times in The Book of Mormon, and 32 times in the Bible.

The tranquility of this outwardly stable cultural milieu was shattered in the 66th year of the reign of the Judges, when Gadianton's robbers murdered Cezoram and the son who succeeded him as they sat upon the judgment seat. (V. 15, see V. 19). As domestic security evaporated, "the people began to grow exceedingly wicked again." (V. 16). Their culture twisted into only a caricature of stability, and they increasingly resembled the Band of Gadianton, for "they began to commit secret murders, and to rob and to plunder, that they might get gain." (V. 17).

Throughout his abridgement, Mormon repeatedly warned of these terrorists within the infrastructure of Nephite society. (V. 18). This chapter and Ether Chapter 8 give us important insights into secret combinations, including what motivated them, how they came into power, what sustained them, who supported them, and how they operated. Combinations then and now have used immorality, money, seduction, deception, sophistry, intimidation, and violence to achieve their goals. Assassination by these groups is a recurring scenario in The Book of Mormon. (See V. 23).

Mormon reported of the Lamanites that, to their everlasting credit, they attempted "to destroy (the Band of Gadianton from) off the face of the earth. But behold, Satan did stir up the hearts of the more part of the Nephites, insomuch that they did unite with those bands of robbers, and did enter into their covenants and their oaths." (V. 20-21). Here, we have a fine turn of events, with Lamanites exhibiting faithfulness and Nephites flaunting their heritage and their sacred covenants.

Alma had recognized the power of "these secret oaths and covenants," and the danger of making them known among the people. (V. 25, see Alma 37:27 & 29). But these have existed from the time of Cain, the first murderer, and since then have been revealed to man by Satan himself. For "behold, those secret oaths and covenants did not come forth unto Gadianton from the records which were delivered unto Helaman; but behold, they were put into the heart of

Gadianton by that same being who did entice our first parents to partake of the forbidden fruit." (V. 26). Who could argue that the devil is the prime motivator of these organizations?

"And it came to pass that they did have their signs, yea, and their secret words; and this that they might distinguish a brother who had entered into the covenant." (V. 22). Oaths and covenants are intrinsic to the Gospel Plan, and so when they are perverted by Satan to satisfy worldly desires, they are pleasing to the natural man with itching ears. (See 2 Timothy 4:3).

There were other points of similarity as well. Just as the Church today disciplines its members, so in Book of Mormon times, the Band of Gadianton tried its members, but did so "according to the laws of their wickedness" instead of the laws of God. (V. 24). Theirs was a caricature of the true order, but the façade of legitimacy was compelling to their carnal nature, and so was particularly persuasive to their impressionable minds.

Mormon was familiar with The Book of Ether and knew that it contained the record of the Jaredites who had been dragged "down to an entire destruction, and to an everlasting hell." (V. 28). The one responsible for that was "he who is the author of all sin." (V. 30). After all, it is Satan's desire that all men might be as miserable, as he is. (See 2 Nephi 2:27).

Verse 31 provides a contrast to the gold and silver mentioned in verse 11, which was given for the blessing and enjoyment of the covenant people. In just five years, the Nephites had taken those precious metals, mistakenly thinking that they had been provided so they might do with them as they pleased, and fashioned their own golden idols. (See Exodus 32:1-4). "And it came to pass that all these iniquities did come unto them in the space of not many years." (V. 32). In fact, the majority of the corruption of the Nephites had occurred in just one year, and consequently "the Spirit of the Lord began to withdraw from the Nephites, because of the wickedness and the hardness of their hearts." (V. 35). Of the modern age, Joseph Fielding Smith, Jr. said: "Because of the wickedness of the world, the Spirit has been withdrawn, and when the Spirit of Christ is not striving with men, the Spirit of Satan is." ("The Predicted Judgments", Brigham Young University Speeches of the Year, 3/21/967). He is always ready to move into the vacuum created by our own empty-headed behavior.

Elder Smith continued: "All the world today, with the exception of a handful of people who have obeyed the new and everlasting covenant, are suffering spiritual death. They are cast out from the presence of God. They are without God, without Gospel truth, and without the power of redemption, for they know neither God nor His Gospel. ("Gospel Doctrine," p. 432-433). The world, or spiritual Babylon, has sacrificed its fortunes to the harsh reality of justice, and when the repayment date for the pleasure of the moment arrives, when it has to pony up and pay for the flavor of the day, truly there will be "weeping, wailing and gnashing of teeth." (D&C 19:5). When the world is measured, it will be found wanting, and mercy will have no claim on it.

A child who had been raised in the home of consistently faithful parents asked what he wanted to be when he grew up. His answer was articulated in just one word: "Obedient." By 24 B.C., the Lamanites in the land had finally developed testimonies of the principle of obedience. Alma had asked the Zoramites to "try the virtue of the word of God." (Alma 31:5). Now his approach was validated as the elect followed the counsel that had for so long been proffered.

Mormon's careful abridgement of the records of Helaman must have amazed him, for those that he had previously studied contained a similar account of the largely unsuccessful mission of Alma to reclaim the apostate Zoramites, who "were dissenters from the Nephites." (Alma 31:8). Of that group of people, Mormon had written: "And now, as the preaching of the word had a great tendency to lead the people to do that which was just ... therefore Alma thought it was expedient that they should try the virtue of the word of God." (Alma 31:5). Some of these dissenters had finally opened their hearts to the truth, as had their Lamanite counterparts. "And thus, we see that the Lord began to pour out his Spirit upon the Lamanites, as well, because of their easiness and willingness to believe in his words." (V. 36).

Perhaps only as converts can, these Lamanites appreciated the new-found stability and confidence that Gospel knowledge and obedience bring. They came to understand that "force and compulsion will never establish an ideal society. This can only come through transformation of the individual soul, and through a life redeemed from sin and brought in harmony with divine will." (David O. McKay, C.R. 10/1962).

Consequently, they became missionaries who did not take the easy way out. Rather, they followed the road less traveled that led down a difficult path to those who most needed the Gospel. "And it came to pass that the Lamanites did hunt the band of robbers of Gadianton; and they did preach the word of God among the more wicked part of them, insomuch that this band of robbers was utterly destroyed from among the Lamanites." (V. 37, see Mosiah 18:21, Alma 5:61, 31:5, 34:3, Helaman 3:29, & Mormon 8:2). Their actions reflect Alma's teaching style and approach to missionary work among apostate people.

We remember that after the disappearance of Alma: "The saying went abroad in the church that he was taken up by the Spirit, or buried by the hand of the Lord, even as Moses." (Alma 45:19). In other words, he was translated for a wise purpose known only to the Lord. Perhaps when "angels came down out of heaven and ministered" to the Lamanites, Alma was among their number, giving encouragement and direction. (Helaman 5:48). For "they were bidden to go forth and marvel not, neither should they doubt." (Helaman 5:49).

As it turned out, it was the Nephites who built up and supported the secret combinations. "Vice is a monster of so frightful mien, as to be hated, needs but to be seen. Yet seen too oft, familiar with her face, we first endure, then pity, then embrace." (Alexander Pope). These combinations finally "seduced the more part of the righteous until they had come down to believe in their works and partake of their spoils, and to join with them in their secret murders and combinations." (V. 38). Secret combinations are abominable in the sight of God precisely because they seduce the unwary, tempting them by deceit and enticement to forsake allegiance to true principles. By stripping their victims of the opportunity to exercise agency, they thwart the Plan of Happiness.

Thus, the Band of Gadianton "did obtain the sole management of the government." (V. 39). In other words, there was no longer any significantly righteous influence exercised by those vested with temporal power. The stage had been set for terrible abuses, allowing the "Gadianton robbers to fill "the judgment-seats, having usurped the power and authority of the land; laying aside the commandments of God, and not in the least aright before him; doing no justice unto the children of men; condemning the righteous because of their righteousness; letting the guilty go because of their money; and moreover to be held in office at the head of government, to rule and do according to their wills, that they might get gain and glory of the world, and, moreover, that they might the more easily commit adultery, and steal, and kill, and do according to their own wills." (Helaman 7:4-5).

The objective of the combination was power and gain. Of Satan, who made a covenant with Cain, the scriptures record that: "He sware unto Cain that he would do according to his commands. And all these things were done in secret. And Cain said: Truly I am Mahan, the master of this great secret, that I may murder and get gain. Wherefore, Cain was called Master Mahan, and he gloried in his wickedness." (Moses 5:30-31). Ever since then, taking over the reins of government has been a primary goal of subversive groups, since such control is a source of great worldly power. But Cain and others like him become so thoroughly debauched and so completely forfeit their agency, that they forgot that the awful oath of fealty was made by the deceiver himself, who was a liar from the beginning. When men sell their souls to the Devil, generally for nothing more than a mess of pottage, they are in his grasp, and they become his faithless disciples.

In these conditions, the Nephites "were in an awful state." (V. 40). More than ever, they needed the Balm of Gilead to dress their wounds. (See Bible Dictionary, p. 618). Instead, they distanced themselves from its healing influence. The Savior's birth was close at hand. Could anyone preach the word with such power and authority that it might make a difference in the lives of at least some of these apostate Nephites? Mormon gave us the Prophecy of Nephi, the son of Helaman, to help us to put things in perspective in these pivotal times that bear such a strong similarity to our own. (See Helaman Chapters 7-16).

"And it came to pass
that the Lamanites did hunt
the band of robbers of Gadianton;
and they did preach the word of God
among the more wicked part of them,
insomuch that this band of robbers
was utterly destroyed from
among the Lamanites."
(Helaman 6:37).

Helaman
Chapter 7

The superscription to chapter 7 that is part of the original text of Mormon's abridgement, identifies the last 10 chapters of The Book of Helaman as "The Prophecy of Nephi." Inasmuch as Helaman's death was recorded in Helaman 3:37, it is unclear why Nephi's prophecy did not formally begin until this chapter. Perhaps Mormon used writings of Nephi's brother Lehi in preparing Helaman 3:37-6:41. But Mormon did not reveal if this was actually the case.

In chapters 7-9, Mormon recorded the events of just 3 of the 51-year time span of The Book of Helaman. He said that he could not record the hundredth part of the history of his people, so he must have considered the content of these chapters to be very important for us to have. (See Words of Mormon 1:5, Helaman 3:14, & 3 Nephi 5:8). If all the other chapters of Helaman were given similar weight, the book would be 1,600 chapters long, instead of just 16.

Since his release as Chief Judge, Nephi had been in the land northward, preaching to the people who had emigrated there around 46 B.C. from the Land of Zarahemla. (V. 1-2, see Helaman 3:3-5 & 8). Mormon had reported that, before long, these Nephites were "scattered upon the face of the earth, and mixed with the Lamanites until they (were) no more called the Nephites, being wicked, and wild, and ferocious, yea, even becoming Lamanites." (Helaman 3:16). Several hundred years later, when all genealogical distinctions between "Lamanite" and "Nephite" had been erased, the land northward would be the likely birthplace of Mormon, who at eleven years of age was carried by his father "southward, even to the land of Zarahemla." (Mormon 1:6, see Alma 50:11).

But by 23 B.C., the population in the land northward must have been composed of inactive and apostate members of the Church as well as non-members unreceptive to Nephi's message, because the record states that "they did reject all his words, insomuch that he could not stay among them." (V. 3). Perhaps, the pressure to leave came from the people themselves, or it may have come at the direction of the Spirit. Whatever the case, circumstances made it impossible for Nephi to tarry there. The terrible consequence was that, cut off from their last connection and only lifeline to righteous influences, these people sank into the deepest depths of apostasy and carnality, as Mormon reported they would.

'A number of years earlier, the Lord had given the people in Ammonihah every reasonable opportunity to repent, but they had proven beyond a doubt that they had no intention of doing so. They were past repentance. That was the fatal symptom of their hard-heart disease. They were in the terminal stage of spiritual sickness.

The terrible thing about losing spiritual elasticity in the walls of our hearts is that understanding of "the word" is withheld, which leaves us vulnerable to all sorts of secular and sacred sickness. The scriptures identify the consequences of sin in very plain language. The effect of sin on those of us who have previously been taught the principles of the Gospel in plainness is that the guidance of the Spirit is withdrawn, and we are left alone to grope in darkness. Guilt causes us to shrink from Church activity, and in the absence of the Spirit, we have no claim on promises, prosperity, or preservation. Tragically, feeling uncomfortable in proximity to spiritual experiences, we withdraw to lifestyles devoid of such associations. Thus, begins a downward spiral that gains momentum as sinful practices, more easily committed, become entrenched.

Even worse, when we do this, we come out "in open rebellion against God." (Mosiah 2:37). "Thus saith the Lord concerning all those who know my power, and have been made partakers thereof, and suffered themselves through the power of the devil to be overcome, and to deny the truth and defy my power: They are they who are the sons of perdition." (D&C 76:31-32). Nephi hit the nail on the head, when he wrote that Satan "leadeth them by the neck with a flaxen cord until he bindeth them with his strong cords forever." (2 Nephi 26:22). After all is said and done, it is the wicked, and not the righteous, who are so horribly treated by the devil.

Nephi knew what the inevitable consequences of the rejection of his message by the people in the land northward would be, and he desperately wanted them to avoid that fate. Therefore, he persevered until the situation became intolerable, giving the people additional doctrine that illuminated the principles of the Plan of Happiness.

The great lessons from the scriptures should not have been lost on these Nephites. Salem had repented, and such was their subsequent righteousness that they had been translated. Whatever the fate of the people, the responsibility was on their shoulders, for Nephi warned them of the consequences of disobedience. Then, he had properly taught what they ought to do to avoid that misfortune. It is disconcerting to realize that, in our day, the world faces similar challenges but largely ignores the voice of warning raised by the servants of God who bear the same message of impending destruction.

When Nephi returned to the land of his nativity, he found the situation equally desperate, with his own people in a state of "awful wickedness, and those Gadianton robbers filling the judgment-seat, having usurped the power and authority of the land." (V. 4). Although they had no legitimate right to government, and their rule was a mockery of justice, they were able to exert a powerfully negative influence on the full spectrum of Nephite society in Zarahemla because of their key positions. Put quite simply, these wicked judges did "no justice unto the children of men." (V. 4).

They condemned "the righteous, because of their righteousness; letting the guilty and the wicked go unpunished because of their money; and moreover, to be held in office at the head of government, to rule and do according to their will, that they might get gain and glory of the world, and, moreover, that they might the more easily commit adultery, and steal, and kill, and do according to their own wills." (V. 5). One immediately feels very uncomfortable reading about these abuses of power in government among the Nephites, because the description of their wicked behavior sounds eerily familiar, since the same scenarios are evident within the supposedly enlightened and self-regulated governments of today's free societies.

In our own time, men and women of respect, reason, and responsibility shudder to think of the excesses committed by freely elected representatives, and feel with Nephi, whose "heart was swollen with sorrow" and who suffered with "agony of his soul." (V. 6). President Kimball once reflected: "The sad, simple truth is that when we do not act preventively in the earlier years, we must later on act redemptively, but with less efficiency and fewer and more labored results." This is as true of societies, as it is of individuals.

Nephi must have felt that, in spite of his best efforts, he was losing ground. "Now, here, you see," said the rabbit to

Alice in Wonderland, "it takes all the running you can do, to keep in the same place. If you want to get somewhere else, you must run at least twice as fast as that! (Lewis Carroll, "Through the Looking Glass," p. 41).

Nephi revealed his human side, when he lamented: "Oh, that I could have had my days in the days when my father Nephi first came out of the land of Jerusalem. Yea, if my days could have been in those days, then would my soul have had joy in the righteousness of my brethren." (V. 7-8). This is ironic, for certainly, he was familiar with Jacob's farewell, wherein he had actually characterized his family as "a lonesome and a solemn people, wanderers, cast out from Jerusalem, born in tribulation, in a wilderness, and hated of (their) brethren, which caused wars and contentions; wherefore, (they) did mourn out (their) days." (Jacob 7:26).

The grass always looks greener in the neighbor's yard (even though it may be over the septic tank). Ultimately, we must all recognize that Heavenly Father knows each of us better than we know ourselves, and has optimally designed our mortal experiences to help us to grow as much as possible. One group is permitted to gain familiarity with, endure, and finally triumph over a set of circumstances carefully tailored to stimulate its maximum growth, and another group has its own unique challenges. Nephi must have appreciated this, when he wrote: "But behold, I am consigned that these are my days, and that my soul shall be filled with sorrow because of this the wickedness of my brethren." (V. 9).

"For yesterday is but a dream, and tomorrow is only a vision. But today well lived makes yesterday a dream of happiness and every tomorrow a vision of hope." (Sanskrit Poem). Nephi took his stewardship responsibilities very seriously, and if he wondered "Who is working harder, I or the devil?" it must have been because he wanted to make sure that his efforts bore fruit. Again and again, though, Heavenly Father reinforced the lesson for Nephi that his reward for a job well done would be the opportunity to do even more.

Interestingly, Nephi chose a very conspicuous spot to pour out his soul unto God. "It was upon a tower, which was in the garden of Nephi, which was by the highway which led to the chief market, which was in the city of Zarahemla." (V. 10). Mormon labored to paint a vivid word picture of the setting, so that we might better understand the powerful effect it would have had on passersby, for "they ran and told the people what they had seen, and the people came together in multitudes." (V. 11).

Had Nephi announced in advance his intention to hold a revival meeting, he might never have enjoyed such an enthusiastic response. After all, his purpose was to express his concerns for the people, call them to repentance, and bear his testimony. His scathing indictment that followed confirms this. Your desire is "to get gain, he declared, "to be praised of men, yea, and that ye might get gold and silver. And ye have set your hearts upon the riches and the vain things of this world, for the which ye do murder, and plunder, and steal, and bear false witness against your neighbor, and do all manner of iniquity." (V. 21). The devil had a great hold upon the hearts of the people of Zarahemla, just as the world today groans under the burden of sin (See V. 15).

Nephi's experience is reminiscent of that of Abinadi. King Noah, with his wicked priests, had broken most if not all of the Ten Commandments. "If ye teach the law of Moses," the prophet had asked, "why do ye not keep it?" (Mosiah 12:29). Abinadi had paid with his life for his bold denunciation of their behavior. Now, it was mandatory that Nephi follow the guidance of the Spirit, for he was in an equally precariously dangerous situation.

Nephi wondered why his made-to-order audience had come to his doorstep, in the first place. "Why have ye gathered yourselves together?" he asked. Is it "that I may tell you of your iniquities? (V. 13). Moths are drawn to the light, but if they venture too closely, they are overcome by the heat, and die. Just so, a wicked and an adulterous generation seeks for a sign. (See Matthew 16:4). Perhaps these multitudes were so jaded that they thought it would be theologically titillating to witness the servant of God performing his strange antics on a tower that had been erected in his yard. They were going to get more than they had bargained for.

Nephi demanded to know how the people had gotten themselves into such a sorry state of affairs. He vividly described how the devil was, at that very moment, "seeking to hurl (their) souls down to everlasting misery and endless wo." (V. 16). His question: "Why will ye die?" should have penetrated even the most hardened hearts. (V. 17, see v. 18). If they refused to repent, he promised that they would be scattered and become "meat for dogs and wild beasts." (V. 19).

The Preacher had written: "I have seen all the works that are done under the sun; and, behold, all is vanity and vexation of spirit." (Ecclesiastes 1:14). Nephi's people had set their hearts upon the vain things of the world. It was this behavior that was at the root of the great evils enumerated in verse 21. Their vanity had led to pride, thereby stifling humility and access to the Spirit. As a result, they could no longer feel the necessity of obedience to the commandments. Instead, they relied on their own efforts and capabilities; on the arm of flesh. Consequently, the quantity and quality of service to their fellowmen diminished, as selfishness overwhelmed selflessness. They were wrapped up in themselves and made very small packages, indeed.

In reality, their actions actually enhanced the vice-like grip of their bondage, instead of giving them the freedom they craved, because they had forfeit their agency as they became imprisoned in the grip of bad habits. Five hundred years earlier, Nephi had written: "There are also secret combinations, even as in times of old, according to the combinations of the devil, for he is the founder of all these things; yea, the founder of murder, and works of darkness; yea, and he leadeth (the unwary) by the neck with a flaxen cord, until he bindeth them with his strong cords forever." (2 Nephi 26:22).

A Psalm of David had warned "Except the Lord keep the city, the watchman waketh but in vain." (Psalms 127:1). Nephi echoed his warning to the people of Zarahemla, declaring that except they speedily repent, that "great city, and also all those great cities which (were) round about, which (were) in the land of (their) possession, (should) be taken away" by conquering armies, or be destroyed by the wrath of God. (V. 22).

None of us must ever be found asleep at our posts. Inspired counsel is not given as a sedative, but rather as a stimulant. It is a simple prescription: The Lord will strengthen and bless those who repent and keep the commandments, but not necessarily with telestial toys that might lead the faithful on detours leading away from the strait and narrow path. Nor will He strengthen us by making our way easy, lest we be pacified and lulled into a false sense of carnal security.

Instead, He will much more subtly fortify us. He will see that we have opportunities to be anxiously engaged in good causes. (See D&C 58:27). He will help us to work out our salvation with fear and trembling before the Lord. (Philippians 2:12, Alma 34:37, & Mormon 9:27). He will cause us to move out of our comfort zones into the stimulating environment of service, and even onto the uncomfortable road that leads to Gethsemane. Socrates had said: "Know thyself," Cicero admonished, "Control thyself" and the Apostles taught in the shadow of the Greatest Example of all, saying "Give thyself" completely and without reservation. (1 Timothy 4:14).

These principles had become alien to the people of Zarahemla, because they had united themselves with "that secret band which was established by Gadianton." (V. 25). Nephi declared: "Except ye repent ye shall perish; yea, even your lands shall be taken from you, and ye shall be destroyed from off the face of the earth." The people had so many temporal blessings that their lifestyle had become "beyond that which is good." (V. 26). In other words, their prosperity had inflated their self-confidence and collective self-reliance to their ultimate detriment. The key to remaining in God's good graces was to be dignified and yet humble, and to take satisfaction in the worthy results of their accomplishments, while giving God the credit.

Nephi wanted to teach his people that peace only comes through personal integrity, and that we must keep our covenants, no matter the cost. We "should have the integrity of Abraham, and not be like those who say: 'Yes, I will obey the Lord! But first, I must move my sheep to another pasture, and mend my tents. I should be able to obey by the end of the week, or by the first of next week, at the very latest.'" (Spencer W. Kimball, "The Example of Abraham").

The frightening reality was that violating their covenants left the people of Zarahemla in Satan's power, the personification of which was the terrifying Band of Gadianton. Joseph Smith wrote: "When we undertake to cover our sins, or to gratify our pride, our vain ambition, or to exercise control or dominion or compulsion upon the souls of the children of men, in any degree of unrighteousness, behold, the heavens withdraw themselves; the Spirit of the Lord is grieved; and when it is withdrawn, Amen to the priesthood or the authority of that man." (D&C 121:37). Although we may still hold the office, we can lose the power, if our actions reflect our vanity, profanity, or mockery. In these circumstances, we voluntarily trade the character traits of our Heavenly Father for those of the wily old fox who is Satan.

The fox that appears in Old Testament passages is likely the jackal, who is a beast that "devours the bodies of the dead, and even digs them up from their graves." ("Smith's Bible Dictionary", p. 198). How fitting, then, that the devil would be associated with such an animal. Denied a physical body, he ravages those whose faith is weak, spiritually murdering them in a twisted attempt to gain dominion over the bodies he so desperately craves.

Finally, Nephi bore strong testimony, affirming the truth of the things he had said. "I know that these things are true because the Lord God has made them known unto me, therefore I testify that they shall be." (V. 29).

"Gadianton robbers
(filled) the judgment seats,
having usurped the power and
authority of the land; laying aside
the commandments of God, and not in
least aright before him; doing no justice unto
the children of men; condemning the righteous
because of their righteousness; letting the guilty and
the wicked go unpunished because of their money; and
moreover, to be held in office at the head of government, to
rule and do according to their wills, that they might get
gain and glory of the world, and, moreover, that they
might more easily commit adultery, and steal,
and kill, and do according to their own
wills." (Helaman 7:4-5).

Helaman
Chapter 8

By strongly affirming his faith in God and bearing testimony of these things, Nephi placed his personal safety in great jeopardy, for among the people who had listened to him "were judges, who also belonged to the secret band of Gadianton, and they were angry." (V. 1, see Helaman 7:4).

The judges asked the people: "Why seest thou this man, and hearest him revile against this people, and against our law?" (V. 2). Since it was not a crime in Zarahemla to revile against the people in general, there can be little doubt that the judges were seeking to bring charges against Nephi for false prophecy. The priests of Noah had used the same strategy against Abinadi. To Noah, the people had reported: "He saith that thou shalt be as a stalk, even as a dry stalk of the field, which is run over by the beasts, and trodden under foot." (Mosiah 12:11). This is a classic Near Eastern curse, or "oath of adjuration," and the charge was that Abinadi had pretended that the Lord had spoken it. The claim of the people was that Abinadi had "prophesied in vain." (Mosiah 12:13). Inasmuch as false prophecy was a crime in ancient Israel, Abinadi had been delivered into the hands of Noah, setting the stage for the king and his priests to rule in the case. They had been unsuccessful, and so would the judges in Zarahemla who now sought to ensnare Nephi by a similar stratagem.

In the beginning of the Dispensation of the Fulness of Times, Joseph Smith was repeatedly forced to deal with the same type of malicious accusations, and often found himself in courts of law facing trumped-up charges of no substance. Today, such legal harassment would be called "malicious prosecution," but in times past the righteous had no protection from this type of intimidation. Satan's strategies never seem to change.

Likewise, the wicked never seem to learn from the mistakes and bad examples of their forbearers. Because they are faithless, they see no alternative but to rely on the arm of flesh. After all, it is the natural thing to do. To Nephi, they said: "We are powerful, and our cities great, therefore our enemies can have no power over us." (V. 6). Suffering from congenital short sightedness it was impossible for them to recognize the irony of their arrogant declaration. They were blinded to any sense of historical perspective, and could not draw a parallel between their situation and that of the wicked City of Ammonihah, whose inhabitants had said essentially the same thing to Alma, shortly before their own destruction. In 34 A.D., the voice of the Lord would declare to a New World Order: "Behold, that great city of Zarahemla have I burned with fire, and the inhabitants thereof." (3 Nephi 9:3).

However, Nephi's pointed testimony concerning the iniquities of the people had convinced some of them that he was a true prophet. These were moved to declare in his defense: "Let this man alone, for he is a good man, and those things which he saith will surely come to pass, except we repent." (V. 7). Since he had correctly identified their sins, they reasoned that his predictions regarding Zarahemla's fate would also come to pass. "He knoweth, as well, all things which shall befall us as he knoweth of our iniquities." (V. 8).

Whether these individuals were truly converted and had obtained testimonies is questionable. The ebb and flow of Nephite repentance and apostasy moved so quickly in Zarahemla that it became blurred. Those in Nephi's audience who were inclined to defend him might have been among those who soon thereafter would slide back into apostasy.

Perhaps a more prudent approach by the people would have been that which was advocated by Gamaliel, in Jerusalem. The scriptures report that he advised the Pharisees there to "refrain from these men, and let them alone; for if this counsel or this work be of men, it will come to naught. But if it be of God, ye cannot overthrow it; lest haply ye be found even to fight against God." (Acts 5:38-39).

As is often the case, though, such advice was summarily rejected as the disobedient moved forward doggedly and determinedly with their plans. Those who wanted to take Nephi's life would have preferred to cover their sins, for secret combinations prefer to do just that. They work within small cells and go to great lengths to carry out their terrorist acts under the cloak of anonymity. Theirs are truly works of darkness. Therefore, because of the publicity associated with his ministry, "those people who sought to destroy Nephi were compelled because of their fear, that they did not lay their hands on him." (V. 10).

Mobs are very effective and do great damage within short time spans, but they have poor staying power. As soon as their anonymous faces begin to take on recognizable identities, their members hesitate, and, unsure of themselves, shrink from active participation.

Secret combinations are more insidiously dangerous, inasmuch as they are composed of those who have taken solemn oaths. They are driven by obsessive ideology, however misguided it may be. This is why the prophets were so afraid of the secret combinations in The Book of Mormon. They recognized that their capacity for fanaticism empowered them with the ability to do lasting damage.

Because of the hesitation of his adversaries, however, Nephi was given another opportunity to speak to the people. When he did so, he avoided a dispute over his interpretation of the Law by teaching from the scriptures that God did give prophets the power to foretell future events. (V. 11-12). By citing the example of Moses, who parted the waters of the Red Sea, Nephi reminded the people that God does confer tremendous power on His agents. "Why should ye dispute among yourselves, and say that he hath given unto me no power?" he asked. (V. 12).

To Nephi, the real power given to Moses was manifest in his witness of Jesus Christ. "Yea, did he not bear record that the Son of God should come?" (V. 14). In these scriptures and in Numbers 21:8-9 are recorded the account of the brazen serpent. However, there is no Old Testament record of the testimony of Moses concerning the Son of God. Surely, this is one of the plain and precious parts that have been taken from the Bible. (See 1 Nephi 13:26-29, 34:40 & 14:23).

Nephi explained: "As he lifted up the brazen serpent in the wilderness, even so shall he be lifted up who should come. And as many as should look upon that serpent should live, even so as many as should look upon the Son of God with faith, having a contrite spirit, might live, even unto that life which is eternal." (V. 14-15, see 1 Nephi 17:41, Alma 33:19, 37:45-47, & John 3:14-15). When Nephi emphasized to his audience of scoffers and unbelievers that not only did Moses "testify of these things, but also all the holy prophets, from his days even to the days of Abraham," we are presented with more evidence of plain and precious parts of the Bible that are missing from the King James Translation. (V. 16).

Could the account of the serpent on The Plates of Brass be the model for the serpent motif that is so enduring in Meso-American art and architecture? It was the Great White God of the Maya, after all, who was Quetzalcoatl, or the bird serpent of precious plumage.

Today, the quetzal is the national bird of Guatemala, because of its vibrant color, and 'coatl' means 'serpent' in the Nahuatl language. Kukulkan roughly translates as 'feathered serpent' in the Mayan language. The earliest worship of a feathered serpent was in Teotihuacan, between the first century B.C. and the first century A.D.

Nephi then pointed out to those who had made the claim that he had reviled against the Law that "Abraham not only knew of these things, but there were many before the days of Abraham who were called by the order of God … a great many thousand years before his coming." (V. 18). In effect, Nephi explained that all the prophets of old, by virtue of their holy calling, taught the same truths that he, by the same authority, now expounded to the people. (See D&C 107:8). Samuel the Lamanite would also shortly make his appearance to reinforce for the people of Zarahemla the point that Nephi was now making. That is to say, the prophets of old had foretold the birth and mission of the Messiah. Why should these people, who were living in such close temporal proximity to His mortal ministry, doubt the words of the prophets? (See Commentary Reference to Helaman 16:20).

Even the wicked inhabitants in Zarahemla would recognize in Nephi's reference to Abraham that their ancestral patriarch had a testimony of the Savior. "Your father Abraham rejoiced to see my day" said the Savior, "and he saw it, and was glad." (John 8:56). We find the biblical antecedent to this "plain and precious" passage only in the Joseph Smith Translation of the Bible. "It came to pass," reads that text, "that Abram looked forth and saw the days of the Son of Man, and was glad, and his soul found rest, and he believed in the Lord; and the Lord counted it unto him for righteousness." (J.S.T. Genesis 5:12)

Then Nephi cited additional prophets with whom the people of Zarahemla would be familiar. The prophet Zenos, referenced 12 times in The Book of Mormon, had testified of Christ, and suffered martyrdom for his efforts. (V. 19). Zenock, mentioned 5 times in The Book of Mormon, had been a powerful witness, as well. (V. 20). Ezias is also identified by Nephi as a witness. (V. 20). This is the sole reference to this prophet in The Book of Mormon. "We are left to wonder whether perhaps this man is the same as the one called Esaias, a contemporary of Abraham, one who is twice mentioned in the revelations given to Joseph Smith." (Robert L. Millet, "Doctrinal Commentary on The Book of Mormon," V. 3, p. 377, see D&C 76:100, & 84:12-13).

Nephi then identified Isaiah and Jeremiah as prophets whose witnesses were recorded on The Plates of Brass, and who knew by the spirit of prophecy that the Savior should come. (V. 20). Abraham had lived about 2,000 B.C. His antiquity was to the Nephites about the same as the Nephites are to us. Perhaps there is a subtle message here for latter-day readers of The Book of Mormon. Perhaps we should give heed to the counsel of Nephi, just as he exhorted his brethren to listen to Abraham, Isaiah, and others of the ancient brotherhood.

Nephi continued to attack the credibility of those in his audience who were members of the secret Band of Gadianton. He asked: "Will you dispute that Jerusalem was destroyed? Will ye say that the sons of Zedekiah were not slain, all except it were Mulek?" Of course, they could not say this, because their very presence in Zarahemla confirmed the fact, for many of them were descendants of the very party that had fled Jerusalem with Mulek at the time of the destruction of Jerusalem by the Babylonians. (See Helaman 6:10, 2 Kings 25:7, & Commentary Reference to Omni 1:15). As Nephi said: "Do ye not behold that the seed of Zedekiah are with us" even now? (V. 21). The Nephites knew very well that the reason that the Jews at Jerusalem had been destroyed was because they had lost the protection of the Lord when they no longer kept the commandments.

Finally, Nephi invoked the memory of one of their greatest forbearers, the prophet "Lehi (who) was driven out of Jerusalem because he testified of these things." (V. 22). Those who speak the truth always draw the fire of the disobedient. Lashish Letter #8, discovered in 1938 but written at the time of Lehi, complained: "The prophets of doom are undermining the morale of the people in town and country." (Hugh Nibley, "Since Cumorah," p. 311). The comparison that Nephi drew could not have been lost on his audience.

Nephi said: "Almost all of our fathers (perhaps with the sole exceptions of Omni, Amaron, Chemish, and Abinadom) have testified of the coming of Christ." (V. 22, see Commentary References to Omni 1:10-13). Of those faithful witnesses, Nephi assured the assembled multitude that God was "with them, and he did manifest himself unto them; that they were redeemed by him." (V. 23).

Having turned the accusation of the judges into an effective forum for his own sermon, Nephi was able to use the power of the word, rather than rhetoric or violence, to defeat the judges. (V. 24-26, see v. 1). Once again, the anger of the disobedient, and those who could not control themselves, had ultimately destroyed their own credibility. It had required a cool head and spiritual sensitivity on the part of Nephi, but he had risen to the occasion.

To confirm his priesthood office and the validity of his message in the eyes of the people, Nephi lastly made an easily verifiable short-term prophecy. He said: Destruction "is now even at your doors; yea, go ye in unto the judgment-seat, and search; and behold, your judge is murdered, and he lieth in his blood; and he hath been murdered by his brother, who seeketh to sit in the judgment-seat. And behold, they both belong to your secret band, whose author is Gadianton and the evil one who seeketh to destroy the souls of men." (V. 27-28).

Helaman
Chapter 9

In the Book of Deuteronomy, we read: "If the thing follow not, nor come to pass, that is the thing which the Lord hath not spoken." (Deuteronomy 18:22). The multitude that had gathered at Nephi's garden by the highway that led to the chief market in the City of Zarahemla sought to know if Nephi's prophecy regarding the murder of the Chief Judge was true. (See Helaman 7:10 & 8:27). If it were not, they were prepared to condemn him to death according to the Law. Therefore, five messengers were dispatched to the judgment-seat. These men "said among themselves, as they went: Behold, now we will know of a surety whether this man be a prophet." (V. 1-2). How much better it would have been if they had already been converted by the power of Nephi's priesthood directed teaching, and if they had received a witness by the Spirit of his prophetic mantle.

When they saw the Chief Judge lying dead beside his judgment-seat, "they were astonished exceedingly, insomuch that they fell to the earth." (V. 4). They were overcome by the sudden realization that all that Nephi had prophesied would surely come to pass. Feeling acutely vulnerable, their knees buckled, and "they did quake, and had fallen to the earth." (V. 5). They were as Belshazzar, who saw the handwriting on the wall, so to speak. "His countenance was changed, and his thoughts troubled him, so that the joints of his loins were loosed, and his knees smote one against another." (Daniel 5:6).

Meanwhile, the servants of the Chief Judge, who had earlier discovered the body, had sounded the alarm, and when they returned to find the five unconscious men nearby, it was naturally assumed that they were the murderers. (V. 6-8). They were summarily cast into prison. Only later did matters get straightened out, so that they were released on the recognizance of the judges who had been at the garden of Nephi and had dispatched them in the first place. (V. 9-15).

These judges "belonged to the secret band of Gadianton." (Helaman 8:1). Both Seezoram, the Chief Judge, and Seantum, his own brother who had murdered him, belonged to that band as well. (V. 23 & 26, see Helaman 8:28). A real power struggle seems to have been in full swing, with fratricide of no concern to members of a renegade faction of the secret combination jockeying for position within the organization.

The judges thought nothing of falsely condemning a prophet of God, for murder was in their hearts. They "did cry out against Nephi" and caused that he "should be taken and bound and brought before the multitude, and they began to question him in divers' ways that they might cross him, that they might accuse him to death." (V. 16 & 19). With their band in control of the government, they believed that it just might be possible to condemn him under the guise of legal procedure.

But Nephi continued to withstand their pressure tactics of intimidation. Again, he rebuked his accusers, declaring: "O ye fools, ye uncircumcised of heart, ye blind, and ye stiffnecked people, do ye know how long the Lord your God will suffer you that ye shall go on in this your way of sin? O ye ought to begin to howl and mourn, because of the great destruction which at this time doth await you, except ye shall repent." (V. 21-22).

He deflected their questions, and once again challenged them by identifying the true murderer and ordering them to prove his words. (V. 25-35). "And then shall ye know that I am an honest man, and that I am sent unto you from God." (V. 36). Thus, would his authority be firmly established, and his accusers would have no basis for further argument. It came to pass exactly as Nephi had said it would, and he obtained his liberty, for the cause to detain him had evaporated. (V. 37-38). Interestingly, these events led some to believe Nephi's words. Some said he was a prophet, and others that he was a god, "for except he was a god he could not know of all things." (V. 39-41). To these people, Nephi's prophetic power was more important than his message. They were star-struck, but blind to the light, nevertheless.

And so, we come, finally, to what may be the real reason for the inclusion by Mormon of this rather lengthy account of Nephi's experiences in Zarahemla shortly before the birth of the Savior. Can it be that Mormon saw our day, and understood that the prophets of God who would stand at the head of the Restored Church would be ignored by the world even as it was carried by the floodwaters of sin toward the precipice of eternal damnation?

Today, all save the elect of God brush off the message of the Restoration of the Gospel, and spiritual Babylon waits for the theological titillation of priesthood power. But it is not a change in the inner vessel that it desires. It is a wicked and adulterous generation that seeks a sign. It is a society that is "past feeling" and thus needs greater and greater stimulation of the physical senses, mistakenly substituting an adrenalin rush for the sustaining influence of the Spirit.

In the Last Days, the Savior has published the commandment that we might "give diligent heed to the words of eternal life. For you shall live by every word that proceedeth forth from the mouth of God." (D&C 84:43-44). Nephi's ministry in Zarahemla was focused on leading the people to that level of commitment, so that they might become a people who would stand as independent witnesses in the days prior to Christ's mortal ministry.

The Word and Will of the Lord, given to Brigham Young at the Winter Quarters of the Camp of Israel, declared: "Marvel not at these things, for ye are not yet pure; ye can not yet bear my glory; but ye shall behold it if ye are faithful in keeping all my words that I have given you, from the days of Adam to Abraham, from Abraham to Moses, from Moses to Jesus and his apostles, and from Jesus and his apostles to Joseph Smith." (D&C 136:37). Today, we could add: "And from Joseph Smith to our current living prophets, seers, and revelators."

As we read The Book of Helaman, and marvel at the faith of men like Nephi, we should remember to apply the message to our own circumstances, as we try to live "by every word that proceedeth forth from the mouth of God" and from His authorized servants, the prophets, as we prepare to receive the Lord of all the Earth at His Second Coming.

Joseph F. Smith wrote: "The greatest event that has ever occurred in the world since the resurrection of the Son of God from the tomb and His ascension on high, was the coming of the Father and of the Son to that boy Joseph Smith, to prepare the way for the laying of the foundation of his kingdom." ("Joseph Smith & The Restoration," p. 54). The ministries of men like Nephi rank high in importance among those events that occurred before the mortal mission of Jesus Christ.

Nephi hoped his message would help the people to experience the exhilaration of personal revelation. He wanted them to understand that each one of them mattered to personally to Heavenly Father.

In our Dispensation, B.H. Roberts "wrote repeatedly that without the renewing insights of modern revelation, no official creed or statement of faith, and no high-sounding abstractions of the philosophers really answered the question: 'Why did God create man?' For him the gloriously emancipating truth was that the self-existence of God is paralleled by the uncreated spark in the spirit of man, and that God transmitted to his sons and daughters the highest potential in the universe - his likeness." (Truman Madsen, "Defender of The Faith," p. 192).

Nephi loved the People of Zarahemla. He recognized them as sons and daughters of God, and felt that they were so important that he was willing to devote his life, even give his life, to minister to their needs. It is a measure of their apostasy that they did not return the favor of his love and respect. The people largely rejected Nephi, a prophet of God! The Savior spoke truly, when He declared: "No prophet is accepted in his own country." (Luke 4:24, see Matthew 13:57).

Valiant defenders of the faith in our own day have offered contrasting examples to the unbelievers in Zarahemla, and striking parallels to Nephi. "B.H. Roberts was once asked an intricate question on the life and teaching of the Prophet. As he answered, the elders saw their beginning curiosity expanded to vast proportions. They nodded in grateful appreciation. All of a sudden, he looked up and raised his hands and exclaimed: 'Brother Joseph, I have fought for you, I have defended you, I have loved you,' and made one of the most spiritual and emotional outbursts. Those present declared that they had never heard a stronger testimony of the Prophet." (Truman Madsen, "Defender of The Faith, p. 388).

Because the people in Zarahemla were morally and spiritually bankrupt, they had no reserves from which to draw strength when Nephi preached among them. Once again, contrast their experience with that of Elder Roberts: "Having gone word by word and line by line through the writings of Joseph Smith, and having read everything he could find on his life, he found Joseph to be possessed of a deeper and richer comprehension of Christ than anyone he had read in the Christian tradition since the apostles. Through all Roberts' buffetings and his intellectual probings, honing his own mind with the major figures in the history of Western thought, this conviction never diminished. And as his extensive knowledge of the alternatives increased, his convictions deepened: Joseph Smith told the truth. Joseph Smith was a prism of the Lord Jesus Christ." ("Defender of The Faith," p. 93). The same could be said of Nephi. He told the truth and was a prism of the Lord Jesus Christ, and had the people looked to him, they would have understood the many faceted Plan of Salvation and recognized its relevance. Their hearts would have been changed through faith on His name, and they would have been made free. (See Mosiah 5:7-8).

Instead, Nephi was constrained to characterize the people of the City of Zarahemla as fools, uncircumcised of heart, blind, and stiffnecked. (See V. 21). These qualities prevented them from participating in the ordinances of salvation that would have been as the gateway leading to the path of progression toward eternal life in the Celestial Kingdom.

Reading about it, or hearing about it, is not enough. Joseph Smith taught: "Could we read and comprehend all that has been written from the days of Adam, on the relation of man to God and angels in a future state, we would know very little about it. Reading the experience of others, or the revelations given to them, can never give us a comprehensive view of our condition and true relation to God. Knowledge of these things can only be obtained by experience through the ordinances of God set forth for that purpose. Could you gaze into heaven five minutes, you would know more than you would by reading all that has ever been written on the subject." (H.C., 6:50).

Moses held up the Brazen Serpent as a Type of Christ and yearned for the people to look to it and live. Nephi held up the example of Moses and all the other prophets and urged the Nephites to do the same. Through laborious means and at great personal sacrifice, Mormon provided us with the Prophecy of Nephi for the same reasons. "And behold," his son Moroni wrote, "these things which we have desired concerning our brethren, yea, even their restoration to the knowledge of Christ, are according to the prayers of all the saints who have dwelt in the land." (Mormon 9:36).

Why did Mormon
include this rather lengthy account of Nephi's
experiences in Zarahemla shortly before the birth of the
Savior? (See Helaman 9). Can it be that Mormon saw our
day, and understood that the prophets of God who would
stand at the head of the Restored Church would be
ignored by the world even as it was carried
by the floodwaters of sin toward
the precipice of eternal
damnation?

Helaman
Chapter 10

Following the three-year ministry of Jesus Christ, and after He had shown Himself to His apostles subsequent to His resurrection, Simon Peter was nevertheless moved to declare: "I go a fishing." (John 21:3). In Peter's mind, there was nothing left to do but resume business as usual. In Zarahemla, in spite of the priesthood power manifested by Nephi, "the people divided hither and thither and went their ways, leaving Nephi alone, as he was standing in the midst of them." (V. 1).

He must have concluded that he had given his best effort to a futile cause, and he turned "towards his own house, pondering upon the things which the Lord had shown unto him." (V. 2). As he was doing so, the voice of the Lord came to him, "saying, blessed art thou, Nephi, for those things which thou hast done; for I have beheld how thou hast with unwearyingness declared the word, which I have given unto thee, unto this people. And thou hast not feared them, and hast not sought thine own life, but hast sought my will, and to keep my commandments." (V. 4).

"A favorite theme of Brigham Young was that the dominion God gives to us is designed to test us and enable us to show to ourselves, our fellows, and all the heavens just how we would act if entrusted with God's power." (Hugh Nibley, "Subduing the Earth," p. 89-90). The Lord told Nephi that because he had been unwavering, he would be made "mighty in word and in deed, in faith and in works." (V. 5). He would be given the unlimited power of God, because he could be trusted to do exactly as God would do in similar circumstances.

The exercise of priesthood power is based solely upon the principles of righteousness. If, in the capacity of the priesthood, we "undertake to cover our sins, or to gratify our pride, our vain ambition, or to exercise control or dominion or compulsion upon the souls of the children of men, in any degree of unrighteousness," the authority of our priesthood is taken from us. (D&C 121:34-37).

"You are, and always will be, independent in that stage of development to which your voluntary decisions and divine powers have led," wrote Truman Madsen. "There are limits all along the way to what you can be and do. But you are not a billiard ball. No power in the universe can coerce your complete assent or dissent. This thesis on capacity translates Bergson's metaphor into breath-taking fact: 'The universe is a machine for the making of gods.'" ("Eternal Man," p. 18).

Of all His creations, we are the only one with the capacity to willful disobey natural laws. We are the recipients of agency; of independent action. Squirrels gather nuts, bears eat berries, and birds fly south as the winter approaches; bees produce honey, and beavers build dams. Salmon return to their streams to spawn. But we have free will, and more than that, we have moral agency, or the power one the one hand to choose to live in harmony with God and nature, or on the other hand to "walk in crooked paths." (Alma 7:20).

Nor does the foreknowledge of God diminish our moral agency. James E. Talmage taught: "Our Heavenly Father knows the nature and dispositions of each of His children, a knowledge gained by long observation and experience in the past eternity of our primeval childhood; a knowledge compared with which that gained by earthly parents through mortal experience with their children is infinitesimally small. By reason of that surpassing knowledge, God reads our future individually and collectively as communities and nations. He knows what each will do under given conditions, and sees the end from the beginning. His foreknowledge is based on intelligence and reason; He foresees the future as a state which naturally and surely will be; not as one which must be because He has arbitrarily willed that it should be." ("The Great Apostasy." p. 20).

In the case of Nephi, God had cause to be supernally confident, with unshakable faith. "Behold, I give unto you power," he said, "that whatsoever ye shall seal on earth shall be sealed in heaven; and whatsoever ye shall loose on earth shall be loosed in heaven; and thus, ye shall have power among this people. And thus, if ye shall say to this temple it shall be rent in twain, it shall be done. And if ye shall say unto this mountain, Be thou cast down and become smooth, it shall be done. And behold, if ye shall say that God shall smite this people, it shall come to pass." (V. 7-10). Nephi held the priesthood power to act in the name of Almighty God, as it were by divine investiture of authority.

"Every one being ordained after this order and calling (of the Melchizedek Priesthood) should have power, by faith, to break mountains, to divide the seas, to dry up waters, to turn them out of their course; to put at defiance the armies of nations, to divide the earth, to break every band, to stand in the presence of God; to do all things according to His will, according to His command, subdue principalities and powers; and this by the will of the Son of God which was before the foundation of the world." (J.S.T. Genesis 14:30-31).

The concept of priesthood and its offices can have real meaning only if we have accepted God and Christ, have entered the fold in the waters of baptism, and have received the Holy Ghost. (See D&C 20:37, & 1 Corinthians 2:14). The Apostle Peter sent a second epistle "to them that have obtained like precious faith with us through the righteousness of God and our Saviour Jesus Christ. According as his divine power hath given unto us all things that pertain unto life and godliness, through the knowledge of him that hath called us to glory and virtue; whereby are given unto us exceeding great and precious promises: That by these ye might be partakers of the divine nature." (2 Peter 1:1, 3 & 4). These are they who know the power of God and experience the whisperings of the Spirit. "He that keepeth his commandments receiveth truth and light until he is glorified in truth and knoweth all things." (D&C 93:28).

In this dispensation, only the President of the Church of Jesus Christ of Latter-day Saints holds priesthood keys in their fulness. When Joseph Smith conferred upon Brigham Young, who was at that time the President of the Council of The Twelve, the keys of the sealing power, Parley P. Pratt said: "This last key of the priesthood is the most sacred of all, and pertains exclusively to the First Presidency of the Church, without whose sanction and approval or authority, no sealing blessing shall be administered pertaining to things of the resurrection and the life to come." ("Millennial Star 5:151).

Thus armed, Nephi was once again enjoined by God to "go and declare unto (the people of Zarahemla) that thus saith the Lord God, who is the Almighty: except ye repent ye shall be smitten, even unto destruction." (V. 11). It would have been impossible for Nephi to deliver the message more powerfully than by invoking the name of the Lord when doing so.

The discouragement evident in Nephi's lament recorded in Helaman Chapter 7:7 was now gone. With firm conviction and without the slightest hesitation, "he did not stop, and did not go unto his own house, but did return unto the multitudes and began to declare unto them the word of the Lord." (V. 12).

Likewise did Peter, James, and John, with Andrew, immediately respond to the Savior's invitation: "Come follow me." (Luke 18:19). "And Jesus, walking by the sea of Galilee, saw two brethren, Simon called Peter, and Andrew his brother, casting a net into the sea ... And he saith unto them, Follow me, and I will make you fishers of men. And they straightway left their nets, and followed him. And going on from thence, he saw other two brethren, James ... and John his brother ... with Zebedee, their father, mending their nets; and he called them. And they immediately left the ship and their father, and followed him." (Matthew 4:18-22).

For his part, Nephi was received no more graciously than he had been previously, but he persevered, and went forth in the power of the Spirit "from multitude to multitude, declaring the word of God, even until he had declared it unto them all, or sent it forth among all the people." (V. 17). We have been warned that if we have had the opportunity to teach others correct principles, but have failed to do so, we may be responsible for their sins. We are led to the sobering conclusion that Nephi did not return to his own house for some time, until every accountable person in the Land of Zarahemla had received his personal witness and warning to repent.

To their potential good fortune, the Lord loved the Nephites so much that he sent a prophet of God to minister among them, bearing the promise of every blessing available through the priesthood. Unfortunately, they rejected his message and the opportunity for Nephi to administer the Gospel and confer the gifts of the Spirit. Therein lie the keys of the mysteries of the Kingdom of God and of the knowledge of God. All spiritual blessings of the Church flow through these priesthood channels. We are "born again" through sanctification by the Spirit that only is made possible by ordinances that are driven by the power of the priesthood.

It is the priesthood that administers salvation to mankind, and its bearers represent the Savior in order to benefit those who have proven their worthiness. Thus, may men and women become sons and daughters of Christ, to be adopted into His family, and to be one with Him, as He is One with the Father. (See Mosiah 5:7).

"This unity is a Type of completeness. The mind of any one member of the Godhead is the mind of the others. Seeing, as each of them does, with the eye of perfection, they understand alike, guided by the same principles of unerring justice and equity." (James E. Talmage, "Articles of Faith," p. 41). There is a physical and spiritual rapport between the Father and the Son, and between them and true believers. Through this rapport, that is perfected within us by the Holy Ghost, we become one in a spiritual sense.

The Priesthood facilitates this unity by administering Gospel ordinances in the temple, where God's children enter into the patriarchal order of celestial marriage, and are organized into eternal family units. There, we learn to govern temporally and spiritually, so it is only natural that we would covenant to consecrate our time and talents to the Church and Kingdom, and would put our shoulders to the wheel in preparation for the millennial reign of Jesus Christ.

These priesthood powers include the means to gain eternal life, or the kind of life that God lives. This is done with an oath and a covenant. (See D&C 84:39). Included therein is the opportunity to have our calling and election made sure, by "the more sure word of prophecy." (2 Peter 1:10 & 19). Finally, it even includes the power to see the Savior face to face. (See D&C 93:1). Faithful members of the Church are "entitled and expected to seek and obtain all the spiritual blessings of the Gospel, including the crowning blessing of seeing the Lord face to face." (Bruce R. McConkie, "The Promised Messiah," p. 594-595).

"Verily, thus saith the Lord: It shall come to pass that every soul who forsaketh his sins" through repentance, "and cometh unto me" by the strait and narrow gate of baptism, "and calleth on my name" in prayer, "and obeyeth my voice" by listening to the promptings of the Holy Ghost, "and keepeth my commandments" in obedience, "shall see my face and know that I am." (D&C 93:1).

The Savior was quite clear when He said: "Not every one that saith unto me, Lord, Lord, shall enter into the kingdom of heaven, but he that doeth the will of my Father which is in heaven." (Matthew 7:21). He explained that if we do his will, we "shall know of the doctrine, whether it be of God, or whether I speak of myself." (John 7:17). Today, the humanist school of apologists recites platitudes about the great teacher Jesus of Nazareth. But make no mistake. Either He was what He said He was, or He was the greatest imposter the world has ever seen. There is no middle ground.

As for Nephi, he set the standard for righteous priesthood stewards everywhere. In fact, he raised the bar for future missionaries, for the circumstances under which he conducted his ministry are not so very different from our own. He provided a personal role model for each of us to emulate. If Nephi was still a young man during these times, he had certainly internalized guiding principles at an early age. When we think of Nephi, these lines seem applicable: "The stars fade away, the sun himself grow dim with age, and nature sink in years. But (Nephi) shall flourish in immortal youth, unhurt amidst the war of elements, the wreck of matter, and the crash of worlds." (Joseph Addison, "Cato," Act 5, Scene 1).

Helaman
Chapter 11

"Heaven lies about us in our infancy! Shades of the prison-house begin to close upon the growing boy. But he beholds the light, and whence it flows; he sees it in his joy. The youth, who daily farther from the east must travel, still is nature's priest, and by the vision splendid, is on his way attended. At length, the man perceives it die away, and fade into the light of common day." (William Wordsworth, "Ode: Intimations of Immortality").

Nephi and Lehi were two men who did not lose the wide-eyed wonder of youth. In their childhood, their father Helaman surely had told them stories about their heritage, and they must have been proud of their given names. "Helaman taught his sons; yea, he did teach them many things which are not written, and also many things which are written." (Helaman 5:13, see Helaman 5:5-12).

They needed all the faith, resilience, self-assurance, and self-confidence that good upbringing could give them, because conditions continued to deteriorate badly "insomuch that there were wars throughout all the land among all the people of Nephi." (V. 1). Rather than the Lamanites, it was instead the "secret band of robbers" that was responsible for the "work of destruction and wickedness." (V. 2).

Lest latter-day readers become too complacent when learning about these ancient conspiracies, it should be remembered that Nephi, the son of Father Lehi, described our day in these words: "And there are also secret combinations, even as in times of old, according to the combinations of the devil, for he is the founder of all these things; yea, the founder of murder, and works of darkness; yea, and he leadeth them by the neck with a flaxen cord, until he bindeth them with his strong cords forever." (2 Nephi 26:22).

We are taught to love our enemies, and to pray for them that despitefully use us, but at the same time we are also cautioned to have an "everlasting hatred against sin and iniquity." (Alma 37:32, see Matthew 5:44). Nephi now focused the power of the priesthood on the immediate problem at hand. He cried "unto the Lord, saying: O Lord, do not suffer that this people should be destroyed by the sword; but O Lord, rather let there be a famine in the land, to stir them up in remembrance of the Lord their God, and perhaps they will repent and turn to thee." (V. 4).

Too often, when threatened, we become anti-enemy, rather than pro-gospel. Nephi, though, did not lose his eternal perspective. He had been given the awesome power of God, but he did not use it to curse the people. Rather, he determined that they deserved one last desperate chance to come to their senses, and to repent of their iniquities, after much needed chastisement.

"And so, it was done." (V. 5). The famine became so intense that the people "were smitten that they did perish by thousands in the more wicked parts of the land." (V. 6). When "the people saw that they were about to perish by famine, they began to remember the Lord their God; and they began to remember the words of Nephi." (V. 7). But, as we shall see, they could change their lives only by first changing their hearts.

Conditions in the very Last Days will be similar. "And thus, with the sword and by bloodshed the inhabitants of the earth shall mourn; and with famine, and plague, and earthquake, and the thunder of heaven, and the fierce and vivid lightning also, shall the inhabitants of the earth be made to feel the wrath, and indignation, and chastening hand of an Almighty God, until the consumption decreed hath made a full end of all nations." (D&C 87:6). In the judgments that precede the Second Coming, all earthly kingdoms will come to an end, and the Kingdom of God will triumph and become the one political power during a thousand years of peace and righteousness. (See D&C 87:6). During the critical years before the Savior's birth, and before His appearance to the Nephites, the same physical processes were taking place to prepare the people for the arrival of their Sovereign.

"Because of the famine and the pestilence and destruction which (had) come unto them," the people did repent. (V. 15). They even "swept away the band of Gadianton from amongst them insomuch that they (had) become extinct." (V. 10). "The whole face of the land was filled with rejoicing; and they did no more seek to destroy Nephi, but they did esteem him as a great prophet, and a man of God, having great power and authority given unto him from God. And behold, Lehi, his brother, was not a whit behind him as to things pertaining to righteousness." (V. 18-19).

For three years, the people lived in peace and harmony, "and the church did spread throughout the face of all the land; and the more part of the people, both the Nephites and the Lamanites, did belong to the church." (V. 21). Unfortunately, in time, "dissenters from the people of Nephi, who had some years before gone over unto the Lamanites, and taken upon themselves the name of Lamanites, and also a certain number who were real descendants of the Lamanites," renewed hostilities with their former brethren. (V. 24).

This group "did search out all the secret plans of Gadianton; and thus, they became robbers of Gadianton." (V. 26). They were forerunners of the terrorist organizations with which we are familiar today, mirroring the activities reported in our media. "They did commit murder and plunder, and then they would retreat back into the mountains, and into the wilderness and secret places, hiding themselves that they could not be discovered, receiving daily an addition to their numbers." (V. 25).

The government recognized the serious nature of the threat to society posed by the Gadianton robbers. Therefore, a joint venture of Nephites and Lamanites serving together under one command was put together. This army "did go forth against this band of robbers, and did destroy many." (V. 30). But the enemy proved to be too strong, "insomuch that they did defy the whole armies of the Nephites, and also of the Lamanites." (V. 32).

This calamity "came unto the people because of their iniquity." (V. 34). During the next four years, as their wickedness intensified, "they were ripening again for destruction." (V. 37). There were only 7 years left until the birth of the Savior, and the time-bomb was ticking. During His mortal ministry, Jesus said to the Jews at Jerusalem: "Wo unto you, scribes and Pharisees, hypocrites. For ye make clean the outside of the cup and of the platter, but within they are full of extortion and excess. Thou blind Pharisee, cleanse first that which is within the cup and platter, that the outside of them may be clean also." (Matthew 23:25-26). He just as well could have directed this denunciation toward the Nephites and Lamanites living in the Land of Zarahemla, in 7 B.C. Perhaps members of The Church of Jesus Christ of Latter-day Saints should take notice, as well.

Helaman
Chapter 12

The content of this chapter provides a powerful prophetic insight into our nature, and includes one of the greatest summaries found anywhere in the scriptures of a basic human tendency. From a perspective few have been privileged to have, Mormon shared his innermost thoughts on human frailty.

Having sifted through so many plates kept by Nephite prophets for a thousand years, Mormon realized there was a common thread running through the chronicle of their experiences. He identified a fatal flaw in the character of those who put their trust in their own capabilities and in their material possessions. That is, before they know it, "their treasure is their god." (2 Nephi 9:30). As Ben Johnson said of our peculiar fascination with bright yellow metal: "That for which all virtue is sold, and almost any vice - Almighty Gold!" (In a 1599 letter he wrote to a countess named Elizabeth).

Ideally, we are spiritual beings having mortal experiences. In practical terms, the mission field that we call mortality is made up of worldly experiences, constantly hammered by the influences of carnality, sensuality, and devilishness. There is a wide gulf between the spiritual and temporal. The purpose of the Plan of Salvation is to reconcile the two, or bring us into a state of holiness, richer for having had the experiences of mortality. We are not to be worn down by life, but rather to be refined and polished by adversity and challenge. We are as Joseph Smith described himself. We are rough stones rolling, and in the midst of the abrasive elements of mortality, we need the learning and wisdom of a heavenly curriculum.

Truman Madsen wrote: "We have intelligent initiative that can go astray. In this realm, the role of Christ is to break the bonds of our diminishing freedom and re-enthrone our becoming. In critical ways, only He can do this. Our destiny is to become more and more free in the widening circles of fulfilment called Eternal Life." ("Eternal Man," p. 69-70).

Mormon recognized "the unsteadiness of the hearts of the children of men." (V. 1). At the same time, he also saw the fulfilment of a grand principle of the Gospel, namely, that "there is a law, irrevocably decreed in heaven before the foundations of this world, upon which all blessings are predicated, and when we obtain any blessing from God, it is by obedience to that law upon which it is predicated." (D&C 130:20-21).

When we respond to the whisperings of the Spirit, we correspond to Hamlet's description of humanity at its finest: "What a piece of work is man! How noble in reason! How infinite in faculty! In form and moving how express and admirable! In action how like an angel! In apprehension how like a god! The beauty of the world! The paragon of animals!" (Shakespeare). The irony of it all is that "at the very time when he doth prosper his people, then is the time that they do harden their hearts, and do forget the Lord their God, and do trample under their feet the Holy One - yea, and this because of their ease, and their exceedingly great prosperity." (V. 2).

It seems, Mormon observed: "That except the Lord doth chasten his people with many afflictions, they will not remember him." (V. 3). If it brings us to repentance, we are allowed to suffer terror, famine, all manner of pestilence, and even death. It is all part of our mortal experience, and if it serves a useful purpose, it is not in vain. Even Joseph Smith was comforted with these words of the Savior: "Know thou, my son, that all these things shall give thee experience, and shall be for thy good." (D&C 122:7). But how quickly are we "lifted up in pride; yea, how quick to boast, and do all manner of that which is iniquity; and how slow are (we) to remember the Lord (our) God, and to give ear unto his counsels, yea, how slow to walk in wisdom's paths!" (V. 5).

It is so easy for us to "hearken unto the words of the evil one." (V. 4). Our natural tendency seems to be to make mistakes, violate law, and suffer the consequences. It must be one of the critical lessons of mortality to deal with opposition, exercise agency, and experience the natural and inevitable positive and negative consequences of independent action.

But central to the Plan of Salvation is complete and unequivocal dependence upon God. Those who allow themselves to be worn down by the vicissitudes of life "do not desire that the Lord their God, who hath created them, should rule and reign over them; notwithstanding his great goodness and his mercy towards them, they do set at naught his counsels, and they will not that he should be their guide." (V. 6).

Brigham Young clearly understood his relationship with God and declared: "There is no man who ever made a sacrifice on the earth for the Kingdom of Heaven, except the Savior. I would not give the ashes of a rye straw for that man who feels that he is making sacrifices for God. We are doing this for our own happiness, welfare, and exaltation, and for nobody else's. What we do, we do for the salvation of the inhabitants of the earth, not for the salvation of the heavens, the angels, or God." (J.D., 16:114, see Commentary Reference to 3 Nephi 15:1).

In this sense, Mormon wrote: "O how great is the nothingness of the children of men; yea, even they are less than the dust of the earth." (V. 7). As King Benjamin had done, Mormon related our "nothingness" to our debt to God. (See Mosiah 4:2, & Moses 1:10). "For behold," Mormon continued, "the dust of the earth moveth hither and thither, to the dividing asunder, at the command of our great and everlasting God. Yea, behold at his voice do the hills and the mountains tremble and quake. And by the power of his voice, they are broken up, and become smooth, yea, even like unto a valley. Yea, by the power of his voice doth the whole earth shake. Yea, by the power of his voice do the foundations rock, even to the very center. Yea, and if he say unto the earth - Move - it is moved. Yea, if he say unto the earth - Thou shalt go back, that it lengthen out the day for many hours - it is done." (V. 7-14). In other words, the earth and all things in it obey the will of God. It is only our agency that give us the capacity to willfully violate the order of nature.

King Benjamin had urged his people to thank God, and not him, for their peace and prosperity. (Mosiah 2:19). He said that if they praised Him, and served Him "with all (their) whole souls, yet (they) would be unprofitable servants. (Mosiah 2:20-21). That is because our debt to God is completely beyond our ability to pay. We can do nothing that puts Him in our debt. (See 2 Nephi 25:23). But God does not ask us to settle our account with Him; He only asks that we keep His commandments. The marvel of God's love is that the more we try to serve Him, the more He blesses us. Therefore, we become even more deeply indebted to Him and remain so forever. When, ultimately, the precious blood of Christ redeems us, it is by His grace alone that we enjoy salvation.

One of the greatest sins, therefore, is that of ingratitude. Gratitude is deeper than thanks. Thankfulness is the beginning of gratitude and may consist merely of words, but gratitude is shown in action. It is independent of circumstances, penetrates the deepest undercurrents of life, and is founded upon God. We show our ingratitude to God by our willful disobedience to His commandments. Ingratitude, then, is the companion of sin.

Mormon continued his discourse on human frailty by comparing our agency to the course of the planets, suggesting that the orbit of the earth is fixed according to physical laws, but that if God wills it to be otherwise, it is done. "And thus, according to his word the earth goeth back, and it appeareth unto man that the sun standeth still; yea, and behold, this is so; for surely it is the earth that moveth and not the sun." (V. 15).

Other Old Testament prophets had also written about the movement of the earth and sun: "Then spake Joshua to the Lord in the day when the Lord delivered up the Amorites before the children of Israel, and he said in the sight of Israel, sun, stand thou still upon Gibeon; and thou, moon, in the valley of Ajalon. And the sun stood still, and the moon stayed, until the people had avenged themselves upon their enemies. Is not this written in the book of Jasher? So, the sun stood still in the midst of heaven, and hastened not to go down about a whole day." (Joshua 10:12-13). "The sun and moon stood still in their habitation." (Habakkuk 3:11).

Mormon seems to have been blessed by the Lord with a clearer understanding of the cosmos, as was his lineal ancestor, Abraham. "But the record of the fathers, even the patriarchs, concerning the right of Priesthood, the Lord my God preserved in mine own hands; therefore a knowledge of the beginning of the creation, and also of the planets, and of the stars, as they were made known unto the fathers, have I kept even unto this day, and I shall endeavor to write some of these things upon this record, for the benefit of my posterity that shall come after me." (Abraham 1:31).

In verses 16-22, Mormon continued his description of the omnipotence of God and the impotence of man. He finally concluded: "Therefore, for this cause, that men might be saved, hath repentance been declared." (V. 22). Without the Atonement of the Savior, we would forever be less than the dust of the earth, because we would not be able to live in obedience to the laws of God, as does the earth.

The Atonement makes possible our redemption from sin. "Therefore, blessed are they who will repent and hearken unto the voice of the Lord their God; for these are they that shall be saved. And may God grant, in his great fulness, that men might be brought unto repentance and good works, that they might be restored unto grace for grace, according to their works." (V. 24).

Nephi, the son of Father Lehi, had outlined his mission as a prophet-leader, as a teacher, and as a parent: "For we labor diligently to write, to persuade our children, and also our brethren, to believe in Christ, and to be reconciled to God; for we know that it is by grace that we are saved, after all we can do." (2 Nephi 25:24, see Commentary Reference to 2 Nephi 10:25).

The grace to which he referred is an attribute of perfection possessed by Deity and consists of His love, mercy, and condescension toward His children. (See D&C 66:12, 84:102, and especially 93:6-20). It consists of the gifts and power of God by which we may be brought to perfection.

Jacob explained in 2 Nephi 10:25 how the grace of God operates. We are raised from physical death by the power of the Resurrection, and from spiritual death by the power of the Atonement. We are granted grace proportionately as we conform to the standards of personal righteousness that are part of the Gospel Plan. Thus, the Saints are commanded to "grow in grace". (D&C 50:40), until they are sanctified and justified "thru the grace of our Lord and Savior Jesus Christ." (D&C 20:30-32, see "Mormon Doctrine," p. 339). This is why Nephi declared that we are saved by grace "after all we can do," and this is why repentance is so important. When the day of repentance is past, so is the day of grace.

(See Mormon 2:15, see Commentary Reference to Jacob 6:11). But perhaps in the actual nuts and bolts operation of the Plan, it is the journey that is most important to God. Perhaps, in the ultimate sense, there are as many routes leading to the Celestial Kingdom as there are individuals making their way along the path, and God will leave the light on for late arrivals.

It may come down to the fact that mortality is not our natural dimension. It may be that we cannot ever be entirely comfortable in our present circumstances. "Thus, it is that we are never really at home in time. Alternately, we find ourselves impatiently wishing to hasten its passage, or to hold back the dawn. We can do neither, of course. Whereas the bird is at home in the air, we are clearly not at home in time, because we belong to eternity. Time, as much as any one thing, whispers to us that we are strangers here. If it were natural to us, why is it that we have so many clocks and wear wristwatches?" (Neal Maxwell, B.Y.U. Speeches of The Year, 1979). "Time is the fire in which we burn". (Delmore Schwartz).

Growing old may be strictly and uniquely a quality of mortality, and a built-in mechanism that affords us an opportunity to gauge the approach of our reunion with our Heavenly Father. The passage of time is so subtle that we overlook it. Perhaps this is why we so often say "Let us eat, drink, and be merry, for tomorrow we die; and it shall be well with us." (2 Nephi 28:7). Death seems so distant, and its consequences so remote.

In Winston Churchill's view, however: Time "stands at attention, obedient, expectant, ready to serve; ready, if called upon, to pulverize, without hope of repair, what is left of civilization. It awaits only the word of command". ("The Gathering Storm," p. 37). As a matter of fact, most people spend their time far less wisely than they spend their money. As disciples of Christ, we learn to budget our time as carefully as we budget our money. One measure of our success is not only the frugality with which we spend our time, but also the diligence with which we make time, the care with which we find time, the joy with which we give time, the wisdom with which we invest time, the care with which we find time, the pleasure with which we share time, and the discipline with which we take time. We learn to manipulate the mercurial element of time so that we can not only make the most of our gift of mortality, but also insure our happiness and continued progression in eternity. This creative process, if you will, allows us more time for the accomplishment of the things that matter most in our busy lives. Perhaps this is why idle minds are the devil's workshop. When we kill time, we damage our own eternal selves, for sin is a waste of time.

Mormon wrote: "They that have done good shall have everlasting life; and they that have done evil shall have everlasting damnation." (V. 26). But the Lord Himself declared: "Nevertheless, it is not written that there shall be no end to this torment, but it is written endless torment. Again, it is written eternal damnation; wherefore it is more express than other scriptures, that it might work upon the hearts of the children of men. Behold, I am endless, and the punishment which is given from my hand is endless punishment, for Endless is my name. Wherefore eternal punishment is God's punishment. Endless punishment is God's punishment." (D&C 19:6-7 & 10-12).

All the principles, commandments, and ordinances of the Gospel are structured to enable us to realize the goal set forth in one single verse of scripture, which is the very mission statement of God: "This is my work and my glory," He declared, "to bring to pass the immortality and eternal life of man." (Moses 1:39). It is inconceivable that He would concentrate His efforts and focus His energy on an activity that was doomed to failure because there was a flaw in the instruments, the free agents, that were critical to its success, and that were the center of His attention. The little boy's expression that "God don't make junk" betrays wisdom beyond his years. Perhaps Victor Hugo also heard the majestic clockwork when he wrote: "Be like a bird that pausing in her flight a while on boughs to light, feels them give way beneath her and yet sings, knowing that she hath wings."

Helaman
Chapter 13

"The prophecy of Samuel the Lamanite, to the Nephites" comprises chapters 13-15 of The Book of Helaman. (Superscription to Chapter 13, see Commentary Reference to Helaman 5:49-52). That the resurrected Savior held Samuel in high regard is evident from the fact that during His post-mortal ministry among the Nephites, He commanded that a complete record of the fulfilment of Samuel's prophecies be kept. (See 3 Nephi 23:7-13).

In Zarahemla, just before the birth of the Savior, there was a complete reversal of the established order. Mormon recorded that "the Nephites did still remain in wickedness while the Lamanites did observe strictly to keep the commandments of God." (V. 1). Into this society in upheaval "one Samuel, a Lamanite, came ... and began to preach unto the people." (V. 2). But he was cast out. (See 3 Nephi 8:25).

The scriptures provide tantalizing clues to Samuel's origins. About 29 B.C., in response to the missionary efforts of Nephi and Lehi, "the Lamanites had become, the more part of them, a righteous people, insomuch that their righteousness did exceed that of the Nephites." (Helaman 6:1). If Samuel had been among these converted Lamanites, he would have had nearly a quarter of a century to prepare for his ministry in Zarahemla. As a matter of fact, at that time, "many of the Lamanites did come down into the land of Zarahemla, and did declare unto the people of the Nephites the manner of their conversion, and did exhort them to faith and repentance." (Helaman 6:4). As part of this missionary force, Samuel would have received on-site training for his later efforts.

"Yea, and many did preach with exceedingly great power and authority." (Helaman 6:5). Mormon was not a sloppy record-keeper, and when his abridgement needed clarification, he was not hesitant to make the necessary changes. (See Alma 24:19). If he said that these Lamanites taught with power and authority, then we can be sure that they had been ordained with Melchizedek Priesthood power via the proper channels.

Samuel's ministry to the Nephites at the City of Zarahemla in 5 B.C. (See Helaman 14:2) was extremely important to those inhabitants, and gives depth to our understanding of the great forces at work among those people around the time of the birth of Christ. Perhaps, though, there was a more fundamental reason for the Savior's insistence on the inclusion of an account of Samuel's ministry in the records.

The Book of Mormon was written for our day. As its characters play out a drama on an unfamiliar stage, they weave a pattern in the embroidery of history's tapestry that makes a great deal of sense. In 2023, the L.D.S. Church numbered some seventeen million individuals. Church members represented about .002% of the world's population. In that year, only two in a thousand inhabitants of the earth was a member of the Church.

A projection of Church demographics suggests that English-speaking members of the Church are in a minority. To think of the L.D.S. Church as a "Utah based sect" or even an American phenomenon is unsupportable. For generations now, local priesthood leaders have administered the regional affairs of the Church, and now we are witnessing increasing numbers from their ranks joining the brethren of the General Authorities. Many years ago, the President of the Church, Harold B. Lee is alleged to have prepared the Church for its leap onto the international stage with the declaration: "There is no United States of America in heaven!"

The Church basks on an international stage, and its members regularly receive counsel from the brethren of the General Authorities who are the harvest from seeds that have been nurtured in a world-wide garden. "And whatsoever they shall speak when moved upon by the Holy Ghost shall be scripture, shall be the will of the Lord, shall be the mind of the Lord, shall be the word of the Lord, shall be the voice of the Lord, and the power of God unto salvation." (D&C 68:4).

Perhaps in the account of Samuel the Lamanite, there is a message that we must guard against racial bigotry and cultural bias within the quorums and congregations of the Church. If we have not already experienced it, the time will come when our file leaders will have skin of a different color than our own, speak in our language with heavy foreign accents, or even communicate in tongues that are unfamiliar to us. Perhaps they will come from different social or economic classes, or be unlearned as the world measures education. They may lack social graces that we think are important, or have customs unique to their own cultures.

We are not truly converted to the Gospel until we see the power of God resting upon the leaders of the Church. The Nephites in Zarahemla cast Samuel out of their city with an undeniable statement regarding the quality of their commitment to the Gospel and to the established organization of the Church.

Samuel came with proper credentials, and delivered an unimpeachable message that could not be misunderstood. "I, Samuel, a Lamanite, do speak the words of the Lord which he doth put into my heart; and behold he hath put it into my heart to say unto this people that the sword of justice hangeth over this people; and four hundred years pass not away save the sword of justice falleth upon this people." (V. 5, see V. 9-10, Alma 45:10, & Mormon Chapter 6). Samuel denounced not only his generation, but prophesied of the ultimate destruction of the entire Nephite society that is recounted in the Books of Mormon and Moroni. He had been instructed by the voice of the Lord, that had commanded him to "prophesy unto the people whatsoever things should come into his heart." (V. 3). So, he was prompted by the Spirit to make this bold statement.

He explained: "Nothing can save this people save it be repentance and faith on the Lord Jesus Christ, who surely shall come into the world, and shall suffer many things and shall be slain for his people." (V. 6). He said: "An angel of the Lord hath declared it unto me, and he did bring glad tidings to my soul." (V. 7). Samuel may have been speaking specifically of his people, but his words apply generally to all of us. No one, anywhere, at any time, in any circumstance, can be saved without "repentance and faith on the Lord Jesus Christ." (V. 6). The only Good News is the body of Gospel principles that extend the promise of salvation to every man, woman, and child who has ever lived, or who shall ever live, on the earth. The rest of the news is bad. (See Commentary Reference to 3 Nephi 27:13).

When Nephi and Lehi, with three hundred Lamanites, had been "encircled about as if in the midst of a flaming fire," they not only "were filled with that joy which is unspeakable and full of glory," but they also "saw the heavens open; and angels came down out of heaven and ministered unto them." (Helaman 5:44, 45 & 48). They had experienced God's warm embrace, for He dwells in everlasting burnings. As Melvin J. Ballard wrote: "If I ever can receive that of which I had but a foretaste, I would give all I am, all that I ever hope to be, to feel what I then felt." ("Sermons and Missionary Experiences of Melvin Joseph Ballard," p. 156).

In verses 8-20, Samuel directly quoted the angel who had personally instructed him. He said that the worst consequences of the failure of the people to repent would be the withdrawal of the Spirit and the loss of spiritual blessings. (V. 8). Characteristically, the Lord would continue to extend His arm of mercy. (V. 11). The wicked had their righteous brethren to thank for the continuing preservation of their city. Speaking in the name of the Lord, Samuel told the people: "It is because of those who are righteous that it is saved." (V. 12, see Commentary Reference to Alma 10:24). With this scripture in mind, the Latter-day Saints have a far-reaching and all-encompassing responsibility to society to be righteous and to honor their covenants, even if they live in the midst of spiritual Babylon.

The memory of Abraham pleading with the Lord to spare the wicked city of Sodom should have been clear in the minds of the inhabitants of Zarahemla, as they heard Samuel declare the word of the Lord: "Behold, if it were not for the righteous who are in this great city, I would cause that fire should come down out of heaven and destroy it." (V. 13, see 3 Nephi 8:8, & Genesis 18:23-33). In Zarahemla in 6 B.C., Samuel and his Lamanite brethren who had come up into the land exercised priesthood power and authority sufficient to stay the hand of the Lord for yet a while longer. (See Helaman 6:4).

Samuel said that a sign that the people would be ripe for destruction would be when they should cast out the righteous from among them. (V. 14). How ironic that the wicked themselves should so ignorantly carry out the very acts that would seal their own fate. A curse was to come upon the land that was tailor made to fit the sins of the people. Since they had substituted the worship of material possessions for the worship of God, Samuel said that it would come to pass "that whoso shall hide up treasures in the earth shall find them again no more, because of the great curse of the land." (V. 18, see Mormon 1:18).

"It is not surprising that in a society where wealth is more important than God, stealing should be raised to a fine art. Theft, fraud, deception, and loss of treasure buried to keep it safe would bring the people to poverty." (Kent P. Jackson, "Studies in Scripture," 8:119). When we stop to think of the sophisticated strategies that have been crafted in the Last Days to separate individuals from their wealth, we can see that the situation is similar to that found in Zarahemla just before the Coming of the Lord.

The Nephites would learn the hard way that if they persisted in setting their hearts upon the things of the world, they would surely lose them. (V. 20). They did not understand the celestial laws of stewardship and consecration, and so they neglected to give thanks to God for all that He had given them. They were cursed because they focused their attention on their material possessions, while ignoring Him who had freely blessed them temporally. "Ye do not remember the Lord your God in the things with which he hath blessed you, but ye do always remember your riches, not to thank the Lord your God for them; yea, your hearts are not drawn out unto the Lord, but they do swell with great pride." (V. 22).

"And in nothing doth man offend God, or against none is his wrath kindled, save those who confess not his hand in all things, and obey not his commandments." (D&C 59:21). "For this cause," warned Samuel, "hath the Lord God caused that a curse should come upon the land, and also upon your riches, and this because of your iniquities." (V. 23).

Six hundred years earlier, Israel had similarly rejected Lehi and his contemporary prophets. Within ten years of Lehi's forced exodus from Jerusalem, the Babylonians were at the city gates. Now, Samuel pronounced a curse of destruction upon the people of Zarahemla for doing the same thing. "Ye do cast out the prophets, and do mock them, and cast stones at them, even as they did of old time." (V. 24).

The Jews had tried to stone Lehi. The Nephites tried to do the same to Samuel, and to shoot him with arrows. (See

Helaman 16:2). Joseph Smith was finally silenced by the musket balls of an angry mob. The techniques of Satan have not changed so very much, and if, in the "enlightened" Twenty-First Century, we are lulled into complacency, we deceive only ourselves and are in danger of suffering a fate similar as the Nephites. (See Commentary Reference to Mosiah 17:30)

Then and now, the wicked justify their behavior as they publicly but superficially distance themselves from those who persecute the Saints. (See v. 25). But Samuel would not accept weak rationalizations. (V. 26-27). "The Nephites were not willing to take the first step of repentance; to acknowledge their sins. Instead, they quieted conscience with the soothing and false counsel of 'foolish and blind guides.'" (Kent P. Jackson, "Studies in Scripture," 8:118).

Samuel told the Nephites in Zarahemla that the day would come when they would cry: "O that we had repented in the day that the word of the Lord came unto us," and "O Lord, canst thou not turn away thine anger from us?" (V. 36-37). Unfortunately, their time of probation would be past. He said of them: "You have procrastinated the day of your salvation until it is everlastingly too late, and your destruction is made sure." (V. 38). "Ye have sought all the days of your lives for that which ye could not obtain," he said, "and ye have sought for happiness in doing iniquity, which thing is contrary to the nature of that righteousness" which is in God. (V. 38, see Commentary Reference to Alma 41:10).

When individuals completely pattern their lives after the divine model, as Samuel had, they earn the right to speak in the name of the Lord. Bruce McConkie composed a statement of belief that is still carried by many of the missionaries of the Church of Jesus Christ of Latter-day Saints. He wrote: "I am called of God. My authority is above that of the kings of the earth. By revelation, I have been selected as a personal representative of the Lord, Jesus Christ. He is my Master, and He has chosen me to represent Him, to stand in His place, to say and do what He Himself would do if He personally were administering among the very people to whom He has sent me. My voice is His voice, and my acts are His acts, my words are His words, and my doctrine His doctrine, for I am His agent. My commission is to do what He wants done, to say what He wants said, to be a living modern witness in word and in deed of the divinity of His great and marvelous latter-day work, and he that receiveth me receiveth Him, while he that rejects me rejects Him that sent me. How great is my calling!" (See 2 Nephi 25:17, 27:26, Helaman 3:13-16, 3 Nephi 5:8, 21:9, Moroni 10:3, D&C 4:1, & Isaiah 29:14).

Helaman
Chapter 14

This chapter contains one of the most specific prophesies in all scripture. Perhaps Samuel the Lamanite gave it in order to nurture the budding faith of those in his audience who were turned toward repentance. Mormon wrote, "Samuel the Lamanite, did prophesy a great many more things which cannot be written." (V. 1). Given the doctrinal fluidity with which he proclaimed the Gospel, these prophecies to which Mormon refers must have been truly inspirational. Perhaps these records will one day become available, given the importance the Savior ascribed to the prophecies of Samuel the Lamanite.

He established a specific timeline when the Savior would be born, saying "unto them: Behold, I give unto you a sign; for five years more cometh, and behold, then cometh the Son of God to redeem all those who shall believe on his name." (V. 2, see 3 Nephi 1:13). Then he described the signs accompanying the birth of Christ. It was no coincidence that the signs attendant to the birth of "the light of the world" should be wonders in heaven. "For behold, there shall be great lights in heaven, insomuch that in the night before he cometh there shall be no darkness." (V. 3, see 3 Nephi 1:15). Heaven, it seems, is not so very far away, after all.

An additional sign was to be a new light in the night sky. "And behold, there shall a new star arise, such an one as ye never have beheld; and this also shall be a sign unto you." (V. 5, see 3 Nephi 1:21). Even the Zoroastrian priests from the East beheld the star and intuitively understood its significance. Traveling to Jerusalem after the Savior's birth, they inquired of King Herod: "Where is he that is born King of the Jews? For we have seen his star in the east, and are come to worship him." (Matthew 2:2).

Samuel the Lamanite also prophesied of "many (additional) signs and wonders in heaven." (V. 6). Although there is no mention of these in Third Nephi, we can be sure that they were given as further testimony of the Savior's birth. "And it shall come to pass that ye shall all be amazed, and wonder, insomuch that ye shall fall to the earth." (V. 7, see 3 Nephi 1:16).

Isaiah prophesied of a messenger, whose voice "crieth in the wilderness, Prepare ye the way of the Lord. Make straight in the desert a highway for our God." (Isaiah 40:3). During His mortal ministry, Jesus Christ said of His prophet John the Baptist: "For this is he of whom it is written, Behold, I send my messenger before thy face, which shall prepare thy way before thee." (Matthew 11:10). Samuel the Lamanite was a similar messenger, who said of his ministry: "Thus hath the Lord commanded me, by his angel, that I should come and tell this thing unto you; yea, he hath said unto me: Cry unto this people, repent and prepare the way of the Lord." (V. 9). Thus, his ministry in the New World closely paralleled that of John the Baptist in the Old World.

Joseph Smith recorded Doctrine & Covenants Section 65, that he characterized as a prayer. In it, "one sent down from on high, who is mighty and powerful, whose going forth is unto the ends of the earth, yea, whose voice is unto men, (declared): "Prepare ye the way of the Lord, make his paths straight." (D&C 65:1). Samuel the Lamanite certainly stands with all these other prophets who helped to prepare the way of the Lord. He held the authority of the priesthood, and President Harold B. Lee said of such brethren, "Where there are the keys to the Kingdom, there is the Church of Jesus Christ, and it is the stone which was cut out of the mountain without hands." (See Daniel 2:45). Joseph Smith said: "I calculate to be one of the instruments in setting up the Kingdom of Daniel by the word of the Lord, and I intend to lay a foundation that will revolutionize the whole world." (H.C., 6:364). The same thing could be said of Samuel the Lamanite.

He said to the Nephites in Zarahemla: "Because I am a Lamanite, ye are angry with me and do seek to destroy me." (V. 10). Because of their prejudice directed to the messenger, they could not comprehend his message. But they could not ignore his voice. He said: "Ye shall hear my words, for, for this intent have I come upon the walls of this city." (V. 11). Samuel the Lamanite was literally preaching from the housetops. As Mormon said: "All things which are hid must be revealed upon the housetops." (Mormon 5:8).

Samuel the Lamanite must have had a personal relationship with the Savior. His desire was that the People of Zarahemla "might know of the coming of Jesus Christ, the Son of God, the Father of heaven and of earth, the Creator of all things from the beginning." (V. 12). The Savior introduced Himself in the Doctrine and Covenants as "Jesus Christ, the Great I AM, Alpha and Omega, the beginning and the end, the same which looked upon the wide expanse of eternity, and all the seraphic hosts of heaven, before the world was made." (D&C 38:1-2).

In 1980, President Spencer W. Kimball told the Los Angeles Area Conference congregation: "The Savior lives, and He tells us what to do through the Holy Scriptures, and by revelation of Himself and His Holy Father to the prophets." On another occasion, he said: "I know that God lives, for as in the words of my predecessor, John Taylor, I have seen him." (Priesthood Session, General Conference, 4/1978). His associate General Authorities have also borne powerful testimonies: "I know of the divinity of the Lord Jesus Christ, for it has been revealed to me in a most interesting, complete, and beautiful way," declared L. Tom Perry, in a fireside at the Spokane Washington North Stake. (5/10/1986). During the same stake conference, he said at the close of another address: "I leave with you that special witness which is mine to bear, for I have witnessed it with my own eyes, and heard it with my own ears, and this I do in the name of Jesus Christ, Amen." Enzio Busche said: "I know Him. I know that He is real. I testify as a witness." (Spokane North Stake Conference, 11/1980).

Because Samuel the Lamanite preached with such power and authority, we can be confident that his witness was just as sure. Even though his ministry predated the birth of the Lord, he knew with certainty that the Savior "must die that salvation may come ... to bring to pass the resurrection of the dead, that thereby men may be brought into the presence of the Lord." (V. 15). Thereby, we would overcome the effects of physical death and live again. We would also temporarily overcome the effects of spiritual death. "Behold, the resurrection of Christ redeemeth mankind, yea, even all mankind, and bringeth them back into the presence of the Lord" so that the Judgment might take place. (V. 17).

Then, if we have repented while in the probationary state of mortality we will stand before the judgment bar of Christ and will be redeemed from "spiritual death, yea, a second death." (V. 18). That is, we will be allowed to come into the presence of God, because the Atonement of Christ will have paid the price that was demanded by Justice for our sins. Those who are without mercy, however, will be "cut off again as to things pertaining to righteousness." (V. 18). Having been brought into the presence of the Lord, they will not be able to endure His Holiness, because they will be filthy still. Therefore, Samuel the Lamanite said: "Repent ye, repent ye, lest by knowing these things and not doing them ye shall suffer yourselves to come under condemnation, and ye are brought down unto the second death." (V. 19).

Samuel the Lamanite then gave the people another sign that would signify the death of the Savior. By this sign, the people would know that cosmic forces had been set into motion, and the unalterable decrees spoken of by the prophets had been initiated. For the repentant, this sign would be hopefully anticipated and gladly welcomed, but for those who had wasted the days of their probation and mocked the prophets, it would be a terrible day. Native Americans have a saying: "It is a good day to die." This is only true when one has properly prepared for the birth date of their immortal soul.

The sign to be given was that in the "day that he shall suffer death, the sun shall be darkened and refuse to give his light unto you; and also the moon and the stars; and there shall be no light upon the face of this land, even from the time that he shall suffer death, for the space of three days, to the time that he shall rise again from the dead." (V. 20, see 3 Nephi 8:19-23). That this should be so, is consistent with the true doctrine that the light of Christ is the power that controls the order of the universe. "The earth rolls upon her wings," declared the Savior, "and the sun giveth his light by day, and the moon giveth her light by night, and the stars also give their light, as they roll upon their wings in their glory, in the midst of the power of God. Then shall ye know that ye have seen me, that I am, and that I am the true light that is in you, and that you are in me; otherwise ye could not abound." (D&C 88:45 & 50).

In 33 A.D., when the "Light of the world" was crucified, all nature found itself in upheaval. Momentarily, the order of the cosmos was thrown into turmoil. "Yea, at the time that he shall yield up the ghost there shall be thunderings and lightnings for the space of many hours, and the earth shall shake and tremble; and the rocks which are upon the face of this earth, which are both above the earth and beneath, which ye know at this time are solid, or the more part of it is one solid mass, shall be broken up." (V. 21, see Commentary Reference to Alma 24:19, & 3 Nephi 8:6-7).

"Yea, they shall be rent in twain, and shall ever after be found in seams and in cracks, and in broken fragments upon the face of the whole earth, yea, both above the earth and beneath." (V. 22 see 3 Nephi 8:12, 17 & 18). "And behold, there shall be great tempests, and there shall be many mountains laid low, like unto a valley, and there shall be many places which are now called valleys which shall become mountains, whose height is great." (V. 23, see 3 Nephi 8:5-6). "And many highways shall be broken up, and many cities shall become desolate." (V. 24, see 3 Nephi 8:11 & 13). "And many graves shall be opened, and shall yield up many of their dead; and many saints shall appear unto many." (V. 25, see 3 Nephi 23:9-13, & Matthew 27:52-53).

All the events that were prophetically cited by Samuel the Lamanite had been spoken unto him by an angel from God. They would be terrifyingly real, and all the more so because they would all be carried out while "darkness should cover the face of the whole earth for the space of three days." (V. 27).

Even greater signs than these would be given to the children of men, "to the intent that there should be no cause for unbelief," and also "to the intent that whosoever will believe might be saved, and that whosoever will not believe, a righteous judgment might come upon them; and also, if they are condemned, they bring upon themselves their own condemnation." (V. 28-29).

Samuel the Lamanite taught the people the important principle that the death of the Savior was necessary to make repentance and forgiveness for sin possible. Because of His infinite and eternal sacrifice from before the foundation of the world, a choice was given to all mankind, and the gears of the Plan of Salvation began turning. Without His sacrifice, the whole Plan would have been frustrated, and it would have been impossible for the children of men to exercise true moral agency. With it, the freedom to make difficult choices, and to repent, would become the ultimate expression of free will.

"Behold, ye are free; ye are permitted to act for yourselves; for behold, God hath given unto you a knowledge, and he hath made you free. He hath given unto you that ye might know good from evil, and he hath given unto you that ye might choose life or death; and ye can do good and be restored unto that which is good, or have that which is good restored unto you; or ye can do evil, and have that which is evil restored unto you." (V. 31, see Commentary Reference to Alma 24:19).

Helaman
Chapter 15

This chapter opens with a warning to the people that is similar to the one given by the Savior to the Jews just before the close of his mortal ministry. (See J.S.T. Matthew 1:2 & 16). Samuel the Lamanite told the Nephites that, in spite of the fact that they had been a chosen people, because of their apostasy, God would find it necessary to withdraw their promised blessings that had been conditioned on obedience. The Lamanites, on the other hand, would enjoy the blessings associated with obedience. (See D&C 130:20-21). The Lord had "hated" them, because of their rebellion. (V. 4). That is to say, those people had alienated themselves from the love that our Father has for His children. They had chosen to act in ways that made it impossible for His blessings to get through to them.

The Lord told Joseph Smith: "If you keep not my commandments, the love of the Father shall not continue with you, therefore you shall walk in darkness." (D&C 95:12). Clarifying that same principle, the Apostle John wrote: "Love not the world, neither the things that are in the world. If any man loves the world, the love of the Father is not in him." (1 John 2:15).

"No man can serve two masters," explained the Savior, "for either he will hate the one, and love the other; or else he will hold to the one, and despise the other. Ye cannot serve God and mammon. Therefore, I say unto you, Take no thought for your life, what ye shall eat, or what ye shall drink; nor yet for your body, what ye shall put on. Is not the life more than meat, and the body than raiment?" (Matthew 6:24-25).

Samuel the Lamanite closed his "prophecy," by acknowledging that he, a Lamanite, understood that for nearly 600 years, his people had walked in darkness, and "had done evil continually, and this because of the iniquity of the tradition of their fathers." (V. 4). But because of the sacrifices of the Nephites, who had been to his people as "saviors on Mount Zion," salvation had come to them. (See Isaiah 52:7, & Obadiah 1:31).

Even at this time, the Lamanites were beginning to say of their brethren the Nephites: "How beautiful upon the mountains are the feet of (those) that bringeth good tidings unto (us), that publisheth peace ... that publisheth salvation; that saith unto (us): Thy God reigneth!" (3 Nephi 20:40).

Samuel the Lamanite pointed out that the majority of his brethren were now "in the path of their duty, and they walk(ed) circumspectly before God, and they observe(d) to keep his commandments and his statutes and his judgments." (V. 5). Those who were walking in the light of the Gospel were "striving with unwearied diligence that they (might) bring the remainder of their brethren to the knowledge of the truth." (V. 15).

Theirs was a profound spiritual transformation founded on "the holy scriptures, yea, the prophecies of the holy prophets, which are written." (V. 7). Ezra Taft Benson warned: "Social, ethical, cultural, or educational converts will not survive under the heat of the day unless their taproots go down to the fulness of the Gospel which the Book of Mormon contains." ("A Witness and a Warning," p. 6).

So complete was their conversion, that the Lamanites had "buried their weapons of war, and (were fearful) to take them up lest by any means they should sin." (V. 9). They would rather suffer death than lift their swords even against their enemies. Their steps of repentance involved sorrow for sin, abandonment of sin, confession of sin, restitution for sin, and then continuing obedience to the will of God. The Lamanites could not bring back those Nephites whom they had murdered, but they would never again turn their faces from the Source of eternal happiness, and would earnestly strive to do all they could to walk in His light.

"And now because of their steadfastness (and) their firmness when they are once enlightened," prophesied Samuel, "behold, the Lord shall bless them and prolong their days, notwithstanding their (previous) iniquity." (V. 10). Even in their apostate condition, the Nephites should have seen that it was repentance that had brought to the Lamanites the favor of the Lord.

The Nephite prophets had foretold that their own people would eventually be destroyed because of iniquity. But of the Lamanites, it was prophesied that in the Last Days the promises of the Lord would again be extended to them. (V. 12). "And this is according to the prophecy, that they shall again be brought to the true knowledge, which is the knowledge of their Redeemer, and their great and true shepherd, and be numbered among his sheep." (V. 13).

The Book of Mormon clearly and repetitively teaches this principle of "gathering" which "is always to the waters of baptism, where a covenant is made to take upon oneself the name of Christ. It always embraces being numbered among His sheep, or being an active member of His Church." (Robert L. Millet, "Doctrinal Commentary on The Book of Mormon," v. 3, p. 420).

And so, in the "Prophecy of Samuel", we come to a critical juncture. "Therefore," he said to the Nephites, "I say unto you, it shall be better for them than for you, except ye repent." (V. 14). How could the Nephites fail to recognize the contrasts in the dramatic portrait that Samuel the Lamanite had painted? The experience of the Nephites with their brethren the Lamanites during six hundred years was both direct and dramatic. Now, with the prophetic power of Samuel the Lamanite, they were being told that righteousness, and not lineage, is important to the Lord, and it is righteousness that is the ultimate qualification for salvation.

In a reversal of fortunes, the Nephites were now suffering from the "wicked traditions of their fathers," just as their Lamanite brethren had, for so long. (V. 7). They had a mind set toward their brethren that could not be dislodged by the powerful message of Samuel the Lamanite. They had forgotten the teaching of Nephi: "And now behold, my beloved brethren, I would speak unto you; for I, Nephi, would not suffer that ye should suppose that ye are more righteous than the (Lamanites) shall be. For behold, except ye shall keep the commandments of God, ye shall all likewise perish; and because of the words which have been spoken, ye need not suppose that the (Lamanites) are utterly destroyed. For behold, I say unto you that as many of the (Lamanites) as will repent are the covenant people of the Lord; and as many of the (Nephites) as will not repent shall be cast off; for the Lord covenanteth with none save it be with them that repent and believe in his Son, who is the Holy One of Israel." (2 Nephi 30:1-2).

Samuel the Lamanite closed his message to the Nephites with an expression of his divine investiture of authority: "And now, behold, saith the Lord, concerning the people of the Nephites: If they will not repent, and observe to do my will, I will utterly destroy them, saith the Lord, because of their unbelief notwithstanding the many mighty works which I have done among them; and as surely as the Lord liveth shall these things be, saith the Lord." (V. 17).

This stamp of divine approval on the words of Samuel the Lamanite could not have been lost on the Nephites in Zarahemla. He had ended his address to them by invoking the name of the Lord no less than four times with the awesome solemnity of an Israelite oath. He, a Lamanite, stood before them atop the walls of the great city, as an example for all to see of the type of righteous individual they all could be. Truly, God is no respecter of persons, and he uses the weak things of the world to confound the wise. (See D&C 1:35).

"The weak things of the world shall come forth and break down the mighty and strong ones." (D&C 1:19). Samuel the Lamanite had come out of obscurity in the Land of Nephi. His origin is unknown, and where he went remains a mystery. He arrived in Zarahemla without impressive pedigree or established credentials that we know of. But we do know this: He came with power and authority and with a message of supreme importance to the people. Spencer W. Kimball once wrote: "Christianity did not go from Rome to Galilee; it was the other way around. In our day, the routing is from Palmyra to Paris, and not the reverse." In the day of Samuel the Lamanite, it was from obscurity in the Land of Nephi, to the great city of Zarahemla.

"The more part of (the Lamanites)
are striving with unwearied diligence
that they may bring the remainder of their
brethren to the knowledge of the truth; therefore,
there are many who do add to their numbers daily.
And behold … as many of them as are brought to the
knowledge of the truth, and to know of the wicked
and abominable traditions of their fathers …
are led to believe the holy scriptures (and) to
faith on the Lord, and unto repentance,
which faith and repentance bringeth
a change of heart unto them."
(Helaman 15:6-7).

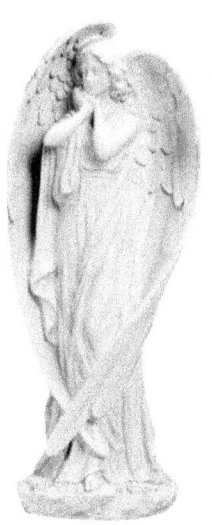

Helaman
Chapter 16

Those who believed the words of Samuel the Lamanite, as he stood upon the city walls of Zarahemla, sought out Nephi that they might be interviewed for baptism. (V. 1). Nephi, who was recognized in Zarahemla as the Presiding High Priest over the Church, "was baptizing, and prophesying, and preaching, crying repentance unto the people, showing signs and wonders, working miracles among the people." (V. 4, see Helaman 3:37)

God always establishes His word in the mouths of two or more witnesses, and in Zarahemla, it was Nephi who added his testimony to that of Samuel the Lamanite. He told the Nephites "of things which must shortly come, that they might know and remember at the time of their coming that they had been made known unto them beforehand." (V. 5). Nephi did this at great personal risk, because of the recent attempts by his brethren, the Nephites, to still the voice of Samuel the Lamanite, after he had delivered his warning. For "they (had) cast stones at (Samuel the Lamanite) upon the wall, and also many shot arrows at him as he stood upon the wall." (V. 2).

Thomas S. Monson has called the priesthood "a robe of responsibility, and not a cloak of comfort." ("Liahona," 7/2009). When carried out with dignity, priesthood duties enlarge the capacity of its bearers to accomplish the tasks at hand. In the case of Samuel the Lamanite, "the Spirit of the Lord was with him, insomuch that (the Nephites) could not hit him with their stones neither with their arrows." (V. 2).

Undaunted, the people "cried unto their captains, saying (of Samuel), take this fellow and bind him, for behold he hath a devil. Away with him." (V. 6). King Noah had said the same thing of Abinadi when that prophet had condemned his monarchy for its debauchery. (See Mosiah 13:1). The Jews would also accuse John the Baptist, the forerunner of Jesus Christ, of having a devil. (See Matthew 11:18). Joseph Smith wrote in his History: "It caused me serious reflection then, and often has since, how very strange it was than an obscure boy, of a little over fourteen years of age ... should be though a character of sufficient importance to attract the attention of the great ones of the most popular sects of the day, and in a manner to create in them a spirit of the most bitter persecution and reviling." (J.S.H. 1:23). This seems to be the standard knee-jerk reaction by the wicked in response to expressions of the truth.

Samuel the Lamanite, fled from his would-be captors and returned to the Land of Nephi, where he "began to preach and to prophesy among his own people." (V. 7). "And behold, he was never heard of more among the Nephites." (V. 8). He had delivered the message, had fulfilled his responsibility, and had magnified his office before the Lord. The sins of the people could no longer be shifted from their own shoulders. Whenever the Lord says "and let every man who hath been warned warn his neighbor," it is to establish accountability, to free the Children of the Covenant from the sins and blood of their generation, as well as to build the Church and Kingdom.

The Savior knew Samuel the Lamanite, and held him in high esteem. When He later appeared among the Nephites, He commanded that a complete account be written in the records concerning the fulfilment of the prophecies of Samuel the Lamanite. (See 3 Nephi 28:7-13).

What does The Book of Helaman say about the effect of the efforts of Samuel the Lamanite, among the inhabitants of the City of Zarahemla? Sadly, "there was but little alteration in the affairs of the people, save it were the people began to be more hardened in iniquity, and do more and more of that which was contrary to the commandments of God." (V. 12). Likewise, in spite of the voice of warning that has been raised by the prophets of God since 1830, there has been little change in the inclination of mankind to disobey the commandments. If anything, there is increasingly flagrant violation of Heavenly Father's laws. Therefore, the behavior of the people in the ancient City of Zarahemla should not seem strange to us or out of character. Neither should their ultimate fate seem harsh, unusual, or unwarranted. "Except the Lord keep the city, the watchman waketh but in vain." (Psalms 127:1).

In Zarahemla, just two years before the birth of the Savior, "there were great signs given unto the people, and wonders; and the words of the prophets began to be fulfilled." (V. 13). "And angels did appear unto men, wise men, and did declare unto them glad tidings of great joy." (V. 14). This situation mirrors exactly conditions in the world today. Many angels, whose visits have been well documented, have also appeared in the Last Days, and the words of the prophets are being fulfilled.

As early as September 15, 1842, the Prophet Joseph Smith wrote an epistle to the Saints: "And again, what do we hear? Glad tidings from Cumorah! Moroni, an angel from heaven, declaring the fulfillment of the prophets - the book to be revealed. A voice of the Lord in the wilderness declaring the three witnesses to bear record of the book! The voice of Michael on the banks of the Susquehanna, the voice of Peter, James, and John in the wilderness declaring themselves as possessing the keys of the kingdom, and of the dispensation of the fulness of times! And again, the voice of God in the chamber of old Father Whitmer ... and at sundry times, and in divers places through all the travails and tribulations of this Church of Jesus Christ of Latter-day Saints! And the voice of Michael, the archangel; the voice of Gabriel, and of Raphael, and of divers angels, from Michael or Adam down to the present time, all declaring their dispensation, their rights, their keys, their honors, their majesty and glory, and the power of their priesthood; giving line upon line, precept upon precept; here a little, and there a little; giving us consolation by holding forth that which is to come, confirming our hope!" (D&C 128:20-21).

In Zarahemla, only the most believing part of the Nephites and Lamanites kept the counsel of Samuel the Lamanite. (V. 15). In Nauvoo, Illinois, Joseph exhorted the people: "Shall we not go on in so great a cause? Let the sun, moon, and the morning stars sing together, and let all the sons of God shout for joy!" (D&C 128:22-23).

But characteristically, in the Land of Zarahemla, Satan stirred up those Nephites most susceptible to his influence "to do iniquity continually; yea, he did go about spreading rumors and contentions upon all the face of the land, that he might harden the hearts of the people against that which was good and against that which should come." (V. 22).

The devil has largely succeeded with his various programs designed to distort true principles and give lies the ring of truth. His deceptions deceive the world. There is only one clear, bright light of truth, but there is a many faceted, flickering, dancing lightshow of deceptive error with many shades of darkness engulfing the world today. It is sometimes difficult to pick out truth and identify it amid its various counterfeits.

The Nephites living in Zarahemla just before the birth of the Savior rationalized their behavior by asking themselves if it was logical that Christ should be born in the distant land of Jerusalem. "It is not reasonable," they argued, "that such a being as a Christ shall come. If so, and he be the Son of God, the father of heaven and of earth, as it has been spoken, why will he not show himself unto us as well as unto them who shall be at Jerusalem?" (V. 18). They said that the prophecies of His birth and ministry were only part of "a wicked tradition" that only supported the reality of events that could not be externally substantiated. (V. 20). They claimed that since they could not witness with their own eyes that they were true, they must forever be in ignorance of their validity. (V. 21).

In our day, the same weak argument is expressed. Jacob Neusner, a Jewish religious scholar, very perceptively observed that "among our colleagues are some who do not really like religion in its living forms, but find terribly interesting religion in its dead ones. That is why an old Christian text, one from the First Century for example, is deemed a worthy subject of scholarship. But a fresh Christian expression (I think in this connection of the Book of Mormon) is available principally for ridicule, but never for study. Religious experience in the First Century is fascinating. Religious experience in the Twentieth Century is frightening or absurd." ("Bulletin of The Council on The Study of Religions," 12/1977).

Those who fault The Book of Mormon are frequently those who have never actually read it, dismissing the coherence of the text as a fabrication of "the cunning and the mysterious arts of the evil one." (V. 21). They claim that it is he who will work "some great mystery which we cannot understand, which will keep us down to be servants to their words, and also servants unto them ... and thus will they keep us in ignorance unto them, all the days of our lives." (V. 21). But where are the doctrinal loopholes that would betray as a deception the fulness of the Gospel as it is manifest in The Book of Mormon, and where are the conceptual cul-de-sacs ad doctrinal dead-ends that would expose it as a fabrication of the adversary? They do not exist!

It is likely that many individuals will not read The Book of Mormon because it just might be true. One is reminded of the sign board seen outside an evangelical church that warned: "Don't pray about The Book of Mormon. That's how they get you!" If they were familiar with the promise extended by Moroni to those who do read it, they would probably still decline the invitation, offering the same flimsy excuses as the people in Zarahemla who had heard the exhortations of Samuel the Lamanite. (See Moroni 10:4).

Suffice to say that since the events in The Book of Helaman reflect the powerful forces shaping our own society, a study of its themes and messages will help us to prepare for the Second Coming of Christ. The parallels are too striking to be dismissed as insignificant or coincidental by careful students of the scriptures and faithful disciples of Christ.

"Satan did get great hold upon the hearts of the people upon all the face of the land." (Helaman 16:23).

Third Nephi

The Book of Nephi, The Son of Nephi, Who Was The Son of Helaman

Around 1-4 A.D. - 34-35 A.D.

Third Nephi
Chapter 1

This book was given the title "Third Nephi - The Book of Nephi" by Orson Pratt, in the 1879 edition of The Book of Mormon in order to clarify its authorship. Mormon had called it "The Book of Nephi," in honor of Helaman's son Nephi. As Mormon wrote: "And Helaman was the son of Helaman, who was the son of Alma, who was the son of Alma, being a descendant of Nephi who was the son of Lehi, who came out of Jerusalem in the first year of the reign of Zedekiah, the king of Judah." (Superscript to Third Nephi - The Book of Nephi, see Commentary Reference to Ether 1:6-33).

Chapters 1-7 of Third Nephi - The Book of Nephi chronicle events in the New World that occurred during the mortal ministry of Christ in the Old World. Ninety-one years had passed away since King Mosiah had given up the throne in the Land of Zarahemla when the Reign of the Judges had been initiated, with Alma as the first Chief Judge. It was A.D. 1, the year of the Lord's birth, that was "six hundred years from the time that Lehi left Jerusalem." (V. 1).

The Elder Nephi, together with his brother Lehi, had grown up "unto the Lord," (Helaman 3:21), and had enjoyed a tremendous ministry, beginning about 45 B.C. By 30 B.C., Nephi had determined to follow the great example of Alma the Younger, to "preach the word of God all the remainder of his days, and his brother Lehi also, all the remainder of his days." (Helaman 5:4).

Now, in the year of the birth of the Savior, Nephi "departed out of the land of Zarahemla, giving charge unto his son Nephi, who was his eldest son, concerning the plates of brass, and all the records which had been kept, and all those things which had been kept sacred from the departure of Lehi out of Jerusalem." (V. 2). In other words, the young man was given all the emblems of authority, just as Mosiah had received them from his father, King Benjamin. (See Commentary Reference to Mosiah 1:16).

Then, his father "departed out of the land, and whither he went, no man knoweth." (V. 3). We never again encounter Nephi, or for that matter his brother Lehi, in The Book of Mormon. The circumstances of his disappearance were similar to that of Alma the Younger, 78 years earlier. (See Alma 45:18-19, & Essay: "A Whirlwind into Heaven").

Then, although the prophecies "began to be fulfilled more fully; for there began to be greater signs and greater miracles wrought among the people," many "began to rejoice," saying the time was past and the words of Samuel would not be fulfilled. (V. 4 & 6). The receipt of signs is the evidence of faith that only comes after believing and accepting the truth.

Some people take a fiendish delight in the lost hopes and broken dreams of others, and revel in destroying their faith. These individuals are happy when they mistakenly believe that the prophets are wrong, because they think they have found a justification for their unrighteous behavior. Flushed with a sense that they have the power to carry their desires to the extreme, they stone the prophets, cast them out, and put them to death. (See 3 Nephi 8:25).

This is why, in Zarahemla, "there was a day set apart by the unbelievers, that all those who believed in those traditions should be put to death, except the sign should come to pass, which had been given by Samuel, the prophet." (V. 9). Significantly, in this verse Mormon confirmed that Samuel was indeed a prophet of God. Heretofore, he had been referred to as "Samuel the Lamanite." Now, those who believed in his prophecies were under a death threat. False prophecy was blasphemous in ancient Israel, and was a capital offense. It was because the unbelievers would not acknowledge the reality of Samuel's prophecy or the legitimacy of his authority that they determined to destroy all those who looked forward to the Savior's birth. (See Commentary References to Mosiah 12:12 & 14, 17:7, Helaman 9:2, & Deuteronomy 18:22).

Nephi, the son of Nephi, had a great testimony of the Savior, and believed all the words of his father, and of Samuel, the Prophet. Living with his family "by the highway which led to the chief market, which was in the city of Zarahemla," (Helaman 7:10), he had surely heard Samuel deliver his prophecy of the birth of the Savior from the walls of the great city.

Therefore, "it came to pass that he went out and bowed himself down upon the earth, and cried mightily to his God on behalf of his people, yea, those who were about to be destroyed because of their faith in the tradition of their fathers." (V. 11). He knew that the prophecy was true, and now he begged Heavenly Father to protect His faithful servants.

After an entire day of mighty prayer, "the voice of the Lord came unto him, saying: Lift up your head and be of good cheer; for behold, the time is at hand, and on this night shall the sign be given, and on the morrow come I into the world, to show unto the world that I will fulfil all that which I have caused to be spoken by the mouth of my holy prophets." (V. 12-13, see 1 Nephi 10:5, & Enos 1:5). Nephi's prayer had been answered in a most glorious way. The Lord Himself had validated to Nephi the prophecies of his forefathers.

Alma had prophesied of Christ. (Mosiah 18:1-10, see Alma 5:11-12). Alma the Younger had added his testimony. (Alma 5:44-48). Helaman, and Helaman's brothers Shiblon and Corianton, had been just men and walked uprightly before God, and did good continually to keep the commandments. (Helaman 63:2). Helaman, the son of Helaman, did "that which was right in the sight of God continually." (Helaman 3:20), and Nephi's own father had taken it "upon himself to preach the word of God" as his life's mission. (Helaman 5:4).

Now Samuel, the prophet, had added his own personal witness. In hindsight, we know that all of his specific prophecies of the birth and death of the Savior were ultimately confirmed. Biblical records and The Book of Mormon attest to these truths. But for Nephi, it was strictly a matter of faith. After the trial of his faith came the anticipated blessing in a most marvelous and unforeseen way.

The Lord confirmed that He would come into the world "to do the will, both of the Father and of the Son - of the Father because of me, and of the Son because of my flesh." (V. 14). In other words, the Savior was the Firstborn spiritual child of Heavenly Father, to Whom was given the responsibility to bring about the spiritual rebirth of all mankind. Christ is the Father of our spiritual regeneration. (See Mosiah 15:1-8). It was His responsibility, by divine investiture of authority, to come to earth as the Savior and Redeemer of the world, according to the great Plan that had been initiated before the foundation of the world, "when the morning stars sang together, and all the sons of God shouted for joy." (Job 38:7).

The scriptures teach us that the Light of Christ is "the light which is in all things, which giveth life to all things, which is the law by which all things are governed, even the power of God, who sitteth upon his throne, who is in the bosom of eternity, who is in the midst of all things." (D&C 88:13). How appropriate that the sign of the birth of the Savior should be the dissolution of the night. "And it came to pass that there was no darkness in all that night, but it was as light as though it was mid-day. And it came to pass that the sun did rise in the morning again, according to its proper order; and they knew that it was the day that the Lord should be born, because of the sign which had been given." (V. 19).

So powerful was the sign, that many fell to the earth "because of their iniquity and their unbelief." (V. 18). In a most dramatic way, those who had relied on their own might, and had denied God the power to influence their lives, were suddenly left without even the strength to stand. "And thus we see, that the devil (quite literally) will not support his children at the last day." (Alma 30:60).

In both the Eastern and the Western Hemispheres, "a new star did appear, according to the word." (V. 21). The Wise Men would inquire of Herod: "Where is he that is born King of the Jews? For we have seen his star in the east, and have come to worship him." (Matthew 2:2). All the prophets have testified of Christ, and many signs and wonders have been given. Types and shadows have been raised up in similitude of the Only Begotten. God has been generous not only to Nephites, but to all men and women who have eyes to see, and ears to hear. God has manifest Himself not only to "those who believed after he came in the meridian of time, in the flesh, but (also to) all those from the beginning, even as many as were before he came, who believed in the words of the holy prophets, who spake as they were inspired by the gift of the Holy Ghost, who truly testified of him in all things." (D&C 20:26).

But even as these vibrant testimonies have been given, and in the midst of so many evidences of the love of God in the world, "there began to be lyings sent forth among the people, by Satan, to harden their hearts to the intent that they might not believe in those signs and wonders which they had seen." (V. 22). Satan is the source of unbelief in the world, and his goal is to quickly and effectively countermand every good desire, deed, and spiritual manifestation.

To combat this evil influence, Nephi continued to go forth among the people, "baptizing unto repentance, in the which there was a great remission of sins." (V. 23). With the Savior yet a Babe in Bethlehem, Nephi never ceased to invoke His worthy Name and perform this ordinance, the effect of which was particularly dramatic among the Nephites.

Because of the preaching of the Word of God and the acceptance by the people of the covenant of baptism, peace was maintained in the Land of Zarahemla. (V. 23). By a careful study of the scriptures, the people understood that the birth of the Savior notwithstanding, the Law of Moses was not yet fulfilled. Alma had clearly taught by these same scriptures that the Law of Moses would only be fulfilled when the "great and last sacrifice" had been made. (See Alma 34:13, see 2 Nephi 25:24, 3 Nephi 9:17 & 12:18). Signs and wonders on the American continent would commemorate that sacrifice.

The Angel had declared unto the shepherds tending their flocks in the fields near Bethlehem: "Fear not, for behold, I bring good tidings of great joy, which shall be to all people," including Nephites and Lamanites who gratefully accepted the invitation from Nephi and his brethren to join the fold of God. (Luke 2:10). They brought "glad tidings unto the people because of the signs which did come to pass, according to the words of the prophecy of all the holy prophets." (V. 26).

The Gospel was the breastwork protecting their hearts, and obedience to the covenants was their sanctuary against the rising winds of wickedness stirring in the land. The ominous threat of the Gadianton Robbers was fanning the flames of apostasy. In just three years' time, "they began to increase in a great degree, because there were many dissenters of the Nephites who did flee unto them." (V. 28). It was then, as it is now. Before we joined the Church, we were unconverted and uncommitted. We were open-minded and tolerant to all points of view. We were libertarian. Having made the covenant of baptism, though, we can never again have it both ways, or all ways, and those who apostatize often become the most vocal enemies of the Church and of Christ. Mormon observed "that after a people have been once enlightened by the Spirit of God, and have had great knowledge of things pertaining to righteousness, and then have fallen away into sin and transgression, they become more hardened, and thus their state becomes worse than though they had never known these things." (Alma 24:30).

Joseph Fielding Smith, Jr. cautioned the Saints: "Before you joined this Church you stood on neutral ground. When the Gospel was preached, good and evil were set before you. You could choose either or neither. There were two opposite masters inviting you to serve them. When you joined the Church you enlisted to serve God. When you did that, you left the neutral ground, and you can never get back on to it. Should you forsake the Master you enlisted to serve, it will be by the instigation of the evil one, and you will follow his dictation and be his servant." (C.E.S. Manual, p. 258).

King Benjamin taught the people of the Nephite Church that when a man "cometh out in open rebellion against God ... he listeth to obey the evil spirit, and becometh an enemy to all righteousness; therefore, the Lord has no place in him, for he dwelleth not in unholy temples." (Mosiah 2:37). When the Spirit is withdrawn, darkness supersedes the light and apostasy will follow. "This is one of the greatest evidences of the divinity of the Latter-day work. In other organizations, men and women may commit all manner of sin and still retain their membership, because they have no companionship with the Holy Ghost to lose, but in the Church when they sin and continue without repentance, the Spirit is withdrawn, and when they are left to themselves, the adversary takes possession of their minds, and they deny the faith." (Joseph Fielding Smith, Jr., "Doctrines of Salvation," 3:309).

It was this behavior among the apostate Nephites of Alma's day that had moved Mormon to observe: "It is strange to relate, (but) not long after their dissensions they became more hardened and impenitent, and more wild, wicked and ferocious than the Lamanites - drinking in with the traditions of the Lamanites; giving way to indolence, and all manner of lasciviousness; yea, entirely forgetting the Lord their God." (Alma 47:36).

Those who followed Satan in the years before the crucifixion of the Lord also began to enjoy success with the youth of the Church. Among the converted Lamanites in the Land of Zarahemla, there were "many children who did grow up and began to wax strong in years, that they became for themselves, and were led away by some who were Zoramites, by their lyings and their flattering words, to join those Gadianton robbers." (V. 29).

These youngsters were old enough to make their own decisions, and many chose to follow the Zoramites, who had years earlier both physically and spiritually "separated themselves from among the Nephites." (Alma 30:59). "And thus, were the Lamanites afflicted also, and began to decrease as to their faith and righteousness, because of the wickedness of the rising generation." (V. 30). The same thing had happened in the days of Benjamin and Mosiah. (See Mosiah 26:1-4). It is happening today as well, as the endless cycle repeats itself.

Third Nephi
Chapter 2

Three years after the birth of the Savior, the people in Zarahemla "began to forget those signs and wonders which they had heard, and began to be less and less astonished at a sign or a wonder from heaven." (V. 1). Perhaps, because their spiritual sensitivities were dulled, they only desired "theological titillation," and were thus "hard in their hearts, and blind in their minds, and began to disbelieve all which they had heard and seen." (V. 1).

For a variety of reasons, the wicked are occasionally given signs. Sometimes they demand signs from the ministers of the Lord as proof of their authority. (See John 2:18, 6:30). Those who have adulterous hearts seek signs for the satisfaction of their desires that require an ever-greater intensity of validation for the same level of gratification. (See Matthew 12:39). Signs are sometimes given for no reason other than to vindicate the prophets. (See Mosiah 20:21). Signs leave the wicked without excuse but with responsibility for what happens. Since consequences follow actions, signs establish accountability. (See D&C 63:7 & 11).

Mormon wrote that the people attributed the signs that had been given to "the power of the devil, to lead away and deceive the hearts of the people." (V. 2). This is a classic illustration of the subtle craftiness of Satan, who would even bring attention to himself if it would somehow serve his own evil purpose.

In reality, the devil himself was the source of their rationalizations: "And thus did Satan get possession of the hearts of the people again, insomuch that he did blind their eyes, and lead them away to believe that the doctrine of Christ was a foolish and a vain thing." (V. 2). As Paul wrote: "The natural man receiveth not the things of the Spirit of God: for they are foolishness unto him: neither can he know them, because they are spiritually discerned." (1 Corinthians 2:14).

When Mormon observed: "The people began to wax strong in wickedness and abominations," he might have been drawing particular attention to those who had made covenants with God, and who should have known better when they chose to conspicuously compromise their standards. (V. 3). It is one thing for an ignorant people to live in opposition to the laws of God, but it is quite another for those who have had the light to turn from it, willfully rebel, and intentionally seek a path of darkness. That behavior is an abomination, because it represents unfaithfulness to God, in what is essentially a marriage contract. (See Revelation 19:7). It is not easy for such individuals to obtain forgiveness. (See Alma 39:6).

In these decaying circumstances, 9 years passed away from the time of the birth of Christ. (V. 5-7). A new reckoning of time was established. The first calendaring system, used from 600 B.C. to 92 B.C., measured time from the departure of Lehi from Jerusalem. (V. 6, see Mosiah 29:44-47, & Alma 1:1). The second system was used for 100 years, during the Reign of The Judges. (91 B.C. - 9 A.D.). (V. 5). Now "the Nephites began to reckon their time from this period when the sign was given, or from the coming of Christ." (V. 8, see Commentary Reference to Alma 24:19).

As Mormon read these accounts from The Large Plates of Nephi, he may have asked himself: "Where was the great leader and prophet Nephi, when the people so desperately needed him?" He wrote: "And Nephi, who was the father of Nephi, who had the charge of the records, did not return to the land of Zarahemla, and could nowhere be found in all the land." (V. 9, see 3 Nephi 1:3).

In spite of the efforts of the younger Nephi and his brethren, "the people did still remain in wickedness" as the next two years passed away. (V. 10). Then, conditions deteriorated even more dramatically, as the Gadianton robbers spread "death and carnage throughout the land," as they boldly engaged in open warfare against the government. (V. 11).

So grave was the situation, that Mormon reported: "The Nephites were threatened with utter destruction." Extraordinary circumstances were met with an unusual response, as the Nephite and Lamanite brethren of the Church once again raised the "Title of Liberty" in the land, in order "to maintain their rights, and the privileges of their church and of their worship, and their freedom and their liberty." (V. 12-13, see Alma 46:12-13).

Because the Gospel had driven the law into their inward parts, and had written it upon their hearts, (Jeremiah 31:33), and because their fathers had embraced the word, which had wrought a mighty change in their hearts, (Alma 5:13-14), these Lamanites had experienced the process of sanctification. No longer were they under the condemnation of their fathers. (See 2 Nephi 5:21). Instead, "the curse was taken from them, and their skin became white like unto the Nephites. And their young men and their daughters became exceedingly fair, and they were numbered among the Nephites, and were called Nephites." (V. 15-16).

Years earlier, Jacob had made a cultural distinction between the Lamanite and Nephites. "I, Jacob, shall not hereafter distinguish them by these names, but I shall call them Lamanites that seek to destroy the people of Nephi, and those who are friendly to Nephi I shall call Nephites, or the people of Nephi." (Jacob 1:14, see Commentary Reference to Alma 4:13).

Now the conflict of the people of Nephi with the group of dissenters known as the Gandianton robbers was characterized by a series of pitched battles, with the fortunes of war shifting first to one side, and then to the other. The same disputes are common in the world today, with no clear resolution in sight. Negotiators may sue for peace while the antagonists try to gain a military advantage, but there will be no peace in the world until the supremacy of The Prince of Peace is recognized, and until every faction acknowledges its individual responsibility and accountability for behavior that is inconsistent with His program. In Zarahemla, "the sword of destruction did hang over them, insomuch that they were about to be smitten down by it, and this because of their iniquity." (V. 19).

Third Nephi
Chapter 3

In this chapter, Mormon recorded the details of a correspondence between Lachoneus, the governor of the land, and Giddianhi, the Gadianton leader. Their epistles are interesting, not so much because of their actual content, but because they reveal the contrasting characters of the antagonists.

The Nephite apostate Giddianhi began with exaggerated flattery of Lachoneus. (V. 2). His praise was insincere, disingenuous, overstated, and twisted. Then he resorted to the same tired clichés that had been so frequently employed by the Lamanites. First, he characterized the Gandianton band as having an "unconquerable spirit." (V. 4). What sweet irony is this? Yes, their spirits were unconquerable, but only in the sense that they were unteachable. Then, he blamed the Nephites for creating the animosity between their two cultures. He talked of the Gadianton band recovering "their rights and government," as if they had been wrongfully taken in the first place. (V. 10). Today's "Nephite dissenters" have their own bias to overcome, as they struggle with perceived ecclesiastical, social, economic, political, and cultural discrimination.

More flattery followed, with the ominous promise that if the Nephites submitted to him, they would not be their slaves, but would rather be their "brethren, and partners of all (their) substance." (V. 7). No matter that the substance of the Gadianton Robbers consisted only of whatever property of the Nephites they could steal.

Giddianhi swore an oath to Lachoneus that the Nephites would not be destroyed if they would submit to the demands of the Band. But his offer was a fabrication and a lie. The Gadianton Robbers had always been parasites who lived off the efforts of others. Their habit was to take what they pleased by whatever means were necessary, with no regard for the property rights of others. To them, the end justified the means. Their lifestyle was utterly corrupt, "for there was no way that they could subsist save it were to plunder and rob and murder." (3 Nephi 4:5). In his epistle, Giddianhi offered no evidence at all that they had reformed their ways. As a matter of fact, he proclaimed himself the governor of "the secret society of Gadianton," crying havoc against the Nephites if they did not yield. (V. 8-9). Satan's ugly fingerprints were smeared all over the pages of this epistle from Giddianhi.

As for Lachoneus: "He was exceedingly astonished, because of the boldness of Giddianhi." (V. 11). If the situation had not been so critical, it would have been laughable. But Lachoneus "was a just man, and could not be frightened by the demands and the threatenings of a robber." (V. 12). He would call a spade a spade. Lachoneus would not give this man any undeserved respect, or his "office" any legitimacy, nor would he negotiate with a terrorist. Giddianhi was nothing more than a "wicked and abominable robber." (V. 11).

Would that today's political leaders could have the moral courage of Lachoneus. In contrast to the oaths and threats of Giddianhi, Lachoneus declared to his brethren: "As the Lord liveth, except ye repent of all your iniquities, and cry unto the Lord, ye will in nowise be delivered out of the hands of those Gadianton robbers." (V. 15). In contrast to Giddianhi's oath, his carried real power, for it was supported by personal righteousness. Its effect was to immediately instill in the people a fear of God, to the end that "they did exert themselves in their might to do according to the words of Lachoneus." (V. 16, see Commentary Reference to Mosiah 4:1).

Central to the Nephite military strategy "was the custom to appoint ... some one that had the spirit of revelation and also prophecy" to be commander of the army. (V. 18). Gidgiddoni was chosen. Lachoneus had counseled the people to inquire of the Lord concerning the best course of action, using an oath to give his instruction emphasis, and to convey its spiritual power. (V. 15). Now Gidgiddoni's inspired leadership would prove to be the key to the temporal salvation of the people. (V. 21).

No offensive war was to be undertaken against the Lamanites. (V. 21, see D&C 98:32-39). Instead, all those who would call themselves Nephites assembled in the Land of Zarahemla to defend themselves against their enemies." (V. 22-23). In all, "there were a great many thousand people" who responded to the call of Gidgiddoni. (V. 24). In these circumstances, "they did put up their prayers unto the Lord their God, that he would deliver them in the time that their enemies should come down against them to battle." (V. 2, see Commentary Reference to Mormon 6:1-5).

The Lord helps those who help themselves. Therefore, while they waited, "Gidgiddoni did cause that they should make weapons of war of every kind, and they should be strong with armor, and with shields, and with bucklers, after the manner of his instruction." (V. 26).

Third Nephi
Chapter 4

By 18 A.D., the Gadianton Band felt strong enough to "sally forth from the hills, and out of the mountains, and the wilderness, and their strongholds, and their secret places." (V. 1). At first, they probably felt that the conquest of the Land of Zarahemla was going to be easy, as they "began to take possession of all the lands which had been deserted by the Nephites, and the cities which had been left desolate." (V. 1).

But then, their desire for spoils became their undoing. They were accustomed to plundering to obtain whatever they wanted, but the Nephites had left nothing of value behind when they had retreated to the City of Zarahemla from the outlying districts. (V. 2-4). Therefore, because their supply of provisions was critically low, it became necessary for Giddianhi to lead his army directly against the Nephites. (V. 5-6).

The ensuing battle was great for the Nephites and terrible for the Gadianton Robbers, who symbolically bore witness of their corruption by mimicking the physical characteristics of apostate Lamanites. They even changed the color of their exposed skin, "because of their being dyed in blood." (V. 7, see Commentary Reference to Mormon 5:15).

Today, dissenters from the true faith do not dye their skins with blood to broadcast their apostasy. Instead, they adopt other equally obvious qualities. Just as surely, and just as unwittingly, do these modern-day apostates label themselves. Their skin is "dyed" with the bloodstains of corrupt cultural, political, economic, sociological, and religious ideology.

The sight that met the Nephite army must have been almost overwhelming, for "when they saw the appearance of the army of Giddianhi, (they) had all fallen to the earth, and did lift their cries to the Lord their God, that he would spare them and deliver them out of the hands of their enemies." (V. 8). Mistaking this action of the Nephites for unequivocal surrender, Giddianhi rushed forward with his army to fulfil the terrible oath he had sworn to Lachoneus. (See 3 Nephi 3:8).

But "notwithstanding the threatenings and the oaths which Giddianhi had made, behold, the Nephites did beat them back." (V. 12). Giddianhi had taken the name of the Lord in vain. He had used it without priesthood power, direction, or authority, and it was to no effect. Moreover, it was an abomination in the sight of God, Who will not be mocked. In this instance, the consequence for such action was the temporal and spiritual destruction of his Gadianton Band. "There never was known so great a slaughter among all the people of Lehi since he left Jerusalem." (V. 11).

Now it was Gidgiddoni's turn to "Cry Havoc - Take No Prisoners." His order was "that they should not spare any that should fall into their hands by the way; and thus, they did pursue them and did slay them, to the borders of the wilderness." (V. 13). Giddianhi the robber was among those who fell that day. (V. 14).

Because of their victory, the security of the Nephite nation was maintained for three years. (V. 14-16). Then, a new Band of Gadianton laid siege upon them. Their leader, named Zemnarihah, did not realize that the Nephites were well prepared, "having reserved for themselves provisions, and horses and cattle, and flocks of every kind, that they might subsist for the space of seven years, in the which time they did hope to destroy the robbers from off the face of the land." (V. 4, see 3 Commentary Reference to Nephi 6:1).

The Gadiantons, on the other hand, had only scanty resources and were forced to live off the land. Soon, they began to suffer physical depravation. (V. 19-21). Therefore, Zemnarihah gave the order to abandon the siege, and to "march into the furthermost parts of the land northward." (V. 23). Ironically, this was beyond the land that was called Desolation. (V. 23, see Alma 22:30-31). That field of battle would indeed leave the Gandianton Robbers desolate.

The Nephite army, under the command of Gidgiddoni, cut off the Gadianton Band, engaged them in battle, and soundly defeated them. Of the enemy, "there were many thousands who did yield themselves up prisoners unto the Nephites, and the remainder of them were slain." (V. 27). With the fortunes of war changing, the Nephite captains could afford to be more tolerant of their enemies. In fact, Mormon reported in 3 Nephi Chapter 5 that "they did cast their prisoners into prison, and did cause the word of God to be preached unto them; and as many as would repent of their sins and enter into a covenant that they would murder no more were set at liberty." (3 Nephi 5:4, see Helaman 6:37). The Nephites were rediscovering the principle that the only really effective weapon against evil and darkness is truth and light. Ideology can be the most persuasive influence on earth.

Zemnarihah, on the other hand, was dealt with more severely, perhaps because he was more culpable. He "was taken and hanged upon a tree, yea, even upon the top thereof until he was dead. And when they had hanged him until he was dead they did fell the tree to the earth." (V. 28). The manner of his death became symbolic for the Nephites, who had sacrificed so much in defense of their "rights, and the privileges of their church and of their worship, and their freedom and their liberty." (3 Nephi 2:12). With one unified voice, they proclaimed: "May the Lord preserve his people in righteousness and in holiness of heart, that they may cause to be felled to the earth all who shall seek to slay them because of power and secret combinations, even as this man hath been felled to the earth." (V. 29). Zemnarihah's death was not an act of revenge, but rather the dramatic exclamation point on a chapter of history that should never have happened in the first place, and that hopefully would never be repeated.

The Nephites were grateful for their deliverance, which "was because of their repentance and their humility." (V. 33). They had prepared properly, followed counsel, fought courageously, and then thanked the Lord for his intervention. They knew that He would watch over His "people in righteousness, so long as they (should) call on the name of their God for protection." (V. 30). As 22 A.D. drew to a close, the Nephites must have hoped the new year would bring them the peace and prosperity they so desired.

Third Nephi
Chapter 5

Quite remarkably, Mormon reported that at this time "there was not a living soul among all the people of the Nephites who did doubt in the least the words of all the holy prophets who had spoken; for they knew that it must needs be that they must be fulfilled." (V. 1). They believed in the signs of the times, forsook their sins, and "did serve God with all diligence day and night." (V. 2-3).

They had come to a clearer understanding of the dynamics of interactive relationships, had recognized that all things have their opposites, and realized that the only effective weapon against evil and darkness is truth and light. (See 2 Nephi 2:11). Therefore, the Nephites "did cast their prisoners into prison, and did cause the word of God to be preached unto them; and as many as would repent of their sins and enter into a covenant that they would murder no more were set at liberty." (V. 4, see Helaman 6:37).

"Force and compulsion will never establish an ideal society," said David O. McKay. "This can only come through transformation of the individual soul, and through a life redeemed from sin and brought in harmony with Divine will." (C.R., 10/1962). For all we know, the converted Gadianton robbers remained faithful, and their righteous descendants helped to form the core of the Zion society that was later established in Zarahemla. (See Commentary Reference to 4 Nephi 1:2-3).

Lehi had taught that "men are free according to the flesh, and all things are given them which are expedient unto man. And they are free to choose liberty and eternal life, through the great Mediator of all men, or to choose captivity and death, according to the captivity and power of the devil; for he seeketh that all men might be miserable like unto himself." (2 Nephi 2:27).

The Nephites were eager to model their behavior after that of the Savior, for their prophets had revealed Him to them. They had been taught to show mercy to former adversaries on condition of their true repentance. But of the Gadianton robbers "who did not enter into a covenant, and who did still continue to have those secret murders in their hearts, yea, as many as were found breathing out threatenings against their brethren were condemned and punished according to the law." (V. 5). Nephite justice required that all stand accountable for their actions.

Mormon was almost overwhelmed as the sheer volume of material within The Large Plates of Nephi confronted him. He had but a short time to do the work of abridgement, and did it in straitened circumstances, because Nephite society in 385 A.D. was imploding. (See Mormon 6:6). Little wonder that he wrote only briefly of these events that transpired in Zarahemla: "They cannot all be written in this book (meaning his abridgment on The Plates of

Mormon), yea, this book cannot contain even a hundredth part of what was done among so many people in the space of twenty and five years." (V. 8, see Words of Mormon 1:5).

Nevertheless, Mormon indulged in frequent asides in his abridgement. Perhaps as he labored with the many records at his disposal, he had occasion to pause and reflect on the lessons learned from the unique perspective he had been given. We are fortunate that he had the sensitivity, not to mention the time, to reveal something of his personality within The Plates of Mormon. It is a testament to his spiritual powers to realize that not only was Mormon able to communicate his feelings in writing, but that Joseph Smith preserved their essence through the translation of the "Reformed Egyptian" into English. It is a miracle of nearly equal magnitude that the latter-day translation of The Book of Mormon into dozens of languages has not diminished in the slightest its power of conversion.

Mormon assured his readers that "there are records which do contain all the proceedings of this people; and a shorter but true account was given by Nephi." (V. 9). He was referring to Third Nephi - The Book of Nephi, the book written by Nephi. Mormon wrote: "Therefore, I have made my record of these things according to the record of Nephi, which was engraven on the plates which were called the (Large) plates of Nephi." (V. 10). But, Mormon clarified, "I do make the record (or abridgment) on plates which I have made with mine own hands," that is, on The Plates of Mormon. (V. 11).

Mormon wanted us to know that he was named "after the land of Mormon, the land in which Alma did establish the church among the people." (V. 12, see Mormon 1:5). If the people of Mormon's own day could have only rallied around the standard of his name, perhaps they too could have re-established The Church of Jesus Christ, and it could have been "the first church which was established among them after their transgression." (V. 12). There is so much irony in his name when we link its historical significance with the cultural circumstances surrounding his life and ministry.

Visualize Mormon, sitting alone at the Hill Cumorah, with danger lurking in every shadow. He felt compelled to declare in his abridgement: "Behold I am a disciple of Jesus Christ, the Son of God. I have been called of him to declare his word among his people, that they might have everlasting life." (V. 13). This is the same man who wrote, at about the same time, that "a continual scene of wickedness and abominations has been before mine eyes ever since I have been sufficient to behold the ways of man." (Mormon 2:18, see Mormon 4:11 & 8:8).

When Mormon made this declaration, he surely realized that he was one of only a few disciples of Jesus Christ that were left among the Nephites. He also must have resigned himself to the reality that his words had fallen on deaf ears, and his ministry, unlike that of Nephi, had not been able to generate saving faith among his people. For "every heart was hardened ... and there never had been so great wickedness among all the children of Lehi ... as was among this people." (Mormon 4:11-12). His editorial aside reads as if he just had to tell someone, anyone, that there was one disciple left in the land who had faith in Christ, and who would bear a testimony of His mission, regardless of the consequences.

The only thing left to sustain him was "the will of God ... and the prayers of those who have gone hence, who were the holy ones." (V. 14). It was their spiritual power, directed in his behalf, that enabled him to "make a record of these things which have ... taken place from the time that Lehi left Jerusalem, even down unto the present time." (V. 14-15). Nearly a thousand years of Nephite history had been abridged from the records at his disposal. (V. 16).

This abridgment would be preserved for us in The Book of Mormon, including "the things which (he had) seen with (his) own eyes." (V. 17). Nevertheless, he wrote from Cumorah that "it is impossible for the tongue to describe, or for man to write a perfect description of the horrible scene of the blood and carnage which was among the people" in 385 A.D. (Mormon 4:11).

At this point, Mormon felt inspired to bear his testimony of the record, that it was "just and true." (V. 18). He also offered a small apology that he was not able to make the record even more powerful. The limitations of language, he said, impeded that effort. (V. 18, see Mormon 9:31-33).

In verse 19, Mormon concluded his personal reflections and emphasized his determination to complete his abridgment of the mass of records that were before him at Cumorah. He desired to focus on the task at hand, that was to distill the religious and secular history of the Nephites down into a manageable chronicle that would be hidden in the earth until it was time to bring it forth as a marvelous work and a wonder in the Last Days. (See 2 Nephi 25:17, 27:26, Helaman 3:13-16, 3 Nephi 21:9, Moroni 10:3, D&C 4:1, & Isaiah 29:14).

As he neared the completion of the work, Mormon was blessed to see the larger picture. He wrote: "I am Mormon, and a pure descendant of Lehi. I have reason to bless my God and my Savior Jesus Christ, that he brought our fathers out of the land of Jerusalem, (and no one knew it save it were himself and those whom he brought out of that land) and that he hath given me and my people so much knowledge unto the salvation of our souls." (V. 20).

He repeated the theme that has been so faithfully preserved throughout the text of The Book of Mormon: "Insomuch as the children of Lehi have kept his commandments he hath blessed them and prospered them according to his word." (V. 22). He also repeated the promise given to Lehi's descendants, that "surely shall he again bring a remnant of the seed of Joseph to the knowledge of the Lord their God." (V. 23). He then repeated the promise to the Children of The Covenant: "And as surely as the Lord liveth, will he gather in from the four quarters of the earth all the remnant of the seed of Jacob, who are scattered abroad upon all the face of the earth." (V. 24).

Mormon wanted those who would live in the Last Days and would read his words to know that the promises of the Lord are unequivocal. "As the Lord liveth, so shall it be. Amen." (V. 26).

"They did cast their
prisoners into prison, and
did cause the word of God to be
preached unto them; and as many
as would repent of their sins and enter
into a covenant that they would murder
no more were set at liberty."
(3 Nephi 5:4).

Third Nephi
Chapter 6

With war no longer a threat, the people returned to their homes, both in the land northward and the land southward. They took with them all their temporal possessions. (V. 1). In one of the very few references to horses in The Book of Mormon, this verse states that they took these animals with them, as well. (See 3 Nephi 4:4, & Commentary References to Ether 9:32 & 10:19).

Do we discern in Mormon's description the seeds of apostasy? The record states that the people carried with them "their gold, and their silver, and all their precious things." (V. 2). There is nothing intrinsically wrong with possessing these things, but the Nephites never seemed to pull it off well, and Mormon always made a point of identifying particular possessions that typify our focus of attention on telestial trinkets that have no lasting value. Also, this verse stands in stark contrast to Nephi's description of Father Lehi's departure into the wilderness from the land of Jerusalem, when "he left his house, and the land of his inheritance, and his gold, and his silver, and his precious things, and took nothing with him, save it were his family, and provisions, and tents." (1 Nephi 2:4, see 2 Nephi 12:7).

Interestingly, verse 3 indicates that those former Gadianton robbers who had "entered into a covenant to keep the peace of the land, who were desirous to remain Lamanites," were given land to farm so that they might enjoy the fruits of their own labors. These Lamanites were not compelled to become Nephites, nor were they pressured to join the Church, but they were given the means to provide for their own families. It would have been critically important that these former Gadianton robbers have every opportunity to experience the success of working within the system, because only a dozen years earlier, Mormon had reported that "there was no way that they could subsist save it were to plunder and rob and murder." (3 Nephi 4:5). It was the only lifestyle they had known.

All the people were once again focusing on their responsibilities as functioning members of society, and "there was great order in the land, and they had formed their laws according to equity and justice." As a matter of fact, "there was nothing in all the land to hinder the people from prospering continually, except they should fall into transgression." (V. 5, see V. 18, & Commentary Reference to 3 Nephi 7:2).

Mormon emphasized this fact in his record, because it was his sad duty to record that within a year's time, "there began to be a great inequality in all the land," that culminated in the flagrant violation of the law by the leaders themselves. (V. 14, see V. 21-30).

How could this be so? Mormon revealed that it had been "Gidgiddoni, and the judge, Lachoneus, and those who had been appointed leaders, who had established this great peace in the land." (V. 6). It was only by the righteous example and influence of these two men that the Nephites were able to prosper in the land. Left on their own, the people in general could not sustain their forward momentum.

In the very next year, that was the 29th since the sign of Christ's birth had been given, "there began to be some disputings among the people." (V. 10). Some of the Nephites, who should have known better, "were lifted up unto pride." (V. 10). Today, we ought to take very seriously the relevant counsel from the Doctrine and Covenants: "Beware of pride, lest ye become as the Nephites of old." (D&C 38:39).

In time, the people began to be ranked according to their economic or educational opportunities. "Some were ignorant because of their poverty, and others did receive great learning because of their riches." (V. 12). This verse is critically relevant in light of similar circumstances today and commands our thoughtful attention. It has always been extremely important to the welfare of all that men and women be given opportunities to explore their potential. In fact, "we hold these truths to be self-evident, that all men are created equal, that they are endowed by their Creator with certain unalienable rights, that among these are life, liberty and the pursuit of happiness." (Declaration of Independence). When economic circumstances, in particular, preclude an educational pathway leading to life, liberty, and the pursuit of happiness, individuals, the Church, and the state would do well to examine their moral responsibility to provide assistance, because these individuals and institutions have a vested interest in the national resource represented by the educational development of their members.

Truman Madsen wrote in an appeal for contributions to Brigham Young University: "The Jews have an ancient saying: 'The world is saved by the breath of students. Even to rebuild the temple, the schools must not be closed.' Today, some of the finest schools are closed, and not just by a padlock on the doors. They are closed to the highest values of our culture, especially religious values; closed by taut admission standards or by exorbitant tuition; closed by an 'openness' that retreats under the clamor for rights without duties, and promotes laxity instead of discipline; closed by the intrusion of federal controls. Brigham Young University remains open and remarkably unimpeded by these trends. It is one of the most creative undergraduate environments in America. As it extends its reach to hundreds of thousands in the wider world, its geographic location will be less important than its influence. It is already one of the world's leading institutions in adult education. The choice here is not between rebuilding the temple or closing the school. The university is crowned by a temple. As society disintegrates, the need for a rooted, prepared, expert, spiritually sensitive citizenry is not only clear, but also crucial. It is no mere cliché to say the future of mankind is being made here. If, as someone said, 'the greatest thing in life is to give yourself for something that outlasts you', this university is one of the bastions of perpetual opportunity. For its product is, in the ultimate perspective, eternal. There could not be a better investment."

From a slightly different perspective, Will and Ariel Durant have written: "If education is the transmission of civilization, then our finest contemporary achievement is our unprecedented expenditure of wealth and toil in the provision of higher education for all. We have raised the level and average of knowledge beyond any age in history. The heritage that we can now transmit is richer than that of Pericles, for it includes all the Greek flowering that followed him; richer than Leonardo's, for it includes him and the Italian Renaissance; richer than Voltaire's, for it embraces all the French Enlightenment and its ecumenical dissemination. If progress is real, it is because we are born to a richer heritage, born on a higher level of that pedestal which the accumulation of knowledge and art raises as the ground and support of our being. The heritage rises, and men and women rise in proportion as they receive it.

What would be the full fruitage of instruction if every child should be schooled till at least his twentieth year, and should find free access to the universities, libraries, and museums that harbor and offer intellectual and artistic treasures? Consider education as the transmission of our mental, moral, technical, and aesthetic heritage as fully as possible to as many as possible, for the enlargement of our understanding, control, embellishment, and enjoyment of life." ("The Lessons of History," p. 100-102).

Perhaps, "the best education is to be perpetually thrilled with life". (Edward Everett Hale). Emerson wrote on one occasion that those who have "seen the rising moon break out of the clouds at midnight have been present like archangels at the creation of light and of the world," and on another that "if the stars should appear but one night in a thousand years, how would we believe and adore, and preserve for many generations the remembrance of the city of God which had been shown?" Too often, the problem with education, Hugh Nibley declared, "is that when we ask for the bread of life, we instead get only processed academic factory food served at an automat." ("An Intellectual Autobiography," p. xxiii).

In any event, in the Church in Zarahemla in A.D. 30, "there became a great inequality in all the land, insomuch that the church began to be broken up." (V. 14). There is a subtle relationship between knowledge and liberty, and because the Nephites did not place a high value on providing educational opportunities for all their people, their society as a whole suffered. They ultimately lost their individual and collective freedom, even as they clamored for personal rights.

"Knowledge will forever govern ignorance, and a people who mean to be their own governors must arm themselves with the power which knowledge gives. What spectacle can be more edifying or more seasonable than that of liberty and learning, each leaning on the other for their mutual and surest support?" (James Madison). Had the Nephites determined to be a free people in every sense of the world, their independence from ignorance would have focused their attention on more diligently nurturing themselves as their most significant natural resource.

In Zarahemla, the only people who resisted the pressures tearing away at the fabric of their society were "a few of the Lamanites who were converted unto the true faith; and they would not depart from it, for they were firm, and steadfast, and immovable, willing with all diligence to keep the commandments of the Lord." (V. 14, see Commentary Reference to 1 Nephi 2:10). Is it possible that these Lamanites were the intended recipients of the blessing first given to the sons and daughters of Laman, by Lehi? Six hundred years earlier, he had said to those ancestors of these people: "Because of my blessing the Lord God will not suffer that ye shall perish; wherefore, he will be merciful unto you and unto your seed forever." (2 Nephi 4:7). Lemuel's children received "the same blessing which (Lehi) left unto the sons and daughters of Laman; wherefore, (neither would they) utterly be destroyed; but in the end (their seed should) be blessed." (2 Nephi 4:9). If Lehi's patriarchal blessing to his grandchildren had been partially confirmed at this pivotal time in Zarahemla, we are led to the conclusion that the ministries that had focused on the elder sons of Lehi and their posterity had not been entirely in vain. (See Commentary reference to 2 Nephi 1:28).

Quite clearly, the cause of the apostasy of the disobedient "was that Satan had great power, unto the stirring up of the people to do all manner of iniquity, and to the puffing them up with pride, tempting them to seek for power, and authority, and riches, and the vain things of the world." (V. 15). However, the power of the devil was not absolute. These people had not lost their moral agency to decide their own fate. "They did not sin ignorantly, for they knew the will of God concerning them, for it had been taught unto them; therefore, they did willfully rebel against God." (V. 18, see 4 Nephi 1:38, & Commentary Reference to Alma 56:47).

In the midst of this wickedness, "there began to be men inspired from heaven and sent forth, standing among the people in all the land." (V. 20). These missionaries testified boldly of Christ and His resurrection, which though yet in the future, was to them as a present reality. In the same way, in our day, missionaries go into all the world to preach the Gospel, that encompasses the broad scope of the Plan of Salvation including the Millennial Reign of Christ, the restoration of the Kingdom of God on earth, and the eventual celestialization of this world.

As it is today, among the Nephites "there were many of the people who were exceedingly angry because of those who testified of these things." Certainly, the wicked take the truth to be hard. These individuals were classed as "chief judges, and they who had been high priests and lawyers." (V. 21). In this chapter, we see the terrible conditions within a society when the laws of the land are of no effect because the leaders are wicked. These Nephites even entered into satanic covenants and conspiracies to overthrow the legitimate government. (See v. 27-28 & 30).

In contempt of the law, because they loved Satan more than God, these men secretly put to death many of the missionaries. (V. 23, see Moses 5:18). To defend their murderous acts, they covenanted with "the devil, to combine against all righteousness." (V. 28). Cain had done the same thing after he had slain Abel. (See Moses 5:29-31). "And they did set at defiance the law and the rights of their country." (V. 30). Well did Edmund Burke observe of such, whose "passions forge their fetters." These people had sold their birthright for a mess of pottage and had made a compact with the devil, forgetting that one of his goals is to make all men, not just the righteous, but the wicked as well, as miserable as he is, and that he will not support his followers at the last day. In just three years, these people who had revived the secret oaths and covenants of Master Mahan would face their day of judgment terrifyingly alone. (See Moses 5:30-31)

Third Nephi
Chapter 7

In the thirtieth year, the people had become so depraved that they assassinated the righteous chief Judge Lachoneus as he sat upon the judgment seat. Unwittingly, they had eliminated the protector of their rights and privileges. (V. 1).

The fabric of their society was in a process of disintegration. "The people were divided one against another; and they did separate one from another into tribes, every man according to his family and his kindred and friends; and thus, they did destroy the government of the land." (V. 2). As we read the account, we worry that it prefigures our own day. The order of government collapsed because the society was degenerate and had decayed from within. "There were no wars as yet among them; and all this iniquity had come upon the people because they did yield themselves unto the power of Satan." (V. 5). "The regulations of the government were destroyed, because of the secret combination" that was dedicated to anarchy. (V. 6). Conditions were so disgusting to Mormon that he resorted to revolting figures of speech to describe them: "The people had turned from their righteousness, like the dog to his vomit, or like the sow to her wallowing in the mire." (V. 8, see Proverbs 26:11, & 2 Peter 2:22).

Even though the various familial tribes co-inhabiting the land mistrusted each other and were jealous of their rivals' power, "yet they were united in the hatred of those who had entered into a covenant to destroy the government." (V. 11, see V. 14). They recognized that the secret combination was a common enemy. If its power remained unchecked, reasoned the leaders of these tribes, it would destroy them, as well as the government.

The tribes, therefore, "had come to an agreement that they would not go to war one with another," and "in some degree they had peace in the land." (V. 14). There are different qualities of peace that these people enjoyed by the most liberal of definitions. (See Commentary Reference to Mosiah 25:19-29). "Nevertheless, their hearts were turned from the Lord their God, and they did stone the prophets and did cast them out from among them" in the most ignorant manner. (V. 14).

For the previous 30 years, Nephi had been testifying and preaching to the people. He was a special witness, and bore the name "Nephi" with honor and distinction. He had heard the voice of the Lord on the night before His birth. (3 Nephi 1:13). Mormon testified that Nephi had "been visited by angels and also the voice of the Lord, therefore having seen angels, and being eyewitness, and having had power given unto him that he might know concerning the ministry of Christ" he pursued his ministry with enthusiasm, "and began to testify, boldly, (of the necessity of) repentance and remission of sins through faith on the Lord Jesus Christ." (V. 15-16).

Sometimes in the ministry, experiences are so personal in nature that they are only meaningful to the participants.

In these cases, it serves no useful purpose to record them. Because they are so profoundly moving and testify so sweetly of sacred principles, they cannot be shared with others whose frame of reference may be more profane. Mormon wrote of such experiences of Nephi: "All of them cannot be written, and a part of them would not suffice, therefore they are not written in this book." (V. 17). More than once, Joseph Smith told the Saints: "Would to God I could tell you what I know. But you would call it blasphemy, and there are men upon this stand who would want to take my life. If the Church knew all of the commandments, one half they would reject through prejudice and ignorance." (Ivan Barrett, "Joseph Smith & The Restoration," p. 522, see D&C 76:114-118).

Joseph wrote in his History: "Reading the experience of others, or the revelation given to them, can never give us a comprehensive view of our condition and true relation to God. Knowledge of these things can only be obtained by experience through the ordinances of God set forth for that purpose. Could you gaze into heaven five minutes, you would know more than you would by reading all that has ever been written on the subject." (H.C., 6:50). For example, the ordinances of the priesthood, particularly those that are taught in the temple, bring us to a greater understanding of the nature of God. This is why the temple endowment cannot be revealed to those who are unworthy of its blessings.

Sometimes, it can be dangerous to teach principles of the Gospel to those who are not prepared to receive them. Joseph Smith said: "The moment you teach them some of the mysteries of the Kingdom of God that are retained in the heavens, and are to be revealed to the children of men when they are prepared for them, they will be the first to stone you and put you to death. It was this principle that crucified the Lord Jesus Christ, and will cause the people to kill the prophets in this generation." (Ivan Barrett, "Joseph Smith & The Restoration," p. 521).

In the spring of 1844, conspirators who were apostates from the Church sought the life of Joseph Smith with the following oath: "You solemnly swear, before God and all holy angels, and before your brethren of whom you are surrounded, that you will give your life, your liberty, your influence, your all, for the destruction of Joseph Smith, so help you God!" Each person who so swore placed his hand on the Bible and signed his name. ("Joseph Smith & The Restoration," p. 590). The activity of the secret combinations, which sought the overthrow of both civil and Church government, was not restricted to the days of Nephi shortly before the Lord visited the Americas. One is reminded of the Wehrmacht Oath of Loyalty to Adolph Hitler (adopted by the German people on August 2, 1934): "I swear by God this sacred oath that I shall render unconditional obedience to Adolph Hitler, the Leader of the German empire, supreme commander of the armed forces, and that I shall at all times be prepared, as a brave soldier, to give my life for this oath."

Joseph declared: "No man knows my history; I cannot tell it. I shall never undertake it. If I had not experienced what I have, I should not have believed it myself." ("Teachings of Presidents of the Church: Joseph Smith", p. 520-25). On another occasion he said: "If I had not actually got into this work, and been called of God, I would back out. But I cannot back out. I have no doubt of the truth." (Lyndon Cook & Andrew Ehat, "The Words of Joseph Smith," p. xx).

Nephi ministered among his people "with power and with great authority." (V. 17). Authority is received by the laying on of hands, but priesthood power granted by God is commensurate with personal righteousness. (See Helaman 10:6). The rabble understood the source of Nephi's influence, and "were angry with him, even because he had greater power than they. It were not possible that they could disbelieve his words, for so great was his faith on the Lord Jesus Christ that angels did minister unto him daily." (V. 18). He performed many miracles, "and the people saw it, and did witness of it, and were angry with him because of his power." (V. 20). Signs lack the power of conversion, and the gifts of the Spirit are given only for the edification of the faithful.

Nephi was successful in his ministry, although initially "there were but few who were converted unto the Lord." (V. 21). "There were none who were brought unto repentance who were not baptized with water." (V. 24). The purpose of

Nephi's ministry in the last years before the destruction of the wicked in Zarahemla was to bring as many souls as possible to repentance, that they might be numbered among the faithful, and enter into the fold of Christ through baptism.

"Therefore, there were ordained of Nephi, men unto this ministry, that all such as should come unto them should be baptized with water, and this as a witness and a testimony before God, and unto the people, that they had repented and received a remission of their sins." (V. 25). The Lord is patient and long-suffering, and extends His arm of mercy long after others would have thrown up their hands in frustration and given up. Thirty-three years after the sign of the birth of Christ had been given, "there were many that were baptized" by those who held priesthood authority. These faithful missionaries were as Saviors on Mount Zion to the repentant. (V. 26, see Obadiah 1:31).

"Now I would have you
remember … that there were none
who were brought unto repentance who
were not baptized with water. Therefore, they
were ordained of Nephi, men unto this ministry,
that all such as should come unto them should be
baptized with water, and this as a witness and a
testimony before God, and unto the people,
that they had repented and received
a remission of their sins."
(3 Nephi 7:24-25).

Third Nephi
Chapter 8

In the beginning of this chapter, Mormon went to great lengths to validate the legitimacy and accuracy of the record of Nephi. It is a story without parallel in the history of the world or of the scriptures, and he wanted latter-day readers to be prepared to accept it at face value. He wrote that what was to follow came from Nephi, who was "a just man who did keep the record." (V. 1).

The Nephites had some idea of when the Savior would be crucified. Perhaps they received this information from The Plates of Brass or from their prophets. They realized that, according to Hebrew custom, thirty years after the sign had been given of His birth, the mortal ministry of the Savior would have begun. In any event, they "began to look with great earnestness for the sign which had been given by the prophet Samuel the Lamanite, yea, for the time that there should be darkness, for the space of three days over the face of the land." (V. 3, see Helaman 14:20).

Once again, Samuel the Lamanite, was referred to in the scriptures as a prophet. During his ministry among the Nephites in Zarahemla, his message had been generally rejected. Thirty-nine years later, the spiritual preparedness of the population was not so very different, for "there began to be great doubtings and disputations among the people, notwithstanding so many signs had been given." (V. 4).

But the fulfilment of the prophecy was recorded with great accuracy. "In the thirty and fourth year, in the first month, on the fourth day of the month, there arose a great storm, such as one as never had been known in all the land." (V. 5). This scripture, the New Testament, and the Doctrine & Covenants, all indicate that the Savior might have been crucified the very week that He turned 33 years of age. The first month in the Hebrew calendar was in the springtime of the year, between the middle of March and the middle of April.

Verses 5-18 detail the destruction that subsequently occurred in the lands of The Book of Mormon. It appears that it was one of the greatest natural disasters in the history of the world. It was the physical manifestation of the revolt of the earth against the crucifixion of its Creator. In these verses, the adjectives "great and terrible" are used 7 times; "great" is used 8 times, and "terrible" is used 6 times. Clearly, it was difficult to find adequate words to describe the massive devastation.

The "whole face of the land was changed" with such a physical contortion that "the face of the whole earth became deformed." (V. 12 & 17). "The thunderings, and the lightnings, and the storm, and the tempest, and the quakings of the earth … did last for about the space of three hours." (V. 19). It is almost impossible to conceptualize a storm of this magnitude, or an earthquake lasting for more than a few seconds. Indeed, "it was said by some that the time was greater." (V. 19). To them, it must have seemed an eternity.

"And then behold, there was darkness upon the face of the land." (V. 19, see Matthew 27:51). So overpowering, complete, total, and universal was the murky blackness, that "those who had not fallen could (actually) feel the vapor of darkness." (V. 20, see Exodus 10:21-23). The Spirit of Christ had been withdrawn. Thus, "there could not be any light at all." (V. 21, see D&C 84:45-46, & 88:7-23). The survivors of the storm could see neither "the sun, nor the moon, nor the stars, for so great were the mists of darkness which were upon the face of the land." (V. 22).

Perhaps the record of the experience of the Nephites is as close as any of us will come to understanding just how overwhelming will be the spiritual darkness that will prevail among those who are resurrected to a kingdom without glory, which is as a "lake which burneth with fire and brimstone, which is the second death." (D&C 63:17). For those who experience it, such a spiritual vacuum will be a living hell.

As the abridgment of Nephi's record continued, it is important to remember that this thick darkness prevailed for 3 days before it "dispersed from off the face of the land, and the earth did cease to tremble, and the rocks did cease to rend, and the dreadful groanings did cease, and all the tumultuous noises did pass away." (3 Nephi 9:10). It must have been a very long 72 hours for the survivors.

During this whole time, "there was great mourning and howling and weeping among all the people continually." (V. 23). "They were heard to cry and mourn, saying: O that we had repented before this great and terrible day, and had not killed and stoned the prophets, and cast them out." (V. 25). In light of the Savior's later declaration to these people, that they were spared because they had been more righteous than their brethren, we might conclude that they had not literally done these things. (See 3 Nephi 9:13).

Mormon reported that those who survived the destruction were "they who received the prophets and stoned them not; and it was they who had not shed the blood of the saints." (3 Nephi 10:12). But perhaps they had not been as valiant in the testimony of Jesus as they could have been. Perhaps they had figuratively stoned the prophets, ignored their counsel, and denied their authority. That they were "more righteous than their brethren" might not be saying much, inasmuch as their brethren had been destroyed "because of their sins and their wickedness, which was above all the wickedness of the whole earth, because of their secret murders and combinations; for it was they that did destroy the peace of my people and the government of the land; therefore I did cause them to be burned, to destroy them from before my face, that the blood of the prophets and the saints should not come up unto me any more against them." (3 Nephi 9:9). "And thus were the howlings of the people great and terrible." (V. 25).

Third Nephi
Chapter 9

In the midst of the darkness, "there was a voice heard among all the inhabitants of the earth, upon all the face of this land." (V. 1). Here is another interesting application of the Hebrew word "eretz," that can be translated either as "earth" or as "land," depending upon the context in which it is being used. (See Commentary References to Alma 24:19 & Ether 1:6 & 1:38, and Commentary References to Ether 1:35 & 13:2).

The voice cried: "Wo, wo, wo unto this people." (V 2, see Commentary Reference to 2 Nephi 18:9). In Hebrew, it is impossible to express a statement more strongly than to repeat it three times. These people were surely in a sorry state. The devil had surveyed the destruction in the land, had laughed at the spiritual wasteland that it had become, and with his angels reveled in the suffering and misery of its wretched survivors.

In the ensuing verses, the "voice" made it clear that it was He who was responsible for the great destruction in the land. "Behold, that great city Zarahemla have I burned with fire. And behold, that great city Moroni have I caused to be sunk in the depths of the sea. And behold, that great city Moronihah have I covered with earth." (V. 3-5). There is a very subtle undercurrent to these declarations. The power of the inhabitants of these great cities, that were thought to be invincible, was nothing compared to the might of God. (See v. 6-10).

"And many great destructions have I caused to come upon this land, and upon this people, because of their wickedness and their abominations." (V. 12). The Lord explained that He had done it "to hide their iniquities and their abominations from before my face, that the blood of the prophets and the saints shall not come any more unto me against them." (V. 5, see v. 7, 8, 9 & 11). The wrath of God requires the destruction of the wicked. (See 1 Nephi 22:16). God is long suffering, but when the people are past repentance, the point of no return is reached. Then, mercy can no longer stay the hand that wields the sword of Justice, and it must fall. (See Alma 26:19 & 60:29, Helaman 13:5, & 3 Nephi 2:19).

Nevertheless, to those who were "more righteous than they," the Lord offered His arm of mercy. (V. 13-14). What follows is one of the clearest declarations in all scripture that Jesus Christ is the Creator, Who acted under the direction of the Father to form the earth. "Behold, I am Jesus Christ the Son of God, I created the heavens and the earth, and all things that in them are. I was with the Father from the beginning. I am in the Father, and the Father in me; and in me hath the Father glorified his name." (V. 15). This verse not only addresses the plurality of Gods (See Genesis 1:26, 3:22, Moses 2:26 & 4:28), but it also enlarges our understanding of the unity of the Godhead. (See Mosiah 15:4, Helaman 14:12, Moses 1:33, & D&C 45:1).

Christ has all power to grant unto men that they might become "the sons of God." (V. 17). His promise is to all who "shall believe on (His) name, for behold, by (Him) redemption cometh, and in (Him) is the law of Moses fulfilled." (V. 17, see V. 19 & 20, Mosiah 5:7, & Ether 3:14).

To the Nephites who listened to this voice out of the darkness enveloping the land, the words of Christ must have been powerful indeed, as He declared: "I am the light and the life of the world." (V. 18). Again, He declared that by His sacrifice, the Law of Moses was fulfilled. (V. 19).

Instead of burnt offerings, He commanded: "Ye shall offer for a sacrifice unto me a broken heart and a contrite spirit. And whoso cometh unto me with a broken heart and a contrite spirit, him will I baptize with fire and with the Holy Ghost." (V. 20). Christ came "unto the world to bring redemption unto the world, to save the world from sin." (V. 21). The only way that can be done is through sincere repentance. (V. 22).

In verse 13, the Savior had indicated that the people who had been spared were "more righteous" than their less fortunate contemporaries. They were not perfect by any means, but the Savior recognized that at least they still had the capacity to repent. Therefore, He urged them: "Will ye not return unto me, and repent of your sins, and be converted, that I may heal you?" As this pivotal chapter ended, so too the Voice fell silent, and the people were given many hours to consider the words that had pierced their souls. (3 Nephi 10:1).

Third Nephi
Chapter 10

Perhaps, in order to really let the invitation to come unto Christ sink in, "there was silence in the land for the space of many hours." (V. 1). Because of the powerful effect of the message, the people were speechless; therefore, "they did cease lamenting and howling." (V. 2).

"And it came to pass that there came again a voice unto the people, and all the people did hear, and did witness of it." (V. 3). They recognized it as the Savior's voice they had heard earlier. He again extended the invitation to make the journey to Him, saying: "Repent and return unto me with full purpose of heart." (V. 6). But let them come in faith, nothing wavering, as the Apostle James had instructed. (See James 1:6).

In spite of the reassurance of the message, the people were overwhelmed by "the loss of their kindred and friends" and so they recommenced their lamentation. (V. 8). "Thus, did the three days pass away." (V. 9). Finally, "the darkness dispersed from off the face of the land, and the earth did cease to tremble, and the rocks did cease to rend, and the dreadful groanings did cease, and all the tumultuous noises did pass away. And the earth did cleave together again, that it stood." (V. 9-10). Even after the initial 3 hours of earth in upheaval, there had been 3 days of unsettled commotion, all experienced while the people were enveloped in pitch-blackness.

Then, the nightmare was over, and the people could hardly believe it. But it was true, "and their mourning was turned into joy, and their lamentations into the praise and thanksgiving unto the Lord Jesus Christ, their Redeemer." (V. 10). Unlike their less fortunate brethren who had been "sunk and buried up in the earth, they were not drowned in the depths of the sea; and they were not burned by fire, neither were they fallen upon and crushed to death; and they were not carried away in the whirlwind; neither were they overpowered by the vapor of smoke and of darkness." (V. 13).

A thousand years before Mormon undertook his abridgment, Nephi had written: "For I did liken all scriptures unto us, that it might be for our profit and learning." The past is prologue. (See Commentary Reference to Alma 43:1). Now Mormon wrote, somewhat chiastically: "Whoso readeth, let him understand; he that hath the scriptures, let him search them." (V. 14). In other words, the events surrounding the crucifixion of the Savior could easily be applied to our day. The events attendant to His Second Coming will be equally spectacular.

Nephi's counsel had been to press forward with complete dedication and steadfastness, or confidence and a firm determination in Christ, having a perfect brightness of hope, or perfect faith, and charity, or a love of God and of all men. If we do this, he promised, feasting upon the word of Christ, or receiving strength and nourishment from the scriptures, and endure to the end in righteousness, we shall have eternal life, that is the greatest gift God can bestow upon His children. (2 Nephi 31:20). The problem with men is that "they will not search knowledge, nor understand great knowledge, when it is given unto them in plainness, even as plain as word can be." (2 Nephi 32:7).

The Nephite and Lamanite survivors in the greater Land of Zarahemla had been literally forced to press forward through the night of spiritual darkness and endure the three days that followed. How very different was their experience, when compared to that of the Savior, Whose body rested peacefully in the sepulchre for three days before His resurrection. Perhaps their understanding of the Vision of The Tree of Life in the Nephite scriptures had prepared them for their own agonizing struggle to reach the Tree of Life beyond the swirling mists where so many had lost their way.

When men "are led, that in many instances they do err because they are taught by the precepts of men," then "wo, wo, wo be unto them, saith the Lord God Almighty." (2 Nephi 28:14-15). These voices of warning have been raised not only by Nephi and Mormon, but also by many others, including Jacob, Zenos, and Zenock. (V. 15-16, see 1 Nephi 19:11-12). Verses 16 and 17 suggest that The Plates of Brass were a family history and that Zenos and Zenock prophesied of the Nephites, "who (were) a remnant of their seed."

Mormon's editorial comment at the end of this chapter has created some confusion in the minds of some, because it suggests that it was "in the ending of the thirty and fourth year ... soon after the ascension of Christ into heaven (that) he did truly manifest himself unto them" and that He began His ministry among them. (V. 18, see Mosiah 18:2, Alma 40:20, & 3 Nephi 11:12). If this is the case, then nearly a year elapsed between the 3 days of darkness and destruction and Christ's visit to the Nephites. In fact, the chronology relating to the Savior's visit to the Americas remains undecided. As Alma counseled his son Helaman: "Now these mysteries are not yet fully made known unto me; therefore, I shall forbear." (Alma 37:13).

3 Nephi 17:3 suggests that some time must have passed after the time of the destruction before Christ's ministry, because the people once again had homes to which they could retreat. Either their homes had miraculously been spared, or more likely, there had been time to rebuild them. That verse reads: "Therefore, go ye unto your homes, and ponder upon the things which I have said." (3 Nephi 19:1).

Also, 3 Nephi 11:1 states that after the destruction, the people were gathered "round about the temple which was in the land Bountiful; and they were marveling and wondering one with another, and were showing one to another the great and marvelous change which had taken place." This is not the description of a people who had been very recently traumatized by the worst natural disaster in the history of the world. Nor is it reasonable to assume that the temple itself had been left undamaged. Evidently, the people had time to repair and rebuild it, as well, before Christ's appearance.

On the other hand, Joseph Fielding Smith, Jr. believed that Christ's visit came immediately after the darkness and destruction had ceased. (See "Answers to Gospel Questions," 4:25-29). It really doesn't matter when Christ appeared to the more righteous Nephites and Lamanites in Zarahemla. Evidently the exact chronology of the visit was unimportant to Mormon, who did not clarify in his abridgment just when it occurred. He was much more interested in the messages Christ brought to those people, and by association, to us. He knew these principles would be important for us to learn in the Last Days.

To us he wrote: "Behold, I speak unto you as if ye were present, and yet ye are not. But behold, Jesus Christ hath shown you unto me, and I know your doing." (Mormon 8:35). "Behold, the sword of vengeance hangeth over you (also); and the time soon cometh that he avengeth the blood of the saints upon you, for he will not suffer their cries any longer." (Mormon 8:41).

Third Nephi
Chapter 11

The people were gathered in Bountiful, that was north of Zarahemla, just below the narrow neck of land and that region further north which the Nephites called Desolation. (See Helaman 22:27-31). There a temple stood, where the people gathered, "marveling and wondering one with another" regarding "the great and marvelous change which had taken place" in the land. (V. 1). As we read the story of His appearance to these people, we should remember that the Coming of Christ to the Nephites and Lamanites is a pattern of His Second Coming in the Last Days.

The people "heard a voice as if it came out of heaven." It was a "small voice (which) did pierce them that did hear to the center, insomuch that there was no part of their frame that it did not cause to quake; yea, it did pierce them to the very soul, and did cause their hearts to burn." (V. 3, see Luke 24:32). In a letter written to William W. Phelps, the Prophet Joseph Smith revealed: "The still small voice ... whispereth through and pierceth all things, and often times it maketh my bones to quake while it maketh manifest." (D&C 85:6). It was this voice of the Spirit that pierced the people in Bountiful to the very marrow of their bones.

The third time that it called to them, "they did hear the voice, and did open their ears to hear it; and their eyes were towards the sound thereof; and they did look steadfastly towards heaven, from whence the sounds came. And behold, the third time they did understand the voice which they heard." (V. 5-6, see Commentary Reference to Helaman 5:33). The Spirit speaks directly to the soul. As Joseph Smith wrote after his own baptism: "Our minds, being now enlightened, we began to have the scriptures open to our understandings, and the true meaning and intention of their more mysterious passages revealed unto us in a manner which we never could attain to previously, nor ever before had thought of." (J.S.H. 1:74).

The voice declared unto the people: "Behold my Beloved Son, in whom I am well pleased, in whom I have glorified my name - hear ye him." (V. 7, see J.S.H. 1:17, Matthew 3:17 & 17:5, & J.S.T. John 1:19). "There are many places in the scriptures where it appears to be the Father speaking, inasmuch as references are made to 'mine Only Begotten Son.' It should be understood (though) that it is the Savior giving the (actual) revelations and that at (these) times He speaks by divine investiture of authority. He speaks for the Father, in the name of the Father, and as if He were the Father." (Robert L. Millet, "Studies in Scripture," 2:332).

J.S.T. John 1:19 reads: "No man hath seen the Father at any time, except He hath borne record of the Son." Joseph Fielding Smith, Jr. taught: "All revelation since the Fall has come thru Jesus Christ. The Father has never dealt with man directly and personally since the Fall, and He has never appeared except to introduce and bear record of the Son." ("Doctrines of Salvation", 1:27).

With His introduction understood, the Savior descended "out of heaven; and he was clothed in a white robe; and he came down and stood in the midst of them." (V. 8). His appearance was marvelous and unique and was almost beyond the comprehension of the people, who "wist not what it meant, for they thought it was an angel that had appeared unto them." (V. 8).

But He unequivocally declared to the multitude: "I am Jesus Christ, whom the prophets testified shall come into the world." (V. 10). He had figuratively experienced his own ordeal by water, having "drunk out of that bitter cup" that the Father had given Him. (V. 11, see 1 Nephi 17:26, 18:8-23, & Ether 6:1-12). The Father had sent him, to suffer "the will of the Father in all things from the beginning." (V. 11, see Ether 4:12).

The people were so overwhelmed by the appearance of the Son, and by His declaration that "it had been prophesied among them that (He) should show himself unto them after his ascension into heaven," that they fell to the earth. (V. 12, see Commentary Reference to 3 Nephi 10:18). But the Savior invited them to stand and feel the tokens in His hands and his feet, that they might know that He was "the God of Israel, and the God of the whole earth, and (had) been slain for the sins of the world." (V. 14, see Zechariah 13:6, & D&C 45:51-52). The Savior boldly confirmed that He, and not Satan, is the God of the earth, although the deceiver would have us believe otherwise. (See Moses 1:12).

It must have taken some time, but the multitude did come forth, "and did feel the prints of the nails in his hands and in his feet; and this they did do, going forth one by one until they had all gone forth, and did see with their eyes and did feel with their hands, and did know of a surety and did bear record, that it was he, of whom it was written by the prophets, that should come." (V. 15). Mormon went to great length to verify that these people "had witnessed for themselves" that it was the Redeemer of Israel Who stood before them. (V. 16).

As soon as His identity had been established, the people "did cry out with one accord, saying; Hosanna! Blessed be the name of the Most High God! And they did fall down at the feet of Jesus, and did worship him." (V. 16-17). In Hebrew, "Hosanna" means "Oh Grant Salvation" which is what Jesus immediately did for these people, teaching them the basic principles and ordinances of the Gospel.

Previously, the people had been baptized under the Law of Moses. Now, the Lord gave to Nephi and others the authority of the Aaronic Priesthood, and "the power to baptize." (See Commentary Reference to 3 Nephi 19:10). "And he said unto them: On this wise shall ye baptize; and there shall be no disputations among you." (V. 22, see 3 Nephi 18:36-37). Then, He carefully taught these newly ordained priests the proper method of the administration of the ordinance. (V. 23-28).

He instructed them that only the repentant who have the desire should be baptized, and He made clear by inference that they must first have reached an age of accountability and have the capacity to choose for themselves. (V. 23). In other scriptures, the age of accountability is established at 8 years. (See D&C 18:42, 20:71, 68:25 & 27, & Commentary Reference to Moroni 8:5-26).

He also taught that immersion in water was symbolic of the burial of Christ. (V. 23, see v. 26). The repentant, Joseph Smith said, "were baptized after the manner of his burial, being buried in the water in his name, and this according to the commandment which he has given - That by keeping the commandments they might be washed and cleansed from all their sins." (D&C 76:51-52). "Consequently, the baptismal font was instituted as a similitude of the grave." (D&C 128:13). As Paul wrote: "Therefore, we are buried with him by baptism into death: that like as Christ was raised up from the dead by the glory of the Father, even so we also should walk in newness of life. For if we have been planted together in the likeness of his death, we shall be also in the likeness of his resurrection." (Romans 6:4).

Paul taught that there is "one Lord, one faith, (and) one baptism." (Ephesians 4:5). There was no disputation regarding the doctrine of Christ as long as the Apostles walked the earth. When they were martyred, though, and their priesthood authority died with them, confusion arose concerning the simplest policies and procedures of the Church and doctrines of the Kingdom, and there was no enlightened solution to the problem. The resulting apostasy required the direct latter-day intervention of Heavenly Father and His Son Jesus Christ. (See J.S.H. 1:16-20).

Paul had prophesied of the coming apostasy from the faith. He wrote to the Thessalonian Saints: "Be not soon shaken in mind, or be troubled, neither by spirit, nor by word, nor by letter as from us, as that the day of Christ is at hand. Let no man deceive you by any means: for that day shall not come, except there come a falling away first." (2 Thessalonians 2:2-3).

In the third century A.D., the Church Historian Eusebius provided a glimpse of the falling away spoken of by Paul: "But with our greater freedom a change came over us. We yielded to pride and sloth. We yielded to mutual envy and abuse. We warred upon ourselves as occasion offered, and we used the weapons and the spears of words. Leaders fought with leaders, and laity formed factions against laity. Unspeakable hypocrisy and dissimulation traveled to the farthest limits of evil." ("The Essential Eusebius," P. 177).

Later, in the Age of Chivalry, Charlemagne urged his churchmen to engage in faithful Gospel scholarship. "In a letter to abbots and bishops he complained of illiterate monks: 'What pious devotion had faithfully prompted in their hearts, their uneducated tongues could not put into words without stumbling.' Hardly a Bible existed that was not riddled with the gross errors of untutored copyists." (Thomas Bulfinch, "The Age of Chivalry," p. 61, see 1 Nephi 13:26).

A leader of the Reformation in America, Roger Williams complained: "There is no regularly constituted church on earth, nor any person authorized to administer any church ordinance; nor can there be until new apostles are sent by the Great Head of the Church, for Whose Coming I am seeking." ("Picturesque America," p. 502).

Finally, Thomas Jefferson declared: "The religion builders have so distorted and deformed the doctrines of Jesus, so muffled them in mysticisms, fancies and falsehoods, have caricatured them into forms so inconceivable, as to shock reasonable thinkers. Happy in the prospect of a restoration of primitive Christianity, I must leave to younger persons to encounter and lop off the false branches which have been engrafted into it by the mythologists of the middle and modern ages." ("Jefferson's Complete Works," 7:210 & 257).

In order to establish the performance of the ordinance of baptism with absolute finality, Christ gave the Nephites upon whom He had conferred priesthood authority the specific words that they should employ in the baptismal prayer. "And now behold, these are the words which ye shall say, calling them by name, saying: Having authority given me of Jesus Christ, I baptize you in the name of the Father, and of the Son and of the Holy Ghost. Amen." (V. 24-25).

The baptismal prayer given by the Lord in the Doctrine & Covenants reads: "Having been commissioned of Jesus Christ, I baptize you in the name of the Father, and of the Son, and of the Holy Ghost. Amen." (D&C 20:73). The textual variation might have to do with translation differences, or to the fact that these disciples received their authority directly from Jesus Christ, whereas those in the Last Days have received theirs as a commission from John The Baptist, who came to earth on assignment to restore that authority. (See D&C 13).

The essence of both prayers authorizes the officiator to invoke the Holy Names of all three members of the Godhead. The words of this sacred ordinance convey power, and suggest the sanction and approval of God Himself. "Thus saith the Lord" is an equally authoritative declaration. As the Savior taught Nephi: "And thus will the Father bear record of me, and the Holy Ghost will bear record unto him of the Father and me; for the Father, and I, and the Holy Ghost are one." (V. 36, see V. 32).

The members of the Godhead are one in purpose, and are completely unified. (V. 27). They are "One Eternal God." (Alma 11:44, see Mosiah 15:4). There is a physical and spiritual rapport between the Father and the Son, and between them and true believers. Through this rapport, that is for us effected by the Holy Ghost, we become "one" in the spiritual sense. The unity of the Godhead expressed in the scriptures is a type of completeness. The mind of any one member is the mind of the others. Seeing, as each of Them does with the eye of perfection, they see and understand alike, guided by the same principles of unerring justice and equity. (See James E. Talmage, "Articles of Faith," p. 41).

This principle, so beautifully illustrated in many different teaching moments throughout the scriptures, stands in bold contrast to the incomprehensible doctrine of the Trinity that was formulated by a church council hundreds of years after the inspired Apostolic Ministry came to a close. Of that doctrine, Thomas Jefferson wrote: "Three are one and one is three, and yet the one is not three, and the three are not one. This constitutes the craft, the power and profit of the priests. Sweep away their gossamer fabric of factious religion, and they would catch no more flies." (Milton Backman, "American Religions and The Rise of Mormonism," p. 202).

As a distinct member of the Godhead, the Holy Ghost has the commission to be a witness of the truth to the souls of men, to quell disputations among the people concerning the points of the doctrine of Christ. (V. 28). "For verily, verily," said the Savior, "he that hath the spirit of contention is not of me, but is of the devil, who is the father of contention, and he stirreth up the hearts of men to contend with anger, one with another." It was on these very points of doctrine that the clergy and their congregations argued, in Palmyra, New York in the early 1800s. "A scene of great confusion and bad feeling ensued - priest contending against priest, and convert against convert; so that all their good feelings one for another, if they ever had any, were entirely lost in a strife of words and a contest about opinions." (J.S.H. 1:6, see Commentary Reference to Mormon 8:26-32).

The true doctrine of Christ is simply that all men and women, everywhere, must repent and believe in Him. Then they must be baptized in strict accordance with the ordinance authorized by the Savior Himself, and performed by the servants ordained to that ministry under His hands, or by those whose priesthood line of authority traces back to Him. "And whoso believeth in me, and is baptized, the same shall be saved; and they are they who shall inherit the kingdom of God." (V. 33).

Those who do not believe in the power of God unto salvation and decline baptism will not be able to continue their eternal progression and will therefore be damned. (V. 34). Participation in this ordinance is not some arbitrary requirement established by man, with corollaries, footnotes, variances, and exceptions to the rule. It is central to the Plan of Salvation, and is the hinge upon which swings the gate leading to eternal life with Heavenly Father. It is central to His ordained Plan and is all the more beautiful because of its simplicity and symmetry. It is clearly codified and clarified in the Bible's companion cannon. It is given in The Book of Mormon so that there will not be disputations among the people concerning this vital point of doctrine. (See V. 28).

As King Benjamin said: "Under this head ye are made free, and there is no other head whereby ye can be made free. There is no other name given whereby salvation cometh; therefore, I would that ye should take upon you the name of Christ, all you that have entered into the covenant with God that ye should be obedient unto the end of your lives. And it shall come to pass that whosoever doeth this shall be found at the right hand of God, for he shall know the name by which he is called; for he shall be called by the name of Christ. And now it shall come to pass, that whosoever shall not take upon him the name of Christ must be called by some other name; therefore, he findeth himself on the left hand of God." (Mosiah 5:8-10). The discourse by King Benjamin clearly and simply stated the position taken by God and reiterated by His prophets. For "surely the Lord God will do nothing, but he revealeth his secret unto his servants the prophets." (Amos 2:7).

In the Third Century, Eusebius wrote of "the unspeakable hypocrisy of men who crept into the Church and who took on the name and character of Christians." ("The Essential Eusebius," p. 208). The world uses the term "Christian" in an almost profane way, because it does not understand the significance of covenants made with the Lord. "Covenants are binding contracts, and since God is a party to every Gospel covenant, they must come by revelation, and no person enters into a Gospel covenant except on the basis of direct revelation from God. It follows that the only ones who have entered into covenants are members of the Church." (Bruce R. McConkie, "Mormon Doctrine," p. 166, see Commentary Reference to 3 Nephi 27:5).

Because God is a party to every Gospel covenant, those who make sacred promises with Him will be visited "with fire and with the Holy Ghost." (V. 36). Fire and smoke have always been symbolic of the presence of the Lord and the glory of God. They are frequently used to depict celestial realms. In the language of Joseph Smith: "God Almighty Himself dwells in eternal fire. Our God is a consuming fire." ("Teachings," p. 367, see Deuteronomy 4:24, & Hebrews 12:24). The Spirit of God is like a burning fire.

One of the responsibilities of the Holy Ghost is to bear the most Holy Witness of the validity of every Gospel ordinance. Because there can be no greater or more unimpeachable witness, with the "baptism" of fire and the Holy Ghost comes the remission of sins, that are symbolically purged or burned out of the sinews of the penitent. (See 2 Nephi 31:17).

The Savior taught the principle and repeated it almost verbatim, so important was it. Together with little children, Jesus is cited as the only perfect example. In these verses, He said (twice, for emphasis?): "Ye must repent, and become as a little child, and be baptized in my name, or ye can in nowise receive these things. And again, I say unto you, ye must repent, and be baptized in my name, and become as a little child, or ye can in nowise inherit the kingdom of God." (V. 37 - 38). This is the doctrine of Christ, simply stated in unambiguous language. When his people build upon this doctrine, "the gates of hell," that are the doors to the spirit prison of the unjust, "shall not prevail against them." (V. 39, see 2 Nephi 9:13, D&C 76:73, 138:8 & 28, Isaiah 61:1, 1 Peter 3:19, & Moses 7:57). Hell is where the unrepentant go to await the day when they shall come forth in the Second Resurrection of the Damned. (See D&C 21:6).

His message was so important that the Savior instructed Nephi and his brethren: "Go forth unto the people, and declare the words which I have spoken, unto the ends of the earth." (V. 41).

"I am Jesus Christ, whom
the prophets testified shall come
into the world And behold, I am the
light and the life of the world."
(3 Nephi 11:10-11).

Third Nephi
Chapter 12

This chapter is similar to the Savior's Sermon on the Mount. (Matthew 5). The differences in the text that are found in The Book of Mormon correspond to those found in the J.S.T. version of Matthew. In this Sermon, the Lord gave a revelation of His own character, or "an autobiography, every syllable of which He had written down in deeds." ("Gospel Doctrine Lesson Manual," 38). So doing, He gave us a blueprint to follow in the conduct of our own lives.

Verses 1 and 2 are introductory, and are found only in The Book of Mormon and in J.S.T. Matthew 5:3-4. They clarify for whom the Sermon was intended. It was not for the whole world, or for the chosen disciples only, but was for all those who were willing to accept Christ and keep His commandments.

The twelve whom Christ had chosen from among the people were given the power and authority to baptize. (V. 1, see 3 Nephi 11:23-28). Later, the Savior gave them the authority to administer the spiritual affairs of the Church as well. (See 3 Nephi 18:36-37). Nephi and others held the Melchizedek Priesthood. Now, they received authority from Christ to use that priesthood to administer the government of the Church He had established in the land.

These twelve were specifically called to be the servants of the people. (V. 1). The only authority they were given was the power to bless the lives of their brethren. "God does notice us, and He watches over us. But it is usually through another person that He meets our needs. Therefore, it is vital that we serve each other. The abundant life is achieved as we magnify our view of life and expand our view of others and our own possibilities. Thus, the more we follow the teachings of the Master, the more enlarged our perspective becomes. We see many more possibilities for service that we would have seen without this magnification. There is great security in spirituality, and we cannot have spirituality without service." (Spencer W. Kimball, "Ensign", 10/1985).

Some who read The Book of Mormon object to the distinct biblical language found throughout its pages. "Resemblances between the Bible and The Book of Mormon," though, "are not hard to explain. Far from being evidence of fraud, they are rather confirmation of authenticity. If The Book of Mormon is what it says it is, we should expect to find a strong biblical influence in it. Its prophets sound like those of the Old Testament because they studied and consciously quoted the words of those prophets, and all prophets moreover are programmed to sound alike, being called for the same purpose under much the same conditions." (Hugh Nibley, "Churches in The Wilderness").

"The Book of Mormon makes fittingly few alterations in Bible language. However much consolation such close parallels may give to those cynical of the book's origins, it must be conceded that at least The Book of Mormon knows a good thing when it sees it. Consistence with the peerless King James Version, whatever its implications for originality, is highly stylistic tribute." (Steven C. Walker, "More Than Meets the Eye: Concentration of The Book of Mormon").

Before we study 3 Nephi Chapter 12, we should know something of the background of those who translated the King James Version of the Bible, and of Joseph Smith, who translated The Book of Mormon. "When the King James translators began their work, they did so with fasting and prayer. For the most part, they were pious men who sought the inspiration of the Lord in their work. We believe they received it. The preservation of the Bible through the ages is itself a miracle. It was accomplished only through the hand of God. Then why not its translation? The King James translators did everything they knew how to obtain divine inspiration for their task. Knowing the great value of that book for the Gentiles, as Nephi himself said, would God withhold the necessary inspiration? Those humble translators were instruments in the hands of the Almighty to further His purposes among the Gentiles." (Mark E. Petersen, "Those Gold Plates," p. 52 & 56).

In just over six weeks' time, Joseph Smith translated the plates on which was recorded the thousand-year history of the Nephites. During that process, "through strenuous effort in exercising faith and with the operation of the inspiration of God upon his mind, Joseph obtained the thought represented by the Nephite characters, understood it in the Nephite language, and then expressed it in the language such as he was master of, which language was reflected and held in vision in the Urim and Thummim until written by the scribe. The language used was brightened, illuminated, and dignified by the spiritual light that radiated throughout his mind. In any event, one must concede that the stock of words used in The Book of Mormon is far beyond the vocabulary of an unlettered youth." (Ivan Barrett, "Joseph Smith and The Restoration," p. 83).

Whether or not the Savior delivered the words that we know as the Sermon on the Mount in the exact language as recorded in 3 Nephi is irrelevant. What is important is that those living in the Last Days are given a scripture in their own, familiar biblical language.

The Savior told the Nephites he had taught "the Beatitudes" to his disciples in Galilee, in the Old World. (See 3 Nephi 15:1). Perhaps this acknowledgement sheds light on the similarity of language in the biblical and Book of Mormon accounts. The emphasis of the Beatitudes is changed, however, by subtle word additions and substitutions in the Book of Mormon text. For example, each Beatitude begins with the coordinating conjunction "and" that helps to relate it back to the introductory statements in verses 1 and 2.

In verse 3, we read: "Yea, blessed are the poor in spirit *who come unto me*, for theirs is the kingdom of heaven." That portion in italics is not found in the K.J.T., possibly because the clause relates the passage back to the introductory verse 1. When people are "poor in spirit" they are humble and teachable, and are more likely to accept Christ when the invitation comes.

"And again, blessed are all they that mourn, for they shall be comforted." (V. 4). We who have been baptized and have received the Holy Ghost are truly blessed. (See Mosiah 18:9). This is because our heaviest burdens are those that have to do with our unresolved sin. Obedience to the Gospel principles of repentance and forgiveness helps us to live abundantly. When we have been liberated from the burden of our sins, we look forward with great enthusiasm to life's experiences, and have no cause to mourn.

In another way, when we have trials, if we are rooted deeply in Gospel soil, the Lord may bless us with "good grief." Although emotions can overflow at times, maintaining an eternal perspective can ennoble even the most difficult moments, for example, at the passing of a loved one. The Savior taught: "Thou shalt live together in love, insomuch that thou shalt weep for the loss of them that die, and more especially for those that have not hope of a glorious resurrection. And it shall come to pass that those that die in me shall not taste of death, for it shall be sweet unto them." (D&C 42:45-46). "They shall never die the second death, and feel the torment of the wicked when they come face to face with eternity." (Joseph Fielding Smith, Jr., Church History and Modern Revelation, 1:186). Death is only bitter when we are unprepared to meet God. (See Alma 48:23). "Death," as a matter of fact, "hath passed upon all men to fulfil the merciful plan of the Great Creator." (2 Nephi 9:6).

Spencer W. Kimball declared: "I am confident that there is a time to die. I am not a fatalist. I believe that many people 'die before their time' because they are careless, abuse their bodies, take unnecessary chances, or expose themselves to hazards, accidents, and sickness. God controls our lives, guides and blesses us, but gives us our agency. We may live our lives in accordance with His Plan, or we may foolishly shorten or terminate them. I am positive in my mind that the Lord has planned our destiny. We can shorten our lives, but I think we cannot lengthen them very much." ("Tragedy or Destiny," p. 9 & 11).

"And blessed are the meek, for they shall inherit the earth." (V. 5). The meek are not weak, but their strength lies in neither taking nor giving offense. When faced with the challenge of adversity, they become "Pro-Gospel" rather than "Anti-Enemy." They delight in the grace of God and understand the Lord's intention when He said: "If men come unto me I will show unto them their weakness. I give unto men weakness that they may be humble; and my grace is sufficient for all men that humble themselves before me; for if they humble themselves before me, and have faith in me, then will I make weak things become strong unto them." (Ether 12:27). Those who develop the quality of meekness qualify to inherit the celestialized earth.

"And blessed are all they who do hunger and thirst after righteousness, for they shall be filled with the Holy Ghost." (V. 6, see 3 Nephi 18:4 & 9). Nephi taught that "if ye shall press forward" with complete dedication, "feasting upon the word of Christ" or receiving physical and spiritual strength and nourishment, "and endure to the end" with continuing responsibility and accountability, "behold, thus saith the Father: Ye shall have eternal life," which is the greatest of God's gifts. (2 Nephi 31:20).

The Lord said we should "seek not for riches, but for wisdom; and, behold, the mysteries of God shall be unfolded unto you, and then shall you be made rich. Behold, he that hath eternal life is rich." (D&C 11:7, see Commentary Reference to 4 Nephi 1:23). The mysteries of God are those truths that can only be known by revelation from the Holy Ghost. When we "hunger and thirst after righteousness," the doctrine of the priesthood will distill upon our souls as the dews from heaven, and the Holy Ghost will be our constant companion. (See D&C 121:45-46).

"And blessed are the merciful, for they shall obtain mercy." (V. 7). "For with what judgment ye judge, ye shall be judged: and with what measure ye mete, it shall be measured to you again." (Matthew 7:2). What goes around comes around, and if you cast your bread upon the waters, after many days it shall return to you.

"And blessed are all the pure in heart, for they shall see God." Our capacity for worship is proportional to our comprehension of God. This is why He sends His prophets to declare His word. "I give unto you these sayings that you may understand and know how to worship, and know what you worship, that you may come unto the Father in my name, and in due time receive of his fulness." (D&C 93:19). As Nephi prophesied of the remnant of his seed, so it might be said of us, "that they shall come to the knowledge of their Redeemer and the very points of his doctrine, that they may know how to come unto him and be saved." (1 Nephi 15:14).

Jesus also said: "I was in the world and received of my Father, and the works of him were plainly manifest." (D&C 93:5). In other words, Jesus came into the world to perform the works of His Father, that we might know our Father.

(See John 5:19). In this sense, He became the revelation of God to the world; therefore, He was known as "the Word, even the messenger of salvation." (D&C 93:8).

"And blessed are all the peacemakers, for they shall be called the children of God." (V. 9). The spiritually begotten sons and daughters of Christ are the fashioners of peace who actively seek peace, and their behavior models the Master, who was the Prince of Peace. Theirs is not the peace of this world, although that sometimes comes as a fringe benefit of living a Christ-centered life. Theirs is the peace that surpasses understanding, that comes from obedience to Gospel principles.

"And blessed are all they who are persecuted for my name's sake, for theirs is the kingdom of heaven." (V. 10). True believers pray for those who find fault with the Church, for their behavior will ultimately be their own undoing. How sad it will be, when they finally admit: "It ain't my ignorance that done me in, but what I knowed that warn't so!"

Someone once observed, tongue in cheek, that they regretted their inability to preach the Gospel with such power that it would result in mob violence. The point is that, in the Last Days, discipleship will be lived in crescendo, and the polarity resulting when the Gospel standard is measured against the shifting sands of sectarianism will only highlight the behavior of those who are true to their covenants. By standing out, the Saints will sometimes come under fire from those who feel uncomfortable because of their example.

"And blessed are ye when men shall revile you and persecute (you), and shall say all manner of evil against you falsely, for my sake; for ye shall have great joy and be exceedingly glad, for great shall be your reward in heaven; for so persecuted they the prophets who were before you." (V. 12, see D&C 122:7-9). If anything, when men and women endure persecution, they are in the good company of holy men of God. As the Psalmist declared: "I had rather be a doorkeeper in the house of my God, than to dwell in the tents of wickedness." (Psalms 84:10).

The Savior next told his assembled disciples that they were "to be the salt of the earth." (V. 13). In the Book of Mormon account, this is stated as a goal toward which worthy members of the Church should be constantly striving. He revealed: "When men are called unto mine everlasting gospel, and covenant with an everlasting covenant, they are accounted as the salt of the earth and the savor of men. (D&C 101:39-40).

Jesus established the same goal in the next verse. He said: "I give unto you to be the light of this people." (V. 14). "Therefore, let your light so shine before this people, that they may see your good works and glorify your Father who is in heaven." (V. 16). The Book of Mormon account clarifies to whom these disciples are to be a light. Also, the subtle use of the pronoun "who," personalizes the relationship we have with our Heavenly Father.

Then the Savior taught that He had not "come to destroy the law or the prophets" but rather to fulfil the Law of Moses. He clarified the teaching from Matthew, that in Him the Law "had all been fulfilled." (V. 17-18, see 3 Nephi 15:2-10).

The next verse relates back to 3 Nephi 9:20, that identified the sacrifice required of those who would take up their cross and follow the Savior. "To enter into the kingdom of heaven," Jesus said that we must come to Him "with a broken heart and a contrite spirit." (V. 19-20). The next few verses clarify the teaching of the Savior that it is impossible to come unto Him with unresolved feelings. (V. 21-24). This is why it is wrong to partake of the Sacrament without having first been reconciled to our brethren. We drink damnation to our souls if we participate in the ordinance of the Sacrament hypocritically, because when we do so our outward gesture of contrition is in vain, and our fraudulent profession of faith actually severs our connection to the covenant.

Then, in verses 27-30, the symbolical admonitions of Matthew 5:29-30 are eliminated. Instead, the Book of Mormon verses focus on the true and intended meaning of how to avoid lust. When we take up our cross, we deny ourselves all ungodliness. (V. 30, see Jacob 1:8, & Alma 39:9). The vivid imagery of Christ laboring along the Via Dolorosa toward Calvary should sear our individual and collective consciousness. Because we are also asked to bear heavy burdens, the Savior wanted us to know that we will not walk alone.

There follows a frequently misunderstood passage that reads: "It hath been written, that whosoever shall put away his wife, let him give her a writing of divorcement. Verily, verily, I say unto you, that whosoever shall put away his wife, saving for the cause of fornication, causeth her to commit adultery; and whoso shall marry her who is divorced committeth adultery." (V. 31-32).

Heavenly Father instituted marriage as an ordinance of exaltation, legally binding a man and a woman together in time and eternity. It was only later under the Lesser Law that divorce was permitted, and that because of the hardness of the hearts of the people. In other words, because Israel could not live the fulness of the Gospel, or could not observe Celestial Laws, she was given a lesser law to which she could be obedient.

Divorce was unheard of in the days of the Patriarchs, but by the time of the Savior's ministry it was common among the Jews. He was familiar enough with the practice to incorporate into His teaching a call to greater righteousness, and a return to the principles of perfection typified by the eternal marriage covenant that is taught in the temple.

The New and Everlasting Covenant is completely antithetical to Divorce, which is so foreign to celestial standards that the Lord has said of marriage: "Therefore, prepare thy heart to receive and obey the instructions which I am about to give unto you; for all those who have this law revealed unto them must obey the same. For behold, I reveal unto you a new and everlasting covenant; and if ye abide not that covenant, then are ye damned; for no one can reject this covenant and be permitted to enter into my glory." (D&C 132:3-4).

Bruce R. McConkie wrote: "As far as the record reveals, (Christ) merely specifies the high law that his people should live, but that is beyond our capability even today. If husbands and wives lived the law as the Lord would have them live it, they would neither do nor say the things that would even permit the fleeting thought of divorce to enter the mind of their eternal companions. Though we today have the Gospel, we have yet to grow into that high state of marital association where marrying a divorced person constitutes adultery. The Lord has not yet given us the high standard he here named as that which ultimately will replace the Mosaic practice of writing a bill of divorcement." ("The Mortal Messiah," 2:139).

The next commandment the Savior gave the people was an injunction against swearing, "neither by heaven, for it is God's throne, nor by the earth, for it is his footstool." (V. 34-35). He was referring to the inappropriate expression of oaths by those without self-control or power over others. Such weaklings resort to making oaths in vain, merely as expressions of their frustration at their inability to determine their own destiny, influence others, or shape the world around them. Christ calls us to a higher plane of existence, where our word is our bond, and where our honesty and integrity are woven into the very sinews of our being.

He continued to systematically supplant the Mosaic Law with admonitions to seek perfection. (V. 38-45). Whereas the people had been taught to seek retribution from those who had harmed them, for example, "and eye for an eye, and a tooth for a tooth," He urged them: "Ye shall not resist evil, but whosoever shall smite thee on thy right cheek, turn to him the other also." (V. 39). "And if any man will sue thee at the law and take away thy coat, let him have thy cloak also. And whosoever shall compel thee to go a mile, go with him twain." (V. 40-41). This is not a doctrine of passive resistance, but of active cooperation. "Love your enemies," He counseled, and "bless them that curse you, do good to them that hate you, and pray for them who despitefully use you and persecute you." (V. 44).

"He scribed a circle that drew me out. Heretic, rebel, a thing to flout! But love and I had the wit to win. We scribed a circle that drew him in." (Edwin Markham). This attitude describes the love that God feels for all of us. He is no respecter of persons. He does not draw up sides, or pick and choose which of us He will favor and which He will neglect or ignore. His impartiality is eminently fair. We are all "the children of (our) Father who is in heaven; for he maketh his sun to rise on the evil and on the good." (V. 45). "And he inviteth them all to come unto him and partake of his goodness; and he denieth none that come unto him, black and white, bond and free, male and female; and he remembereth the heathen; and all are alike unto God, both Jew and Gentile." (2 Nephi 26:33).

In the Nephite version of The Sermon on The Mount, the Savior carried His people along on a wave of self-discovery, gently lifting them to higher levels of self-actualization, that they might be prepared to receive His concluding injunction: "Therefore I would that ye should be perfect even as I, or your Father who is in heaven is perfect." (V. 48). This statement is a significant departure from the wording in Matthew 5:48, which reads: Be ye therefore perfect, even as your Father which is in heaven is perfect." The Nephite version makes sense, though, inasmuch as Christ appeared to them as "the way, the truth, and the life", a resurrected, perfected God of Glory, with the implication that no man or woman could hope to come "unto the Father, but by (Him). (John 14:6). In his ministry among the Nephites, He gloried in the possibility that they, and we, might experience a spiritual re-birth and become like Him and His Father.

Third Nephi
Chapter 13

The Savior repeatedly stressed that it is more blessed to observe the spirit of the law. He was all too familiar with the Pharisees of His own day, who were obsessed with blind obedience to outward ordinances and observances. But they were as a whited sepulchre, full of dead men's bones. (See Matthew 23:27). In other words, they were hypocrites, for they pretended to be pious, when they were only going through the motions.

In the opening verses of this chapter, the Savior urged His true disciples to engage in acts of "Quiet Christianity," not for the praise of men, but for the glory of God. (See v. 1-5). "How carefully most men creep into nameless graves," observed Phillips Brooks, "while now and again one or two forget themselves into immortality."

Next, the Savior taught His disciples how to pray. In 3 Nephi 19:22, He said of the Nephites: "They pray unto me because I am with them." In effect, they were acknowledging in their prayers that Jesus is the God of this earth, for He had earlier declared this truth to them. (See 3 Nephi 11:14). We read also that they were purified because of their faith in Christ. (See 3 Nephi 19:29). Because of their sanctification, Jesus prayed to the Father with this wish: "That I may be in them as thou, Father, art in me, that we may be one." (2 Nephi 19:29).

When the penitent forsake the world and go down into the waters of baptism, there is a harmony that describes them, for they "are no more strangers and foreigners, but (are) fellowcitizens with the saints, and of the household of God." (Ephesians 2:19). Perhaps, at least for the Nephites and Lamanites, the unity of the Father, Son, and Holy Ghost made it relatively unimportant to whom they prayed while the Savior ministered among them. In any event, Christ's personal ministry provided the perfect opportunity to teach them how to pray. This He did, which is documented in 3 Nephi Chapters 13, 18, 19, & 20.

He first instructed His disciples: "Enter into thy closet, and when thou hast shut thy door, pray to thy Father who is in secret; and thy Father, who seeth in secret, shall reward thee openly." (V. 6). We should not "pray as the Zoramites do," Alma had cautioned, "for ye have seen that they pray to be heard of men, and to be praised for their wisdom." (Alma 38:13).

One who was present when Joseph Smith prayed, said of the experience: "There was no ostentation, no raising of the voice as by enthusiasm, but a plain conversational tone, as a man would address a present friend. It appeared to me as though, in case the veil were taken away, I could see the Lord standing facing His humblest of all servants." (Hyrum & Helen Mae Andrus, "They Knew the Prophet," p. 52).

The Lord asked that we "use not vain repetitions." (V. 7). Alma taught that when "your prayer is vain, (it) availeth you nothing, and ye are as hypocrites who do deny the faith." (Alma 34:28, see Mosiah 4:16-27). Thoughtless repetition in prayer suggests a dulling of the senses, slothfulness, and faithlessness. This is why such prayers are generally ineffectual.

If we are full of faith, however, we will ask only for those blessings that we ought to have, for Heavenly Father "knoweth what things ye have need of, before ye ask him." (V. 8, see Matthew 6:8). Moreover, we have been instructed: "If ye are purified and cleansed from all sin, ye shall ask whatsoever you will in the name of Jesus, and it shall be done. But know this, it shall be given you what you shall ask." (D&C 50:29-30).

We are to pray "after this manner," said the Savior. (V. 9). There follows the Lord's Prayer, adapted to the circumstances of the Nephite Saints. (V. 9-13, see Matthew 6:9-13). For example, the words "Thy kingdom come" is omitted in The Book of Mormon, perhaps because the Church had already been established among the Nephites. "And lead us not into temptation" is rendered in the J.S.T. "and suffer us not to be led into temptation." This clarification suggests the need for companion scriptures that shed light on passages from the Biblical text that are either confusing, distorted, or contradict established Gospel doctrine.

The Savior then taught the principle of forgiveness. (V. 14-15). He had obtained forgiveness for the sins of mankind only after the most excruciating suffering on His part. Is it, then, too much for Him to ask us to forgive each other? He recognized that without forgiveness, the Plan of Redemption is rendered ineffectual for both the penitent and those who have been wronged by others. Exoneration is really a celestial characteristic that demands forgiveness of sinners by disciples. Christ requires it of those who would in every other way observe the laws of the Celestial Kingdom. He commanded Joseph Smith: "I, the Lord, will forgive whom I will forgive, but of you it is required to forgive all men." (D&C 64:10). Brigham Young declared: "He who takes offense when none was intended is a fool, and he who takes offense when one was intended is usually a fool." Withholding love negates the Spirit of Christ, and is the proof that we never really knew Him, and that, for us, He lived in vain. It means that His teachings fell on deaf ears, and that we were never near enough to Him to be enveloped within the spell of His compassion for the world.

Next, Jesus taught the disciples how to fast. (V. 16-18). Fasting is an intensely personal experience that doesn't draw the attention of others. In fact, the Lord condemns those who "appear unto men to fast (for) they have their reward." (V. 16).

The Master called His disciples to a higher plane of spirituality and to a commitment to selfless consecration of effort. He said: "Lay not up for yourselves treasures upon earth, where moth and rust doth corrupt, and thieves break through and steal; But lay up for yourselves treasures in heaven, where neither moth nor rust doth corrupt, and where thieves do not break through nor steal." (V. 19-20). The key is to lose ourselves in service, even as we let our light shine before men. (See 3 Nephi 12:16).

Verses 22 and 23 are a study in contrasts, and then verse 24 sums up the whole point. "The light of the body is the eye," reads the first verse. "If, therefore, thine eye be single, thy whole body shall be full of light." (V. 22). Elsewhere, the Savior taught: "If your eye be single to my glory, your whole bodies shall be filled with light, and there shall be no darkness in you, and that body which is filled with light comprehendeth all things." (D&C 88:67).

These scriptures help us to understand Moroni's visit to Joseph Smith, in his chamber on September 21, 1823. Joseph recalled the experience in these words: "I discovered a light appearing in my room, which continued to increase until the room was lighter than at noonday, when immediately a personage appeared at my bedside ... He had on a loose robe of most exquisite whiteness. It was a whiteness beyond anything earthly I had ever seen; nor do I believe that any earthly things could be made to appear so exceedingly white and brilliant ... Not only was his robe exceedingly white, but his whole person was glorious beyond description, and his countenance truly like lightning. The room was exceedingly light, but not so very bright as immediately around his person." (J.S.H. 1:30-32).

The Savior dramatically described the antithesis of this glorious state, when He taught: "But if thine eye be evil, thy whole body shall be full of darkness. If, therefore, the light that is in thee be darkness, how great is that darkness!" (V. 23). The influence of Satan that gripped Joseph in the Sacred Grove just before his deliverance illustrates how overwhelmingly intense darkness can be. Joseph recalled: "I was seized upon by some power which entirely overcame me, and had such an astonishing influence over me as to bind my tongue so that I could not speak. Thick darkness gathered around me, and it seemed to me for a time as if I were doomed to sudden destruction ... I was ready to sink into despair and abandon myself to destruction - not to an imaginary ruin, but to the power of some actual being from the unseen world." (J.S.H. 1:15-16). We are again reminded of Lehi's Vision of The Tree of Life, and of those who lost their way in mists of darkness. (See 1 Nephi 8:23).

Then the Savior taught the great principle: "No man can serve two masters; for either he will hate the one and love the other, or else he will hold to the one and despise the other. Ye cannot serve God and Mammon." (V. 24). A house divided against itself cannot stand. The Church cannot modify its standards so that it becomes popular with the world, for then all hell would want to join it. The Saints cannot hold membership in both the Church of God and the Great and Abominable Church of the Devil. They cannot live in Zion, but have a summer home in Babylon. They cannot engage in a leisurely journey through Idumea, stopping along the way to sample its worldly pleasures.

There is a basic instability associated with hypocrisy, and when we walk what we perceive to be the fine line between righteousness and wickedness. we will suffer eternally damaging consequences. We are faced with a conundrum of cosmic proportion. Agency was preserved as the crown jewel of mortality in order to avoid this dilemma. We are free to choose, but choose we must. We are free to follow one lifestyle or another, but not both. That desire runs counter to the laws of nature and is fatally flawed. When we pursue that path, we travel down a one-way road that leads inevitably to a personality precipice.

We do not have the option to walk "in (our) own way, and after the image of (our) own god, whose image is in the likeness of the world, and whose substance is that of an idol." (D&C 1:16). One of the greatest contributions of Joseph Smith was to share with the world his knowledge of what is to come after death. He clarified our understanding of heaven, and taught that it was an attainable goal for which we should expend every effort. He created desire in the hearts of millions to follow the difficult road to Gethsemane. What he did, validated the promises made by our Father to each of us, that the struggles of mortality would be worth every effort, and that we would look back on our experiences in appreciation for the personal growth and development that occurred only because of our willing participation and effort. But only if the drama is played out within the context of the Gospel, according to the rules established by the Plan of Salvation, do our anticipated blessings come. There is no other way.

This has been the pattern from the foundation of the world. "And thus, the Gospel began to be preached, from the beginning, being declared by holy angels sent forth from the presence of God, and by his own voice, and by the gift of the Holy Ghost. And thus, all things were confirmed unto Adam, by an holy ordinance, and the Gospel preached, and a decree sent forth, that it should be in the world, until the end thereof; and thus, it was. Amen." (Moses 5:58-59).

Those of us who have consecrated our time, talents, energy, and our very lives to the Kingdom of God, have long since "crossed over Jordan". We stand with Joshua, who declared: "Choose you this day whom ye will serve; whether the gods which your fathers served that were on the other side of the flood, or the gods of the Amorites, in whose land ye dwell: but as for me and my house, we will serve the Lord." (Joshua 24:15).

The Book of Mormon text makes clear that the counsel in the balance of this chapter was reserved for the Twelve. "And now it came to pass that when Jesus had spoken these words, he looked upon the twelve whom he had chosen, and said unto them: Remember the words which I have spoken. For behold, ye are they whom I have chosen to minister unto this people. Therefore, I say unto you, take no thought for your life, what ye shall eat, or what ye shall drink; nor yet for your body, what ye shall put on. Is not the life more than meat, and the body than raiment?" (V. 25, see Moroni 2:1). The ministry of the Twelve was to be a full-time engagement. There could be no anxieties, uncertainties, or distractions associated with earning a livelihood. The Lord would provide, as the next verses indicate. After all, He asked, does He not watch over the fowls of the air, as well as His other creations? (V. 26).

"Consider the lilies of the field how they grow; they toil not, neither do they spin; And yet I say unto you, that even Solomon, in all his glory, was not arrayed like one of these." (V. 28-29). God does show Himself to us, but He usually does it in the form of "love letters." Ralph Waldo Emerson wrote: "I see the spectacle of morning from the hilltop over against my house, from daybreak to sunrise, with emotions which an angel might share. The long, slender bars of cloud float like fishes in a sea of crimson light. From the earth, as a shore, I look out into that silent sea. I seem to partake its rapid transformations; the active enchantment reaches my dust, and I dilate and conspire with the morning wind. How does nature deify us with a few and cheap elements! Give me health and a day, and I will make the pomp of emperors ridiculous!"

The admonition of the Lord is to "seek ye first the kingdom of God and his righteousness, and all these things shall be added unto you." (V. 33). The J.S.T. renders this verse: "Wherefore, seek not the things of this world, but seek ye first to build up the kingdom of God, and to establish His righteousness, and all these things shall be added unto you." This translation individualizes the charge given by Jesus with a specific call to action with a divine commission of responsibility. At the same time, it promises that temporal treasures that promote personal righteousness will be given to the faithful.

"Sufficient is the day unto the evil thereof." (V. 34). In other words, there is enough to worry about today without adding to it the burden of fretting about the future. We should not get in the thick of thin things. There are, after all, only three types of control in life. First are those circumstances over which we have direct control, then those over which we have indirect control, and finally those over which we have no control. We need to learn where we should most profitably direct our energies.

Third Nephi
Chapter 14

Now Jesus "turned again to the multitude, and did open his mouth unto them again, saying: verily, verily, I say unto you, Judge not, that ye be not judged." (V. 1). This verse from Matthew has been grossly misinterpreted; many have thought it to mean that we should not take a stand or judge the actions of others under any circumstances. This is simply incorrect. The Light of Christ is given to every person who comes into the world in order to provide a discriminating standard by which righteous judgments may be made.

Once again, the J.S.T. provides the required clarification. In that text, this verse is rendered: "Judge ye not unrighteously, that ye be not judged, but judge righteous judgment." (J.S.T. Matthew 7:1). Therefore, righteousness is the essential quality that must accompany the judgments by which we are continually confronted. We must emulate the Savior when necessity requires us to pass judgment. (See Mormon 8:19).

The Savior would never require of us a standard of behavior that He was not willing to observe Himself. This is why, in the next few verses, He employed the metaphor of the mote and beam, to illustrate that it is human nature to highlight or accentuate the sins of others, even when we are guilty of far more serious transgressions. (V. 3-5).

The observation has been made that none of us would come to Church if all our sins smelled like tobacco. In other words, sometimes individuals wear their sins on their coat sleeves, which keeps them from activity in the Church, regardless of the magnitude of the transgression. When other, far more serious sins committed by active members of the Church remain unseen and unrevealed, the casual transgressor may find it easier to maintain Church activity. He or she might even call attention to the imperfections of others. It is this hypocrisy that Jesus condemned.

When the Savior again spoke metaphorically, He did so in a manner that could not be misinterpreted. He said: "Give not that which is holy unto the dogs, neither cast ye your pearls before swine, lest they trample them under their feet, and turn again and rend you." (V. 6). Who could be more holy than Jesus Christ, "the Holy One of Israel?" The seraphim surrounding the throne of God cried one "unto another" in the superlative, "and said: Holy, holy, holy, is the Lord of Hosts; and the whole earth is full of his glory." (2 Nephi 16:2). "In the language of Adam, Man of Holiness is his name, and the name of his Only Begotten is the Son of Man (of Holiness), even Jesus Christ." (Moses 6:57).

The point is that when dealing with topics of the most sacred nature, that by very definition include Jesus Christ as their centerpiece, it is very important to treat them with the utmost respect, and sometimes this requires figures of speech. As the Lord taught Joseph Smith: "That which cometh from above is sacred, and must be spoken with care, and by constraint of the Spirit and in this there is no condemnation." (D&C 63:64).

The J.S.T. renders verse 6: "Go ye into the world, saying unto all, Repent, for the kingdom of heaven has come nigh unto you. And the mysteries of the kingdom ye shall keep within yourselves; for it is not meet to give that which is holy unto the dogs; neither cast ye your pearls unto swine, lest they trample them under their feet. For the world cannot receive that which ye, yourselves, are not able to bear; wherefore ye shall not give your pearls unto them, lest they turn again and rend you." (J.S.T. Matthew 7:9-11). When we understand that the mysteries of the kingdom are the saving principles and ordinances of the Gospel of Jesus Christ that are only spiritually discerned, we can better understand how those who have chosen to ignore the Light of Christ or the influence of the Holy Ghost could figuratively trample these principles and ordinances, as well as the Savior Himself, under their feet. When presented with concepts they are unprepared to receive, they set them at naught, since they cannot comprehend their true value. (See 1 Nephi 19:7).

Nephi, the son of Father Lehi, wrote: "The things which some men esteem to be of great worth, both to the body and soul, others set at naught and trample under their feet. Yea, even the very God of Israel do men trample under their feet; I say, trample under their feet, but I would speak in other words - they set him at naught, and hearken not to the voice of his counsels." (1 Nephi 19:7). "These are they who are not valiant in the testimony of Jesus; wherefore, they obtain not the crown over the kingdom of our God." (D&C 76:79). "To be valiant in the testimony of Jesus is to take the Lord's side on every issue. It is to think what He thinks, to believe what He believes, to say what He would say, and to do what He would do." (Bruce R. McConkie, C.R., 10/74).

Perhaps this is what the Lord had in mind when He next exhorted the multitude to "ask, and it shall be given unto you; seek, and ye shall find; knock, and it shall be opened unto you." (V. 7). What could be more natural than the simple statement expressed in the 9th Article of Faith: "We believe all that God has revealed, all that He does now reveal, and we believe that He will yet reveal many great and important things pertaining to the Kingdom of God." The world does not need more revelation. What it needs is a listening ear. Many of us deny ourselves the blessings of heaven simply because we do not wait for the answers to our prayers.

In verses 8-11, the Savior explained how anxious Heavenly Father is to grant the righteous requests of His children. Comparing His benevolence to that of our earthly fathers, the Savior declared: "How much more shall your Father who is in heaven give good things to them that ask him?" (V. 11).

Thus, Jesus established in the minds of the multitude the principle that Father in Heaven will bless us, conditional only upon our preparation. Earthly parents feel the same way when they properly understand their own guardianship responsibilities. This sets the stage for the introduction of The Royal Law. (See James 2:8). "Therefore, all things whatsoever ye would that men should do to you, do ye even so to them, for this is the law and the prophets." (V. 12).

The Royal Law requires total obedience, for it is a celestial Law. Its frees us to reach our potential. Failing in any of its requirements can rob us of eternal life in the mansions of the Celestial Kingdom. "For whosoever shall keep the whole law, and yet offend in one point, he is guilty of all." (James 2:10). In other words, "He who cannot abide the law of a celestial kingdom cannot abide a celestial glory." (D&C 88:22).

The conditions of admission to the Lord's Church are stringent, and yet they are attainable. They are strict, but they are not elitist. They include all who have broken hearts and contrite spirits. They invite all who are bowed down in the depths of humility. "Enter ye in at the strait gate," said the Savior, "for wide is the gate, and broad is the way, which leadeth to destruction, and many there be who go in thereat." (V. 13).

The waters of baptism invite the penitent, the humble, the meek, the poor in spirit, and the pure in heart. When Elisha directed Naaman to wash in the River Jordan seven times in order to be cured of his leprosy, this proud captain of the host of the King of Syria refused, at first. But "his servant came near, and spake unto him, and said, My father, if the prophet had bid thee do some great thing, wouldest thou not have done it? How much rather then, when he saith to thee, Wash, and be clean? Then went he down, and dipped himself seven times in Jordan, according to the saying of the man of God: and his flesh came again like unto the flesh of a little child, and he was clean." (2 Kings 5:13-14).

"Strait is the gate, and narrow is the way, which leadeth unto life, and few there be that find it." (V. 14). When our hearts are set upon temporal things, our spirituality is weakened until our relationship with God is no longer a part of our daily experiences. Thus, we are exhorted to "lay aside the things of this world, and seek for the things of a better." (D&C 25:10).

But what are we to do? How can we find the truth? Where can we turn for guidance and direction? Is there no one on the earth authorized to speak in the name of God, who can help us? Have the heavens closed? Are they silent? Are we to be left alone, to wander to and fro, like flotsam on the sea of life? Does God answer our prayers? Has revelation ceased? The Book of Mormon, and the Savior's instruction in Third Nephi - The Book of Nephi, confirm that the source material of the Gospel is revelation, and "if any man preach any other Gospel unto you than that ye have received, let him be accursed." (Galatians 1:9, see D&C 50:13-20).

The Savior warned against "false prophets, who come to you in sheep's clothing, but inwardly they are ravening wolves." (V. 15, see Matthew 7:15, & Commentary Reference to Alma 31:30). Some enemies have ignorantly used this scripture to attack the Church, claiming that it addresses the President and Prophet. This is quite an assertion, coming as it does from a people "who never had faith enough to call down one scrap of revelation from heaven, and for all they have now are indebted to the faith of another people who lived hundreds and thousands of years before them. Does it remain for them to say how much God has spoken and how much he has not spoken?" (Joseph Smith, H.C., 2:17-18).

If their assertion is reasonable, where then are the true prophets suggested by Christ's warning? They must exist, for "Adam's revelation did not instruct Noah to build his ark; nor did Noah's revelation tell Lot to forsake Sodom; nor did either of these speak of the Exodus. These all had revelations for themselves, and so had Isaiah, Jeremiah, Peter, Paul, John, and Joseph Smith." (Henry D. Moyle, "Teachings of The Living Prophets Student Manual," Religion 333 & "The Gospel Kingdom," p. 34).

His children think of Heavenly Father in the present tense; He is the Great I Am. In the Doctrine & Covenants, the Lord testified that Joseph Smith was given "power from on high, by the means which were before prepared, to translate the Book of Mormon; which contains a record of a fallen people, and the fulness of the gospel of Jesus Christ to the Gentiles and to the Jews also; which was given by inspiration and is confirmed to others by the ministering of angels, and is declared unto the world by them - Proving to the world that the holy scriptures are true, and that God does inspire men and call them to his holy work in this age and generation, as well as in generations of old; Thereby showing that he is the same God yesterday, today, and forever." (D&C 20:8-12).

Something wonderful nourishes our testimonies of the living Prophet, Seer, and Revelator of the Church of Jesus Christ of Latter-day Saints. Over 150 years ago, John Greenleaf Whittier said of "these modern prophets, I discovered, as I think, the great secret of their success in making converts. They speak to a common feeling; they minister to a universal want. They speak a language of hope and promise to the weak, weary hearts, tossed and troubled, who have wandered from sect to sect, seeking in vain for the primal manifestations of the divine power." ("Whittier Attends a Mormon Conventicle," in "Among the Mormons: Historic Accounts by Contemporary Observers", p.59).

In the following verses, the Savior gave a key. (V. 16-20). "By their fruits ye shall know them." (V. 20). Do these prophets, or teachers who speak in the name of the Lord, bless the lives of their people? Is their doctrine edifying and uplifting? Do they encourage a religion that promotes chastity, morality, and fidelity to family values? Do they hold dear the sanctity of life and the rights of the unborn? Do they believe that moral agency is an eternal principle vital to the successful completion of our probation on earth? Do they believe in obeying, honoring, and sustaining the law of the land? Do they believe in being honest, true, chaste, benevolent, virtuous, and in doing good to all men? Do they believe all things, hope all things, have they endured many things and hope to be able to endure all things? If there is anything virtuous, lovely, or of good report or praiseworthy, do they seek after these things? (See Philippians 4:8, & the 13th Article of Faith).

It is vital that those who seek the Church of Christ recognize the fruits of faith, because "not every one that saith unto me, Lord, Lord, shall enter into the kingdom of heaven; but he that doeth the will of (our) Father who is in heaven." (V. 21). This is a particularly significant verse in light of the various evangelical movements sweeping the land. Many claim that it is only necessary to "Confess Christ," or to declare faith in Him, in order to be saved. They miss the critical point the Savior made in verse 21 / Matthew 7:21. The action verb "to do" implies more than desire; it demands active obedience to the requirements established by Heavenly Father.

"Faith, if it hath not works, is dead, being alone." (James 2:17). There is no more power in faith that does not include works, than there is strength in food that is not eaten, or warmth in clothes that are not worn. The teachings on faith and works by Luther and the other Reformers who founded Protestantism are often misunderstood. "By faith, Luther meant no merely intellectual assent to a proposition, but vital, personal self-committal to a practical belief. He heartily approved of good works; what he denied was their efficacy for salvation. 'Good works,' he said, "do not make a good man. But a good man does good works.' And what makes a man good? Faith in God, and Christ." (Wil Durant, The Story of Civilization, "The Reformation," p. 374-375). This is consistent with the doctrine of The Church of Jesus Christ of Latter-day Saints that we are saved by grace, after all that we can do. (See Commentary Reference to 2 Nephi 25:23)

"And they who keep their second estate," being obedient to every commandment of God, "shall have glory added upon their heads for ever and ever." (Abraham 3:26). This scripture speaks of "eternal life, which God, that cannot lie, promised before the world began." (Titus 1:2). The doctrine of Christ is to "do these things," as Nephi of old said, "which I have told you I have seen that your Lord and your Redeemer should do; for, for this cause have they been shown unto me, that ye might know the gate by which ye should enter. For the gate by which ye should enter is repentance and baptism by water; and then cometh a remission of your sins by fire and by the Holy Ghost." (2 Nephi 31:17).

Then, when we are on the path leading to eternal life, it is important that we move forward with purpose. It is not enough to have been baptized and to have received the Holy Ghost. We must not camp out on the path and remain stationary, in a passive or vegetative state. The dictionary is the only place where success comes before work. Hence, we read the Savior's observation that "many will say to me in that day: Lord, Lord, have we not prophesied in thy name, and in thy name have cast out devils, and in thy name done many wonderful works?" (V. 22).

This verse applies particularly to members of the Church who have held the priesthood. A problem is created when confusion arises between priesthood authority and power. The former comes by the laying on of hands, and the latter through righteousness. Sometimes, when those who hold the priesthood are asked to officiate in the ordinances, they do so without the supporting power of Christ. Their acts are only valid because of their ordination and because of the sustaining faith of those to whom they minister. Thus, the Savior's recurring admonition: "Be ye clean that bear the vessels of the Lord." (3 Nephi 20:41).

The verse also suggests that there will be many at the Judgment Bar of Christ who will continue to press a point that is stubbornly advocated on earth. Namely, they will argue if it mattered so much whether one had been a Methodist,

Quaker or Lutheran. They will advocate the position that, as long as they accepted Christ, their efforts could not have been in vain.

But, in these verses, Christ clearly stated that at the Bar of Justice, He will declare the simple fact: "And then, I will profess unto them: I never knew you; depart from me, ye that work iniquity." (V. 23). What a contrast this will be to those who come to the Lord with their sheaves of good works. (See Psalms 126:6). These will be as Job, who was known by the Lord, Who said of him: "There is none like him in the earth, a perfect and an upright man, one that feareth God, and escheweth evil." (Job 1:8).

Interestingly, the J.S.T. renders this verse: "Ye never knew me." (J.S.T. Matthew 7:33). This translation is more in harmony with the following verses that tie discipleship in with performance. "Therefore, whoso heareth these sayings of mine and doeth them, I will liken him unto a wise man." (V. 24). The key is spiritual consistency. As Brigham Young declared: "I never count the cost of anything. I just find out what the Lord wants me to do, and I do it."

It must be remembered, though, that the Lord rewards the simple faith of those who are trying to press forward with whatever light they have received. Their righteous efforts will be acknowledged. For example, in the springtime of the year 1820, a young boy approached God in a quiet grove of trees. He was not yet a member of the Church of Jesus Christ, did not have a clear conception of God, and had never before engaged in vocal prayer. Nevertheless, his humble petition was answered with spectacular results. That drama is replayed hundreds of thousands of times each year, as the Holy Ghost falls upon those who earnestly seek the truth

For members of the Church, though, the expectations of the Savior are much higher. "For of him unto whom much is given much is required; and he who sins against the greater light shall receive the greater condemnation." (D&C 82:3). Since the law to which we were responsible while on the earth will judge us, we will vary in our culpability to answer for our deeds. Therein lies the power of the Gospel to give us the eternal perspective to see beyond the limited horizon of our vision. One of our greatest temptations is to confuse our dreams with reality, but a defeat of cosmic proportion comes when our dreams are surrendered to the narrow reality that is dictated by our present circumstances.

"Life is a sheet of paper white, where each of us may write a line or two, and then comes night. Greatly begin. If thou hast time but for a line, make that sublime. Not failure, but low aim is crime." (James Russell Lowell). Bruce R. McConkie was asked: "How can we reach the Celestial Kingdom." His answer was: "Set your course, and move along it." The Restored Gospel of Jesus Christ provides the way to do just that, as the Church builds upon the rock of continuing revelation, or instruction from God. (See V. 24-25).

We acknowledge His leadership and emulate His example. He sets the course, and we follow the established guidelines. He gives the commands, and we yield to His will. He requires obedience, and we humbly accept the rewards for following through, as well as dealing with the consequences for willful neglect of our responsibilities. What makes the Plan fair is that it is interactive; it gives us continual guidance and feedback from the Master. We accepted the risks attendant to mortality because we believed in the Plan, and we knew our Father would never leave us alone, or abandon us to fend for ourselves. When we leave Him, though, our vulnerability is exposed. When our love for Him dominates our lives so that our foundation is grounded on the bedrock of the Gospel of Jesus Christ, we can be sure of our success, that was ordained in the heavens before the world was. After all, it is the Plan of Redemption. It is our key to immortality and eternal life. (See Moses 1:39).

"Behold, there are save two churches only; the one is the church of the Lamb of God, and the other is the church of the devil." (1 Nephi 14:10).

Third Nephi
Chapter 15

Again, the Lord emphasized to the multitude that "whoso remembereth these sayings of mine and doeth them, him will I raise up at the last day." (V. 1). The disciples of Christ follow Him because the love Him. Their love harmonizes with the Law of Obedience, which was "irrevocably decreed in heaven before the foundation of this world, upon which all blessings are predicated. And when we obtain any blessing from God, it is by obedience to that law upon which it is predicated." (D&C 130:20-21).

That is to say, obedience to specific commandments is always accompanied by associated blessings. These rewards for obedience are sometimes temporal but are always spiritual. Now and then, men and women recognize the eternal immutability of that grand law, but in general, they do not. As they come to a greater appreciation of the Plan of Salvation and begin to understand the nature of God, they see more clearly what the Lord meant, when He said: "I am bound when ye do what I say; but when ye do not what I say, ye have no promise." (D&C 82:10).

Brigham Young once declared: "There is no man who ever made a sacrifice on the earth for the kingdom of heaven ... except the Savior. I would not give the ashes of a rye straw for that man who feels that he is making sacrifices for God. We are doing this for our own happiness, welfare, and exaltation, and for nobody else's. What we do, we do for the salvation of the inhabitants of the earth, not for the salvation of the heavens, the angels, or God." (J.D., 16:114, see Mosiah 2:25).

There are really two dimensions to this statement by President Young. At first we are struck with the reality that much of what we do in this life we do for ourselves. As our altruistic sensitivities coalesce into a single-minded sense of purpose, we will labor on behalf of others and gladly begin to lose ourselves in service. Then, when we really catch the vision and our eternal perspective snaps into focus, we will give ourselves to the Savior. We will yield our agency to Him because of our implicit trust in His goodness and because of the positive reinforcement we receive from our philanthropic experiences. His expectations for us are uncompromising, but His firmness has a noble purpose. (See 3 Nephi 12:48).

The Saints in Zarahemla had enjoyed a special relationship with Christ during the centuries before His mortal ministry, albeit on again and off again. Now, even with the Resurrected Lord in their midst, they did not understand that the law, that had governed Israel all that time, was done away. "They understood not the saying that old things had passed away, and that all things had become new." (V. 2).

The nation of Israel had run away from her opportunities and was content to have a lesser law to govern her. The same conditions prevail among some of the Latter-day Saints today. Many in the Church seem to be camped out at the base of Sinai, waiting for the prophet to bring them a highly anticipated law of carnal commandments. But the scriptures say that the power of the Gospel is to drive the law into our inward parts, and write it upon our hearts. (See Jeremiah 31:33). It motivates us to do good not because we are compelled to do so, or because we expect a reward for doing so, but because it is the right thing to do, and because it becomes our very nature to wish to do so.

Possibly the most significant difference that accounts for the superiority of the Gospel over the Law of Carnal Commandments is the process whereby we internalize the Gospel. This is called sanctification by the Spirit. It is a testament to its power that after the ministry of Christ among the Nephites and Lamanites, they dwelt in peace for two centuries. There had been earlier religious reformations among the Nephites, but this dedication to the doctrine of Christ was unprecedented.

In our day, (in the Dispensation of the Fulness of Times), the government of the Church is as well established as it has ever been, and with the blessings of electronic and print media, the world has the words of Christ as it has never had them before. The First Presidency of the Church, the Twelve Apostles, and the Quorums of The Seventy travel throughout the world testifying of Christ. Temples grace many lands. Opportunities for sanctification by the Spirit have never been greater. The Lord is fulfilling His promise, when He said that in the Last Days: "It shall come to pass ... that I will pour out my spirit upon all flesh; and your sons and your daughters shall prophesy, and your old men shall dream dreams, your young men shall see visions." (Joel 2:28).

Christ taught the multitude: "The law is fulfilled that was given unto Moses." (V. 4). Abinadi had said that the Law of Moses was given to point the attention of the people to Christ, and that its elements were types of things to come. (See Mosiah 13:27-32, Galatians 3:24, & D&C 84:27). Now the Savior confirmed: "I am he that gave the law, and I am he who covenanted with my people Israel; therefore, the law in me is fulfilled ... therefore it hath an end." (V. 5). It is clear from this verse that Christ is the God of the Old Testament. (See Mosiah 15:1). By that authority, He set aside the Law of Moses that had formerly governed Israel, inasmuch as its purpose had been accomplished.

Christ then declared: "The covenant which I have made with my people is not all fulfilled; but the law which was given unto Moses hath an end in me." (V. 8). Salvation is in Christ, and not in the Law. (See Mosiah 13:27-28, & 2 Nephi 11:4). We sometimes observe of the ancient Jews that they were caught up in the mechanics of the Law, and forgot to whom it pointed. Our challenge today is to see that we are converted to the Gospel rather than just to the Church. When we get caught up in its machinery, without making contact with the Savior and without being spiritually begotten of Him, life can become a treadmill. The Gospel is a springboard that propels us to greater spiritual heights.

That is because the Gospel brings us to Christ, Who is "the law, and the light. He told the Nephites: "Look unto me and endure to the end, and ye shall live; for unto him that endureth to the end, will I give eternal life." (V. 9). With His ministry, the Law of Moses became "dead", as the Melchizedek Priesthood was given the responsibility to direct the spiritual affairs of the Church. (See 2 Nephi 25:23-25). Since Christ and the Law were inseparable, the power lay within Him to grant eternal life to the Nephite Saints in accordance with the laws and ordinances of the Fulness of The Gospel. When they conformed their lives to its every element, and followed his example in every whit, spectacular results ensued. In describing the conditions in Zarahemla following the ministry of the Savior, Mormon wrote: "Surely there could not be a happier people among all the people who had been created by the hand of God." (4 Nephi 1:16). This has been the case since the foundation of the world in every dispensation, when the people have enjoyed every element of the Gospel Plan of Salvation. As Joseph Smith taught: "Happiness is the object and design of our existence and will be the end thereof, if we follow the path that leads to it. And this path is virtue, uprightness, faithfulness, holiness, and keeping all the commandments of God. In obedience there is joy and peace

. . . and as God has designed our happiness ... He never has, He never will, give a commandment to His people that is not calculated in its nature to promote that happiness which He has designed." (History of the Church, 5:134-135.)

The commandments we have received that testify of Christ are "the law and the prophets." (V. 10). The Preparatory Gospel was called the Torah, and was the Law for Israel. This was given to Moses on Sinai when he received the second set of tablets in place of the Gospel Covenant that Israel had rejected. (See V. 8). Even though Israel did not enjoy the benefits and blessings of the Fulness of the Gospel, their prophets held the Melchizedek Priesthood. Moses alone held that authority among the Israelite nation during the Exodus.

When Moses was about to be translated, he ordained Joshua to be the Israelite prophet to the nation. He bestowed upon Joshua all of the keys, powers, and privileges necessary to carry out his responsibilities. Through the ages, the Hebrew prophets all held the Melchizedek Priesthood, that they received by the laying on of hands by either mortal servants or heavenly messengers who were in authority.

While Joshua held the keys to minister to the spiritual needs of the Israelites, Eleazar, the son of Aaron, held the keys of the temporal affairs of Israel. This was the Presidency of the Aaronic or Levitical Priesthood, that was passed on by patriarchal succession. The Church, then, was cared for in its temporal affairs by a Presiding Bishopric, and in its spiritual affairs by a prophet/leader who held the Melchizedek Priesthood.

Through those ancient leaders came prophecies that were not fulfilled, and promises and covenants that were not satisfied, at the Resurrection of Christ. They are still in force and will yet testify of the Savior in the most powerful way, and so continue to be an integral part of "the law and the prophets." (V. 10).

Then Christ revealed to His twelve disciples that He had never told their brethren at Jerusalem of their existence, or that of the Ten Tribes, who had been "led away out of the land." (V. 15, see Commentary References to 2 Nephi 20:21, & to Alma 7:10). He had only told them "that other sheep I have which are not of this fold; them also I must bring, and they shall hear my voice; and there shall be one fold, and one shepherd." (V. 17).

Jesus had been commanded by the Father to reveal no more to Israel. This was "because of stiffneckedness and unbelief." (V. 18). Had they been given more insight into their brethren in the New World, they would probably not have understood it anyway. As Joseph Smith said: "As far as we degenerate from God, we descend to the devil and lose knowledge." ("Teachings," p. 217). His counsel applies equally to all of Heavenly Father's children.

Most Christians today believe the "other sheep" mentioned by the Savior refers to the Gentiles, who would at some subsequent day receive the Gospel. But The Book of Mormon makes crystal clear that this is not the case. The Savior explained: "And verily I say unto you, that ye are they of whom I said: Other sheep I have which are not of this fold; them also I must bring, and they shall hear my voice; and there shall be one fold, and one shepherd. And they understood me not, for they supposed it had been the Gentiles; for they understood not that the Gentiles should be converted through their preaching. And they understood me not that I said they shall hear my voice; and they understood me not that the Gentiles should not at any time hear my voice - that I should not manifest myself unto them save it were by the Holy Ghost. But behold, ye have both heard my voice, and seen me; and ye are my sheep, and ye are numbered among those whom the Father hath given me." (V. 21-24).

The Gentile nations of the earth will receive the Gospel, and the elect among them will be converted by the power of the Holy Ghost. Peter, who brought the Gospel to the Gentiles, reported: "On the Gentiles also was poured out the gift of the Holy Ghost." (Acts 10:45). Quoting the prophet Joel, Luke declared: "And it shall come to pass in the last days, saith God, I will pour out of my Spirit upon all flesh: and your sons and your daughters shall prophesy, and your young men shall see visions, and your old men shall dream dreams. And on my servants and on my handmaidens I will pour out in those days of my Spirit; and they shall prophesy." (Acts 2:17-18. This was on the Day of Pentecost, when around 3,000 souls heard the preaching of the apostles and "were pricked in their heart, and said unto Peter and to the rest of the apostles, Men and brethren, what shall we do? Then Peter said unto them, repent and be baptized every one of you in the name of Jesus Christ for the remission of sins, and ye shall receive the gift of the Holy Ghost." (Acts 2:37-38).

The gifts of the Spirit were sufficient to carry the Gentiles along the path leading to eternal life, but it was the Word that was given to Israel in both the Old and the New World. As Peter said: "Of a truth I perceive that God is no respecter of persons: But in every nation he that feareth him, and worketh righteousness, is accepted with him. The word that God sent unto the children of Israel, preaching peace by Jesus Christ." (Acts 10:34-36).

Third Nephi
Chapter 16

Next the Savior identified yet "other sheep, which are not of this land, neither of the land of Jerusalem, neither in any parts of that land round about whither I have been to minister." (V. 1). These other sheep refer to groups of people who had previously been scattered through war, conquest, or other means. The Allegory of The Olive Tree given by Zenos clearly teaches that such migrations have taken place. (See Jacob 5). The Jaredites are also a good example, as is the colony of the Elephantine Jews from the 5th century B.C. Perhaps even the Qumran Covenantors (134-104 B.C.) would qualify as other sheep.

Whereas Christ had been specifically forbidden by the Father to tell those at Jerusalem of His other sheep, because of their stiffneckedness and unbelief, to these disciples He explained: "I have received a commandment of the Father that I shall go unto them, and that they shall hear my voice, and shall be numbered among my sheep, that there may be one fold and one shepherd." (V. 3, see 3 Nephi 15:15 & 18).

The Lord commanded Nephi that a record be kept so that when the Gentiles should receive The Book of Mormon in the Last Days, they might obtain a knowledge of its divine authenticity from the Holy Ghost. (V. 4). The Gentiles, Christ said, were to be blessed because of their belief in Him, "in and of the Holy Ghost, which witnesseth unto them" of Him and the Father. (V. 6).

The Savior acknowledged the awesome power of the Holy Ghost as a Witness of the Father and the Son. In the Last Days, He has probably been responsible for more real conversions than in all other ages of the world combined. As Joseph Fielding Smith said: "The impressions on the soul that come from the Holy Ghost are far more significant than a vision. It is where spirit speaks to spirit, and the imprint upon the soul is far more difficult to erase." ("Improvement Era", 11/1966).

On another occasion, he wrote that because of the Holy Ghost, "there should be no laymen in The Church of Jesus Christ of Latter-day Saints. If there are any such, then they have neglected their responsibilities and obligations which the Lord has placed upon them." ("Melchizedek Priesthood Personal Study Guide," 1972-73, p. 190). In the Last Days, "they shall teach no more every man his neighbor, and every man his brother, saying, Know the Lord; for they shall all know me, from the least of them unto the greatest of them." (Jeremiah 31:34).

In our day, the Holy Ghost is being poured out in rich abundance. The Lord has promised: "God shall give unto you knowledge by his Holy Spirit, yea, by the unspeakable gift of the Holy Ghost, that has not been revealed since the world was until now." This is a time when "nothing shall be withheld ... All thrones and dominions, principalities, and powers, shall be revealed ... And also, if there be bounds set to the heavens or to the seas, or to the dry land, or to the sun, moon, or stars, (all this) shall be revealed in the days of the dispensation of the fulness of times." (D&C 121:26-31).

If this is the promise, then worthy members of the Church should strive to be the agents through whom this knowledge comes. The Prophet Joseph Smith wrote to the Saints: "As the dews of Carmel, so shall the knowledge of God descend upon" the Latter-day Saints. (D&C 128:19). There is more to the Gospel than obedience and covenants. The acquisition of knowledge and its application for the benefit of man is progress too. "In one sense of the word, the keys of the kingdom ... consist in the key of knowledge." (D&C 128:14).

In the Church today, there are many striking evidences of the sanctifying and unifying influence of the Holy Ghost. For example, in spite of the many translations of the scriptures used by members worldwide, there is remarkably little disagreement as to their meaning. In Church organization and Church government, ecclesiastical leaders enjoy virtual harmony in spite of cultural, social, racial, political, and economic differences. The ordinances of the Gospel, from baptism to the endowment in the temple, are universally understood and faithfully administered.

Every six months, Saints from all over the world gather at Church headquarters to hear the word of the Lord from His authorized servants. As Harold B. Lee explained in his closing remarks at General Conference: "If you want to know what the Lord has for this people at the present time, I would admonish you to get and read the discourses that have been delivered at this conference, for what these brethren have spoken by the power of the Holy Ghost is the mind of the Lord, the will of the Lord, the word of the Lord, and the power of God unto salvation." (D&C 68:4, C.R. 4/1973).

Today, it is as it was when Ammon ventured as a missionary among the People of Limhi in the Land of Nephi. He told Limhi about a man in Zarahemla who was "a seer, (and) a revelator, and a prophet also, and a gift which is greater can no man have." (Mosiah 8:16). "A seer is one who may see God, who may talk with God, who may receive personal instruction from God. Our prophet is a seer and a revelator. There must be someone to whom the people can turn and trust, who can speak for God. God must have someone on earth who can point the way and say, "This is true!" God has given us a living seer and prophet (who) reveals personal testimony that Jesus is in very deed the Risen Savior, the Living God." (Theodore Burton, C.R., 10/1961). In summary, "a prophet is a teacher of known truth, a seer is a perceiver of hidden truth, and a revelator is a bearer of new truth". (John A. Widtsoe, quoted in "Evidences and Reconciliations", p. 257-58).

When asked what made the Church different from others, Joseph Smith replied: "We have the Holy Ghost." ("The Wentworth Letter"). During the Renaissance, Western Europe enjoyed a rebirth of ideas, whose stimulus was the Holy Ghost. The Age of Enlightenment followed, and ushered in the Reformation and then the Restoration. Today, we enjoy an Age of Inspiration by the Spirit.

The Holy Ghost will lift us upward toward God our Father and Jesus Christ. Ultimately, the Holy Ghost is the wind beneath our wings. He gives us the power to slip the surly bonds of earth and dance the skies, joining the tumbling mirth of sun-split clouds. With Him, we will wheel and soar in the sunlit silence. Hovering there, we'll chase the shouting wind along through footless halls of air. Up in the long, delirious burning blue, we'll top the windswept heights with easy grace, where never lark or even eagle flies. And, while with silent, lifting mind we'll skirt the high untrespassed sanctity of space, we'll put out our hands, and with His help, touch the face of God. (Adapted from John G. Magee, Jr., "High Flight").

The Savior used His forum among the Nephites to explain that because of the belief of the Gentiles and the unbelief of the house of Israel, "in the latter day shall the truth come unto the Gentiles, that the fulness of these things shall be made known unto them." (V. 7). For millennia, the Jews had been waiting for the Messiah. In the Meridian of Time, Israel rejected Him. Now, in the Last Days, the third member of the Godhead is manifesting His power to change lives in Israel, giving her yet another opportunity to accept the Messiah. But she must do so without dictating the terms of her covenant relationship with the Master.

None of us can afford to be complacent regarding the status of our salvation. Even while he accompanied the Lord through much of His mortal ministry, Peter was not converted to the Gospel in every sense of the word. After Christ's betrayal, he followed the Savior only at a distance, as far as the courtyard of the high priests, "to see the end." Before the cock crowed, Peter, chief among the Apostles, had denied Christ three times. (See Matthew 26:58-75). Today, many of us follow at a distance, "to see the end," and by our inaction deny the Savior. "These are they who are not valiant in the testimony of Jesus; wherefore, they obtain not the crown over the kingdom of our God." (D&C 76:79). We are courageous when we "take the Lord's side on every issue, when we think what He thinks, believe what He believes, say what He would say, and do what He would do." (Bruce R. McConkie).

Even after the appearance of the Resurrected Lord to the Apostles, Peter resumed his former occupation and announced to the others, "I go a fishing." (John 21:3). When the Savior later appeared on the shore beside the Sea of Galilee, He instructed the Apostles and said to Peter: "Follow me." (John 21:19). We are assured by the accounts of Peter's subsequent ministry that he did just that. He finally recognized that he was "elect according to the foreknowledge of God the Father, through sanctification of the Spirit, unto obedience and sprinkling of the blood of Jesus Christ." (1 Peter 1:2). He had obtained "precious faith," and became a partaker "of the divine nature." (2 Peter 1:1 & 4).

Alma had taught his son Helaman these same principles of true conversion beginning with a clear realization of iniquity and a deep godly sorrow for sin. Next came suffering and torment that motivated Alma's appeal to the Savior, Who granted forgiveness and bestowed spiritual enlightenment culminating in great joy. Born again through a process of renewal, Alma awakened to new possibilities in a life of righteousness and service. (Alma Chapter 36, see Mosiah 4:1-3, & 5:1-7). As Parley P. Pratt declared: "I have received the Holy Anointing and I can never rest until the last enemy is conquered, death destroyed, and truth reigns triumphant." (J.D., 1:15).

To "the unbelieving of the Gentiles" in the Last Days, the Savior issued a stern warning. (V. 8). These are they who have scattered, cast out, and trodden under their feet the Children of the Covenant. (See V. 8). With spiritual darkness blinding them, they have viciously persecuted Israel and caused her "to be smitten, and to be afflicted, and to be slain, and to be cast out from among them, and to become hated by them, and to become a hiss and a byword among them." (V. 9, see Commentary References to 1 Nephi 19:14, & to 3 Nephi 29:8). Since members of the Church are, largely by adoption, heirs of the Covenant, they too can expect similar treatment at the hands of the Gentile nations of the earth. As Neal A. Maxwell once observed: "With fractious religion, Satan is indifferent. But when the Church was restored with the Priesthood, all hell broke loose." ("B.Y.U. Devotional", 8/1977).

The Savior said that the day would soon come when the Gentiles "shall sin against my gospel, and shall reject the fulness of my gospel, and shall be lifted up in the pride of their hearts above all nations, and above all the people of the whole earth, and shall be filled with all manner of lyings, and of deceits, and of mischiefs, and all manner of hypocrisy, and murders, and priestcrafts, and whoredoms, and of secret abominations; and if they shall do all those things, and shall reject the fullness of my gospel, behold, saith the Father, I will bring the fulness of my gospel from among them." (V. 10). Today, the behavior of the Gentiles is leading them in the direction of the rejection of both the Savior and the Plan of Salvation. Their carnality, sensuality, and devilishness are clear evidence that Satan has made significant inroads among the Gentiles in our day.

Ezra Taft Benson, quoting Laurence Gould, declared: "I do not believe the greatest threat to our future is from bombs or missiles. I do not think our civilization will die that way. I think it will die when we no longer care, when the spiritual forces that make us wish to be right and noble die in the hearts of men, when we disregard the importance of law and order, and the basic principles upon which this nation has been built. Great nations are never conquered from outside, unless they are rotten inside. Our greatest national problem today is erosion of the national morality". (Cited in: "The American Challenge", see Commentary Reference to Alma 4:19).

The problem today is not only within the "Gentile" population, but also within the congregations of the Saints. Joseph Fielding Smith warned: "We should wake up to the realization that it is because of the breaking of covenants, especially the new and everlasting covenant, which is the fulness of the Gospel as it has been revealed, that the world is to be consumed by fire and few men left. Since this punishment is to come at the time of the cleansing of the earth when Christ comes again, should not Latter-day Saints take heed unto themselves? We have been given the new and everlasting covenant, and many among us have broken it, and many are now breaking it; therefore, all who are guilty of this offense will aid in bringing to pass the destruction in which they will find themselves swept from the earth when the great and dreadful day of the Lord shall come." ("Deseret News", 10/17/1936).

One of the best-known teachings of the Jews is that when we alienate ourselves from God, all nature becomes our enemy. The converse is also true. In the days of Enoch, because of the wickedness of the people, when he spoke the word of the Lord by the power of the priesthood, "the earth trembled, and the mountains fled, even according to his command; and the rivers of water were turned out of their course; and the roar of the lions was heard out of the wilderness." (Moses 7:13).

In the Last Days, "plagues shall go forth, and they shall not be taken from the earth" until the Lord has completed His work. (D&C 84:97). "And thus, with the sword and by bloodshed the inhabitants of the earth shall mourn; and with famine, and plague, and earthquake, and the thunder of heaven, and the fierce and vivid lightning also, shall the inhabitants of the earth be made to feel the wrath, and indignation, and chastening hand of an Almighty God, until the consumption decreed hath made a full end of all nations." (D&C 87:6). As Brigham Young declared, when people refuse the Gospel, their "land will eventually become desolate, forlorn, and forsaken" as nature refuses her bounties. ("Ancient and Modern Perspectives on The Book of Moses", p. 394).

The time will come when the Gentile nations of the earth will reject the invitation to accept the Gospel and will refuse to join Israel, to be numbered among the Children of the Covenant. Then, the times of the Gentiles will be fulfilled, and the Gospel will be taken to Israel. "And then," said the Lord, "will I remember my covenant which I have made unto my people, O house of Israel, and I will bring my gospel unto them." (V. 11). In those days, "as many of the Gentiles as will repent (shall become) the covenant people of the Lord; and as many of the Jews as will not repent shall be cast off; for the Lord covenanteth with none save it be with them that repent and believe in his Son, who is the Holy One of Israel." (2 Nephi 30:2).

Israel will come to the knowledge of the fulness of the Gospel largely after the Second Coming. (V. 11). At that time, the covenant people of the Lord "shall go through among (the wicked) and shall tread them down, and they shall be as salt that hath lost its savor." (V. 15). "Then," after the initiation of the millennial reign of Christ, "the words of the prophet Isaiah shall be fulfilled, which say: Thy watchmen shall lift up the voice; with the voice together shall they sing, for they shall see eye to eye when the Lord shall bring again Zion." (V. 17-18, see Isaiah 52:8-10). A Zion society, composed of the pure in heart, shall see the ultimate triumph of good over evil, and it shall "break forth into joy" and shall "sing together." (V. 19). "All the ends of the earth shall see the salvation of God." (V. 20).

Third Nephi
Chapter 17

At this point in His ministry among the Nephites, Jesus announced: "Behold my time is at hand." (V. 1). In other words, He would return to "the Father, and also show (Himself) unto the lost tribes of Israel." (V. 4). The Lord had promised that in the mouths of 3 great scriptural witnesses, His divinity would be established. (See 2 Nephi 29:11-14). Now, the resurrected Lord would appear to all the people who would record these witnesses.

Before He left, He commanded the multitude to return to their homes "and ponder upon the things" that He had said, and to pray to the Father for understanding, so that when He returned the next day, they would be prepared to receive further instruction. (V. 3). Moroni included "pondering," a form of prayer, as one of the essential requirements for gaining a testimony of The Book of Mormon. (See 1 Nephi 11:1, & 2 Nephi 4:16).

Incidentally, the fact that the multitude had homes to which they could return suggests that these events must have taken place some time after the great devastation in the land, that is chronicled in 3 Nephi chapter 8. (See 3 Nephi 19:1). In verse 7, the Savior asked if there were any sick or injured among the multitude, which also suggests there had been time for them to at least begin the process of healing from the terrible days of destruction. (See Commentary Reference to 3 Nephi 18:1). "All the multitude, with one accord, did go forth with their sick and their afflicted," and the Savior healed every one. (V. 9). Then, "He commanded that their little children should be brought." (V. 11). This was a very sacred moment, and so the Savior "commanded the multitude that they should kneel down upon the ground." (V. 13).

The Savior then offered a prayer to the Father that was so special that it could not "be written, and the multitude did bear record who heard him. And after this manner do they bear record: The eye hath never seen, neither hath the ear heard, before, so great and marvelous things as we saw and heard Jesus speak unto the Father. And no tongue can speak, neither can there be written by any man, neither can the hearts of men conceive so great and marvelous things as we both saw and heard Jesus speak; and no one can conceive of the joy which filled our souls at the time we heard him pray for us unto the Father." (V. 15-17). So great was the faith of the multitude that the Savior declared His joy was full, and he wept. (V. 20). After taking "their little children, one by one, (He) blessed them, and prayed unto the Father for them." (V. 21). And then, He wept again. (V. 22).

The Spirit was overwhelming. As the multitude raised their eyes, "they saw the heavens open, and they saw angels descending out of heaven as it were in the midst of fire; and they came down and encircled those little ones about, and they were encircled about with fire; and the angels did minister unto them." (V. 24, see Commentary References to 2 Nephi 16:2, & to Helaman 5:43-47).

Truly did the poet declare: "Not in entire forgetfulness, and not in utter nakedness, but trailing clouds of glory do we come, from God, Who is our Home." (Wordsworth, "Ode on Intimations of Immortality"). These special children probably numbered in the hundreds, because they came from a group of "about two thousand and five hundred souls; and they did consist of men, women, and children." (V. 25). Perhaps they formed the nucleus of those who would soon form a Zion society in Zarahemla, where "the people were all converted unto the Lord, upon all the face of the land, both Nephites and Lamanites." (4 Nephi 1:2, see Commentary References to 3 Nephi 6:14, & 4 Nephi 1:2). Certainly, after such an experience, they would desire to be obedient to the Master, that they might be "partakers of the heavenly gift" and be "one, the Children of Christ, and heirs to the kingdom of God." (4 Nephi 1:3 & 17).

Third Nephi
Chapter 18

Before He left, the Savior "commanded his disciples that they should bring forth some bread and wine unto him." (V. 1). Here is another evidence that time had passed since the destruction in the land, for the disciples were able to obtain enough to serve a congregation of 2,500 people. Jesus broke the bread, blessed it, and gave it to His twelve disciples, who in turn served it to the multitude. The entire assembly was "filled" with the Spirit. (V. 3-4). He then explained that this was to be an observance among the people, and that the ordinance should be administered by one bearing the Aaronic Priesthood. "Behold, there shall be one ordained among you," He said, "and to him will I give power that he shall break bread and bless it and give it unto the people of my church, and unto all those who shall believe and be baptized in my name. And this shall ye always observe to do." (V. 5-6).

The Sacrament, then, was to be administered to members of the Church. Today, when non-members attend Church services and partake of the Sacrament, it is of no binding effect, since they have not entered the Fold of the Shepherd through baptism and no covenant relationship has been established. As the Savior taught: "This shall ye do in remembrance of my body, which I have shown unto you. And it shall be a testimony unto the Father that ye do always remember me. And if ye do always remember me ye shall have my Spirit to be with you." (V. 7, see Commentary References to Mormon 9:29, & to Moroni chapter 4.)

Then Jesus introduced the wine, and the disciples and congregation were "filled" with the Spirit. (V. 8-9, see D&C 27:2, & Commentary References to Moroni chapter 5). "And this," He said, "ye shall always do to those who repent and are baptized in my name; and ye shall do it in remembrance of my blood, which I have shed for you, that ye may witness unto the Father that ye do always remember me. And if ye do always remember me ye shall have my Spirit to be with you." (V. 11).

The J.S.T. reads: "For this is in remembrance of my blood of the new testament, which is shed for as many as shall believe on my name, for the remission of their sins." (J.S.T. Matthew 26:24). In other words, Christ's Atonement was for the remission of sins, and the emblems of the Sacrament are tokens in remembrance of that sacrifice.

Moroni knew that his father Mormon had not included verbatim the words of the covenant in his abridgment of Third Nephi - The Book of Nephi. Therefore, when he wrote his appendices upon The Plates of Mormon, he included the exact words of both prayers. (See Moroni Chapters 4 & 5). Constantly in The Book of Mormon, we encounter specific explanations of principles and pointed Gospel doctrine. The record is replete with precept and example. Truly, did the Savior say to those who read The Book of Mormon: "If ye shall always do these things blessed are ye, for ye are built upon my rock." (V. 12).

Jesus Christ is the personification of the Rock of Revelation. He is the physical expression of the One Eternal God. His message is "the only and true doctrine of the Father, and of the Son, and of the Holy Ghost, which is one God, without end." (2 Nephi 31:21). He "doth not walk in crooked paths, neither doth he turn to the right hand nor to the left, neither doth he vary from that which he hath said, therefore his paths are straight, and his course is one eternal round." (D&C 3:2).

Because He is the Rock, "no power on earth or hell can overthrow or defeat that which God has decreed. Every plan of the adversary will fail, for the Lord knows the secret thoughts of men, and sees the future with a vision clear and perfect, even as though it were in the past." (Joseph Fielding Smith, Jr., "Doctrine & Covenants Institute Student Manual," Section 3). "O how great the holiness of our God!" cried Jacob. "For he knoweth all things, and there is not anything save he knows it." (2 Nephi 9:20). "Else He would cease to be God, and man could not have faith in him." (Joseph Fielding Smith, Jr. "Doctrines of Salvation," 1:7-10).

"But whoso among you shall do more or less than these are not built upon my rock, but are built upon a sandy foundation." (V. 13). Unstable telestial turf is Satan's home ground, and when we venture onto it, we "reel to and fro, and stagger like a drunken man, and are at (our) wit's end." (Psalms 107:27). The quicksand of secular humanism and other false ideologies lies ready to suck us into the underworld of the adversary. When we fall, as we inevitably will, "the gates of hell" will be open to receive us. (V. 13).

But because faithful Saints hold to the iron rod, "no unhallowed hand can stop the work from progressing; persecutions may rage, mobs may combine, armies may assemble, calumny may defame, but the truth of God will go forth boldly, nobly, and independent, until it has penetrated every continent, visited every clime, swept every country, and sounded in every ear, 'til the purposes of God shall be accomplished and the Great Jehovah shall say 'The work is done.'" (Joseph Smith, in The Wentworth Letter, H.C., 4:540).

Immediately after teaching the Nephites how to always have the Spirit to be with them, the Lord gave the disciples the key to successfully remembering Him. "Verily, verily," He said to them, "ye must watch and pray always, lest ye be tempted by the devil, and ye be led away captive by him." (V. 15). He then revealed: "For Satan desireth to have you, that he may sift you as wheat. Therefore, ye must always pray unto the Father in my name." (V. 18-19).

He is the Standard of Righteousness, Who said: "Behold I am the light; I have set an example for you." (V. 16). As He had prayed, so He urged the Nephites to pray: "Therefore, ye must always pray unto the Father in my name. (V. 19). "Pray in your families unto the Father, always in my name." (V. 21). All were to be welcome at their meetings. To the members of the congregation of the faithful, the Savior reiterated: "Ye shall pray for them unto the Father, in my name." (V. 23).

Christ was to be the Light that they were to hold up, and He was the Example they were to follow. (V. 24). When He said: "Let your light so shine before this people that they may see your good works and glorify your Father who is in heaven," He meant that He should be reflected in all that they did, so that when men saw their good works, their thoughts would turn to Him. His disciples were to do more than "simply multiply mirrors and study the angles without increasing the light." (B.H. Roberts, "The Truth, The Way, The Life," p. 263). They were not to be as peas in a pod. Of such, Emerson wrote: "I cannot tell them apart. It is the old story again; once we had wooden chalices and golden priests. Now we have golden chalices and wooden priests." ("Lectures and Biographical Sketches," p. 180).

At the same time, the Savior in His own turn gave the glory to His Father. He said: "Behold, ye see that I have prayed unto the Father, and ye all have witnessed." (V. 24). We learn from chapters 4 and 5 in The Book of Moroni and in Doctrine & Covenants Section 20 that the Sacrament Prayer is addressed to the Father in the name of Jesus Christ.

This is the proper form that prayer in general should take, that the Savior reiterated many times to the Nephites. (See verses 19, 21, & 23 above, and 3 Nephi 19:6).

Turning his attention to the Twelve, Jesus said: "I give unto you another commandment, and then I must go unto my Father that I may fulfil other commandments which he hath given me." (V. 27, see 3 Nephi 16:3). Reminding the congregation that He had counseled them that they should deny the Sacrament to no-one, He instructed the Twelve, who were to preside over Church services and were common judges in Israel, that there was one serious limitation to His injunction. "Ye shall not suffer any one knowingly to partake of my flesh and blood unworthily, when ye shall minister it." (V. 28, see Mormon 9:29). "For whoso eateth and drinketh my flesh and blood unworthily eateth and drinketh damnation to his soul." (V. 29). Partaking of the emblems of Christ unworthily blocks the channels through which spiritual power flows. Those who would do so, would partake of sacred emblems in vain, or to no effect. The progression of such individuals would be stalled, with damnation the eternal consequence in the absence of sincere repentance

When the Savior later administered the Sacrament to the Nephites, He said of those who had partaken, that their souls "shall never hunger nor thirst, but shall be filled … with the Spirit." (3 Nephi 20:8-9). James Talmage taught: "The Sacrament has not been established as a specific means of securing remission of sins, nor for any other special blessing, aside from that of a continuing endowment of the Holy Spirit." ("Articles of Faith," p. 175). That, Joseph Smith taught, should be enough to bring us into the presence of God.

"Nevertheless," the Savior continued, "ye shall not cast him out from among you, but ye shall minister unto him and shall pray for him unto the Father, in my name." (V. 30). These verses might also apply to non-members of the Church, who, if they partook of the Sacrament, would be doing so "in vain," and might therefore be mocking God. For the Savior continued: "If it so be that he repenteth and is baptized in my name, then shall ye receive him, and shall minister unto him of my flesh and blood." (V. 30).

This verse might also refer to the restriction of privileges to partake of the Sacrament by members of the Church who had committed sins. When they had repented, and were again true to their baptismal covenants, they would be allowed to participate in the ordinance of the Sacrament. But if such a person would not repent, said the Savior, "he shall not be numbered among my people, that he may not destroy my people." (V. 31). His rights and privileges of membership would be withdrawn.

"Nevertheless," the Savior continued, "ye shall not cast him out of your synagogues, or your places of worship, for unto such shall ye continue to minister; for ye know not but what they will return and repent, and come unto me with full purpose of heart, and I shall heal them; and ye shall be the means of bringing salvation unto them." (V. 32, see Commentary Reference to Alma 16:13).

Jesus gave the twelve disciples these instructions in order to clear up any disputations that they might have had, concerning how they ought to carry out their duties. (V. 34). They had only recently been called, and the rock of revelation from the Master would anchor them securely to the administration of their ecclesiastical responsibilities.

He gave each of them His divine stamp of approval by setting them apart in their new callings. "And it came to pass that when Jesus had made an end of these sayings, he touched with his hand the disciples whom he had chosen, one by one, even until he had touched them all, and spake unto them as he touched them." (V. 36, see Alma 31:36).

Among other things, the twelve were given the Melchizedek Priesthood, that is the power to administer the spiritual affairs of the Church. (See D&C 84:19-20). "He gave them power to give the Holy Ghost." (V. 37, see Commentary

Reference to Moroni 2:1). These ordinances were documented in Moroni 2:1, as Mormon said they would be: "And I will show unto you hereafter that this record is true." (V. 37).

When He "had touched them all, there came a cloud and overshadowed the multitude that they could not see Jesus." (V. 38). In scripture, the cloud always represents the presence of the Lord. (See Exodus 19:9). The symbolism was not lost on the multitude, to whom the disciples bore record that "he ascended again into heaven." (V. 39).

Third Nephi
Chapter 19

Again, we are led to believe that a significant amount of time had passed from the events surrounding the crucifixion of the Lord. Conditions had stabilized in the land to such an extent that "every man did take his wife and his children and did return to his own home" after Jesus had ascended into heaven. (V. 1).

The Savior had promised the people that he would return the next day. (V. 2, see 3 Nephi 17:3). Preparations were made by "an exceedingly great number, (who) did labor all that night, that they might be on the morrow in the place where Jesus should show himself unto the multitude." (V. 3).

Among these were those whom Jesus had chosen to be his "disciples." Spencer W. Kimball taught: "There is no question that they acted as apostles." The names of these special witnesses were "Nephi, and his brother whom he had raised from the dead, whose name was Timothy, and also his son whose name was Jonas, and also Mathoni, and Mathonihah, his brother, and Kumen, and Kumenonhi, and Jeremiah, and Shemnon, and Jonas, and Zedekiah, and Isaiah." (V. 4).

The people who gathered were divided, with each of the twelve disciples taking charge of one group. Now, they prayed as they had been taught to do so by the Savior. (See 3 Nephi 18:21). The disciples "did cause that the multitude should kneel down upon the face of the earth, and should pray unto the Father in the name of Jesus." (V. 6, see 3 Nephi 18:24).

The twelve set the example themselves, praying "unto the Father also in the name of Jesus." (V. 7). Then "they arose, and ministered unto the people. And when they had ministered those same words which Jesus had spoken - nothing varying from the words which Jesus had spoken - behold, they knelt again and prayed to the Father in the name of Jesus." (V. 8-9).

Their desire was to receive the Holy Ghost. (V. 10). They had previously been baptized for the remission of sins, but whereas the Church had operated under the Law of Moses, it was now restructured under the Law of the Gospel. This same organizational format was repeated in 1829 and 1830, at the time of the restoration of the Gospel in the Last Days. (See D&C 13, & Commentary Reference to 3 Nephi 11:22).

Accordingly, "Nephi went down into the water and was baptized." (V. 11). This was most likely done by one of his brethren who had recently received the authority to do so from the Savior. (See 3 Nephi 12:1 & 18:36-37). After Nephi baptized the others of the twelve, "the Holy Ghost did fall upon them, and they were filled with the Holy Ghost and with fire," just as the Savior had promised. (V. 13, see 3 Nephi 12:2 & 18:36-37).

It was truly a Pentecostal experience, and both Nephi and Mormon pointedly documented the reality of the episode, recording that "they were encircled about as if it were by fire; and it came down from heaven, and the multitude did witness it, and did bear record; and angels did come down out of heaven and did minister unto them." (V. 14). They were standing upon holy ground, and when the Savior appeared in their midst, He "commanded them that they should kneel down again upon the earth." (V. 16).

It was as it had been in the days of the Exodus, when the Lord commanded Moses: "Put off thy shoes from off thy feet, for the place whereon thou standest is holy ground." Then, for emphasis, He invoked the name of God three (or even four!) times. For "I am the God of thy father, the God of Abraham, the God of Isaac, and the God of Jacob." (Exodus 3:5-6). Now, the Lord "commanded his disciples that they should pray. And behold, they began to pray; and they did pray unto Jesus, calling him their Lord and their God." (V. 17-18, underlining mine). We can understand why the people would again focus their petitions upon the God of Israel Who was standing in their midst. When He commanded them to pray, they would naturally address Immanuel: "God with us." (See V. 22). Mormon was guided by the Spirit to record the private conversation that occurred between the Savior and His Father during this prayer meeting. Jesus said: "Father, thou hast given them the Holy Ghost because they believe in me; and thou seest that they believe in me because thou hearest them, and they pray unto me; and they pray unto me because I am with them." (V. 22).

The Savior supplicated the Father, asking that there might be complete harmony in the household of faith, and "that I may be in them as thou, Father, art in me, that we may be one." (V. 23, see Ephesians 2:29). This is the peace that surpasses all understanding, and is the unity that eludes the world. It is a concept that is alien to the carnal mind. When the Spirit brings men and women to a correct understanding of the nature of God, they are poised to embark on the journey of eternal progression leading to eternal life. As the Savior said: "This is life eternal, that they might know thee the only true God, and Jesus Christ, whom thou hast sent." (John 17:3).

When Jesus returned to the multitude, He found that "they did still continue, without ceasing, to pray unto him." (V. 24). In language unique in the scriptures, Mormon wrote: "His countenance did smile upon them, and behold they were as white as the countenance and also the garments of Jesus; and behold the whiteness thereof did exceed all the whiteness, yea, even there could be nothing upon earth so white as the whiteness thereof." (V. 25, see V. 30).

Again, He went a little way off from the multitude, and prayed to the Father, thanking Him for giving the Twelve the sanctifying influence of the Holy Ghost. (V. 27-28). They would form the nucleus of His salvation army and would be instrumental in extending to thousands the invitation to join the Church.

The Savior made a careful distinction between those who use their agency to make poor choices and who delight in temporal pleasures that are carnal, sensual, and devilish, and those who choose to take up their cross and follow the sometimes-difficult path leading to the Celestial Kingdom of God. He said: "Father, I pray not for the world, but for those whom thou hast given me out of the world, because of their faith, that they may be purified in me, that I may be in them as thou, Father, art in me, that we may be one, that I may be glorified in them." (V. 29). His was a totally selfless dedication to the eternal welfare of His brethren. He was the Great Exemplar, the Master, the Author of Salvation, and the Redeemer of any and all who make legitimate claims upon the blessings of the Abrahamic Covenant.

"He did smile upon (the multitude) again; and behold they were white, even as Jesus." (V. 30, see v. 25). They had been purified in His redeeming blood, and by the grace of God were saved. They enjoyed the companionship of the

Second Comforter, and their faces reflected His Light. (See D&C 88:3-7, & Commentary Reference to 3 Nephi 18:24). To the Latter-day Saints, the Lord re-affirmed: "And if your eye be single to my glory, your whole bodies shall be filled with light, and there shall be no darkness in you." (D&C 88:67).

He then spoke to the Father in language that could not be corrupted by Mormon's profane abridgement. (V. 31-33). Mormon wrote: "So great and marvelous were the words which he prayed, that they cannot be written, neither can they be uttered by man." (V. 34). Sometimes the gulf between the sacred and the secular is just too great to bridge with words.

But the multitude was spiritually prepared to receive these things, and so they did hear and "bear record; and their hearts were open, and they did understand in their hearts the words which he prayed." (V. 33). Their faith was greater than the Savior had "seen among all the Jews," and it was rewarded in a most marvelous way. Jesus told them: "There are none of them that have seen so great things as ye have seen, neither have they heard so great things as ye have heard." (V. 36).

This lesson from ancient scripture gives us hope that Christ will come again, and manifest Himself among the faithful, and that when He does, it will be a supernal experience. "Sanctify yourselves," we are told, "that your minds become single to God, and the days will come that you shall see him; for he will unveil his face unto you." (D&C 88:68, see D&C 93:1).

"And when Jesus had spoken these words, he came again unto his disciples; and behold, they did pray steadfastly without ceasing unto him; and he did smile upon them again."
(3 Nephi 19:30).

Third Nephi
Chapter 20

When the Savior commanded that the multitude cease their prayers, He made it clear that He desired that they continue to always to carry a prayer in their hearts. "And it came to pass that he commanded the multitude that they should cease to pray, and also his disciples. And he commanded them that they should not cease to pray in their hearts." (V. 1, see Commentary Reference to Alma 24:19). He then "brake bread again and blessed it, and gave to the disciples to eat." (V. 3). Then He commanded the disciples to offer the emblems of the Sacrament to the multitude. (V. 4-5).

No bread or wine had been provided by the disciples or by the multitude that had gathered, "but he truly gave unto them bread to eat, and also wine to drink." (V. 7). The Creator of the earth provided the emblems.

"And he said unto them: He that eateth this bread eateth of my body to his soul; and he that drinketh of this wine drinketh of my blood to his soul; and his soul shall never hunger nor thirst, but shall be filled. Now, when the multitude had all eaten and drunk, behold, they were filled with the Spirit", just as food nourishes the physical body. (V. 8-9). In the Sacrament, and in the other ordinances of the priesthood, "the power of Godliness is manifest. And without the ordinances thereof, and the authority of the priesthood, the power of godliness is not manifest unto men in the flesh. For without this no man can see the face of God, even the Father, and live." (D&C 84:20-22). But these chapters in Third Nephi are a testament to the fact that these Nephites, who entertained the Resurrected Savior in their midst, did enjoy the power of godliness.

James Talmage taught: "The Sacrament has not been established as a specific means of securing remission of sins, nor for any other special blessing aside from that of a continuing endowment of the Holy Spirit." ("Articles of Faith," p. 175, see Commentary Reference to 3 Nephi 18:28). Church members who are bound to a higher standard of obedience by the Covenant of Baptism are particularly blessed to be able to enjoy the ordinance of the Sacrament on a continuing basis. Companionship with the Holy Ghost is essential for those who have moved beyond a law of carnal commandments to a celestial standard.

Then, the Savior declared: "Behold, now I finish the commandment which the Father hath commanded me concerning this people." (V. 10, see 3 Nephi 16:17-20). The people had been brought to the knowledge of God and had been provided with priests and teachers to administer the ordinances. The Nephite society that had been spared during the great destruction in the land of Zarahemla was squarely set on the path leading to eternal life. "The Covenant which the Father (had) made unto his people" had been fulfilled. (V. 12).

The Lord indicated that there would yet be "remnants which shall be scattered abroad upon the face of the earth." (V. 13). When these would come to a knowledge of the truth, He promised that they would "be gathered in from the east and from the west, and from the south and from the north." (V. 13). We see the fulfilment of that promise today, as Israel is gathered from the four corners of the earth and the isles of the sea.

The Lord then confirmed for the Nephite faithful that it was the desire of their Father that they have a land of promise for their inheritance. (V. 14). Whether this refers to the rather narrowly defined geographical location of the land of the Nephites, or the whole of the American continent, is not clear, but from the pronouncements of modern-day prophets, it seems that the Western Hemisphere, in general, qualifies as a "Land of Promise."

There follows a warning to the "Gentiles (who) do not repent after the blessing which they shall receive, after they have scattered" the remnant of Jacob. (V. 16). These Gentiles are those who have not entered into a covenant relationship with God. The Lord said: "Then shall ye, who are a remnant of the house of Jacob, go forth among them; and ye shall be in the midst of them who shall be many; and ye shall be among them as a lion among the beasts of the forest, and as a young lion among the flocks of sheep, who, if he goeth through both treadeth down and teareth in pieces, and none can deliver." (V. 16). This may refer to the mighty missionary army that will march through spiritual Babylon in the Last Days. (See Commentary Reference to 3 Nephi 21:12).

That force of missionaries will be "clear as the moon, and fair as the sun, and terrible as an army with banners." (D&C 5:14, see Song of Solomon 6:10). "And the day shall come when the nations of the earth shall tremble because of her, and shall fear because of her terrible ones." (D&C 64:43). "And it shall be said among the wicked: Let us not go up to battle against Zion, for the inhabitants of Zion are terrible; wherefore we cannot stand." (D&C 45:70). "Fear may seize upon them, and they shall stand afar off and tremble. And all nations shall be afraid because of the terror of the Lord, and the power of his might." (D&C 45:74-75).

Since the Lord's Hand will rule in the Last Days, His people need not fear the threats and oaths of the wicked. "For," He promised, "I will make my people with whom the Father hath covenanted, yea, I will make thy horn iron, and I will make thy hoofs brass. And thou shalt beat in pieces many people; and I will consecrate their gain unto the Lord, and their substance unto the Lord of the whole earth. And behold, I am he who doeth it." (V. 19).

The wicked will be dealt with in a fair and equitable manner. The awful reality, though, will be that they will have no claim upon Mercy, nor upon their telestial treasures or their ill-gotten gain. "The sword of my justice shall hang over them at that day;" warned the Lord, "and except they repent it shall fall upon them, saith the Father, yea, even upon all the nations of the Gentiles." (V. 20).

As the demands of Justice require the destruction of the wicked, the Lord declared: "It shall come to pass that I will establish my people, O house of Israel." (V. 21). He specifically addressed that remnant dwelling in the land of the Americas, saying: "This people will I establish in this land, unto the fulfilling of the covenant which I made with your father, Jacob; and it shall be a New Jerusalem. And the powers of heaven shall be in the midst of this people; yea, even I will be in the midst of you." (V. 22).

The Savior confirmed that it was He of whom Moses had spoken, when he declared: "A prophet shall the Lord your God raise up unto you of your brethren, like unto me; him shall ye hear in all things whatsoever he shall say to you. And it shall come to pass that every soul who will not hear that prophet shall be cut off from among the people." (V. 23, see Deuteronomy 18:15-19, Acts 3:22-23, & D&C 133:63).

All the prophets have testified of Christ, and have confirmed upon Israel the covenant blessings of Abraham. (V.

24-25). Even after their scourging at the hands of the Gentiles, the land promised to Israel would be given to their descendants as an inheritance. (V. 27-29). This promise has only recently been fulfilled; in Joseph Smith's day, it was only the dream of the most visionary Jews and ardent Zionists.

In due time, "the fulness of (the) Gospel shall be preached unto them." (V. 30). "And they shall believe in me, that I am Jesus Christ, the Son of God, and shall pray unto the Father in my name." (V. 31). This prophecy has yet to be fulfilled.

"And then shall be brought to pass that which is written:" Awake, awake again, and put on thy strength, O Zion; put on thy beautiful garments, O Jerusalem, the holy city." (V. 36). The Doctrine & Covenants provides the explanation to this scripture: "What is meant by the command in Isaiah, 52nd chapter, 1st verse, which saith: Put on thy strength, O Zion - and what people had Isaiah reference to? He had reference to those whom God should call in the last days, who should hold the power of priesthood to bring again Zion, and the redemption of Israel; and to put on her strength is to put on the authority of the priesthood, which she, Zion, has a right to by lineage; also, to return to that power which she had lost." (D&C 113:7-8).

God will bring to pass what man has been unable to accomplish for two millennia - the Gathering of Israel. It will be through the efforts of the First Presidency of the Church of Jesus Christ of Latter-day Saints, beginning with the Prophet Joseph Smith, that this will come to pass. When the Kirtland Temple was dedicated, the prayer offered by Joseph included a plea that "the children of Judah (might) begin to return" to the lands which God had given to their father Abraham. (D&C 109:63). Soon thereafter, Moses appeared in that temple and committed to Joseph Smith "the keys of the gathering of Israel from the four parts of the earth, and the leading of the ten tribes from the land of the north." (D&C 110:11). Later, by direction of the Prophet, Orson Hyde traveled to the Holy Land and stood on the Mount of Olives, overlooking the Old City of Jerusalem. From that vantage point, he offered a prayer, dedicating the land for the return of the Jews. (See Commentary Reference to 3 Nephi 29:8).

With the blessing and power of the priesthood of God, Israel shall "loose (herself) from the bands of (her) neck." (V. 37). Joseph Smith explained: "We are to understand that the scattered remnants are exhorted to return to the Lord from whence they have fallen; which if they do, the promise of the Lord is that he will speak to them, or give them revelation ... The bands of her neck are the curses of God upon her, or the remnants of Israel in their scattered condition among the Gentiles." (D&C 113:10).

In the millennial day, when the Lord personally comes to the earth to reign over the righteous for a thousand years, Israel shall certainly "know (His) name; yea, in that day they shall know that (Christ) is he that doth speak. And then shall they say: How beautiful upon the mountains are the feet of him that bringeth good tidings unto them, that publisheth peace; that bringeth good tidings unto them of good, that publisheth salvation; that saith unto Zion: Thy God reigneth!" (V. 39-40).

The Savior is "the founder of peace." (Mosiah 15:18). "His peace is not the peace of the world of ease, of luxury, idleness, absence of turmoil and strife, but the peace born of the righteous life, the peace that lifts the soul, that day by day brings us closer to the home of Eternal Peace, the dwelling place of our Father." (J. Reuben Clark, Jr.).

The Savior loved Isaiah; as a matter of fact, he was the Old Testament prophet whom the Lord most often quoted during His mortal ministry. In the last verses of this chapter, He returned to a quotation of what we know as Isaiah chapter 52.

Six hundred years earlier, Nephi had quoted many of the words that had been spoken by the prophet Isaiah. At that time, he was difficult for his people to understand. As Nephi wrote: "They know not concerning the manner of prophesying among the Jews." (2 Nephi 25:1). Only Nephi and his brother Sam had lived at Jerusalem, and he was admittedly reluctant to teach his children "after the manner of the Jews." (2 Nephi 25:5-6). The Hebrew prophets spoke in figures, using types and shadows to illustrate their points, in a style that was unfamiliar to the Nephites.

When the Savior ministered among the Jews, he had quoted Isaiah to an unbelieving people, who no more recognized His divinity than they had understood the types and shadows used by the prophets of old, Nephi's declaration notwithstanding. (See 2 Nephi 25:5). Fortunately, among members of The Church of Jesus Christ of Latter-day Saints, there has been greater spiritual comprehension.

Third Nephi
Chapter 21

The Savior told the gathered multitude that he would give them a sign, that they might know the time when the gathering of Israel from its long dispersion would take place. (V. 1). This chapter introduces that message, and the Lord's direct quotation of Isaiah chapter 54 that follows completes the prophecy. The sign that would indicate when all these things of which He had prophesied would begin to be fulfilled is clearly related to the descendants of those who were listening to these words of the Savior.

As He said in verse 7: "And when these things come to pass that thy seed shall begin to know these things - it shall be a sign unto them, that they may know that the work of the Father hath already commenced unto the fulfilling of the covenant which he hath made unto the people who are of the house of Israel." Specifically, it is their very knowledge of the Gospel and of The Book of Mormon that is the sign. Acting upon the sign and joining the Church of Christ becomes the key elements in the redemption of Israel.

Because all nations of the earth have been blessed because of the covenants anciently made between God and Abraham, even the Gentiles may join Israel and "repent and come unto (Christ) and be baptized in (His) name and know of the true points of (His) doctrine." (V. 6). As Nephi had taught: "As many of the Gentiles as will repent are the covenant people of the Lord." (2 Nephi 30:2).

The Savior indicated to the Nephites that in the day when the Latter-day Restoration bursts upon the world stage, it will be of such significance "that kings shall shut their mouths." (V. 8). Its destiny is to become the greatest power the world has ever known. "For in that day," declared the Savior, "shall the Father work a work, which shall be a great and marvelous work among them." (V. 9).

The Savior then prophesied that critical to the success of the Restoration would be the activities of a faithful servant in the hand of the Lord. (V. 9-10). We know and testify to the world that this scripture refers to the Prophet Joseph Smith. To reject his testimony is to reject the words of Jesus Christ Himself, and the eternal consequences are as far-reaching. (V. 11).

The Lord revealed His anger toward the wicked in a latter-day revelation to Joseph Smith, declaring: "The arm of the Lord shall be revealed, and the day cometh that they who will not hear the voice of the Lord, neither the voice of his servants, neither give heed to the words of the prophets and apostles, shall be cut off from among the people." (D&C 1:14). To the Nephites, He declared: "My people who are a remnant of Jacob shall be among the Gentiles, yea, in the midst of them as a lion among the beasts of the forest, as a young lion among the flocks of sheep." (V. 12, see Commentary Reference to 3 Nephi 20:16). Surely the word of the Lord "is quick and powerful, sharper than a two-edged sword, to the dividing asunder of both joints and marrow." (D&C 6:2). In a biblical sense, "quick" means "living" or "alive"; for example, "to be quickened by the Spirit" is "to be given spiritual life." The power of God is a source of life energy, which is power in the truest sense, that penetrates to our innermost parts.

In other words, the servants of the Lord who bear the priesthood of God, and who by adoption enjoy the covenant blessings of Abraham, will have tremendous power over the wicked in the Last Days. "Their hand shall be lifted up upon their adversaries, and all their enemies shall be cut off." (V. 13).

The wicked "have strayed from (the) ordinances, and have broken (the) everlasting covenant; They seek not the Lord to establish his righteousness, but every man walketh in his own way, and after the image of his own god, whose image is in the likeness of the world, and whose substance is that of an idol." (D&C 1:15-16). Of such people, the Lord told the Nephites: "Thy graven images I will also cut off, and thy standing images out of the midst of thee, and thou shalt no more worship the works of thy hands." (V. 17). "And it shall come to pass that all lyings, and deceivings, and envyings, and strifes, and priestcrafts, and whoredoms, shall be done away." (V. 19).

Only those who repent, and who hearken unto the words of Christ revealed by His holy prophets and whose hearts are teachable will enjoy the blessings reserved for the righteous. The Savior said: "I will establish my church among them, and they shall come in unto the covenant and be numbered among this the remnant of Jacob, unto whom I have given this land for their inheritance." (V. 22).

Those who have been gathered from among the Gentile nations and who claim the blessings of the Abrahamic Covenant by adoption, will assist "as many of the house of Israel as shall come, that they may build a city, which shall be called the New Jerusalem." (V. 23). This holy city will be as a beacon to scattered Israel. The awakening of the remnant of Jacob to a remembrance of its covenant relationship with the Lord will not be confined to the descendants of Lehi alone, but will be general among all the house of Israel.

Those of The Church of Jesus Christ of Latter-day Saints, in whose veins flows the blood of Ephraim, will "assist (the remnant of Jacob) that they may be gathered in, who are scattered upon all the face of the land, in unto the New Jerusalem." (V. 24). They "shall have the power of heaven come down among them" to assist them in their work. (V. 25).

Even members of "the tribes that have been lost, which the Father hath led away out of Jerusalem" will take advantage of the spirit of gathering, and shall be numbered among the Saints. (V. 26). However, the setting for the greater work of gathering of these tribes is millennial. (See D&C 133:23-34).

The essential point is that Israel will finally be reconciled unto Christ. As Moroni declared to the descendants of Lehi who would read from the pages of The Book of Mormon in the Last Days: "Yea, come unto Christ, and be perfected in him, and deny yourselves of all ungodliness; and if ye shall deny yourselves of all ungodliness, and love God with all your might, mind and strength, then is his grace sufficient for you, that by his grace ye may be perfect in Christ." (Moroni 10:32).

The Lord promised the Nephite Saints: "The work shall commence among all the dispersed of my people, with the Father to prepare the way whereby they may come unto me, that they may call on the Father in my name." (V. 27). Once the people rally around the standard of the Gospel, they will be systematically gathered to the Land of Zion. "Yea, and then shall the work commence, with the Father among all nations in preparing the way whereby his people may be gathered home to the land of their inheritance. And they shall go out from all nations; and they shall not go out in haste, nor go by flight, for I will go before them, saith the Father." (V. 28-29).

Third Nephi
Chapter 22

In this chapter, the Savior quoted Isaiah chapter 54 in its entirety. "And then shall that which is written come to pass." (V. 1). In the Last Days, "more are the children of the desolate than the children of the married wife." (V. 1). In other words, there shall be a great gathering of Israel from among the Gentile nations, and those who enter the Fold shall outnumber those who had previously found their way into the Church, or who were bound by covenant to Christ.

Room must be made for the new Children of the Covenant who will flock to the Gospel standard as the gathering of Israel gains momentum. "Enlarge the place of thy tent, and let them stretch forth the curtains of thy habitations; spare not, lengthen thy cords and strengthen thy stakes." (V. 2). For Zion must increase in beauty, and in holiness; her borders must be enlarged; her stakes must be strengthened; yea, verily I say unto you, Zion must arise and put on her beautiful garments." (D&C 82:14).

In 1833, Joseph Smith was counseled by the Lord to gather Israel from the nations to the land of Zion in Jackson County, Missouri. There they were to remain "until the day cometh when there is found no more room for them; and then I have other places which I will appoint unto them, and they shall be called stakes, for the curtains or the strength of Zion." (D&C 101:21).

The house of Israel was told: "Thou shalt forget the shame of thy youth, and shalt not remember the reproach of thy youth." (V. 4). Isaiah counseled Israel to forsake her past mistakes and the apostasy that had for so long been her recurring inclination, for she had been brought home to the safety and security of the Master to enjoy with Him the most intimate covenant relationship. "For thy maker, thy husband, the Lord of Hosts is his name; and thy Redeemer, the Holy One of Israel - the God of the whole earth shall he be called." (V. 5).

When Israel recognizes the Savior, she shall take upon herself the beautiful garments of the priesthood of God. (See 2 Nephi 8:24). In September 1832, the Lord declared to Joseph Smith in "a revelation on priesthood": "The sons of Moses and of Aaron shall be filled with the glory of the Lord, upon Mount Zion in the Lord's house, whose sons are ye, and also many whom I have called and sent forth to build up my church." (D&C 84:32).

"For a small moment have I forsaken thee, but with great mercies will I gather thee." (V. 7). The Lord seems to be saying that briefly, He had been angry, but that is over now. "In a little wrath I hid my face from thee for a moment, but with everlasting kindness will I have mercy on thee, saith the Lord thy Redeemer." (V. 8). "For can a woman forget her sucking child, that she should not have compassion on the son of her womb?" (Isaiah 49:15).

"For as I have sworn that the waters of Noah should no more go over the earth, so have I sworn that I would not be wroth with thee." (V. 9). Just as I swore to Noah that I would never again destroy the earth by a flood, so do I swear that I will not be angry with you. "For the mountains shall depart and the hills be removed, but my kindness shall not depart from thee, neither shall the covenant of my peace be removed, saith the Lord that hath mercy on thee." (V. 10).

"Behold, I will lay thy stones with fair colors, and lay thy foundations with sapphires." (V. 11). I know that you are so sad now, but I will restore your former beauty unto you. "And I will make thy windows of agates, and thy gates of carbuncles, and all thy borders of pleasant stones." (V. 12).

"And all thy children shall be taught of the Lord, and great shall be the peace of thy children." (V. 13). Even though conditions in the world shall degenerate and peace shall be taken from the wicked, those in Zion shall enjoy the safety and security that only righteousness can guarantee, and there will be such an outpouring of the Spirit that "the earth shall be full of the knowledge of the Lord, as the waters cover the sea." (Isaiah 11:9).

"In righteousness shalt thou be established; thou shalt be far from oppression for thou shalt not fear, and from terror for it shall not come near thee." (V. 14). "And it shall be said among the wicked: Let us not go up to battle against Zion, for the inhabitants of Zion are terrible; wherefore we cannot stand." (D&C 45:70).

Isaiah's visions typically concern only Judah and Jerusalem, but inasmuch as his prophecies were often dualistic, his words may be likened to all. (See 2 Nephi 11:8 & 12:1). He clearly saw the Last Days, when "the mountain of the Lord's house (should) be established in the tops of the mountains." (2 Nephi 12:2). Latter-day Saints are prone to restrict the geographical setting of this scripture to the intermountain west and specifically to the Valley of the Great Salt Lake. But this interpretation may be too narrow. As the Lord warned Joseph Smith: "And let them who be of Judah flee unto the mountains of the Lord's house." (D&C 133:13). Jerusalem, then, must also be considered in connection to it. The word 'mountain' is used both allegorically and figuratively in the scriptures. In this verse, it refers to a high place of God, a place of revelation, and perhaps to the temple of the Lord. Eerdman's Commentary on The Bible likens 'the mountain of the Lord' to Mount Zion, that is, to Jerusalem. There is certainly ample historical precedent to do so.

Moriah has been a sacred place for over 4 millennia and will yet fulfil its ultimate destiny, as foretold in the scriptures. Whether or not the mountain of the Lord's house refers to the temple, every house of the Lord stands as a 'type' of the paradise lost in this world, of the contact point between heaven and earth, and of the final temple that the earth will become when it is renewed to receive its paradisiacal glory.

For the wicked "shall surely gather together against thee, (but they) shall fall." (V. 15). Do not worry, said the Lord, for I will be here to help you. You are not alone. "No weapon that is formed against thee shall prosper; and every tongue that shall revile against thee in judgment thou shalt condemn." (V. 17).

The message that the Lord delivered to the Nephites must have had a familiar ring, for their prophets had for centuries been quoting Isaiah from The Plates of Brass. Nephi had declared: "Yea, and my soul delighteth in the words of Isaiah." (2 Nephi 25: 5). This was so, because he knew that "in the days that the prophecies of Isaiah shall be fulfilled, men shall know of a surety, at the times when they shall come to pass. Wherefore, they are of worth unto the children of men, and he that supposeth that they are not, unto them will I speak particularly, and confine the words unto mine own people, for I know that they shall be of great worth unto them in the last days; for in that day shall they understand them; wherefore, for their good have I written them." (2 Nephi 25:7-8).

Apparently, above all the other Old Testament prophets, Isaiah has become one of our best guides through these perilous

Last Days. The words of Isaiah should strike a resonant chord with the "Lamanites, who are a remnant of the house of Israel; and also (with) Jew and Gentile." ("Title Page to The Book of Mormon"). His prophecies, so authoritatively validated by the events that are unfolding before our eyes in the Last Days, and by the Savior Himself, powerfully bear witness that "Jesus is the Christ, the Eternal God, manifesting himself unto all nations." ("Title Page to The Book of Mormon").

"Enlarge
the place of thy
tent, and let them
stretch forth the curtains
of thy habitations; spare
not, lengthen thy cords and
strengthen thy stakes."
(3 Nephi 22:2).

Third Nephi
Chapter 23

The Book of Mormon is the world's greatest commentary on the book of Isaiah. Thirty percent of Isaiah is quoted directly within its pages, and another three percent is paraphrased. The quotations from Isaiah are laced with prophetic insight by the likes of Nephi, Jacob, Abinadi, Nephi the son of Helaman, and Moroni, set in a refreshing historical matrix. As Nephi wrote: "Now I write some of the words of Isaiah, that whoso of my people shall see these words may lift up their hearts and rejoice for all men. Now these are the words, and ye may liken them unto you and unto all men. (2 Nephi 11:8).

"The version of Isaiah in the Nephite scripture hews an independent course for itself, as might be expected of a truly ancient and authentic record. It makes additions to the present text in certain places, omits material in others, transposes, makes grammatical changes, finds support at times for its unusual readings in the ancient Greek, Syriac, and Latin versions, and at other times no support at all. In general, it presents phenomena of great interest to the student of Isaiah." (Sydney B. Sperry, "Compendium of The Book of Mormon," p. 512).

The Savior commanded: "Search these things diligently; for great are the words of Isaiah." (V. 1). During His ministry among the Nephites, He gave many commandments. The people, in turn, wanted Him to stay and give them even more. They viewed His counsel as instructions to help them to enjoy a better lifestyle. They realized that His commandments were indistinguishable from our blessings associated with obedience, and that both are written, as it were, on a mobius strip, a piece of paper with only one side and one boundary component. They are universally applicable to our circumstances.

In this chapter, the Savior repeatedly commanded the people to study the scriptures. We would do well to be obedient to His encouragement. For the Lord said: "Whosoever will hearken unto my words and repenteth and is baptized, the same shall be saved. Search the prophets, for many there be that testify of these things." (V. 5). Spencer W. Kimball asked all of us "to honestly evaluate our performance in scripture study. It is a common thing to have a few passages of scripture at our disposal, floating in our minds, as it were, and thus to have the illusion that we know a great deal about the Gospel. In this sense, having a little knowledge can be a problem indeed. I am convinced that each of us must, at some time in our lives, discover the scriptures for ourselves, and not just discover them once, but rediscover them again and again." ("Melchizedek Priesthood Teaching Manual - 2007").

Marion G. Romney told the Saints: "I don't know much about the Gospel other than what I've learned from the Standard Works. When I drink from a spring, I like to get the water where it comes out of the ground, not down the stream, after the cattle have waded in it. I appreciate other people's interpretation, but when it comes to the Gospel, we ought to be acquainted with what the Lord says." (C.R., 4/1975, see John 5:39, 1 Nephi 19:23, and the remarks of Dallin Oaks in the Preface to this Commentary).

Jesus loved the scriptures. He not only "expounded all the scriptures unto (the Nephites) which they had received, (but he also) said unto them; Behold, other scriptures I would that ye should write, that ye have not. And it came to pass that he said unto Nephi: Bring forth the record which ye have kept." (V. 7-8).

When He had reviewed these, He asked how it was that an important prophecy by Samuel the Lamanite, relating to the resurrection of Nephite saints at the time of the Savior's resurrection in Jerusalem, had not been included. (V. 9). He held Samuel in such high esteem that He had the Nephite records amended to record the fulfilment of his prophecy. That the desired addition was made is attested by the inclusion of the prophecy of Samuel the Lamanite, in the Book of Helaman. Thus, the record was amended to incude the following: "And many graves shall be opened, and shall yield up many of their dead; and many saints shall appear unto many." (Helaman 14:25).

"And now it came to pass that when Jesus had expounded all the scriptures in one, which they had written, he commanded them that they should teach the things which he had expounded unto them." (V. 14). All scripture springs from, and returns to, a common source, which is Jesus Christ. The primary reason for the scriptures is to speak, teach, and testify of Him. (See Jacob 7:11, & 2 Nephi 25:26). When we preach, teach, expound, and exhort our brothers and sisters to righteousness, our focus is on the Savior. (See D&C 20: 46). Nephi had written: "Behold, my soul delighteth in proving unto my people the truth of the coming of Christ; for, for this end hath the law of Moses been given; and all things which have been given of God from the beginning of the world, unto man, are the typifying of him." (2 Nephi 11:4)

Jacob declared that the scriptures "truly testify of Christ. Behold, I say unto you that none of the prophets have written, nor prophesied, save they have spoken concerning this Christ." (Jacob 7:11). In fact, "we talk of Christ, we rejoice in Christ, we preach of Christ, we prophesy of Christ, and we write according to our prophecies, that our children may know to what source they may look for a remission of their sins." (2 Nephi 25:26).

Third Nephi
Chapter 24

It was important for the Savior to provide the Nephites with the teachings of Malachi, the Old Testament prophet who lived around 400 B.C. His ministry in Israel began two hundred years after Lehi left Jerusalem, so the Book of Malachi would not have been included within The Plates of Brass that were the Nephite scriptures.

An angel Moroni had quoted a prophet of Malachi to Joseph Smith. (See J.S.H. 1:36-40). In response, Joseph declared: "This is good doctrine. It tastes good. I can taste the principles of eternal life, and so can you. They are given to me by the revelations of Jesus Christ; and I know that when I tell you these words of eternal life as they are given to me you taste them, and I know that you believe them. I can taste the spirit of eternal life. I know it is good, and when I tell you of these things which were given me by inspiration of the Holy Spirit, you are bound to receive them as sweet, and rejoice." ("Teachings," p. 355).

"Thus said the Father unto Malachi - Behold, I will send my messenger and he shall prepare the way before me." (V. 1). This almost certainly refers to the Lord Jesus Christ, although the scripture could apply to other heavenly messengers who were instrumental in the work of the Restoration of the Gospel, as well. Latter-day prophets who have been called to lay the foundations of the Kingdom of God might also qualify as messengers of the Father. Joseph Smith would be chief among them, for he was "the Prophet and Seer of the Lord, (who) has done more, save Jesus only, for the salvation of men in this world, than any other man that ever lived in it." (D&C 135:1).

But pre-eminent among the messengers of salvation is the Lord Jesus Christ. There may be a dualistic fulfillment of this prophecy, but the Lord is most probably the messenger of salvation to whom Malachi referred. "In the beginning the Word was, for he was the Word, even the messenger of salvation." (D&C 93:8). Jesus came into the world to perform the works of His Father, that men might know of the Father. (See D&C 93:5 & John 5:19). In this sense, He became the Revelation of God to the world, and therefore He was known as the Word.

"And the Lord whom ye seek shall suddenly come to his temple, even the messenger of the covenant." (V. 1). For the Nephites, this prophecy was fulfilled when the Lord came to the temple in Bountiful. (See 3 Nephi 11:1-12). For the Saints in the Last Days, the prophecy was at least partially fulfilled when the Lord came to the temple at Kirtland. (See D&C 110). The prophecy continues to be fulfilled for the Latter-day Saints, as temples of the Lord are constructed throughout the earth. Of the Kirtland Temple, Jesus Christ said: "I have accepted this house, and my name shall be here; and I will manifest myself to my people in mercy in this house." (D&C 110:7). This is true of every temple built by the Church.

Of the experience in Kirtland, Joseph Smith wrote: "The veil was taken from our minds, and the eyes of our understanding were opened. We saw the Lord standing upon the breastwork of the pulpit, before us; and under his feet was a paved work of pure gold, in color like amber. His eyes were as a flame of fire; the hair of his head was white like the pure snow; his countenance shone above the brightness of the sun; and his voice was as the sound of the rushing of great waters." (D&C 110:1-3).

As Malachi asked: "Who may abide the day of his coming, and who shall stand when he appeareth? For he is like a refiner's fire, and like fuller's soap," which cleanses natural oils from fibers of cloth. (V. 2). "And he shall sit as a refiner and purifier of silver; and he shall purify the sons of Levi, and purge them as gold and silver, that they may offer unto the Lord an offering in righteousness." (V. 3).

When John the Baptist restored the authority of the Aaronic Priesthood, he told Joseph Smith and Oliver Cowdery that it would "never be taken again from the earth, until the sons of Levi do offer again an offering unto the Lord in righteousness." (D&C 13:1). Later, the Lord told Joseph: "Whoso is faithful unto obtaining these two priesthoods ... become the sons of Moses and of Aaron and the seed of Abraham, and the Church and Kingdom and the elect of God." (D&C 84:33-34).

Therefore, the faithful members of The Church of Jesus Christ of Latter-day Saints who bear the priesthood in the Last Days are the Sons of Moses and of Aaron who anciently held the Levitical priesthood. Thus, in September 1842 Joseph Smith wrote an epistle to the Church in which he declared: "Behold, the great day of the Lord is at hand; and who can abide the day of his coming, and who can stand when he appeareth? For he is like a refiner's fire, and like fuller's soap; and he shall sit as a refiner and purifier of silver, and he shall purify the sons of Levi, and purge them as gold and silver, that they may offer unto the Lord an offering in righteousness. Let us, therefore, as a church and a people, and as Latter-day Saints, offer unto the Lord an offering in righteousness; and let us present it in his holy temple, when it is finished." That offering was to be "a book containing the records of our dead." (D&C 128:24). Thus would be fulfilled yet another of Malachi's prophecies: "Behold, I will send you Elijah the prophet before the coming of the great and dreadful day of the Lord: And he shall turn the hearts of the fathers to the children, and the heart of the children to their fathers." (Malachi 4:5-6).

At that day, "shall the offering of Judah and Jerusalem be pleasant unto the Lord, as in the days of old, and as in former years." (V. 4). In other words, in the Last Days, "it shall come to pass that the Jews which are scattered also shall begin to believe in Christ; and they shall begin to gather in upon the face of the land; and as many as shall believe in Christ shall also become a delightsome people. "And it shall come to pass that the Lord God shall commence his work among all nations, kindreds, tongues, and people, to bring about the restoration of his people upon the earth." (2 Nephi 30:8-9).

The Lord will be a "swift witness" against all those whose ways are wicked. (V. 5). Therefore, it will be important for Israel to remember the ordinances of the Gospel that she had forgotten. "Return unto me and I will return unto you, saith the Lord of Hosts. But ye say: wherein shall we return?" (V. 6). Israel would be ignorant of the fact that she had strayed from the Law of Tithing. "Will a man rob God? Yet ye have robbed me. But ye say: Wherein have we robbed thee? In tithes and offerings." (V. 8). If Israel would be obedient to this law, she would qualify for the blessings predicated upon obedience. (See D&C 130:20-21, & Commentary Reference to 3 Nephi 15:1). "Prove me now herewith, saith the Lord of Hosts, if I will not open you the windows of heaven, and pour you out a blessing that there shall not be room enough to receive it." (V. 10).

Israel had been stiff-necked and unteachable. "Your words have been stout against me, saith the Lord. Yet ye say: What have we spoken against thee?" (V. 13). The Lord responded: "Ye have said: It is vain to serve God, and what doth it profit that we have kept his ordinances?" (V. 14). As Joseph Smith counseled the Saints: "Behold, there are many called, but few are chosen. And why are they not chosen? Because their hearts are set so much upon the things of this world, and aspire to the honors of men, that they do not learn this one lesson - That the rights of the priesthood are inseparably connected with the powers of heaven, and that the powers of heaven cannot be controlled nor handled only upon the principles of righteousness." (D&C 121:34-36).

Those who remain faithful will be as "jewels" in the eyes of God. (V. 17). "Shear Jashub" - "A remnant shall return." (See 2 Nephi 18:18). "Then shall ye return and discern between the righteous and the wicked, between him that serveth God and him that serveth him not." (V. 18). "No man can serve two masters." (Matthew 6:24). "For every tree is known by his own fruit." (Luke 6:44).

"Behold, I will send you Elijah the prophet before the coming of the great and dreadful day of the Lord; and he shall turn the heart of the fathers to the children, and the heart of the children to the fathers, lest I come and smite the earth with a curse."
(3 Nephi 25:5-6).

Third Nephi
Chapter 25

This chapter is a continuation of the Lord's quotation from the writings of Malachi. Its message emphasized to the Nephites that before the millennial reign of Christ, the earth would "burn as an oven" and all the proud, yea, and all that do wickedly, shall be stubble." (V. 1). In other words, before the earth can be renewed to receive its paradisiacal glory, it must be cleansed of all iniquity. (See the 10th Article of Faith). Nothing of a telestial quality, that is incompatible with the nature of the Son, will remain.

Furthermore, those who refuse to accept the Gospel, and who consequently do not receive the ordinances of the Priesthood, will be left with "neither root nor branch." That is to say, in the resurrection they will have neither forbearers nor posterity, because they have not participated in the sealing ordinances in the temple.

In contrast to the wicked, those who love the Lord will witness that He has "healing in his wings." (V. 2). The Savior's recitation of this prophecy of Malachi must have been particularly poignant to the Nephites because of their recent experiences. They had witnessed the destruction of their more wicked brethren, and had then enjoyed the personal ministry of the Son of Righteousness. In fact, they had felt for themselves "the prints of the nails in his hand." (3 Nephi 11:15).

The Lord had already made it clear that He would not forget the covenants He had made with Israel, and that in the Last Days, she would be gathered to the lands of her inheritance, where her people could "grow up as calves in the stall." (V. 2). No longer would Israel be as a hunted beast of the forest, with no safe haven to call home.

The Lord then referred to "the law of Moses." (V. 4). Perhaps this refers to the Fulness of the Gospel, and not to the Mosaic Law of Carnal Commandments that Israel had received at the foot of Sinai. (See J.S.T. Exodus 34:1-2). This might be true, in light of the teachings contained in the balance of this chapter from Malachi, that deal with the sealing power of the Melchizedek priesthood and that are essential to the Gospel Plan.

It must be remembered that the Nephites had kept the Law of Moses only because it pointed them to Christ. Six hundred years before the birth of the Savior, Nephi had explained: "Notwithstanding we believe in Christ, we keep the law of Moses, and look forward with steadfastness unto Christ, until the law shall be fulfilled. For, for this end was the law given; wherefore the law hath become dead unto us, and we are made alive in Christ because of our faith; yet we keep the law because of the commandments." (2 Nephi 25:24-25).

The balance of this chapter consists of two verses that are quite familiar to Latter-day Saints because they are found in the Doctrine & Covenants, the Pearl of Great Price, and the Old Testament, as well as in The Book of Mormon. As such, they constitute one of the most carefully documented prophesies of all time.

In The Book of Mormon, these verses read: "Behold, I will send you Elijah the prophet before the coming of the great and dreadful day of the Lord. And he shall turn the heart of the fathers to the children, and the heart of the children to their fathers, lest I come and smite the earth with a curse." (V. 5-6).

Similar verses were placed in the Doctrine & Covenants at the direction of President Brigham Young. (D&C 2:1). It is the first revelation, in chronological order, in the Doctrine & Covenants, inasmuch as it was received on September 21, 1823. In the evening on that date, the Angel Moroni quoted from Malachi to Joseph Smith. His visit was the beginning of the ministering of angels in this dispensation. When people believe in revelation, such communication from the heavens flows steadily. (See Moroni 7:22-29 & 37). The Lord promised to those who are pure vessels bearing the Priesthood: "Thy confidence (shall) wax strong in the presence of God; and the doctrine of the priesthood shall distil upon thy soul as the dews from heaven. The Holy Ghost shall be thy constant companion, and thy scepter an unchanging scepter of righteousness and truth; and thy dominion shall be an everlasting dominion, and without compulsory means it shall flow unto thee forever and ever." (D&C 121:45-46).

The wording of Malachi Chapter 4, in the Bible, is identical to 3 Nephi 25:5-6, in The Book of Mormon, but differs from that in the Doctrine and Covenants, and the Pearl of Great Price, that are also identical. Moroni's alterations from the Bible and Book of Mormon texts were probably for emphasis and clarification rather than for correction, inasmuch as his rendering helps Latter-day Saints to better understand the prophecy.

John Widtsoe wrote: "The beginning and the end of the Gospel are written in section 2 of the Doctrine & Covenants. It is the keystone of the wonderful Gospel Arch, and if that center stone should weaken and fall out, the whole Gospel structure would topple down in unorganized doctrinal blocks." ("Temple Worship", p. 64, cited by ElRay L. Christiansen, C.R. 4/1960).

At the time he visited Joseph, Moroni warned him: "You are but a man. Therefore, you will have to be watchful and faithful to your trust or you will be overpowered by wicked men; for they will lay every plan and scheme to get (the plates) away from you, and if you do not take heed continually, they will succeed." (Lucy Mack Smith, "History of Joseph Smith," p. 110). Satan clearly understood the importance of the restoration of priesthood keys and authority to the earth, and especially of the sealing power, and would go to any length to destroy Joseph Smith or anyone else who held the priesthood. Today, those who bear the priesthood in The Church of Jesus Christ of Latter-day Saints are all marked men and Satan has hired assassins whose sole mission is to destroy their faith and authority.

Malachi's prophecy concerning these keys and covenants was fulfilled April 3, 1836, which, in that year, happened to coincide with the Passover. During the Paschal service each year, the door in Jewish homes is opened, and a place is set at the table with a vacant chair. This is done in order to be ready to admit Elijah so that, as the forerunner of the Messiah, he might partake of the Passover Feast.

The Doctrine & Covenants reads: "Behold, I will reveal unto you the Priesthood, by the hand of Elijah the prophet, before the coming of the great and dreadful day of the Lord." (D&C 2:1). The underlined portion of this verse is different from that which is found in the Bible and Book of Mormon., which reads: Behold, I will send you Elijah the prophet before the coming of the great and dreadful day of the Lord". (V. 5.). Elijah "held the keys of the authority to administer in all the ordinances of the priesthood, and without this authority that is given, the ordinances could not be administered in righteousness." (Joseph Fielding Smith, Jr., "Doctrines of Salvation," 2:113).

The day when the Lord comes will be at once "great and dreadful." (V. 5). For the righteous, it is the day when Christ will come in power and glory; but for the unrighteous, it is when He will take vengeance upon the wicked. "And he shall plant in the hearts of the children the promises made to the fathers, and the hearts of the children shall turn to their fathers." (D&C 2:2). The Doctrine & Covenants emphasizes the Covenant made anciently with Abraham, Isaac, and Jacob that was renewed through the Priesthood keys that Elijah delivered to the Prophet Joseph Smith. The blessings given to the fathers would again be available to the faithful Saints in the Last Days.

Many prophets had held similar keys, but the reason that Elijah was reserved for this mission was that he was the last prophet in Israel to hold the fulness of the power of the priesthood. If God had not sent him to deliver these keys to Joseph Smith, "the whole earth would (have been) utterly wasted at his coming." (D&C 2:3). The Plan of Salvation would have been thwarted, for there would have been no sealing power to eternally bind the faithful to the ordinances of the Gospel.

A righteous people must be prepared to meet Christ, or literally the earth will be wasted at the Second Coming. The sealing power rests with the Melchizedek Priesthood, that "adminstereth the gospel and holdeth the key of the mysteries of the kingdom, even the key of the knowledge of God. Therefore, in the ordinances thereof, the power of godliness is manifest. And without the ordinances thereof, and the authority of the priesthood, the power of godliness is not manifest unto men in the flesh." (D&C 84:19-22).

Even though for over two millennia the Jews have waited in vain for Elijah at the Paschal Service of the Passover, the purposes of God will not be thwarted. The vacant seat at the table has been filled. Elijah has performed his long-awaited mission. "No power on earth or hell can overthrow or defeat that which God has decreed. Every plan of the Adversary will fail, for the Lord knows the secret thoughts of men, and sees the future with a vision clear and perfect, even as though it were in the past." (Joseph Fielding Smith, Jr., "Doctrine & Covenants Institute Student Manual," Section 3).

When Jesus had recited these scriptures to the multitude, He elaborated upon them in such a manner that not a hundredth part of what He said could possibly be written. (See 3 Nephi 25:1 & 6, & 26:6). Suffice to say that these principles are extremely important to Saints of both the former and latter days. For the Nephites, these teachings of the Savior through His prophet Malachi were an affirmation of the promise made by the Lord that He would redeem Israel. In the Dispensation of The Fulness of Times, the House of the Lord, where the sealing ordinances are performed on behalf of the living and the dead, is a dominant feature of the Church and Kingdom and is a tangible confirmation of the fulfilment of Malachi's prophecy concerning the restoration of the priesthood keys of authority.

The Nephites had kept the Law
of Moses only because it pointed them to Christ.
Six hundred years before the birth of the Savior, Nephi
had explained: "Notwithstanding we believe in Christ, we
keep the law of Moses, and look forward with steadfastness
unto Christ, until the law shall be fulfilled. For, for this
end was the law given; wherefore the law hath become
dead unto us, and we are made alive in Christ
because of our faith; yet we keep the law
because of the commandments."
(2 Nephi 25:24-25).

Third Nephi
Chapter 26

After reciting the third and fourth chapters of Malachi, Jesus "expounded them unto the multitude." (V. 1). It must have been wonderful for the people to sit at the feet of the Savior as He unfolded the meaning of the scriptures to them, for "he did expound all things unto them, both great and small." (V. 2).

Jesus explained that the Father had commanded Him to give Malachi's prophecy to the Nephites, inasmuch as it was not found on The Plates of Brass. (See Commentary to 3 Nephi 24, paragraph 1). The doctrines contained therein, He said, would be valuable to future generations. (V. 2). Then, He opened the eyes of their understanding and "he did expound all things, even from the beginning until the time that he should come in his glory." (V. 3, see V. 4-5).

Joseph Smith and Sydney Rigdon enjoyed a similar spiritual manifestation, when they received the revelation known in the Church as "The Vision." Of that experience, Joseph wrote: "By the power of the Spirit our eyes were opened, and our understandings were enlightened, so as to see and understand the things of God - Even those things which were from the beginning before the world was." (D&C 76:12-13).

Mormon abridged Third Nephi - The Book of Nephi from The Large Plates of Nephi. The condensation was quite a challenge, inasmuch as the plates of Nephi contained "the more part of the things which he taught the people." (V. 7). Therefore, he could not abridge onto The Plates of Mormon "even a hundredth part of the things which Jesus did truly teach unto the people." (V. 6).

It is worth noting that the dogma of The Church of Jesus Christ of Latter-day Saints is based almost entirely on a great mass of new revelation given to Joseph Smith between 1820 and 1844. We can be sure, however, that the doctrines we have accepted will continue to be compatible with hidden truth as it is revealed in the due time of the Lord, for example, that which is contained in the sealed portion of The Book of Mormon. After all, a basic tenet of our faith affirms: "We believe all that God has revealed, all that He does now reveal, and we believe that He will yet reveal many great and important things pertaining to the Kingdom of God." (9th Article of Faith).

Those teachings that Mormon did include in his abridgment were "a lesser part of the things which (Jesus) taught the people," but they were written "to the intent that they may be brought again unto this people, from the Gentiles." (V. 8). Malachi made clear, and the Savior reiterated, that in the Last Days the remnant of Jacob would be redeemed. This is being accomplished, in part, by their acceptance of the scripture known as The Book of Mormon.

Covenant Israel, in particular, is on "scripture probation" in the Last Days, to see if it will accept and use that which it already has been given. (See Commentary Reference to 1 Nephi 21:10). The Church emphasizes that it is a scripture-possessing people. It needs to be a scripture-reading people, as well. Mormon wrote that The Book of Mormon would try the faith of the Saints, "and if it shall be so that they shall believe these things then shall the greater things be made manifest unto them." (V. 9, see V. 11, & D&C 82:3).

When the Church is prepared to receive it, the sealed portion of The Book of Mormon will be given. But "if it so be that they will not believe these things, then shall the greater things be withheld from them, unto their condemnation." (V. 10). Mormon had access to many things contained on The Plates of Nephi, "but the Lord forbade (their translation, or abridgment), saying: "I will try the faith of my people" to see if they will believe the things they already have. (V. 11).

"For of him unto whom much is given much is required." (D&C 82:3, see Luke 12:48). We will all be judged by the laws to which we are responsible and will thus vary in our accountability for our deeds. But for members of the Church who live in a covenant relationship with God, the law is exacting, and rigorously tests our obedience. "For it is required of the Lord, at the hand of every steward, to render an account of his stewardship, both in time and in eternity." (D&C 70:9).

The Book of Mormon tests our faith in the sense that we must read and nurture a testimony of its worth and of the role of Joseph Smith as the Prophet of the Restoration. If they do not wholeheartedly embrace the doctrine of Christ in The Book of Mormon, deny the prophetic calling of Joseph Smith, and fail to live up to the covenants they have made, they will be in the power of Satan. (See D&C 1:35, & 20:9). They will receive no witness until after the trial of their faith, but once having passed through the refining fire, they will emerge resolute in their devotion to the Savior. Speaking through Isaiah, the Lord said: "Behold, I have refined thee, but not with silver; I have chosen thee in the furnace of affliction." (Isaiah 48:10).

Mormon continued: "And now I make an end of my sayings, and proceed to write the things which have been commanded me." (V. 12). He indicated that the ministry of the Savior among the Nephites lasted "for the space of three days; and after that he did show himself unto them oft," participating with the people in the ordinance of the Sacrament. (V. 13). In particular, He "did teach and minister unto the children of the multitude." (V. 14). That must have been a particularly gratifying experience for their parents. Through Joseph Smith, the Lord revealed to the Church: "Inasmuch as parents have children in Zion, or in any of her stakes which are organized, that teach them not to understand the doctrine of repentance, faith in Christ the Son of the living God, and of baptism and the gift of the Holy Ghost by the laying on of the hands when eight years old, the sin be upon the heads of the parents." (D&C 68:25).

These Nephite children received a marvelous and unprecedented endowment of spiritual power, as Mormon recorded that the Savior "did loose their tongues, and they did speak unto their fathers great and marvelous things, even greater than he had revealed unto the people." (V. 14). The multitude "both saw and heard these children; yea, even babes did open their mouths and utter marvelous things; and the things which they did utter were forbidden that there should not any man write them." (V. 16).

The Savior's power was demonstrated in other ways as well. He "healed all their sick, and their lame, and opened the eyes of their blind and unstopped the ears of the deaf." (V. 15). Certainly, this comprehensive manifestation of His power to bless the people was enhanced by the tangible element of the Spirit that enveloped those who had survived the destruction, but were not yet members of the Church. It seems only natural that these experiences would lead them to the waters of baptism and with the desire to be "filled with the Holy Ghost." (V. 17).

These were not lukewarm converts; their devotion to Christ was profound. After entering the Fold, "many of them saw and heard unspeakable things, which are not lawful to be written. And they taught, and did minister one to another; and they had all things common among them, every man dealing justly, one with another. And it came to pass that they did do all things, even as Jesus had commanded them." (V. 18-20).

Without being aware of it, they had been transformed into a Zion society, "for this is Zion - THE PURE IN HEART." (D&C 97:21). They "were called the church of Christ." (V. 21). They became a great example for the Saints in the Last Days, who while attempting to embrace the Gospel, remember the counsel of the Master, Who said: "Ye know the things that ye must do in my church; for the works which ye have seen me do, that shall ye also do." (3 Nephi 27:21).

"It came to pass that he did teach and minister unto the children ... and he did loose their tongues, and they did speak unto their fathers great and marvelous things, even greater than he had revealed unto the people, and he loosed their tongues that they could utter."
(3 Nephi 26:14).

Third Nephi
Chapter 27

Those who had been baptized "were journeying and were preaching the things which they had both heard and seen." (V. 1). They had taken their baptismal covenant very seriously. (See Mosiah 18:8-9, & 3 Nephi 11:41). Now they found themselves "gathered together and were united in mighty prayer and fasting." (V. 1). There is great power where two or three gather in the name of Christ and approach the Father in a spirit of fasting. In a Latter-day revelation, the Lord confirmed the principle: "Verily, verily, I say unto you, as I said unto my disciples, where two or three are gathered together in my name ... behold, there will I be." (D&C 6:32).

They had been instructed by Jesus to pray "unto the Father in his name." (V. 2, see 2 Nephi 32:9, 2 Nephi 33:12, & 3 Nephi 19:22). "And Jesus came and stood in the midst of them, and said unto them: What will ye that I shall give unto you?" (V. 2). There had been a difference of opinion among the disciples concerning the name by which the Church should be called, and so the people inquired of the Savior. (V. 3).

He answered with a question, asking them if they had "read the scriptures." (V. 5, see Commentary Reference to 3 Nephi 23:5). These, He said, teach: "Ye must take upon you the name of Christ. For by this name shall ye be called at the last day." (V. 5, see 2 Nephi 31:13). After all, He asked: "How be it my church save it be called in my name?" (V. 8).

Interestingly, when the Lord restored His church in this dispensation, of all the Christian organizations in the world, there was not a single one that bore the name of Jesus Christ. To Joseph Smith, He declared: "For thus shall my church be called in the last days, even The Church of Jesus Christ of Latter-day Saints." (D&C 115:4, recorded April 26, 1838, see D&C 20:1).

Before this revelation was received, the Church had been variously called The Church of Christ, (D&C 20:1), The Church of Jesus Christ, The Church of God, (D&C 84:17), and The Church of The Latter-day Saints. (D&C 115:4, 127:12, 128:21 & 136:2). Even today, it is sometimes inaccurately called The Mormon Church, or The L.D.S. Church.

But "there is no valid reason why the Latter-day Saints should speak of themselves as "Mormons," or of the Church as "The Mormon Church." Missionaries should persuade people to believe in Christ, the Son of God, and to become members of His Church - The Church of Jesus Christ. We should all emphasize that we belong to The Church of Jesus Christ of Latter-day Saints, the name the Lord has given by which we are to be known and called." (Joseph Fielding Smith, Jr., "Answers to Gospel Questions," 4:174-175).

The Lord continued instructing the Nephite Saints more carefully, and defining with greater clarity the significance of the name of His Church. He said of the Church: "If it be called in my name then it is my church, if it so be that they are built upon my gospel." (V. 8). That is the critical point upon which hangs the credibility of any church proclaiming to be the Lord's.

Today, many churches have the name of Christ or its derivative in their titles, and so the essential element that becomes the substance of the issue is embracing the Gospel principles that are taught by the Savior's earthly representatives who bear His priesthood authority. In verse 8, Jesus introduced this truth to His audience. This verse prefaces verses 13-21 that enlarge upon this principle.

Hundreds of years before the birth of the Savior, Nephi had declared to his people: "This is the doctrine of Christ (concerning baptism and receipt of the Holy Ghost) and there will be no more doctrine given until after he shall manifest himself unto you in the flesh. The things that he shall say unto you, shall ye observe to do." (2 Nephi 32:6).

The members of the Church in Zarahemla to whom the Savior personally ministered were now led to understand the doctrine of Christ in even greater detail. Nephi had mourned "because of the unbelief, and the wickedness, and the ignorance, and the stiffneckedness of men; for they will not search knowledge, nor understand great knowledge, when it is given unto them in plainness, even as plain as word can be." (2 Nephi 32:7). He need not have worried about the Saints in 34 A.D., but his concern was real because his focus was on the world in the Last Days. Today, many lack the desire to change, and are swept to and fro like flotsam and jetsam in a sea of mediocrity. Within the Gospel framework our lives are dynamic and changing, for as our knowledge increases, so too does our responsibility and commitment to obedience. As our testimonies of Christ swell, our faith intensifies our desire to repent. In this sense, when our lives are in harmony with Gospel principles, we are in a constant state of improvement leading to perfection. Becoming Christ-like is our ultimate, incredible journey. It is the road less traveled, but the rewards make undertaking and completing the trip worth the effort.

The Savior told His disciples in Zarahemla "and if it so be that the church is built upon my gospel then will the Father show forth his own works in it. But if it be not built upon my gospel, and is built upon the works of men, or upon the works of the devil, verily I say unto you, they have joy in their works for a season, and by and by the end cometh, and they are hewn down and cast into the fire, from whence there is no return." (V. 10-11, see 2 Nephi 1:14, & Commentary Reference to 3 Nephi Chapter 11). The success of the latter-day work of restoration speaks for itself.

An angel of God had taught Nephi: "There are save two churches only; the one is the church of the Lamb of God, and the other is the church of the devil. Wherefore, whoso belongeth not to the church of the Lamb of God belongeth to that great church, which is the mother of abominations; and she is the whore of all the earth." (2 Nephi 14:10, see Commentary References to 2 Nephi 14:10 & 2 Nephi 28:3-4). The so-called "Christian" nations of the earth need to develop a testimony of Jesus just as the heathen nations do. Nephi very clearly saw that "it must needs be that the Gentiles be convinced also that Jesus is the Christ, the Eternal God." (2 Nephi 26:12).

When the Savior counseled the Saints in Zarahemla, in 34 A.D., He was really instructing us to make sure that when we seek His true Church, we look for the works of the Father that serve as the confirmation of the institution's authenticity. "And now I show unto you a parable," He taught. "Behold, wheresoever the carcass is, there will the eagles be gathered together; so likewise, shall mine elect be gathered from the four quarters of the earth." (J.S.M. 1:27).

Verse 11 seems to make a distinction between those churches that are "built upon the works of men," and those that are built "upon the works of the devil." (See 2 Nephi 28:3-4). Certainly, there are many denominational leaders whose intentions are honorable, who were only "blinded by the craftiness of men." (D&C 76:75). The efforts of those who have tried their best to do what is right cannot be categorically condemned. "All who have died without a knowledge of this gospel, who would have received it if they had been permitted to tarry, shall be heirs of the celestial kingdom of God. Also, all that shall die henceforth without a knowledge of it, who would have received it with all their hearts, shall be heirs of that kingdom. For I, the Lord, will judge all men according to their works, according to the desire of their hearts." (D&C 137:7-9). It is only unto those to whom much has been given, that much is expected.

Verse 11 also speaks of those "who have joy in their works for a season." These are they whose intentions were dishonorable. The ungodly may briefly delight in their wickedness because their level of understanding and their behavior harmonize with the lowest common denominator of worldly standards. But as their knowledge increases, the obvious discrepancy between their behavior and Gospel ideals will become so apparent that their short-lived pleasure in their wicked ways will evaporate like the morning mist in the noonday sun. Surely, this is why Alma counseled Corianton that "wickedness never was happiness." (Alma 41:10, see Essay: "Happiness"). "The Lord (will) not always suffer (the wicked) to take happiness in sin." (Mormon 2:13).

In verses 13-21, the Savior enlarged upon the principles that typify His Gospel. When reading these verses, it is instructive to remember that the definition of "gospel" may vary with the circumstances. All words are more or less imprecise, and we derive their special meaning from the context in which they are used.

Jesus said: "Behold, I have given unto you my gospel." (V. 13). He gave to these disciples the first principles and ordinances, and His only and true doctrine. (See v. 20, & 2 Nephi Chapters 31 & 32). The Gospel is "the good news" about Christ, His Kingdom, redemption, and salvation. This is the intent of these verses. The Church has the Gospel, the Good News. The rest of the news is bad. (See Commentary Reference to Helaman 13:6).

D&C 20:8-10 declare that The Book of Mormon contains "the fulness of the Gospel of Jesus Christ to the Gentiles, and to the Jews also." This "has reference to the principles of salvation, by which we attain the glory of the Celestial Kingdom." (Joseph Fielding Smith, Jr.). Summarizing verses 13-21, the Savior said: "If ye do these things blessed are ye, for ye shall be lifted up at the last day." (V. 22).

The good news that Jesus gave to His disciples was that He came into the world to do the will of the Father, to be the Savior of the world when the Plan of Redemption became operative for mankind through His Infinite and Eternal Atonement. (V. 13). "For God so loved the world, that he gave his only begotten Son, that whosoever believeth in him should not perish, but have everlasting life." (John 3:16). Christ became the Author of the Plan of Salvation by divine investiture of authority.

Heavenly Father sent His Son to earth that He "might be lifted up upon the cross." (V. 14). One of the characteristics of the true Church is that its teachings are based upon this principle of the Gospel. As Christ was lifted up upon the cross, so might all men be drawn unto Him as His Gospel message is shared with the world. Because of our unconditional and universal redemption from the time of the Fall of Adam, we will have the opportunity to be lifted up by our Father to stand at the Judgment Bar of Christ, which Moroni called "the pleasing bar of the great Jehovah. (V. 14, see Moroni 10:34).

Jesus was physically lifted up upon the cross, but He was also figuratively lifted up as a light to the world, as the great Teacher and Exemplar, and spiritually lifted up to heaven as a Glorified God. As a result, His intrinsic power to draw men and women to Him through His Gospel is limitless. It is for that purpose that he was lifted up. (V. 15).

As the Savior stated in verse 16: "And it shall come to pass, that whoso repenteth and is baptized in my name shall be filled; and if he endureth to the end, behold, him will I hold guiltless before my Father at that day when I shall stand to judge the world." This is the essence of the Gospel message of salvation.

Lehi had urged his children to "awake and arise from the dust, and hear the words of a trembling parent, whose limbs ye must soon lay down in the cold and silent grave, from whence no traveler can return." (2 Nephi 1:14, see Commentary Reference to 2 Nephi 1:14).

Just so, the Savior now warned the unrepentant: "By and by, the end cometh, and they are hewn down and cast into the fire, from whence there is no return." (V. 11). Then, for added emphasis He reiterated: "And he that endureth not unto the end, the same is he that is also hewn down and cast into the fire, from whence they can no more return." (V. 17). Both the prophet Lehi and the Savior Himself sees to have been caught up in the powerful imagery of Shakespeare. There is a common thread, a majestic clockwork, that inspires us all.

The Gospel was given to mankind so that all who abide by its laws will have the opportunity to enter into God's Rest. (V. 19, see Alma 40:12 & 60:13). His Rest is nothing less than exaltation in His presence within the Celestial Kingdom. (See D&C 84:24). Since "no unclean thing can enter into his kingdom," purification is necessary to prepare those who desire entrance there. The blood shed by the Savior is the symbolical equivalent of the cleansing agent that purifies us and makes us worthy to abide His glory. (V. 19).

Having revealed the key that unlocks the door to God's Rest in His Kingdom, namely His precious blood, Jesus declared: "Now this is the commandment: Repent, all ye ends of the earth, and come unto me and be baptized in my name, that ye may be sanctified by the reception of the Holy Ghost, that ye may stand spotless before me at the last day. Verily, verily, I say unto you, this is my gospel." (V. 20-21).

A major purpose of the Gospel is to provide those principles and ordinances that enable us to become sanctified so that we may be worthy to live once again in a state of holiness in the presence of our Heavenly Father. Sanctification is the process by which the Saints are cleansed from the effects of sin; thus spiritually renewed, they stand prepared to enter the presence of the Lord. We must submit to His will, yield our hearts to Him, and be obedient to all of the teachings of His Church. "Therefore, if ye do these things blessed are ye, for ye shall be lifted up at the last day." (V. 22).

To Nephi, the Savior commanded: "Write the works of this people ... for behold, out of the books that have been written, and which shall be written, shall this people be judged, for by them shall their works be known unto men." (V. 25). Because the Book of Mormon prophets were obedient to this command, Mormon, a pure descendant of Nephi, was able to abridge their records for our benefit.

Jesus revealed that "all things are written by the Father; therefore, out of the books which shall be written shall the world be judged." (V. 26). Whether or not paper and ink, or the Cloud, or even metal plates, survive the ravages of time, God will be able to read the record of our lives, engraven in our very sinews. For Him who created us, the tapestry woven into our souls can be read as easily as any printed or electronically recorded text.

There is an interesting account of Eve's instructions to her children following the death of Adam, that bears on this subject. The Pseudepigraphic Book of Adam and Eve reads: "But hearken unto me, my children. Make ye then tables of stone and others of clay, and write on them, all my life and your father's, all that ye have heard and seen from us. If by water the Lord judge our race, the tables of clay will be dissolved and the tables of stone will remain; but if by fire, the tables of stone will be broken up, and the tables of clay will be baked hard." (Quoted in "Christ's Eternal Gospel," p. 97).

Because the Savior knows that Judgment Day approaches for each of us, He asked: "Therefore, what manner of men ought ye to be? Verily I say unto you, even as I am." (V. 27, see Commentary Reference to 3 Nephi 12:48). This hokmah, or Hebrew aphorism, was given because of its truthful simplicity. It is easy to understand, there is no latitude for error, and its intention cannot be misinterpreted. As Joseph Smith taught, Jesus is the Prototype of a saved being, and the example we should follow. He is our pattern, our guide, and our trusted friend.

Having declared His Gospel message to the faithful, Jesus revealed something of His character and taught a marvelous lesson as well, when He declared: "And now, behold, my joy is great, even unto fulness." (V. 30, see v. 31). Here is the key to an understanding of the Lord our Savior and Redeemer. He did the work His Father gave to Him, because He loves us so much. In doing so, He received a fulness of joy. If we follow His lead, we too will find that joy is the consummate reward for work well done, the work of pure, unselfish love. (See Commentary Reference to 3 Nephi 28:9).

Mahatma Gandhi once declared without hypocrisy: "My life is my message." He was true to his principles, the moral and ethical constants that were to him as guiding stars that would lead him to the safe haven that Christians would call "heaven." The Savior held Himself up as the model of perfection that is our goal. His Gospel holds the key that breaks down the barriers to our personal progress leading to exaltation. Without His divine intervention, though, we would be doomed to failure.

The scriptures often provide examples of contrasting elements, and in the very next verse, the Savior warned us in unmistakable language that a threat to our temporal and spiritual welfare exists. It is hidden in a time bomb called pride, ready to explode and scatter its lethal contents among those who call themselves the disciples of Christ and live within His Fold.

He said: "Behold, it sorroweth me because of the fourth generation from this generation, for they are led away captive by him even as was the son of perdition; for they will sell me for silver and for gold, and for that which moth doth corrupt and which thieves can break through and steal. And in that day will I visit them, even in turning their works upon their own heads." (V. 32). The time of a generation varies with how the word is being used, but the meaning can usually be picked up in context. In the case of the Nephites, 200 years would pass away before the harmony of their Zion society would crumble in disarray. (See 4 Nephi 1:24).

In a general sense, silver and gold represent the idolatry of the world, and when the Savior is sold for such, the symbolism becomes clear. We betray Christ any time that the things of the world become more important to us than He is. The Savior said of members of the Church who will inherit the Terrestrial Kingdom: They "are not valiant in the testimony of Jesus." (D&C 76:79). "To be valiant in the testimony of Jesus is to take the Lord's side on every issue. It is to think what He thinks, to believe what He believes, to say what He would say, and to do what He would do." (Bruce R. McConkie).

To do otherwise, after having received the blessings of the Gospel, is to risk everything. It is the design of the devil to devise "works of darkness; yea, and he leadeth them by the neck with a flaxen cord, until he bindeth them with his strong cords forever." (2 Nephi 26:22). "And thus, the devil cheateth their souls, and leadeth them away carefully down to hell." (2 Nephi 28:21). Verse 32 indicates that such was the case with "the son of perdition," or Judas Iscariot. As an aside, we might ask: Was he a son of perdition? There is real doubt on this question. But that is a subject for an essay. (See the comments by Joseph Fielding Smith, Jr., and by Bruce R. McConkie on this subject, in "Doctrinal Commentary on The Book of Mormon," 4:184).

Finally, the Savior's message came down to one summary statement: "Enter ye in at the strait gate; for strait is the gate, and narrow is the way that leads to life, and few there be that find it; but wide is the gate, and broad the way which leads to death, and many there be that travel therein, until the night cometh, wherein no man can work." (V. 33). The strait gate is baptism by immersion for the remission of sins, and it is the gateway to the path leading to the Celestial Kingdom. (See 3 Nephi 30). Glory with God in His Kingdom is the ultimate purpose of the Gospel Plan. (See Moses 1:39).

Third Nephi
Chapter 28

In this chapter, we gain most of our scriptural understanding relating to the doctrine of translation. (See Essay: "A Whirlwind into Heaven"). The setting was in Zarahemla, at a meeting between Christ and his twelve "disciples." (V. 1). In every instance in The Book of Mormon, these twelve are referred to as "disciples," but they were special witnesses of Jesus Christ among their own people; therefore, they had likely been ordained to the office of Apostle in the Melchizedek Priesthood. (See 3 Nephi 12, 13, 15, 18, 19, 20, 27, 28, 4 Nephi 1, Mormon 1, & Moroni 3).

Latter-day scripture teaches: "The twelve traveling councilors are called to be the Twelve Apostles, or special witnesses of the name of Christ in all the world - thus differing from other officers in the church in the duties of their calling." (D&C 107:23). All men may, by virtue of the priesthood and the gift of the Holy Ghost, be witnesses for Christ. Today, the Twelve hold the fulness of authority, keys, and priesthood to open the way to preach the Gospel to every nation, kindred, tongue, and people. Among the Nephites, the Twelve held the authority to preach the Gospel to their own people. (See 3 Nephi 27:27).

The Savior asked them: "What is it that ye desire of me, after that I am gone to the Father?" (V. 1). Nine of them asked that they might have a speedy resurrection to eternal glory in the Celestial Kingdom after their mortal ministry had been completed. (V. 2). The Savior granted their request, and promised them that after they reached the age of seventy-two, they should come to him. (V. 3). The significance of the age, by the way, is unknown.

Then, the Savior turned to the three remaining disciples and asked what was the desire of their hearts. Perhaps, they felt embarrassed, for they might have thought their request was selfish, and so "they sorrowed in their hearts." (V. 5). But the Master knew their thoughts, and was familiar with the request, inasmuch as it was the same as that of John the Beloved. (V. 6, see John 21:22-23).

Then Jesus introduced to the Nephites the doctrine of translation. The Latter-day Saints are a "peculiar people" in part because they believe in this doctrine. (See John 21:21-23, D&C 7, "Teachings," p. 170-171, and Essay: "A Whirlwind Into Heaven"). He told the three disciples: "Ye shall never taste of death." (V. 7, see D&C 42:45 & 47). They would continue to live as mortals, and would eventually die, but would "never endure the pains of death," but when Christ would return in His glory, they would "be changed in the twinkling of an eye from mortality to immortality." (V. 8). Since "the sting of death is sin" (1 Corinthians 15:56), translated beings in particular are able to avoid the unpleasant side effects of the transition from mortality to immortality.

"Translated beings are still mortal, and will have to pass through the experience of death, although this will be instantaneous. They have not passed through death, that is, they have not had the separation of the spirit and the body." (Joseph Fielding Smith, Jr., "Answers to Gospel Questions," 1:165, & 2:46). Probably all those who were translated before the resurrection of Christ were resurrected themselves, at that time, for example, Enoch (Genesis 5:24), the inhabitants of his city (D&C 38:4 & 45:11-12), Elijah (2 Kings 2:11), and Moses (Deuteronomy 34:5-6). (See also Moses 7:27, & D&C 133:54-55). Those who have been translated since His resurrection will "be changed in the twinkling of an eye," when Jesus comes to earth as the millennial Christ. "Millennial men and women will live in a state akin to translation. Their bodies will be changed so that they are no longer subject to disease or death, as we know it, although they will be changed in the twinkling of an eye to full immortality when they are a hundred years of age." (Bruce R. McConkie, "The Millennial Messiah," p. 644).

The Savior said that translated beings would enjoy other gifts, as well. "And again, ye shall not have pain while ye shall dwell in the flesh, neither sorrow, save it be for the sins of the world." (V. 9). These gifts would be important for these special missionaries, because they had been commissioned to "bring the souls of men unto (Christ) while the world shall stand." (V. 9). In other words, missionary work would be their focus of attention until the Second Coming, regardless of the exigencies of circumstances of their calling.

A fulness of joy comes in the Resurrection (See D&C 93:33), but missionary work can point us toward that same quality of happiness. (See D&C 93:20). The Savior told the three disciples: "And for this cause ye shall have fulness of joy; and ye shall sit down in the kingdom of my Father; yea, your joy shall be full." (V. 10). There is no mistaking here the importance of missionary work in the eyes of the Savior. Because of their desire to continue their missions on the earth, He said: "Therefore, more blessed are ye." (V. 7). Their efforts to bring the Gospel to their less fortunate brethren would eventually bring them into complete harmony with the attributes of their Father in Heaven. "And ye shall be even as I am, and I am even as the Father, and the Father and I are one." (V. 10).

"What man of you," He had asked his disciples in Judea, "having an hundred sheep, if he lose one of them, doth not leave the ninety and nine in the wilderness, and go after that which is lost, until he find it? And when he hath found it, he layeth it on his shoulders, rejoicing. And when he cometh home, he calleth together his friends and neighbours, saying unto them, Rejoice with me; for I have found my sheep which was lost. I say unto you, that likewise joy shall be in heaven over one sinner that repenteth, more than over ninety and nine just persons, which need no repentance." (Luke 15:4-7, see Luke 15:11-32)

After touching the nine disciples with His finger, the Savior departed. (V. 12). Then, the three were "caught up into heaven, and saw and heard unspeakable things". (V. 13). Verse 36 makes very clear that verses 13-23 speak of the three disciples. These three were forbidden to "utter the things which they saw and heard." (V. 14). They had likely received an endowment of spiritual and priesthood power akin to that which is received in the House of The Lord.

"Whether they were in the body or out of the body, they could not tell, for it did seem unto them like a transfiguration," or a special change in appearance and nature wrought upon them by the power of God. (V. 15, see V. 38-39). This transformation was from a lower to a higher state of being, resulting in a more exalted, impressive, and glorious condition. "No man hath seen God at any time in the flesh, except quickened by the Spirit of God", in an attitude of translation. (D&C 67:11, see D&C 76:19-20).

With Moses, the Three Nephites could now declare: "But now mine own eyes have beheld God; but not my natural, but my spiritual eyes, for my natural eyes could not have beheld; for I should have withered and died in his presence; but his glory was upon me; and I beheld his face, for I was transfigured before him." (Moses 1:11). Thus, a difference between translation and transfiguration seems to be that the latter is more temporary in nature. (See V. 37-40).

Exodus records that Moses went up on Mount Sinai to speak with Jehovah. "And the glory of the Lord abode upon mount Sinai ... And the sight of the glory of the Lord was like devouring fire on the top of the mount in the eyes of the children of Israel." (Exodus 24:16-17). "And when Moses came down from mount Sinai ... behold, the skin of his face shone." (Exodus 34:29-30, see Mosiah 13:5-6, Helaman 5:36, D&C 110:3 & J.S.H. 1:32).

To Mormon, as he abridged this account made by Nephi, it seemed that the Three Nephites had been changed in a similar manner "from this body of flesh into an immortal state, that they could behold the things of God." (V. 15). "And now," Mormon wrote, "whether they were mortal or immortal, from the day of their transfiguration, I know not." (V. 17, see V. 36, & Alma 37:8).

The last five verses of this chapter are a postscript, added by Mormon some time later, that explains what the Lord told him in response to a question he had posed about the Three Nephite disciples. Mormon had inquired to know their state, and he was told "that there must needs be a change wrought upon their bodies, or else it needs be that they must taste of death." (V. 37). In other words, the Lord confirmed to Mormon that there was, indeed, a difference between these translated beings, and normal mortals.

"Therefore, that they might not taste of death there was a change wrought upon their bodies, that they might not suffer pain nor sorrow, save it were for the sins of the world." (V. 38). Not only would they not grow older, but also, while tarrying in this special state, they would not experience the challenges of adversity normally associated with mortality. "Now this change was not equal to that which shall take place at the last day; but there was a change wrought upon them, insomuch that Satan could have no power over them, that he could not tempt them; and they were sanctified in the flesh, that they were holy, and that the powers of the earth could not hold them." (V. 39). Indeed, to say that they were mere mortals would be a gross understatement.

In their sanctified state, they remain to this day on the earth, while enjoying dominion over Satan. Although endowed with the power of God, they will not interfere in the course of human events to change history, but will always allow agency to rule in the affairs of men and women. Their mission is focused upon bringing souls unto Christ. They will not allow Satan to thwart that mission, as long as those to whom they minister do not willfully rebel, and reject their invitation to partake of the delicious fruit of the Tree of Life.

Therefore, "they did go forth upon the face of the land, and did minister unto all the people, uniting as many to the church as would believe in their preaching; baptizing them, and as many as were baptized did receive the Holy Ghost." (V. 18). In a demonstration of their power over evil, when "they were cast into prison by them who did not belong to the church ... the prisons could not hold them, for they were rent in twain. And they were cast down into the earth; but they did smite the earth with the word of God, insomuch that by his power they were delivered out of the depths of the earth; and therefore, they could not dig pits sufficient to hold them." (V. 19-20).

Satan clearly understood their power and potential influence, and so he tried desperately to thwart their ministry. Perhaps, they had been foreordained under the hands of Heavenly Father Himself, while yet in the pre-earth existence. Perhaps, Satan had known them well, and was familiar from that time with the ramifications of their future ministry, and in consequence of that knowledge had caused the people to stone to death Nephi's brother Timothy. (See 3 Nephi 7:19 & 19:4).

But it was all futile, for no power on earth could destroy them. Timothy had been restored from death by the power of the priesthood. By the way, we do not know the names of the Three Nephite disciples who tarried, nor do we know if Timothy was one of them. (See 3 Nephi 28:25). But we do know that three times were they "cast into a furnace and received no harm. And twice were they cast into a den of wild beasts; and behold they did play with the beasts as a child with a suckling lamb, and received no harm." (V. 21-22).

Their ministry would be to those who needed the Gospel the most. Even though they were mistreated and even abused, they did not lose sight of their mission statement, that was to bring all men and women unto Christ, to partake of His Divine Nature, to enjoy the blessings of the Gospel, and to participate in the ordinances of salvation and exaltation.

Therefore, "they did go forth among all the people of Nephi, and did preach the gospel of Christ unto all the people upon the face of the land, and they were converted unto the Lord, and were united into the church of Christ, and thus the people of that generation were blessed, according to the word of Jesus." (V. 23, see 4 Nephi 1:1). The Savior rarely intervenes directly in our affairs, but instead gives priesthood assignments to His faithful servants, allowing them to do the work in our behalf. Sacrifice brings forth great blessings, for the scriptures testify, "after much tribulation come the blessings." (D&C 58:4). The Three Nephites are to remain on the earth as translated beings "until the judgment day of Christ; and at that day they (are) to receive a greater change," to be resurrected "into the kingdom of the Father to go no more out, but to dwell with God eternally in the heavens." (V. 40).

Mormon's was personally acquainted with the Three Nephites, for he wrote: "I have seen them, and they have ministered unto me." (V. 26, see Mormon 8:11). Perhaps they revealed to him that they would minister to the Gentiles, and among them "a great and marvelous work (would be) wrought by them, before that judgment day." (V. 27 & 32, see 2 Nephi 25:17, 27:26, Helaman 3:13-16, 3 Nephi 5:8 & 21:9, Moroni 10:3, D&C 4:1, & Isaiah 29:14). Mormon also learned that they would be among the Jews, and among "all the scattered tribes of Israel, and unto all nations, kindreds, tongues and people, and (would) bring out of them unto Jesus many souls, that their desire (might) be fulfilled, and also because of the convincing power of God which (would be) in them." (V. 28-29). Their ministry, it would seem, has known no bounds, as it has ranged over the earth through two millennia. "And they are as the angels of God, and if they shall pray unto the Father in the name of Jesus they can show themselves unto whatsoever man it seemeth them good. Therefore, great and marvelous works shall be wrought by them." (V. 30-31).

But "wo unto him that will not hearken unto the words of Jesus", wrote Mormon. (V. 34). We might well apply his caution to those who reject The Book of Mormon in the Last Days. If they will not accept the message of the Restoration, "it would be better for them if they had not been born." (V. 35). Mortality is the centerpiece of The Plan of Salvation, but if we will not embrace it to come unto Christ, we render it impotent.

In the Lord's Preface to The Doctrine & Covenants, He declared: "Search these commandments, for they are true and faithful, and the prophecies and promises which are in them shall all be fulfilled. What I the Lord have spoken, I have spoken, and I excuse not myself, and though the heavens and the earth pass away, my word shall not pass away, but shall all be fulfilled, whether by mine own voice or by the voice of my servants, it is the same." (D&C 137:38, see D&C 18:34-36).

Third Nephi
Chapter 29

In this chapter, Mormon taught that the publication of The Book of Mormon would be a sign that "the covenant which the Father hath made with the children of Israel, concerning their restoration to the lands of their inheritance, is already beginning to be fulfilled." (V. 1). Interestingly, the implication of this verse is that the children of Israel will be restored to not just the land of Israel, the promised land, or the Holy Land, but to lands of inheritance.

"In the Hellenistic age, the Jews had become dispersed over the whole Greek world. As early as 140 B.C.E., the author of the Sibylline Oracles testified 'that the whole land and seas are full of Jews.' Strabo, a contemporary of Herod, wrote: 'It would have been difficult to find a single place in the world where there are no Jews.' And Josephus added: 'There are no people in the world among whom part of our brethren is not to be found.' Philo spoke of the 'wide expansion of the Jews throughout the world,' and of Jerusalem as 'the center of the scattered nation.'" (Abba Eban, "My People: The Story of The Jews," p. 103-104). Clearly, in the last two or three millennia, the Jews, let alone the other tribes of Israel, have become scattered throughout the earth, and when Israel is gathered into identifiable bodies in the Last Days, their places of habitation will be many.

Verses 2-4, 8 & 9 caution us against a course of action that is contrary to and in ignorance of the great and unmistakable signs of the times. In the Last Days, when The Book of Mormon speaks from the dust, we "need not say that the Lord delays his coming unto the children of Israel," because the Restoration confirms the reality that the Second Coming has already commenced. (V. 2). We "need not imagine in (our) hearts that the words which have been spoken are in vain." (V. 3). All that the prophets have spoken, particularly the Messianic and millennial prophets, is being fulfilled in the most marvelous ways. We "need not any longer spurn at the doings of the Lord." (V. 4). To spurn is to "ignore scornfully, to refuse, or to trample." Since its publication in 1830, the world has tried very hard to ignore The Book of Mormon. But Ezra Taft Benson put great emphasis on it, and cautioned that if we do not carefully and prayerfully study it, we are putting our souls in jeopardy, and neglecting the very thing that could give spiritual and intellectual unity to our lives. (C.R. 4/1986).

His counsel could have applied equally to non-members of the Church. Quite simply, the world needs The Book of Mormon. It was "written to the Lamanites, who are a remnant of the house of Israel; and also, to Jew and Gentile." ("Title Page to The Book of Mormon"). It was preserved for our day, and the cost of its publication was great personal sacrifice, because the world needs, more than anything else, spiritual and intellectual unity.

"Where will you find another work remotely approaching The Book of Mormon in scope and daring? It appears suddenly out of nothing - not an accumulation of 25 years like the Koran, but a single staggering performance, bursting upon a shocked and scandalized world like an explosion, the full-blown history of an ancient people, following them through all the trials, triumphs, and vicissitudes of a thousand years without a break, telling how a civilization originated, rose to momentary greatness, and passed away, giving due attention to every phase of civilized history in a densely compact and rapidly moving story that interweaves dozens of plots with an inexhaustible fertility of invention and an uncanny consistency that is never caught in a slip or a contradiction ... As a sheer tour-de-force there is nothing like it." (Hugh Nibley, "Since Cumorah," p. 156-157).

Like The Book of Mormon, Israel should also muster newfound respect among the nations. The Savior said: "Ye need not any longer hiss, nor spurn, nor make game of the Jews, nor any of the remnant of the house of Israel." (V. 8, see Commentary Reference to 1 Nephi 19:14). After 2,000 years, the State of Israel is a tour de force in the Middle East, and a reality that is here to stay.

Theodore Hertzl founded the Zionist movement in 1897, 57 years after Orson Hyde, acting on the instructions of Joseph Smith, traveled to Jerusalem to dedicate the Holy Land unto the gathering of the Jews. In substance, he offered a (dedicatory) prayer "in behalf of the Jews, that they would be moved upon by the spirit of the return; in behalf of the climate and soil, that they would be favorable to the support of a large population; and in behalf of the political governments of the world, that they would cooperate to make the Jewish settlement possible." ("Ensign," May 1972, p. 94).

"Ye need not suppose that ye can turn the right hand of the Lord unto the left." (V. 9). "What power shall stay the heavens? As well might man stretch forth his puny arm to stop the Missouri river in its decreed course, or to turn it up stream, as to hinder the Almighty from pouring down knowledge from heaven." (D&C 121:33).

"Wo unto him that shall deny the revelations of the Lord, and that shall say the Lord no longer worketh by revelation, or by prophecy, or by gifts, or by tongues, or by healings, or by the power of the Holy Ghost!" (V. 6). "We testify to the world that revelation continues, and that the vaults and files of the Church contain these revelations which come month to month, and day to day." (Spencer W. Kimball, C.R., 4/1977).

"Yea, and wo unto him that shall say at that day, to get gain, that there can be no miracle wrought by Jesus Christ; for he that doeth this shall become like unto the son of perdition, for whom there was no mercy, according to the word of Christ!" (V. 7). It is not often in The Book of Mormon that the text is punctuated by exclamation points for emphasis, but verses 6 & 7 are, and because of that, they should be studied with particular care.

It will be difficult for individuals who have lived a telestial existence in the Last Days to justify their actions before God, in light of the many signs and wonders He has provided to stimulate our inquiry, to turn us from our wicked ways, to prompt our repentance, and to help us to come unto Christ. Anyone who has witnessed these signs and wonders, "who hath seen any or the least of these, hath seen God moving in his majesty and power." (D&C 88:47). "Earth is crammed with heaven," wrote Elizabeth Barrett Browning, "and every common bush with fire of God. But only those who see, take off their shoes. The rest stand around picking blackberries."

Third Nephi
Chapter 30

In Chapter 29, Mormon urged us to avoid a number of things. In this chapter, he turned his attention to the Gentiles of the Last Days, and gave them specific commandments of the Lord regarding behavior that should be avoided, as well as behavior that should be encouraged. "Hear the words of Jesus Christ, the Son of the living God, which he hath commanded me that I should speak concerning you." (V. 1).

His message is summarized in just one verse, in counsel to the Gentiles: "Turn, all ye Gentiles, from your wicked ways; and repent of your evil doings, of your lyings and deceivings, and of your whoredoms, and of your secret abominations, and your idolatries, and of your murders, and your priestcrafts, and your envyings, and your strifes, and from all your wickedness and abominations, and come unto me, and be baptized in my name, that ye may receive a remission of your sins, and be filled with the Holy Ghost, that ye may be numbered with my people who are of the house of Israel." (V. 2).

"Murder" is mentioned at least 43 times in The Book of Mormon, many times on the list of the sins of apostate Nephites, and frequently as a prominent sin among the Gentile nations in the Last Days. Aside from the number of actual homicides committed in the United States (21,570 in 2021), consider the number of abortions that were performed in that "Christian" country in 2020: 930,160. While some of these abortions were morally and ethically justified, others of the nearly one million abortions must certainly fall within the parameters of legalized institutional murder. Food for thought.

The First Presidency of The Church has spoken out officially against abortion, that deals a serious blow to the smooth transition of the spirit children of Heavenly Father from their first to their second estate. They declared: "Abortion must be considered one of the most revolting and sinful practices in this day, when we are witnessing the frightening evidence of permissiveness leading to sexual immorality. The Church opposes abortion and counsels its members not to submit to or perform an abortion except in the rare cases where, in the opinion of competent medical counsel, the life or good health of the mother is seriously endangered or where the pregnancy was caused by rape and produces serious emotional trauma in the mother. Even then, it should be done only after counseling with the local presiding priesthood authority and after receiving divine confirmation through prayer." (Statement by The First Presidency, 2/1973).

Two centuries ago, the British statesman Edmund Burke accurately assessed the character traits that qualify men and women to enjoy the rich blessings of the perfect Law of Liberty. (See James 1:25). He wrote: "We are qualified for liberty in the exact proportion to our disposition to put moral chains on our own appetites; in proportion as our love of justice is above our rapacity; in proportion as our soundness and sobriety of understanding is above our vanity and presumption; in proportion as we are more disposed to listen to the wise and the good in preference to the flattery of names. Society cannot exist unless a controlling power upon will and appetite be placed somewhere; and the less of it there is within, the more of it there must be without. It is ordained in the eternal constitution of things that men and women of intemperate minds cannot be free. Their passions forge their fetters."

The Savior knew that we would live in a world where the distinctions between good and evil are blurred. Spiritual Babylon is all around us, and we need to be vigilant because "vice is a monster of so frightful mien, as to be hated needs but to be seen; Yet seen too oft, familiar with her face, we first endure, then pity, then embrace." (Alexander Pope).

With this in mind, we ponder a statement made by Joseph F. Smith, in 1913, regarding a bellwether of moral standards: "Never, I say, within the period of my life and experience have I seen such obscene, unclean, impure, and suggestive fashions of women's dress as I see today." Over a century after the prophet made that statement, perhaps a reassessment of the standards of our people is in order. Will & Ariel Durant observed: "A little knowledge of history stresses the variability of moral codes, and concludes that they are negligible because they differ in time and place, and sometimes contradict each other. A larger knowledge stresses the universality of moral codes, and concludes to their necessity." ("The Lessons of History," p. 37).

Our generation faces unprecedented challenges, as Satan makes a frontal assault on virtue and chastity. "The new morality is a fad," wrote Robert Collins, M.D.. "It ignores history, it denies the physical and mental composition of human beings, it is intolerant, exploitive, and is oriented toward intercourse, not life. The unity and community that couples seek cannot be accomplished at the pelvic level. One of the students at our university said: 'I've tried everything here. I've had sexual intercourse with 23 different girls, and now that my formal education is about over, I have learned that this did not bring me happiness. My life will be different because of my experience at this university.' Good for him! But has anyone heard from the 23 girls?" ("A Physician's View of College Sex")

Not only are moral codes pertaining to sexuality being hammered, but values such as honesty and integrity are no longer cherished. "Now we are a people of contention with strident and accusatory voices heard in argument across the nation. We rose from scratch to become the greatest industrial power in the history of the earth … We spend millions of our resources in litigation against one another. Our spiritual power is sapped by a flood tide of pornography, by a debilitating epidemic of the use of drugs that destroy both body and mind … In all too many ways, we have substituted human sophistry for the Almighty." (Gordon B. Hinckley, "Church News," 7/2/1988).

We live in a society today that has taken double-speak to a new level. We rationalize away dishonesty by describing it as "misleading others," and transgression as "misbehavior". We justify sin by characterizing it as "poor judgment", looting as "undocumented shopping" or the "redistribution of wealth to the underprivileged". Lying is excused as "hyper-exaggeration".

Our world is filled with smoke and mirrors and artful deception. We are able to clearly see what is real only because we have been blessed to travel a path that affords us a loftier point of view. The Gospel has helped us to avoid the sketchy paths that traverse slippery slopes just above personality precipices. Our scripture mastery has taught us that every wind of doctrine leads nowhere, and does little more than toss us to and fro. The monotony of the landscape adjacent to the roads that wind their way through Idumea can be hypnotic, leading to a stupor of thought, and so we have chosen to avoid going down those paths, because we know that sooner or later, we would be rendered incapable of independent action. We would find ourselves looking forward to the gentle caress of the flaxen cords around our necks that would cause us to lose the desire, and perhaps the capacity, to turn our lives around and retrace our steps to safety. Only too late, we would find that those flaxen cords had been transformed into iron chains that would drag us down to hell.

Envy and covetousness are often at the root of our unrighteousness. As Ben Jonson observed: "That for which all virtue is sold, and almost any vice - almighty gold!" Four thousand years ago, women cast their infants into the mouth of Baal, that fire-breathing god of wood and stone, mentioned so often in scriptural warnings. Now we have abortion mills to accomplish the same purpose. The Savior knew that this would shake the very foundations of our society. The fulness of God's wrath requires the destruction of the wicked. The cup of the wrath of God (Mosiah 3:26) will be full when the evil practices of mankind begin to wield a significant negative influence on the Divine Plan of Salvation for those spirits who have been assigned to come to this earth.

We learn from the word of the Lord to Moses that the Lord selected a place of habitation for the children of Israel, even before they were born. With His foreknowledge, He knew how many spirits would be assigned to become the descendants of Jacob. "Remember the days of old, consider the years of many generations: ask thy father, and he will shew thee; thy elders, and they will tell thee. When the most High divided to the nations their inheritance, when he separated the sons of Adam, he set the bounds of the people according to the number of the children of Israel." (Deuteronomy 32:7-8). "We may well believe that the Lord also parceled out the surface of the earth for all other peoples." (Joseph Fielding Smith, Jr., "Answers to Gospel Questions," 4:11-12).

The idolatry of our day takes an ephemeral form, like a will-o'-the-wisp, and we try to focus on something, anything, that will provide the stability that eludes us. Whether it is a sex goddess, movie queen, the almighty dollar, eternal youth, governmental paternalism, the ivory towers of learning, or the robes of the false priesthood, it is all the same. Many years ago, one of our most popular magazines was "Life." Then came "People," then "US." Next was "Self." Where do we go from there?

Irreligion and self-reliance are becoming the new tenets of our faith, but it is steak without the sizzle. As the religion of the state, irreligion's "orthodoxy would be insistent, and its inquisitors inevitable. Its paid ministry would be numerous beyond belief. Its Caesars would be insufferably condescending. Its majorities, when faced with clear alternatives, would make the Barabbas choice as did a mob centuries ago, when Pilate confronted them with the need to decide. If we let come into being a secular church which is shorn of traditional and divine values, where shall we go for inspiration in the crises of tomorrow?" (Neal Maxwell, "B.Y.U. Today," p. 11, 12/1978).

Better to side with the writer of the Eleventh Hymn of The Dead Sea Covenantors, who wrote: "Behold, for mine own part, I have reached the interview, and through the spirit thou hast placed within me, come to know Thee, my God." ("Christ's Eternal Gospel," p. 111).

The Savior reserved particularly pointed condemnation for those who would pervert the right way of the Lord by distorting the prescribed responsibilities of the priesthood. "But this constitutes the craft, the power, and the profit of the priests. Sweep away their gossamer fabric of factitious religion, and they would catch no more flies." (Thomas Jefferson, "The Writings of Thomas Jefferson," V. 6:192). As Ralph Waldo Emerson wrote: "Once we had golden priests and wooden chalices; now we have wooden priests, and golden chalices." ("Lectures & Biographical Sketches, VIII, The Preacher").

"Where are we? Who are we? We find that we live on an insignificant planet of a humdrum star lost between two spiral arms on the outskirts of a galaxy which is a member of a sparse collection of galaxies, tucked away in some forgotten corner of a universe in which there are far more galaxies than people. Since Aristarchis, every step in our quest has moved us farther from center stage in this cosmic drama." (Carl Sagan, "Cosmos," p. 193). It is as if scientists "have chosen up sides to see who can articulate the most sophisticated despair. These scientists are not describing the broad spectrum of life, but only life without God." (Truman Madsen, "Are Christians Mormons?"). We must not forget the observation of Moroni, who wrote, "if ye have no hope, ye must needs be in despair; and despair cometh because of iniquity." (Moroni 10:22).

Mormon encouraged us as he carried out the will of our Savior. At the close of his record known as Third Nephi - The Book of Nephi, he could leave us with no greater hope than the promise that it is within our power to "be numbered with (Christ's) people who are of the house of Israel." (V. 2).

Fourth Nephi
The Book of Nephi, Who is the Son of Nephi, One of The Disciples of Jesus Christ
About 35 A.D. – 321 A.D.

Fourth Nephi
Chapter 1

In the first edition of The Book of Mormon, this book was called The Book of Nephi, but in 1879, Orson Pratt was authorized by The First Presidency to change the title to Fourth Nephi – The Book of Nephi, for clarification.

This book was written on The Large Plates of Nephi by Nephi, who was the son of Nephi, who was one of the 12 disciples of Christ. Nephi kept the record for about 76 years, and then his son Amos kept the record for another 84 years. Then his son Amos kept the record for 111 years! Finally, Ammaron, who was the brother of Amos, and who must have been quite aged, kept the record for 15 years, (see V. 47) and then hid the record in the land of Antum, at a hill called Shim. (Mormon 1:3). Altogether than, Fourth Nephi – The Book of Nephi spans about 286 years of "Nephite" history.

Following the ministry of the Savior to the Nephites, His disciples had zealously gone "forth among all the people of Nephi, and did preach the gospel of Christ unto all the people upon the face of the land; and they were converted unto the Lord and were united unto the church of Christ." (3 Nephi 28:23). "And as many as did come unto them, and did truly repent of their sins, were baptized in the name of Jesus, and they did also receive the Holy Ghost." (V. 1).

It appears that the disciples were true to their covenants and worked tirelessly to preach the Gospel to all who lived in the Land of Zarahemla. Just how successful they were is eident by a carful reading of verse 2, wherein it is stated that by "the thirty and sixth year, the people were all converted unto the Lord, upon all the face of the land, both Nephites and Lamanites."

These converts internalized the principles of the Gospel so that the conduct of their lives was in complete harmony with the Law of Heaven. "There were no contentions and disputations among them, and every man did deal justly one with another. And they had all things in common among them, therefore, there were not rich and poor bond and free, but they were all made free, and partakers of the heavenly gift." (V. 2-3, see 3 Nephi 26:19).

They wee free from the bondage of sin, and free because they had qualified by worthiness to enjoy the blessings reserved for the obedient. Perhaps they had also received the blessing of the endowment in the temple, because the characteristics of a Zion society are simply the results of a spiritual transformation in the lives of the people that comes about as men and women live the Celestial Law of the Lord.

The disciples of Jesus worked "all manner of miracles" because the power of the priesthood found expression as the fruits of faith. (V. 5). For 23 years these conditions existed, "and the Lord did prosper them exceedingly in the land." (V.

6-7). "The people of Nephi did wax strong, and did multiply exceedingly fast, and became an exceedingly fair and delightsome people." (V. 10). Their families enjoyed the blessings of the priesthood, "according to the multitude of the promises which the Lord had made unto them." Husbands and wives, together with their children, grew up within the secure embrace of the covenants that bind families together forever. (V. 11).

For "they did not walk any more after the performances and ordinances of the law of Moses; but they did walk after the commandments which they had received from their Lord and their God." (V. 12, See 3 Nephi Chapters 10-30). They enjoyed the blessings of the fulness of the Gospel, since with the resurrection of Christ, the Law of Moses had been satisfied. (See 3 Nephi 15:5 & 8).

As Mormon continued his abridgment of the record of Nephi, there was little that he could say, except that "the seventy and first year passed away ... even an hundred years had passed away. And it came to pass that there was no contention in the land, because of the love of God which did dwell in the hearts of the people." (V. 14 & 15). This brief narrative stands in sharp contrast to that of Omni, Amaron, Chemish, and Abinadom, who for 81 years could only write that they knew of "no revelation save that which has been written, neither prophecy." (Omni 1:11).

The 9 disciples of Jesus "lived unto the age of man" and then went to enjoy "the paradise of God." (V. 14, see 3 Nephi 28:3). There they would enjoy a measure of God's Rest, to enjoy life in the Spirit World, free from the cares of this world, prepared to receive their eventual resurrection and enter into the Presence of the Lord in His Kingdom.

As they passed on, "there were other disciples ordained in their stead." (V. 14). This practice evidently continued as long as there was a Church organization among the Nephites. The Three Nephite Disciples, of course, continued to minister among the people. Both Mormon and Moroni both mentioned in the record that they were personally acquainted with them. (See 3 Nephi 28:26-27, & Mormon 8:11).

Unity existed among the people. "There were no envyings, nor strifes, nor tumults, nor whoredoms, nor lyings, nor murders, nor any manner of lasciviousness. There were no robbers, nor murderers. (V. 16-17). There was incredible power in the unity among the people. Their whole was greater than the sum of its parts. "And the Lord called his people Zion, because they were of one heart and one mind, and dwelt in righteousness." (Moses 7:18). What kind of influence is there in Zion? There is power to "break mountains, to divide the seas, to dry up waters, to turn them out of their course; to put at defiance the armies of nations, to divide the earth, to break every band, to stand in the presence of God." (J.S.T. Genesis 14:30-31).

Mormon simply wrote: "Surely there could not be a happier people among all the people who had been created by the hand of God." (V. 16). Imagine his feelings as he continued his abridgment. After reviewing nearly all the records that had been entrusted to his care by Ammaron, and with a unique perspective, Mormon, who would soon witness the complete destruction of his people, wrote: "There were no robbers, nor murderers, neither were there Lamanites, nor any manner of -ites; but they were in one, the children of Christ, and heirs to the kingdom of God." (V. 17). This is the same man whose own mortal experience had been one "continual scene of wickedness and abominations ... ever since (he had) been sufficient to behold the ways of man." (Mormon 2:18).

How satisfying it must have been for Mormon to write of a people who "had come out of the world, who had left the loneliness and estrangement of a fallen creation and entered the realm of divine experience; who had left the orphanage of spiritual alienation, and been received into the family and household of the Lord Jesus Christ. They left the ranks of the nameless, and had taken upon themselves the blessed name of Jesus Christ. They were Christians. Through their Master, they would become, in time, joint heirs to all that the Father has." (Robert L. Millet, "Doctrinal Commentary on The Book of Mormon," 4:202). Mormon simply exclaimed: "How blessed were they!" (V. 18).

Fifty more years passed away, "and there was still peace in the land, save it were a small part of the people who had revolted from the church and taken upon them the name of Lamanites; therefore, there began to be Lamanites again in the land." (V. 20). From this verse on, the digression of the people along the slippery slope leading to apostasy was detailed with increasing concern.

They had "spread upon all the face of the land, and they had become exceedingly rich, because of their prosperity in Christ." (V. 23). It was very perceptive of Mormon to make the fine distinction between wealth and prosperity. An individual or nation prospers in direct relation to obedience to the commandments. However, there is no direct correlation between obedience and wealth, or riches. But if these things do follow, or if, as the Savior said, "ye seek the riches which it is the will of the Father to give unto you, ye shall be the richest of all people, for ye shall have the riches of eternity; and it must needs be that the riches of the earth are mine to give; but beware of pride, lest ye become as the Nephites of old." (D&C 38:39, see D&C 6:7). How insightful are these words in the context of our study of The Book of Mormon!

For "in the two hundred and first year there began to be among them, those who were lifted up in pride. And from that time forth they did have their goods and their substance no more common among them." (V. 24-25, see 2 Nephi 26:9). With an inward focus, the people faltered in their desire to minister to the needs of others. "And they began to be divided into classes; and they began to build up churches unto themselves to get gain, and began to deny the true church of Christ." (V. 26). The Lord's Church made righteous demands upon them that they were unwilling to accept.

In "A Christmas Carol", Charles Dickens related how Ebenezer Scrooge cried: "But you were always a good man of business, Jacob". "Business!" cried the ghost, wringing its hands. "Mankind was my business. The common welfare was my business; charity, mercy, forbearance, and benevolence were all my business. The dealings of my trade were but a drop of water in the comprehensive ocean of my business. At this time of the rolling year," the spectre said, "I suffer most. Why did I walk through crowds of fellow beings with my eyes turned down, and never raise them to that blessed Star which led the Wise Men to a poor abode? Were there no poor homes to which its light would have conducted me?"

Now, in Zarahemla, there began to be distinctions among all the churches that "professed to know the Christ, and yet they did deny the more parts of his gospel." (V. 27). The purpose of the careful counsel given by the Savior to the Saints in Zarahemla 177 years earlier was now obvious. (See 3 Nephi 27:13-21). It is not enough to characterize your organization as the Church of Christ. It must also properly administer the ordinances of the Gospel. That this caricature of the true Church in Zarahemla operated inappropriately is evident by Mormon's remark relating to the Sacrament, that they "did administer that which was sacred, unto him to whom it had been forbidden because of unworthiness." (V. 27, see 3 Nephi 18:28-29).

This church was quite popular with those who sought form without regard to substance, and who enjoyed the relative ease of putting forth minimal effort within an organization that made no demands for personal sacrifice. "And this church did multiply exceedingly because of iniquity, and because of the power of Satan who did get hold upon their hearts." (V. 28). Satan's intent, after all, is to lead us "carefully down to hell." (2 Nephi 28:21).

Another church actually "denied the Christ; and they did persecute the true church of Christ." (V. 29). Nephi had prophesied that in the Last Days even the Gentiles would have to be convinced that Jesus is The Christ. (2 Nephi 26:12, see Commentary to 3 Nephi 27:10-11). Here is an example that in the midst of the Saints in Zarahemla the same lack of faith existed among a people whose testimonies should have been firm. These apostates were moved to exercise what they thought was "power and authority over the disciples of Christ who did tarry with them." (V. 30). They did not realize that power and violence are mutually exclusive; where one is present, the other is absent. Their efforts were puny compared to the power of the Three Nephites, even when these righteous disciples were thrown in jail. "By the power of the word of God, which was in them, the prisons were rent in twain, and they went forth doing mighty miracles among them." (V. 30).

Those who had apostatized from the truth hardened their hearts, and even sought to kill the servants of God, miracles notwithstanding. (V. 31). As the Savior told Joseph Smith: "Faith cometh not by signs, but signs follow those that believe." (D&C 63:9).

The process by which our faith, or power, is developed is one of testing. The Lord gives us certain principles, and by obedience to them, blessings and power follow. But we have no proof or promise until we act on the basis of trust or belief. Then comes confirmation of the reality, but only after we act in faith, or trust. That is why James taught: "Faith, if it hath not works, is dead, being alone." (James 2:17. See John 7:17, & Ether 12:6).

When we understand this process, we can see why sign seeking is condemned. Those who demand outward evidence of the power of God as a condition for belief seek to circumvent the process by which faith is developed. They want proof without price. As with adulterers, they seek results without accepting responsibility.

These faithless apostates took the Three Nephites "and they did cast them into furnaces of fire, and they came forth receiving no harm. And they also cast them into dens of wild beasts, and they did play with the wild beasts even as a child with a lamb; and they did come forth from among them, receiving no harm." Notwithstanding these miracles, "the people did harden their hearts." (V. 32-34).

Contrast this verse with verse 16. 161 years earlier, conditions in Zarahemla were as they had been in the City of Enoch, when "the Lord called his people Zion, because they were of one heart and one mind, and dwelt in righteousness; and there was no poor among them." (Moses 7:18). But now "there was a great division among the people." (V. 35). Ironically, even the Millennium itself, the thousand years of peace, will come to a close because men and women will, in like fashion, begin to deny God. (See D&C 29:22).

The people were now differentiated by religious affiliation rather than by race. It would be so for the rest of "Nephite" and "Lamanite" history. "The true believers in Christ, and the true worshippers of Christ, (among whom were the three disciples of Jesus who should tarry) were called Nephites, and Jacobites, and Josephites, and Zoramites. And it came to pass that they who rejected the gospel were called Lamanites, and Lemuelites, and Ishmaelites." (V. 37-38). Interestingly, there were no "Samites." To understand why, first see Jacob 1:13, and then 2 Nephi 2:4. The apostates "did not dwindle in unbelief, but they did willfully rebel against the gospel of Christ." (V. 38). Mormon emphasized in his abridgement that this was a calculated rebellion by those who should have known better. These people were accountable, and their agency led to a virtual cascade of self-defeating behaviors. The children of these apostates "were taught to hate the children of God, even as the Lamanites were taught to hate the children of Nephi from the beginning." (V. 39).

With the passage of another 29 years, "the wicked part of the people began again to build up the secret oaths and combinations of Gadianton. Forty years later, "both the people of Nephi and the Lamanites had become exceedingly wicked one like unto another." (V. 45). "And there were none that were righteous save it were the disciples of Jesus." (V. 46).

After Amos died, his brother Ammaron kept the record for 15 years, but sadly, there was nothing to report. The pendulum had swung full tilt, "and the people did still remain in wickedness." (V. 47, see Commentary Reference to 4 Nephi 1:14-15).

By 321 A.D., Ammaron was "constrained by the Holy Ghost (to) hide up the records which were sacred ... that they might come again unto the remnant of the house of Jacob, according to the prophecies and the promises of the Lord." (V. 48-49). It is at this point that Fourth Nephi - The Book of Nephi ends, and the personal record of Mormon, known as The Book of Mormon, begins.

"They were one, the children of Christ, and heirs to the kingdom of God. And how blessed were they! For the Lord did bless them in all their doings." (4 Nephi 1:17-18).

The Book of Mormon
321-326 A.D. - 401-421 A.D.

Mormon
Chapter 1

Here begins Mormon's own account, translated by Joseph Smith from The Plates of Mormon. The first seven chapters of The Book of Mormon, commonly referred to as "Mormon," were written by Mormon, and are significant because they serve as an epilogue to his abridgment, and as a final testament to all that he had witnessed. It validates the warning given repeatedly throughout The Book of Mormon: "Serve God and prosper, or reject Him and suffer the consequences."

In verse 1, Mormon indicated that he would make a record "of the things which (he had) both seen and heard, and call it the Book of Mormon." (See Mormon 5:9). He recalled in verses 2-4 that when he was about 10 years of age, around 321 A.D., he had been approached by the prophet and record keeper who was a descendant of Nephi who had been one of the 12 disciples of Christ during His post-mortal visit to the New World. (See 4 Nephi 1:47-49). This man, named Ammaron, had observed Mormon's behavior, and had perceived that he was a "sober child" who was thoughtful and serious minded, and mature beyond his years. Also, he was "quick to observe," which was a necessary trait for a prophet-historian to have. (V. 2). The Holy Ghost had doubtlessly confirmed to Ammaron that God had chosen Mormon to be the next keeper of the sacred emblems, tokens of authority, and records.

Ammaron had faithfully kept the history of the Nephites for 15 years, after his brother Amos had done so for approximately 110 years. Across the span of a century, these brothers had seen their nation disintegrate in a descending spiral of apostasy. For "the people did not dwindle in unbelief, but they did willfully rebel against the gospel of Christ." (4 Nephi 1:38). Now, about 322 A.D., "wickedness did prevail upon the face of the whole land." (V. 13).

Ammaron revealed to Mormon that 14 years hence, he should "go to the land Antum, unto a hill which shall be called Shim." (V. 4). Deposited there were all the sacred engravings that concerned the Nephites. Ammaron knew that these intervening years would not be easy for Mormon. Later in his life, Mormon described "a continual scene of wickedness and abominations (that) has been before mine eyes ever since I have been sufficient to behold the ways of man." (Mormon 2:18).

But Ammaron knew that he would be equal to the task. The young boy knew who he was. He wrote: "And I, Mormon, being a descendant of Nephi, (and my father's name was Mormon) I remembered the things which Ammaron commanded me." (V. 5, see 3 Nephi 5:20). Almost alone among the Nephites, Mormon remembered both his noble lineage and the promises God had made to those who faithfully kept their covenants, even in the midst of great adversity and apostasy.

Ammaron had instructed Mormon to "take the plates of Nephi unto yourself, and the remainder shall ye leave in the place where they are; and ye shall engrave on the plates of Nephi all the things that ye have observed concerning this people." (V. 4). Upon The Large Plates of Nephi had been recorded "an account of the reign of the kings, and the wars and contentions of (the Nephite) people." (1 Nephi 9:4). In other words, those plates contained the history of the Nephites. (See 2 Nephi 4:14). It was upon those Large Plates that Ammaron desired Mormon to record the history of the Nephites, just as all the prophets from the time of Nephi had done. Mormon faithfully discharged this responsibility, taking The Large Plates of Nephi, and making "a record according to the words of Ammaron." (Mormon 2:18).

He later abridged an abbreviated account from The Large Plates upon The Plates of Mormon. (Mormon 2:19). He could not record more comprehensively all that he witnessed, because it was "impossible for the tongue to describe, or for man to write a perfect description of the horrible scene of the blood and carnage which was among the people." (Mormon 4:11).

At the time he received his instructions from Ammaron, Mormon had not yet seen any of the records, because they had been hidden in the Hill Shim. (See 4 Nephi 1:48-49). It was 14 years later, when he had been entrusted with the care of the plates, that he began the monumental task of abridgement of The Large Plates of Nephi onto The Plates of Mormon. (See Words of Mormon 1:3). Additionally, it was only after he had completed that abridgement, when he was about to deliver it to the care of his son, Moroni, that Mormon discovered among all the records The Small Plates of Nephi. These were intact, written in the first-person tense by the prophets from Nephi to Omni, and there were a few blank leaves at the end of the record.

Onto this record, about the year 385 A.D., Mormon added explanatory verses, that were intended to serve as a bridge, or transition, between the body of The Small Plates and Mormon's abridgment of The Large Plates of Nephi, which starts with The Book of Mosiah. (Words of Mormon 1:5).

Mormon hoped that his son Moroni would be able to continue to "write somewhat" concerning his people. (Words of Mormon 1:2). This Moroni did, and his writing was preserved on The Plates of Mormon, and comprises Mormon Chapters 8 and 9, as well as The Book of Moroni. Mormon thought that "perhaps some day it might profit" the remnant of his people in the Last Days to have these records. (Words of Mormon 1:2).

Mormon was likely born in the north country, above the narrow neck of land, possibly in or near the land of Cumorah. (See Alma 22:27-34, & Helaman 6:9-10). When he was 11 years of age, he was carried by his father out of that land, "into the land southward, even to the land of Zarahemla." (V. 6). By 322 A.D., "the whole face of the land had become covered with buildings, and the people were as numerous almost, as it were the sand of the sea." (V. 7).

They had long since distinguished themselves by class status, and there were on the one hand Nephites, Jacobites, Josephites, and Zoramites, all loosely grouped together as Nephites. On the other hand, there were Lamanites, Lemuelites, and Ishmaelites, collectively called Lamanites. (V. 8-9, see Jacob 1:13, & 4 Nephi 1:17).

War broke out between these two groups, and there were "a number of battles, in which the Nephites did beat the Lamanites and did slay many of them." (V. 11). Then, "peace did remain for the space of four years, that there was no bloodshed." (V. 12). This is a remarkably superficial definition of peace that reveals just how bad things really were in Zarahemla.

In spite of the absence of combatants dying on the fields of battle, "wickedness did prevail upon the face of the whole land, insomuch that the Lord did take away his beloved disciples, and the work of miracles and of healing did cease because of the iniquity of the people. And there were no gifts from the Lord, and the Holy Ghost did not come upon any, because of their wickedness and unbelief." (V. 13-14). The specific mission of the disciples had been to bring souls unto Christ. However, conditions were so bad in the land that they were unable to do that. Therefore, they were withdrawn from the mission field. (See V. 16). The same policy exists today in the missions of the Church. When social or political upheaval creates conditions of chaos, the missionaries are withdrawn until the situation improves.

After living in this society for a period of four years, Mormon reported that he "was visited of the Lord, and tasted and knew of the goodness of God." (V. 15). In much the same way, Joseph Smith received the comfort of angels and of the Lord during his moments of greatest trial. While in Liberty Jail, the voice of the Lord came to him and assured him: "Know thou, my son, that all these things shall give thee experience, and shall be for thy good ... Thy days are known, and thy years shall not be numbered less; therefore, fear not what man can do, for God shall be with you forever and ever." (D&C 122:7 & 9).

Even though the last missionaries had been withdrawn, Mormon still "did endeavor to preach unto this people, but (his) mouth was shut, and (he) was forbidden that (he) should preach unto them." (V. 16). The Nephites, who retained their moral agency, were not passive or neutral for "they had willfully rebelled against their God." (V. 16). Now, "because of the hardness of their hearts, the land was cursed for their sake" or "on account of" the fact that the scar tissue of sin had rendered them "past feeling."

Satan revived the secret combinations of old, and "Gadianton robbers, who were among the Lamanites, did infest the land." (V. 18). They were skilled in the dark arts, and were adept at thievery, and so the temporal treasures of the Nephites "became slippery, because the Lord had cursed the land, that they could not hold them, nor retain them again." (V. 18, see Mormon 2:10).

Perhaps the "sorceries, and witchcrafts, and magics, and the power of the evil one" had been sucked into a void that had been created by the withdrawal of the Holy Ghost from among the people. Under these conditions, the normal conventions of human interaction would be dissolved, and a real fortress mentality would develop among the people. Having willfully repudiated the companionship of the Spirit, the people were left to their own devices to fend for themselves in a world where the rules were now defined by Satan, and where behavior was brutally dictated by his will. The people had voluntarily yielded to him their agency, and the words of Nephi had been frighteningly validated: Satan had grasped "them with his awful chains, from whence there is no deliverance," and they were helplessly being dragged down to hell. (2 Nephi 28:20-23).

"Remember the things that ye have observed concerning this people; and … go to the land Antum, unto a hill which shall be called Shim; and there have I deposited unto the Lord all the sacred engravings concerning this people. And behold, ye shall take the plates of Nephi unto yourself, and the remainder ye shall leave in the place where they are; and ye shall engrave upon the plates of Nephi all the things that ye have observed concerning this people." (Mormon 1:3-4).

Mormon
Chapter 2

In Mormon's sixteenth year, open hostilities between the Nephites and Lamanites once again erupted. Even in their depraved state, the Nephites recognized Mormon's virtue as a great asset, and so they appointed him to be "the leader of their armies." (V. 1). How many men can recall in their memoirs, anyone "in (their) sixteenth year (who) did go forth at the head of an army against the (enemy)?" (V. 2).

But it was all in vain. Mormon related: "The land was filled with robbers and with Lamanites; and notwithstanding the great destruction which hung over my people, they did not repent of their evil doings; therefore, there was blood and carnage spread throughout all the face of the land, both on the part of the Nephites and also on the part of the Lamanites." (V. 8, see Commentary Reference to Mormon 8:8). The key element that might have spared the Nephites continued to elude them. In their blinded circumstances, they could not see that recognition of their wickedness, remorse for their behavior, a resolve to reject their apostate ways, repentance for a remission of sins leading to a reformation in behavior, restoration wherever possible for their trespasses, and reliance on God were their only hope. Consequently, complete anarchy ruled, "and it was one complete revolution throughout all the face of the land." (V. 8). Order had broken down among the Lamanites and the Gadianton Robbers as much as it had among the Nephites. The defining characteristics of the antagonists grew less and less distinct.

Fleetingly, it seemed to Mormon that perhaps there was hope for his people, after all. "And it came to pass that the Nephites began to repent of their iniquity, and began to cry even as had been prophesied by Samuel the prophet." (V. 10, see Helaman 13:5-10). Because of the curse upon the land, "there began to be a mourning and a lamentation" among the Lamanites, as well as among the Nephites, but "more especially among the people of Nephi." (V. 11). "But," Mormon wrote, "behold this my joy was vain, for their sorrowing was not unto repentance, because of the goodness of God; but it was rather the sorrowing of the damned, because the Lord would not always suffer them to take happiness in sin." (V. 13, see Moroni 10:22, & 2 Corinthians. 7:10).

These people had become accustomed to taking "joy in their works for a season." (3 Nephi 27:11). Their worldly behavior was in harmony with their lack of spiritual understanding, and so whatever comfort or pleasure they derived from their wicked ways was destined to be short-lived. They could only conduct their lives in opposition to the laws of heaven for so long, before reaching "critical mass". At that point, a readjustment would be required, bringing those errant individuals back into harmony with nature. Sometimes, if the violation of law and the unwillingness to change is so entrenched, the separation of the physical body from the spirit is required. In the end, the principle that Alma taught Corianton is always validated: "Wickedness never was happiness." (Alma 41:10).

Mormon recorded: "They did not come unto Jesus with broken hearts and contrite spirits, but they did curse God, and wish to die ... And I saw that the day of grace was passed with them, both temporally and spiritually; for I saw thousands of them hewn down in open rebellion against their God." (V. 14-15, see Alma 36:15). They had reached the point of no return, beyond which they had either lost the desire to repent, or no longer had the ability to do so.

In a war lasting 15 years, Mormon was powerless to stop the slaughter of the Nephites by the Lamanites. (V. 16). Sometime during that period of time, he "had gone according to the word of Ammaron, and taken the plates of Nephi, and did make a record according to the words of Ammaron." (V. 17). Upon The Large Plates of Nephi, he made a "full account of all the wickedness and abominations" of the people. (V. 18). But he could not bring himself to duplicate that record upon The Plates of Mormon, because, he said, "a continual scene of wickedness and abominations has been before mine eyes ever since I have been sufficient to behold the ways of man." (V. 18). All his life, his heart had been heavy with sorrow because of their wickedness. (V. 19). Nevertheless, he had received the Second Comforter, and the More Sure Word of Prophecy. (See Mormon 1:15). His Calling and Election had been made sure and he could declare with confidence: "I know that I shall be lifted up at the last day." (V. 19).

By this time, Mormon had read of the heroic acts of Moroni that had been recorded upon The Large Plates of Nephi. So impressed was he, that he named his own son after this great military leader. He remembered the Title of Liberty that Moroni had raised throughout the Land of Zarahemla, and how Moroni had exhorted the people to "Come forth in the strength of the Lord, and enter into a covenant that they will maintain their rights, and their religion, that the Lord God may bless them." (Alma 46:20).

Now, Mormon wrote: "It came to pass that I did speak unto my people, and did urge them with great energy, that they would stand boldly before the Lamanites and fight for their wives, and their children, and their houses, and their homes." (V. 23). The people were aroused, if not inspired, and defeated the Lamanites in a great battle. They were even able to regain possession of the lands of their inheritance, including Zarahemla. (V. 27). "Nevertheless," reported Mormon, "the strength of the Lord was not with us; yea, we were left to ourselves, that the Spirit of the Lord did not abide in us; therefore, we had become weak like unto our brethren." (V. 26, see Alma 26:12, & D&C 3:4).

Without the guidance of the Spirit, the Nephites thought it would be in their best interest to negotiate peace with the Lamanites, in the hope that a scrap of paper might guarantee their safety. (V. 28-29). Rather than relying upon the power of God, they focused their energy and efforts on securing a temporal treaty anchored to whatever honor was left among the Lamanites. According to the terms of this agreement, Mormon wrote: "The Lamanites did give unto us the land northward, yea, even to the narrow passage which led into the land southward. And we did give unto the Lamanites all the land southward." (V. 29, see Alma 22:33-34).

The Nephites received the Lands Bountiful and Desolation. Ramah / Cumorah was either part of Desolation or a subdivision of it. The Lamanites received the Land of Zarahemla and the Land of Nephi to the south. (See John L. Sorenson, "An Ancient American Setting for The Book of Mormon," p. 27).

Mormon
Chapter 3

The uneasy peace lasted for 10 years, and then the Lamanites once again came up to battle against the Nephites. (V. 1). The text provides clues regarding the state of affairs during this time. Tensions must have been high, with each side using the lull in the fighting to re-provision, refine military preparedness, and define new tactics, for it was inevitable that hostilities would break out again soon. Gone were the inviolate oaths of both the Nephites and Lamanites. (See V. 10). Whereas, once their word had been their bond, at this stage, promises had value only if they were self-serving. When the treaty between the Nephites and Lamanites no longer gave either party the advantage, its terms were trodden under foot as the armies again took up the march.

The Nephites did not realize that the season had been given to them so that they might change their ways, rather than so that they might prepare for yet another round of bloodshed. "They did not realize that it was the Lord that had spared them, and granted unto them a chance for repentance." (V. 3). Instead, they further hardened their hearts, even though Mormon had been given 10 years to cry unto the people: "Repent ye, and come unto me, and be ye baptized, and build up again my church, and ye shall be spared." (V. 2, see 2 Nephi 19:21).

The terms of the treaty had given the Lamanites the land south of the narrow neck of land, and so the field upon which the armies now met 12 years later was "at the land Desolation ... by the narrow pass which led into the land southward." (V. 5). This was the same battleground north of the Land Bountiful where the Jaredites, at least 500 years earlier, had fought to the last man. (See Omni 1:21, Mosiah 8:8, & Alma 22:30-31).

Because the Nephites won the battle at Desolation, "they began to swear by the heavens, and also by the throne of God, that they would go up to battle against their enemies, and would cut them off from the face of the land." (V. 10). Not only did they forget that the Lord had counseled to avoid an offensive war, but they had also sworn the most vengeful oaths, vowing in the name of God to kill others of His children. (V. 10, see v. 14-15, 3 Nephi 3:20-21, Alma 43:46 & 48:14). This was the final straw for Mormon, who "did utterly refuse from this time forth to be a commander and a leader of this people, because of their wickedness and abomination." (V. 11). He had led them for 38 years, all the while maintaining his standards and trying to reconcile his values with the unprincipled behavior of the Nephite armies under his command.

He had done all that was humanly possible on behalf of his brethren, and wrote: "Notwithstanding their wickedness I had led them many times to battle, and had loved them, according to the love of God which was in me, with all my heart; and my soul had been poured out in prayer unto my God all the day long for them ... And thrice have I delivered them out of the hands of their enemies, and they have repented not of their sins." (V. 12-13).

But all he had done "was without faith, because of the hardness of their hearts." (V. 12). Alma had written: "If ye have faith, ye hope for things which are not seen, which are true." (Alma 32:21). Mormon's hope for his brethren was without faith because there was no confirmation that his prayers would be answered. (See Mormon 5:2). Finally, the Lord intervened on his behalf, but only to release him from the obligation. Mormon wrote: "I did even as the Lord had commanded me; and I did stand as an idle witness to manifest unto the world the things which I saw and heard." (V. 16).

The remaining verses of this chapter concern that witness given by Mormon to the world, that is contained in The Book of Mormon, Another Testament of Jesus Christ. He addressed the Gentiles, the Twelve Tribes of Israel, and the remnant of the Children of Israel in the New World. (V. 17-19). He wrote: "And these things doth the Spirit manifest unto me; therefore, I write unto you all. And for this cause, I write unto you." (V. 20).

There follow 4 specific reasons why The Book of Mormon was preserved for our day:

The first is that everyone in the world may know that "every soul who belongs to the whole human family of Adam ... must stand to be judged of (his or her) works, whether they be good or evil." (V. 20). Everyone will be redeemed from spiritual death, at least briefly, to stand in the presence of God at the Judgment Bar of Christ. This reason for the preservation of The Book of Mormon is critically tied to the fourth reason listed below.

The second is that the book can help us all to "believe the gospel of Jesus Christ." (V. 21). As Joseph Smith stated: "I told the brethren that The Book of Mormon was the most correct of any book on earth, and the keystone of our religion, and a man would get nearer to God by abiding by its precepts, than by any other book." ("Teachings," p. 194, see Commentary Reference to 3 Nephi 29:4).

The third is that The Book of Mormon will serve as another witness to "the Jews, the covenant people of the Lord ... that Jesus, whom they slew, was the very Christ and the very God." (V. 21). As Nephi wrote, The Book of Mormon will be given to the Jews in the Last Days "for the purpose of convincing them of the true Messiah, who was rejected by them; and unto the convincing of them that they need not look forward any more for a Messiah to come ... for there is save one Messiah spoken of by the prophets, and that Messiah is he who should be rejected of the Jews." (2 Nephi 25:18).

The fourth reason for the preservation of The Book of Mormon is that Mormon saw our day, and knew our needs. (See Mormon 8:35). He knew that The Book of Mormon would help us to "repent and prepare to stand before the judgment-seat of Christ. (V. 22).

Mormon
Chapter 4

Because of the Nephites' desire for vengeance, "they began to be smitten; for were it not for that, the Lamanites could have had no power over them." (V. 4, see 3 Nephi 3:21). Sometimes, there is no need for God to intervene in our affairs in order for justice to prevail, when "it is by the wicked that the wicked are punished; for it is the wicked that stir up the hearts of the children of men unto bloodshed." (V. 5).

When "all these things had been done ... there had been thousands slain on both sides, both the Nephites and the Lamanites." (V. 9). "And yet the Nephites repented not of the evil they had done, but persisted in their wickedness continually." (V. 10). "And it is impossible for the tongue to describe, or for man to write a perfect description of the horrible scene of the blood and carnage which was among the people, both of the Nephites and of the Lamanites; and every heart was hardened, so that they delighted in the shedding of blood continually." (V. 11). The entire society was "past feeling." (See 1 Nephi 17:45, & Moroni 9:20).

"There never had been so great wickedness among all the children of Lehi, nor even among all the house of Israel, according to the words of the Lord, as was among this people." (V. 12). The Lamanites began the practice of offering as human sacrifices to their idol gods their women and children prisoners. Naturally, this infuriated the Nephites, who in 367 A.D. "came against the Lamanites with (such) exceedingly great anger ... that they did beat again the Lamanites, and drive them out of their lands." (V. 15, see Commentary Reference to Mormon 5:15).

This was to be the last victory of the Nephite armies in their wars against the Lamanites. "And from this time forth did the Nephites gain no power over the Lamanites, but began to be swept off by them even as a dew before the sun." (V. 18). Undoubtedly at great personal risk, "Mormon, seeing that the Lamanites were about to overthrow the land, therefore (he) did go to the hill Shim, and did take up all the records which Ammaron had hid up unto the Lord." (V. 23). The year was 375 A.D. With the passage of one more decade, the Nephites would cease to exist as a nation.

"Now, I, Mormon
seeing that the Lamanites
were about to overthrow the land,
therefore, I did go to the hill Shim,
and did take up all the records which
Ammaron had hid up unto the Lord."
(Mormon 4:23).

Mormon
Chapter 5

Mormon was filled with compassion for his people, and wrote: I did "repent of the oath which I had made that I would no more assist them; and they gave me command again of their armies, for they looked upon me as though I could deliver them from their afflictions." (V. 1). He was "without hope", though, because he knew that the judgments of the Lord concerning his people would inevitably be pronounced upon their heads. Their immediate problem was that they "did struggle for their lives without calling upon that Being who created them." (V. 2).

The Lamanites' march through the Land of Zarahemla was inexorable, and "so great were their numbers that they did tread the people of the Nephites under their feet." (V. 6). This may have been both a physical description of the might of the Lamanites and an Old-world metaphor for their terrible power over their adversaries. In any event, the Nephites scattered in confusion before them, "and those whose flight was swifter than the Lamanites' did escape, and those whose flight did not exceed the Lamanites' were swept down and destroyed." (V. 7). It was just that simple.

"It is impossible for the tongue to describe, or for man to write a perfect description of the horrible scene ... which was among the people, both of the Nephites and of the Lamanites." (Mormon 4:11). Mormon only wrote "a small abridgment, daring not to give a full account of the things which (he had) seen." (V. 9). It was not his desire "to harrow up the souls of men in casting before them such an awful scene of blood and carnage as was laid before (his) eyes." (V. 8). The use of the words "small abridgement" in this verse is puzzling, inasmuch as Mormon was not abridging records from the Large Plates of Nephi, but was recording his impressions of the scene of destruction directly on the Plates of Mormon. Perhaps he meant "a small account", as he clarified the verse with "daring not to give a full account", and inasmuch as he began his own record with the words: "And now I, Mormon, make a record of the things which I have both seen and heard, and call it the Book of Mormon." (Mormon 1:1, see Commentary Reference to Alma 24:19).

His record was written for the benefit of "the remnant of the house of Jacob" (v. 12), and to "the unbelieving of the Jews" (v. 14), for the following specific purposes. First, that they might "be persuaded that Jesus is the Christ, the Son of the living God." (V. 14). Secondly, "that the Father (might) bring about, through his most Beloved, his great and eternal purpose, in restoring the Jews, or all the house of Israel, to the land of their inheritance, which the Lord their God hath given them, unto the fulfilling of his covenant." (V. 14, see Commentary Reference to Alma 24:19). Thirdly, "that the seed of this people (might) more fully believe his gospel, which shall go forth unto them from the Gentiles." (V. 15).

Mormon warned that the Lamanites would become "a dark, a filthy, and a loathsome people, beyond the description of that which ever hath been amongst us ... and this because of their unbelief and idolatry." (V. 15, see 3 Nephi 4:7).

Chroniclers of the late Middle Ages tell us something of the religious practices of the Aztecs, who may have been descendants of apostate Book of Mormon peoples:

"Eyewitness accounts of Ahuitzotl's spectacular dedication of the great temple in Tenochtitlan in 1487 describe the greatest orgy of human sacrifice in the history of the Aztec Empire. Over eighty thousand victims formed four lines stretching far along the causeways into the city. The kings of the Triple Alliance, in full regalia, assisted by the priests, who held the wretches, offered their hearts to the idols in a sacrifice lasting four days from dawn to dusk." (Gene S. Stuart, "The Mighty Aztecs," p. 110). The caricature of religion was extremely important in the lives of the descendants of the Lamanites who fought at Cumorah. By the Middle Ages, among the people who lived in the vicinity, war was waged primarily for the purpose of obtaining prisoners to sacrifice to idol gods.

It is no wonder that Mormon wrote: "The Spirit of the Lord hath already ceased to strive with their fathers; and they are without Christ and God in the world; and they are driven about as chaff before the wind." (V. 16). Mormon evidently felt that even the Light of Christ had been extinguished in their lives because of their gross wickedness.

He acknowledged that at one time they had been "a delightsome people, and they had Christ for their shepherd; yea, they were led even by God the Father. But now, behold, they are led about by Satan, even as chaff is driven before the wind, or as a vessel is tossed about upon the waves, without sail or anchor, or without anything wherewith to steer her; and even as she is, so are they." (V. 17-18). Everywhere in his record, Mormon skillfully utilized word pictures to draw striking contrasts relating to the behavior of the Nephites, and his talent did not desert him here.

Even though his people no longer had the capacity to call upon Father because they had taught "their children that they should not believe," (4 Nephi 1:38), Mormon acknowledged that "the Lord will remember the prayers of the righteous, which have been put up unto him for them." (V. 21). For nearly a thousand years, the Nephite prophets had prayed to God, begging Him to preserve their records, that they might influence their descendants in the Last Days, to persuade them to come unto Christ once again. (See Moroni 10:32).

Mormon also warned the Gentiles of the Last Days to heed the warnings and counsel of The Book of Mormon, lest the wrath of God be turned to them, and "lest a remnant of the seed of Jacob shall go forth among you as a lion, and tear you in pieces, and there is none to deliver." (V. 24, see 3 Nephi 20:16). The manner in which this prophecy might be fulfilled has not been made clear in the scriptures. The remnant of the seed of Jacob may refer to members of the Church in the latter days who go out into all the world powerfully preaching the Gospel and tearing down apostate teachings, destroying their enemies with the word of God, by turning them into the disciples of Christ.

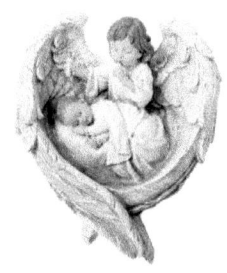

Mormon
Chapter 6

When Mormon began this chapter, he knew that these verses would be the last few passages written upon The Plates of Mormon. Verse 1 states: "And now I finish my record concerning the destruction of my people, the Nephites." As commander of the army, he contacted the king of the Lamanites and proposed that the final battle should be fought at "the land of Cumorah, by a hill which was called Cumorah." (V. 2). This was really the only option available to the Nephites, but it was a desperate gamble, nonetheless. Making an appointment for a battle between armies was actually an established pattern in pre-Columbian times. (John Sorenson, "An Ancient American Setting for The Book of Mormon," p. 346, & "Ancient America," p. 383).

The Lamanite king agreed to the terms, possibly because the location was deep inside the limited territory still under Nephite control. Since the Lamanites were being given an invitation to penetrate to that location for the battle, they would have nothing to lose. (V. 3, & Commentary Reference to Mormon 2:29).

The hill Cumorah was "in a land of many waters, rivers, and fountains." (V. 4). The advantage that Mormon hoped to gain over the Lamanites might have had to do with his intimate knowledge of the area, it being the land of his birth. (See Mormon 1:6). Also, if the lands of The Book of Mormon do have a Meso-American setting, to have retreated further north would have put the Nephites in direct opposition to the culture of Teotihuacan, that by 380 A.D. was a powerful state allied culturally, if not politically, with the Lamanites. (See John L. Sorenson, "An Ancient American Setting for The Book of Mormon," p. 346, & "Ancient America," p. 383).

It is also possible that the Lamanites had some knowledge of the last great battles of the Jaredite civilization that had been fought on this territory. Perhaps the Lamanites thought the setting would be to their advantage, because of superstitions or traditions concerning the Jaredite destruction on the very spot where their own battle would soon take place. In any event, while as many Nephites as possible were gathering to that one location, Mormon took advantage of the calm before the storm to go to the hill Cumorah, there to hide up "all the records which had been entrusted to (him) by the hand of the Lord, save it were (The Plates of Mormon)," which he gave to his son Moroni. (V. 6).

As the Lamanite army approached, at least 23 Nephite captains assembled their forces to meet them, each leading 10,000 soldiers. (V. 10-15). As had been the case in most Book of Mormon military campaigns, families accompanied their fighting men to the fields of battle. So, the inevitable outcome was destined to be genocide, and not merely the military defeat of the twenty-three 10,000-man divisions that made up the Nephite force. All the Nephites, in fact, would be slaughtered on that one day.

"Could Mesa America have been the scene for a war on the impressive scale suggested by The Book of Mormon? The central Mexican chronicler, Ixtlilxochitl, reported of the Tultecas around A.D. 1060 that in a three-year war, 5,600,000 were slain on both sides. Even allowing him considerable room for exaggeration, we are left with little doubt that the battle at Cumorah was within the realm of the plausible in Meso-American terms." (John Sorenson, "An Ancient American Setting for The Book of Mormon," p. 349-350, see Commentary Reference to Ether 15:1-2).

When it was over, Mormon recorded that of all the Nephites present at the commencement of the battle, all "save it were ... twenty and four who were with me, and also a few who had escaped into the south countries, and a few who had deserted over unto the Lamanites, had fallen." (V. 15, see Mormon 8:5). Among the few survivors was his son Moroni. (See v. 11). Mormon had witnessed the final destruction of his people from the top of the hill Cumorah. (V. 11). "And (his) soul was rent with anguish, because of the slain of (his) people." (V. 16). It is reasonable to assume that as many as one million people lay dead on the plains below, counting Nephite and Lamanite soldiers, together with their women and children.

The scriptures clearly teach that the survivors after this last great battle were no longer identified as Nephites. Some escaped into the south countries. (V. 15). Some had dissented from the Nephites and had switched their allegiance to the Lamanites. (V. 15, see Mormon 9:24). Many likely never gathered at Cumorah in the first place, because of the confusion in the Land of Zarahemla during this period of anarchy. (See Mormon 2:7-8). Finally, the Doctrine & Covenants teaches that in the Last Days, many Nephite descendants will be identified. (D&C 3:17-20 & 10:48). But, as far as Mormon was concerned, the thousand-year history of his people was over. They "had fallen, and their flesh, and bones, and blood lay upon the face of the earth, being left by the hands of those who slew them to molder upon the land, and to crumble and to return to their mother earth." (V. 15).

All he could say was: "O ye fair sons and daughters, ye fathers and mothers, ye husbands and wives, ye fair ones, how is it that ye could have fallen! But behold, ye are gone, and my sorrows cannot bring your return." (V. 19-20). Mormon no longer had a Nephite audience, but he continued to record his impressions for our benefit. Therefore, the counsel in the remainder of chapter 6 and in chapter 7 is for those living in the Last Days, as much as it is a lamentation for those of his people who had died.

"O that ye had repented before this great destruction had come upon you." (V. 22). Those words echo to us from an obscure hill rising above a vast plain somewhere in Meso-America, and they should reverberate in our minds and whisper repeatedly to us that we should not procrastinate the day of our repentance.

Mormon
Chapter 7

This is the final chapter written by Mormon, on the Plates of Mormon. It is his last testament to those who are the descendants of "this people who are spared," the "remnant of the house of Israel," the sons and daughters of those who would soon kill him and the remainder of his family. (V. 1).

Mormon desired that this remnant might "know of the things of their fathers." (V. 1). He again reminded them that they were "of the house of Israel." (V. 2). If we find it odd that this remnant would forget their noble lineage, we might then reflect on the "covenant consciousness" of the Church in the Last Days. Sometimes members of the Church of Jesus Christ of Latter-day Saints forget that they are also of the House of Israel, either literally or by adoption, and that they too may claim through righteousness, the covenant blessings promised by God to Abraham and his descendants.

"All have sinned, and have come short of the Glory of God." (James 3:23). Therefore, Mormon reminded the remnant that they "must come unto repentance" in order to be saved. (V. 3). Knowing of their aggressive inclinations, he urged them to "lay down (their) weapons of war, and delight no more in the shedding of blood, and take them not again, save it be that God shall command (them)." (V. 4).

The Savior weighed in on the theme, and counseled Latter-day Israel to "renounce war, and proclaim peace." (D&C 98:16). As President Spencer W. Kimball pointed out: "When threatened, we often become anti-enemy rather than pro-kingdom of God." ("Ensign,"6/1976). In other words, the only real solutions to problems are those that employ Gospel principles, and these are easy to overlook in the heat of the conflict.

But the Savior also said: "Ye shall defend your families, even unto bloodshed." (Alma 43:47). When the Nephites were "not fighting for monarchy nor power but (rather) for their homes, and their liberties, their wives and their children, and their all, yea, for their rites of worship and their church ... they were doing that which they felt was the duty which they owed to their God." (Alma 43:45-46). Sometimes, the actions of others require bold confrontations that inevitably lead to conflict.

Doctrine & Covenants Section 134, a Declaration of Beliefs regarding governments and laws in general, was adopted by unanimous vote at a general assembly of the Church, held at Kirtland, Ohio, 8/17/1835. (See "History of The Church," 2:247-249). It states: "We believe that all men are justified in defending themselves, their friends, and property, and the government, from the unlawful assaults and encroachments of all persons in times of exigency, where immediate appeal cannot be made to the laws, and relief afforded." (D&C 134:11).

Mormon knew that when the descendants of the warlike Lamanites would be brought to a "knowledge of (their) fathers, and repent of all (their) sins and iniquities, and believe in Jesus Christ," they would "blossom as the rose." (V. 5, see D&C 49:24). In other words, the gift of salvation would be theirs. (V. 7). As the Savior promised, through Joseph Smith: "If thou wilt do good, yea, and hold out faithful to the end, thou shalt be saved in the kingdom of God, which is the greatest of all the gifts of God; for there is no gift greater than the gift of salvation." (D&C 6:13, see Commentary Reference to Mosiah 2:25).

Mormon emphasized that the Gospel of Jesus Christ would come to Latter-day Israel in two books: "Not only in this record, but also in the record which shall come unto the Gentiles from the Jews." (V. 8). The Book of Mormon has come forth in a day when many doubt the historical accuracy and the validity of the doctrinal messages of the Bible, and so The Book of Mormon has been given to the world as another testament of Jesus Christ. With this understanding, Mormon's concluding statements have greater impact. "For behold, (The Book of Mormon) is written for the intent that ye may believe (the Bible); and if ye believe (the Bible) ye will believe (The Book of Mormon) also; and if ye believe (The Book of Mormon) ye will know concerning your fathers, and also the marvelous works which were wrought by the power of God among them." (V. 9, see 2 Nephi 25:17, 27:26, Helaman 3:13-16, 3 Nephi 5:8, 20:8, & 21:9, Moroni 10:3, D&C 4:1, & Isaiah 29:14).

Mormon was an amazing individual. He could see beyond the terrible suffering caused by the apostasy of his own people, and he could differentiate their behavior from an intrinsic Nephite and Lamanite nobility. He truly believed that the children of Father Lehi were "numbered among the people of the first covenant," or the magnificent Abrahamic Covenant, that had been made between the Father of The Faithful and God Himself. (V. 10). To the very last, perhaps just hours before he was slain by the Lamanites, he wrote: "If it so be that ye believe in Christ, and are baptized, first with water, then with fire and with the Holy Ghost, following the example of our Savior, according to that which he hath commanded us, it shall be well with you in the day of judgment. Amen." (V. 10).

Mormon's perception was clear and accurate. He could see the autobiographical thread of his people leading backward to Deity. He understood that even the most hardened soul has within it "the acorn of a potential oak, the unsculptured image of a glorified personality." (Truman Madsen, "Eternal Man," p. 17).

Mormon had a great capacity to love his people. In the seventh chapter of The Book of Moroni, Mormon's son felt inspired to include a discourse on the subject of "faith, hope, and charity" that had been given to the people by his father. (Moroni 7:1). The essence of that message is reflected in these lines: "He drew a circle that shut me out, Heretic, rebel, a thing to flout. But Love and I had the wit to win. We drew a circle that took him in." (Edwin Markham).

Mormon felt genuine love for the Nephites and the Lamanites. He surely would have agreed with the following sentiment, articulated on a smaller scale, but nevertheless relevant: "Wouldn't it be nice if, as we tucked our child into bed after a particularly stressful day, we could say something like this. 'I've been watching you, and you are about the most special human being I've ever met. I'm proud to wear your name. I know we had a disagreement today, but that was behavior. It's the person I love. It's behavior that got in the way. I love you unconditionally, not based on achievement, but based on you, and your potential. I love you very much." (Anonymous). This is the charity Mormon felt for his brethren.

Mormon
Chapter 8

The word "Nephite" changed its meaning near the close of The Book of Mormon. From 34 A.D. to 231 A.D. there were no "ites" of any kind, but then a group revolted from the body of the Church who consciously distinguished themselves as Lamanites. (See 4 Nephi 1:20). Those who remained true to the Church were called Nephites. For the remainder of The Book of Mormon, "Nephite" refers to those who remained faithful after 231 A.D.

Mormon had named his son well, after the great Nephite Captain Moroni. In his abridgment of Alma, Mormon had recorded his impression of that great patriot: "Verily, verily I say unto you, if all men had been, and were, and ever would be, like unto Moroni, behold, the very powers of hell would have been shaken forever; yea, the devil would never have power over the hearts of the children of men." (Alma 48:17).

Although Mormon was not personally acquainted with Captain Moroni, he knew of his heroic deeds through the oral and written histories of the Nephites. Even within the pressure-cooker of apostasy in which they lived, Mormon's more righteous contemporaries would have known of the exploits of Captain Moroni, and would intuitively have sought a leader that matched his skills.

Mormon wrote that this first "Moroni was a strong and a mighty man; he was a man of perfect understanding; yea, a man that did not delight in bloodshed; a man whose soul did joy in the liberty and the freedom of his country, and his brethren from bondage and slavery. Yea, a man whose heart did swell with thanksgiving to his God, for the many privileges and blessings which he bestowed upon his people; a man who did labor exceedingly for the welfare and safety of his people. Yea, and he was a man who was firm in the faith of Christ, and he had sworn with an oath to defend his people, his rights, and his country, and his religion, even to the loss of his blood." (Alma 48:11-13).

"Behold, he was a man like unto Ammon, the son of Mosiah, yea, and even the other sons of Mosiah, yea, and also Alma and his sons, for they were all men of God." (Alma 48:18). Largely because of the leadership of Moroni, "there never was a happier time among the people of Nephi, since the days of Nephi, than in the days of Moroni." (Alma 50:23).

This first Moroni sought the word of the Lord through the living prophet (Alma 43:23-26), he was concerned for those who served under him (Alma 43:18-21, 48:7-10), he used strategy (Alma 43:27-35), and he was magnanimous in forgiveness but firm in the right. (Alma 44:1-20). He was patriotic, prayerful, and provided a standard for the righteous to follow. (Alma 46:11-20). He was an example of a noble man of God. (Alma 48:11-18).

Because Moroni was always quick to deal mercifully with a repentant enemy, many of the Lamanites were finally convinced that his policies were superior to theirs, that had espoused hatred and warfare. (See Alma 62:15-17, 27-29). Moroni had a noble heart, and was willing to make the greatest personal sacrifices upon the altar of freedom.

As Ezra Taft Benson declared: "Our stand for freedom is a most basic part of our religion. This stand helped us get to the earth, and our reaction to freedom in this life will have eternal consequences. We have many duties, but we have no excuse that can compensate for our loss of liberty." (C.R., 10/1966).

Moroni, who was the only son of Mormon identified in The Book of Mormon lived up to his namesake in virtually every way. (See V. 5). He was surely one "of the noble and great ones," prepared from before the foundation of the world for his mission on the earth. (See Abraham 3:22). Imagine how difficult it must have been for him to take up The Plates of Mormon and "finish the record of (his) father." (V. 1). Think of how heavy his heart must have been. Little wonder that he recorded in the introductory verse to this chapter: "Behold, I have but few things to write." (V. 1).

But he was true to the commandment given him by his father, and directed his testimony to those living in the Last Days who were the only audience left to receive it. (V. 1). Moroni had little hope of survival after the "great and tremendous battle at Cumorah." (V. 2). He had witnessed the flight of "the Nephites who had escaped into the country southward, (who) were hunted by the Lamanites, until they were all destroyed." (V. 2). Even his father, who had seen ten thousand warriors under his personal command slain on the field of battle, and who then had fallen "wounded in their midst" (Mormon 6:10), was finally killed by the Lamanite horde. (V. 3). Cry havoc / take no prisoners!

Moroni had little inclination to detail the final destruction of his people. He wanted to get the job of writing over with as soon as possible, and then hide the records. "I even remain alone," he recorded, "to write the sad tale of the destruction of my people. But behold, they are gone, and I fulfil the commandment of my father. And whether they will slay me, I know not. Therefore, I will write and hide up the records in the earth, and whither I go, it mattereth not." (V. 3-4). We suppose that Moroni hid the records in the hill Cumorah, although he does not specify.

Moroni felt so badly! He knew why his father had kept the records, and so he knew of their importance. (V. 5). He said: "I would write it also, if I had room upon the plates, but I have not; and ore I have none, for I am alone. My father hath been slain in battle, and all my kinsfolk, and I have not friends nor whither to go; and how long the Lord will suffer that I may live, I know not." (V. 5). In fact, he would live another 21 years.

Probably some time after the great battle at Cumorah, Moroni added the first of a number of postscripts to the record: "And behold, the Lamanites have hunted my people, the Nephites, down from city to city and from place to place, even until they are no more (as a people); and great has been their fall; yea, great and marvelous is the destruction of my people, the Nephites." (V. 7). The Nephites to whom he referred were likely those who had not gathered at Cumorah before the last great battle. There must have been many, perhaps thousands of them, scattered across the land.

The concept of the "destruction" of the Nephites deserves our attention. The definition of the term is "to unbuild, to separate violently into its constituent parts, to break up the structure." Actually, only once in The Book of Mormon are we told of a case of annihilation, when Mormon was careful to employ the unambiguous words: "Every living soul of the Ammonihahites was destroyed." (Alma 16:9, see 1 Nephi 17:31 & 13:30, 2 Nephi 3:3 & 25:9, and especially Moroni 1:2). In 385 A.D., the Nephite nation was obviously destroyed, and was never again reconstructed. But it was certainly not annihilated.

As for the Lamanites, their total victory turned out to be Satan's cruel deception. No-one wins at war, and so, the violence continued unabated. "And behold also, the Lamanites are at war one with another; and the whole face of this land is one continual round of murder and bloodshed; and no one knoweth the end of the war." (V. 8).

Moroni was so disgusted with conditions in the land that he wrote: "And now, behold, I say no more concerning them, for there are none save it be the Lamanites and (apostate Nephite Gadianton) robbers that do exist upon the face of the land." (V. 9). He just wanted to get them out of his mind. "Behold, I make an end of speaking concerning this people. I am the son of Mormon, and my father was a descendant of Nephi." (V. 13). In effect, he was saying that, in sharp contrast to those inhabiting the land, he was the son of a righteous man who was of noble lineage. The trauma of Cumorah could never take away the comfort of that knowledge.

In Moroni's solitary existence, "the stars fade away, the sun himself grow dim with age, and nature sink in years. But (he) shall flourish in immortal youth, unhurt amidst the war of elements, the wreck of matter, and the crash of worlds." (Joseph Addison, "Cato," Act 5, Scene 1). Moroni's world was shattered, and it took time for him to restore his emotional balance. Perhaps he suffered from post-traumatic stress syndrome, and never could fully adjust to his lonely circumstances, but some of the best literature in The Book of Mormon follows the crisis at Cumorah.

In his most straitened circumstances, he was not left entirely alone. He wrote of the Three Nephite "disciples of Jesus, who did tarry in the land" (V. 10), saying, "My father and I have seen them, and they have ministered unto us." (V. 11, see 3 Nephi 28:26-27). It must have been wonderful to have their companionship, counsel, and priesthood blessing. It would be akin to "stepping on shore, and finding it heaven! Of taking hold of a hand, and finding it God's hand. Of breathing a new air, and finding it celestial air. Of feeling invigorated, and finding it immortality. Of passing from storm and tempest to the unbroken calm of God's Rest. Of waking up, and finding it Home." (Anonymous).

Moroni's concern then shifted to how The Book of Mormon would be received by those in the Last Days. He wrote: "And whoso receiveth this record, and shall not condemn it because of the imperfections which are in it, the same shall know of greater things than these. Behold, I am Moroni, and were it possible, I would make all things known unto you." (V. 12, see Title Page to The Book of Mormon, 1 Nephi 19:6, Mormon 9:31-34, Ether 12:23-28, & Essay: "Writing on Plates Was a Pain").

The "imperfections" to which Moroni alluded refer to his perceived inability to communicate in writing as clearly as he would have liked, but not to doctrinal inconsistencies. Later, he was able to elaborate on this subject. In The Book of Ether, he recorded a conversation he had with the Lord: "And I said unto him: Lord, the Gentiles will mock at these things, because of our weakness in writing; for ... thou hast made us mighty in word by faith, but thou hast not made us mighty in writing ... because of the awkwardness of our hands ... Wherefore, when we write we behold our weakness, and stumble because of the placing of our words; and I fear lest the Gentiles shall mock at our words." (Ether 12:23-25, see v. 40, Commentary References to Jacob 4:1, Alma 24:19 & Words of Mormon 1:15 and Alma 24:19, & Jacob 4:1).

Shortly after the carnage at Cumorah, Moroni explained: "And if there be faults, they be the faults of a man. But behold, we know no faults; nevertheless, God knoweth all things; therefore, he that condemneth, let him be aware, lest he shall be in danger of hell fire." (V. 17). The Lord reassured him: "Fools mock, but they shall mourn; and my grace is sufficient for the meek, that they shall take no advantage of your weakness." (Ether 12:26).

Moroni recognized that the plates were "of no worth because of the commandment of the Lord. For truly he saith that no one shall have them to get gain." (V. 14). The records had been preserved by the power of God for a specific purpose, and He would never permit them to be exploited. Their monetary value was negligible, "but the record thereof is of great worth." (V. 14).

When Moroni wrote that "whoso shall bring it to light, him will the Lord bless," he was pointedly speaking of the Prophet of the Restoration, Joseph Smith. (See Mosiah 18:13). But in the most general sense, the verse applies to all those who teach Gospel principles using The Book of Mormon as their guide and as Another Testament of Jesus Christ. (V. 14, see V. 16). The Book of Mormon was literally "brought out of darkness unto light (and) brought out of the earth." But figuratively, it "shall shine forth out of darkness, and come unto the knowledge of the people; and it shall be done by the power of God" by those who teach with the Spirit. (V. 16, see D&C 20:8, 42:14, & H.C., 4:537).

Moroni cautioned those who would seek a sign as confirmation of the divine authenticity of The Book of Mormon. "And he that saith: Show unto me, or ye shall be smitten - let him beware lest he commandeth that which is forbidden of the Lord." (V. 18). "And he that shall breathe out wrath and strifes against the work of the Lord, and against the covenant people of the Lord who are the house of Israel, and shall say: We will destroy the work of the Lord, and the Lord will not remember his covenant which he hath made unto the house of Israel - the same is in danger to be hewn down and cast into the fire." (V. 21, see 3 Nephi 29:8, and Commentary Reference to 1 Nephi 19:14).

In 1921, President Heber J. Grant issued a prophetic warning to the world, concerning conscious persecution of Israel, the Lord's Covenant People: "By the authority of the Holy Priesthood of God, that has again been restored to the earth, and by the ministration, under the direction of the Prophet of God, Apostles of the Lord Jesus Christ have been to the Holy Land and have dedicated that country for the return of the Jews; and we believe that in the due time of the Lord they shall be in the favor of God again. And let no Latter-day Saint be guilty of taking any part in any crusade against these people."

As Moroni declared: "For the eternal purposes of the Lord shall roll on, until all his promises shall be fulfilled ... And as the Lord liveth, he will remember the covenant which he hath made with them. (V. 22-23). See also Enos 1:16, where God promised that The Book of Mormon would come forth unto the Lamanites in the Last Days, and also D&C 3:16-19, that indicates that the Gospel is to go to all the descendants of Book of Mormon peoples. (See V. 25).

In verses 26-32, Moroni described conditions in the Last Days when The Book of Mormon would come forth. It would be revealed in a day when people would be rational and self-reliant, when they would say that "miracles are done away." (V. 26). But it would stir the soul and speak a language inarticulate and yet in harmony with the Spirit, "even as if one should speak from the dead." (V. 26). Joseph Fielding Smith once said: "The impressions on the soul that come from the Holy Ghost are far more significant than a vision. It is where spirit speaks to spirit, and the imprint upon the soul is far more difficult to erase." ("Improvement Era", 11/1966). It is because The Book of Mormon is such a powerful witness of Jesus Christ that it is one of the most effective missionary tools available, and it is also why Satan has tried so hard to prevent its translation, publication, and distribution, and why he continually tries to discredit the work.

The Book of Mormon was to come forth "in a day when the blood of saints shall cry unto the Lord, because of secret combinations, and the works of darkness." (V. 27). These are the agents of Satan who "stare uncomprehendingly with slit eyed skepticism" as the work unfolds before them. (Neal Maxwell). These are they who tried fanatically to disrupt the reformers who paved the way for the Restoration.

In the late Middle Ages in Europe, "theological rabies raged as seldom before or after in history. The Lutheran Pastor Nivander (1582) listed forty characteristics of wolves, and showed that these were precisely the distinctive marks of Calvinists. Said a Lutheran pamphlet of 1590: 'If anybody wishes to be told, in a few words, concerning which articles of the faith we are fighting with the diabolical Calvinistic brood of vipers, the answer is, all and every one of them!' 'These raging theologians,' mourned a Protestant writer in 1610, 'have so greatly aggravated and augmented the disastrous strife among the Christians who have seceded from the papacy, that there seems no hope of all this screaming, abusing, and anathematizing coming to an end before the advent of the Last Day.'" (Wil Durant, "The Age of Reason Begins," p. 552-553).

In contrast, one of the Articles of Faith of the Church of Jesus Christ of Latter-day Saints states: "We claim the privilege of worshiping Almighty God according to the dictates of our own conscience, and allow all men the same privilege, let them worship how, where, or what they may." (11th Article of Faith). Moral agency, or the power to choose in an atmosphere of opposition, is the crowning principle of creation. "Therefore, cheer up your hearts, and remember that ye are free to act for yourselves - to choose the way of everlasting death, or the way of eternal life." (2 Nephi 10:23, see 2 Nephi 2:27). We can choose, but we cannot escape the consequences of our choices.

Moroni prophesied that The Book of Mormon would come in a day when the power of God would be denied, and when churches would "become defiled and be lifted up in the pride of their hearts." (V. 28). Joseph Smith was given the following counsel in the Sacred Grove, in response to his astonishingly profound question: "Which church is right?" "I was answered that I must join none of them," he said, "for they were all wrong; and the Personage who addressed me said that all their creeds were an abomination in his sight, that those professors were all corrupt; that: 'They draw near to me with their lips, but their hearts are far from me, they teach for doctrines the commandments of men, having a form of godliness, but they deny the power thereof.'" (J.S.H., 1:19).

Specifically, the abomination of their creeds was that they had form without substance. Insult was added to injury when hypocrisy became a part of humanized, spiritually impotent dogma. As soon as people did not really believe, but were only professors of religion, it become "magical," because the power by which the church operated was transferred from God to those who professed to be His earthly representatives, but who were only fiercely competing for "market share." The Bible had become a magical book in the eyes of many, conveying power and knowledge without the aid of revelation. Priesthood had acquired the status of an office that automatically bestowed power and grace without regard to the spiritual or moral qualifications of its possessor.

The Lord told Joseph Smith, in the Preface to The Doctrine and Covenants: The religious orders of the day have "strayed from mine ordinances, and have broken mine everlasting covenant. They seek not the Lord to establish his righteousness, but every man walketh in his own way, and after the image of his own god, whose image is in the likeness of the world, and whose substance is that of an idol." (D&C 1:15-16).

Moroni pleaded with those in the Last Days who had "transfigured the holy word of God," or who had changed the appearance and substance of the scriptures, and so had brought damnation upon their souls. (V. 33, see 3 Nephi chapter 28). For Moroni, Jesus Christ was clearly "the way, the truth, and the life." (John 14:6).

In the Last Days, as the Spirit is withdrawn, "there shall be heard of fires, and tempests, and vapors of smoke in foreign lands; and there shall also be heard of wars, rumors of wars, and earthquakes in divers places." (V. 29-30). These are conditions with which Moroni was intimately familiar. He knew that the wrath of God requires the destruction of the wicked, and that our day would be frighteningly similar to the last days of the Nephites. Perhaps, it is because The Book of Mormon speaks to our common feeling that it is so convincing.

Moroni wrote of "great pollutions upon the face of the earth." (V. 31, see v. 36 & 38). He was not necessarily referring to industrial or environmental pollutions, but rather to those qualities that canker the soul and corrupt the expression of the Spirit. It is interesting that Moroni would call our attention to "pollution" in a day when it is fashionable to have an "environmental awareness," but when it is also common to ignore the welfare of our less fortunate neighbors.

In this context, it is worth retelling the story of "reconverted Mormon, Jesse Knight, (who) as a center for the operation of his silver mines (in the late Nineteenth Century) built a town unique in the world of mining. At his own expense, and in a sense of gratitude, he built a chapel and an attractive cultural hall. He set up evening activities, lively and enlightening enough to compete with, and often to defeat, the fleshpots in the nearby town of Eureka. He established a school, hired a first-rate teacher, taxed every miner to contribute to its operation, and kept the town spotless. He sponsored lectures, concerts, town dances, basketball games and socials. Meantime, he paid his men more than the prevailing wage, closed down the operation on the Sabbath, and fired any man who would not leave alcohol alone. His accumulated fortune ended up saving the credit of the Church and substantially underwriting the beginnings of the huge enterprise now known as Brigham Young University." (Truman Madsen, "Defender of The Faith," p. 64-65).

In 1965, David O. McKay was asked what the Savior would feel had been our most important earthly responsibilities. Among a list of six was the following: "He will ask for an accountability on what you have done to contribute in a positive manner to your community, state, country, and the world." ("The Divine Center," p. 55).

One question Moroni posed in this chapter should haunt every casual reader of The Book of Mormon today: "Why are ye ashamed to take upon you the name of Christ?" (V. 38). By direct experience, Moroni knew that there is no room for summer soldiers or sunshine patriots in the missionary army of God. Only as our own faith and testimonies reach the same intensity as Moroni's, will we be able to understand the penetrating quality of his question. B.H. Roberts taught that if you feel a thing, you can express it. If you can't, you do not feel it strongly enough. "Once, in a sermon delivered in Logan, Utah, he described Christ and the raising of Lazarus. So vivid were his images, and so moving his presence, that the audience was carried with him. When, in a loud voice, he repeated the Master's words, 'Lazarus, come forth!', the entire congregation involuntarily came to its feet." (Truman Madsen, "Defender of The Faith," p. 355).

Mormon had wisely chosen a noble name for his son. To the very end of his life, Moroni lived up to the standard of righteousness and excellence that it represented. Although he was unable to positively influence his own people, his name and memory will live always in the hearts of the Latter-day Saints and in the history of the Restoration.

We think of Moroni when we read that "every man and every person who lives in this world wields an influence, whether for good or for evil. It is not what he says; it is not what he does. It is what he is. Every person radiates what he or she really is. It is our energy that affects the people around us. As individuals, we must think nobler thoughts. We must not encourage vile thoughts or low aspirations. We shall radiate them if we do. If we think noble thoughts; if we encourage and cherish noble aspirations, there will be that radiation when we meet people, especially when we associate with them." (David O. McKay, "Man May Know for Himself," p. 108).

"Act now, before it is too late," urged Spencer W. Kimball. "Now is the time to chart the course of action you will follow tomorrow and next week and next year. Now is the time to commit yourself to be as Abraham (or Moroni), to follow the Lord, to refuse to procrastinate, to repent of those sins you have committed, to begin to keep those commandments you have been failing to live. Determine now to attend priesthood and Sacrament meetings every Sabbath, to pay your tithing faithfully, sustain in very deed the programs of the Church, visit the temple often, give service in the organizations, and keep your actions constructive, your attitudes wholesome. Remember that Abraham sought for his appointment to the priesthood. He did not wait for God to come to him; he sought diligently through prayer and obedient living to learn the will of God. Here, then, is the challenge the Lord gives every returned missionary, every single man and woman, every father and mother in the Church: 'Go ye, therefore, and do the works of Abraham' (and Moroni)" (D&C 132:32). ("The Example of Abraham").

Significantly, it was Moroni who visited Joseph Smith as a glorified, resurrected personage. In these verses toward the end of his father's book, if we read between the lines of sadness reflected in many of his words, we can see that he felt as did Paul, who wrote: "For I am now ready to be offered, and the time of my departure is at hand. I have fought a good fight, I have finished my course, I have kept the faith. Henceforth, there is laid up for me a crown of righteousness, which the Lord, the righteous judge, shall give me at that day; and not to me only, but unto all them also that love his appearing." (2 Timothy 4:6-8).

Moroni wrote: "I speak unto you as if ye were present, and yet ye are not. But behold, Jesus Christ hath shown you unto me, and I know your doing." (V. 35). As we study the last two chapters of The Book of Mormon, The Book of Ether, and The Book of Moroni, the Spirit will reveal Moroni to us, and we will know him as intimately as he knows us.

The prophets in The Book of Mormon recorded how hard it was to engrave their thoughts on plates of metal. The remarkable thing is that they were able to do so at all. "We could write but little, because of the awkwardness of our hands ... wherefore, when we write, we behold our weakness, and stumble because of the placing of our words; and I fear lest the Gentiles shall mock at our words". (Ether 12:24-25). "I cannot write but a little of my words, because of the difficulty of engraving our words upon plates". (Jacob 4:1). "And if there be faults, they be the faults of a man". (Mormon 8:17).

Mormon
Chapter 9

This last chapter in The Book of Mormon is directed mainly to non-believers. "And now," wrote Moroni, "I speak also (to) those who do not believe in Christ." (V. 1). Virtually every one of the Nephites with whom Moroni had grown up, his friends and neighbors, and also those of his father's generation, had all gone to the Banquet of Consequences. Now, Moroni asked our worldly contemporaries in the Last Days: "Will ye believe in the day of your visitation?" (V. 2).

No-one had to convince Moroni that each one of us will some day come face to face with our Maker. He had seen tens of thousands of Nephites fall on the fields that stretched out below Cumorah; to those individuals as much as to those in the Last Days he wrote: "Do ye suppose that ye shall dwell with (God) under a consciousness of your guilt? Do ye suppose that ye could be happy to dwell with that holy Being, when your souls are racked with a consciousness of guilt that ye have ever abused his laws?" (V. 3, see Alma 34:32).

We are faced with a dilemma when there are two or more equally unfavorable solutions to a problem. On the one hand, individuals in this predicament could blithely continue to abuse the laws of God. On the other hand, they could feel badly about their transgression, but they would nevertheless stand condemned by the Justice of God, since in mortality they had fallen short of the perfection required by law in order to stand blameless in the presence of God. What is the solution to this dilemma?

The answer lies in Moroni's exhortation to "turn ye unto the Lord: Cry mightily unto the Father in the name of Jesus, that perhaps ye may be found spotless, pure, fair, and white, having been cleansed by the blood of the Lamb, at that great and last day." (V. 6). The only practical solution to the dilemma posed by transgression, or by falling short of perfection in this life, is to grasp the horns of sanctuary and claim Mercy at the feet of the Savior, Who traveled to Gethsemane to atone for our sins.

What of those, Moroni asked, who "deny the revelations of God," and say that the miracle of the Atonement has ceased or is a fable of religious fanaticism? (V. 7). These individuals, because of their skepticism, fail to comprehend the Atonement and its value to their eternal welfare. These are they who "knoweth not the gospel of Christ; yea, (they) have not read the scriptures; if so, (they do) not understand them." (V. 8). It is a question of absolute ignorance or willful rebellion.

A person must approach God in meekness with a heart that is open to the impressions of the Spirit, for we "drink damnation to (our souls, except we humble ourselves) and become as little children, and believe that salvation was, and is, and is to come, in and through the atoning blood of Christ." (Mosiah 3:18, see Matthew 18:4). John Taylor wrote: "No matter what ability and talent we may possess, all must come under this rule if we wish to know the Father and the Son. If knowledge of them is not obtained through revelation it cannot be obtained at all." ("The Gospel Kingdom," p. 112).

"For God is the same yesterday, today, and forever, and in him there is no variableness neither shadow of changing." (V. 9, see 1 Nephi 10:17-19). Policies, plans, practices, pronouncements, procedures, and programs may vary over time, and revelation is adapted to circumstances. Yet, God does not change, and neither do the purposes of His ordinances and covenants. What is constant and everlastingly consistent is revelation itself. God is the same in that He will reveal Himself to all who have faith in Jesus Christ.

"Verily, thus saith the Lord: It shall come to pass that every soul who forsaketh his sins (through repentance) and cometh unto me (in the waters of baptism) and calleth on my name (in mighty prayer) and obeyeth my voice (by responding to the promptings of the Holy Ghost) and keepeth my commandments (in perfect obedience) shall see my face and know that I am ... and that I am in the Father, and the Father in me, and the Father and I are one." (D&C 93:1 & 3, see D&C 67:10 & 88:69).

"This unity of the Godhead is a type of completeness; the mind of any one member is the mind of the others. Seeing, as each of them does, with the eye of perfection, they see and understand alike, guided by the same principles of unerring justice and equity." (James Talmage, "Articles of Faith," p. 41).

Moroni declared, "I will show you a God of miracles, even the God of Abraham, and the God of Isaac, and the God of Jacob." (V. 11. see V. 12-15). Recorded once again is the bold statement, repeated three times, that God in Heaven is the God of Israel.

"The role of Israel as the depository of true religion is almost self evident: the freeing of mankind from the idolatry which obstructs its salvation. For as Isaiah understood, there can be no redemption for man unless he conquers self-deification. He must abandon the worship of his own creations, and liberate himself from his lust for power, avarice, domination, and the cult of the state. There can be no redemption until man recognizes his moral obligations as transcendent and divine. No form of government, no level of material well-being, will save man. He will be redeemed only when 'towers fall, and Jerusalem triumphs over Babylon.' What is at stake, finally, is not only intelligence, but also feeling. Man has to change his heart. Salvation, the prophets tell us, is preconditioned by repentance. The redeeming act of God waits upon our initiative." (Abba Eban, "My People: The Story of The Jews," p. 59-60, see p. 106-107 for a treatment of Israel as the Covenant People of the Lord).

By the time of Moroni's ministry, the God of Israel had patiently waited upon His covenant people for 2,400 years. James Michener described a likely scenario in those earliest years after He had revealed Himself to Abraham: Zadock "was a spiritual man whose tired eyes could see beyond the desert to those invisible summits of the imagination where cool air existed and where the one god, El Shaddai, lived. In later generations, people who spoke other languages would translate this old Semitic name, which actually meant 'He of the mountain', as God Almighty, for El Shaddai was destined to mature into that god whom much of the world would worship. But in these fateful days, when the little group of Hebrews camped while waiting for the signal to march westward, El Shaddai was the god of no one but themselves. They were not even certain that he had continued as the god of those other Hebrews who had moved on to distant lands like Egypt. But of one thing Zadok was sure; El Shaddai personally determined the destiny of this group, for of all the peoples available to him in the teeming area between the Euphrates and the Nile, he had chosen these Hebrews as his predilected people, and they lived within his embrace, enjoying security that others did not know." (James Michener, "The Source," p. 177-178).
The God of Moroni was magnificent; He was a God of miracles. "Are not the things that God hath wrought marvelous

in our eyes? Yea, and who can comprehend the marvelous works of God?" (V. 16). The only reason why He ceases "to do miracles among the children of men is because that they dwindle in unbelief, and depart from the right way, and know not the God in whom they should trust." (V. 20).

Paraphrasing the oft quoted passage at the end of the book that bears his name, Moroni stated: "Whoso believeth in Christ, doubting nothing, whatsoever he shall ask the Father in the name of Christ it shall be granted him; and this promise is unto all, even unto the ends of the earth." (V. 21, see Moroni 10:4). Is this not the greatest miracle of all, that we need but ask in faith, nothing wavering, and it shall be given us? (See James 1:6).

Quoting passages of scripture from the Lord's ministry to the Nephites that are not found in the Book of Mormon text, Moroni explained how His disciples could bring the miracle of the Gospel of Jesus Christ to the world. (V. 22-25). "And whosoever shall believe (these miracles), doubting nothing, unto him will I confirm all my words, even unto the ends of the earth." (V. 25).

The Lord "doeth nothing save it be plain unto the children of men; and he inviteth them all to come unto him and partake of his goodness; and he denieth none that come unto him, black and white, bond and free, male and female; and he remembereth the heathen; and all are alike unto God, both Jew and Gentile." (2 Nephi 26:33). Joseph Fielding Smith taught: "Every soul coming into this world came here with the promise that through obedience he would receive the blessings of salvation. No person was foreordained to sin, or to perform a mission of evil." ("Doctrines of Salvation," 1:61).

With a true comprehension of the worth of every soul, Moroni specifically counseled those in the Last Days: "O then, despise not, and wonder not, but hearken unto the words of the Lord, and ask the Father in the name of Jesus for what things soever ye shall stand in need. Doubt not, but be believing, and begin as in times of old, and come unto the Lord with all your heart." (V. 27).

"Work out your own salvation," he said, "with fear and trembling" before the Lord. (V. 27). In fact, our works are necessary but insufficient, and in the truest sense, we cannot work out our own salvation. But when our works become His works, they are empowered and motivated from On High, and the miracle of salvation by the grace of God is accomplished. (See Philippians 2:12-13).

Moroni was familiar with the power of prayer. (See Moroni 10:4). He cautioned those in the Last Days to be careful about the things for which they prayed. (V. 28). Among the Nephites, he had seen enough of the mockery of God to know that we should "do all things in worthiness." (V. 29).

To give his words deserved impact, Moroni declared: "Behold, I speak unto you as though I spake from the dead; for I know that ye shall have my words." (V. 30). These have come to us in The Book of Mormon, and also in very subtle ways through the ministry of Joseph Smith, who was intimately acquainted with the great personalities from The Book of Mormon. His association with the prophets of that book added wonderful texture to the fabric of the Restored Church, as the complete tapestry was woven over time in the first half of the Nineteenth Century.

"Joseph received instructions from the Lord by inspiration and by visitation from heavenly personages. The angel Moroni communicated with him often. Each year in September, Joseph visited the hill, and the angel enlightened him concerning his labors with the ancient record. Many ancient prophets and apostles appeared to Joseph during his formative years, imparting knowledge and furnishing him direction. Personalities who had once lived on the Western Hemisphere and had contributed to the record Joseph was to receive appeared and acquainted him with particulars about the people mentioned in the book. Nephi, Alma, Mormon, and the disciples chosen by the Savior were among those who revealed themselves to him. These heavenly personages made their appearance to him before he received the Nephite record in September 1827." (Ivan Barrett, "Joseph Smith & The Restoration," p. 68).

Joseph "would describe the ancient inhabitants of this continent, their dress, mode of traveling, and the animals upon which they rode; their cities, their buildings, with every particular; their mode of warfare; and also, their religious worship. This he would do with as much ease, seemingly, as if he had spent his whole life among them." (Lucy Mack Smith, speaking of her son Joseph at age 17, in "History of Joseph Smith," p. 83).

Thinking that their own human frailties might be a stumbling block to some, Moroni asked those who read The Book of Mormon: "Condemn me not because of mine imperfection, neither my father, because of his imperfection, neither them who have written before him, but rather give thanks unto God that he hath made manifest unto you our imperfections, that ye may learn to be more wise than we have been." (V. 31). This tremendous statement expresses real humility and magnanimity. If we embrace The Book of Mormon with open arms and without reservation, it will become a catalyst for personal progress. In every sense, it is a marvelous work and a wonder.

Then, Moroni provided insight into the language of the plates, which has long been of interest to students of The Book of Mormon. Joseph Smith was inclined to allow the book to speak for itself on this matter. (See B.Y.U. Studies. 20:4). However, Moroni wrote: "And now, behold, we have written this record (that is, The Plates of Mormon, but not necessarily The Small Plates of Nephi, or The Large Plates of Nephi) according to our knowledge, in the characters which are called among us the reformed Egyptian, being handed down and altered by us, according to our manner of speech." (V. 32). Only gradually did Nephite writing evolve into what Moroni called the "reformed Egyptian."

Evidently, their speech was a variant of Hebrew, for if the "plates had been sufficiently large we should have written in Hebrew; but the Hebrew hath been altered by us also; and if we could have written in Hebrew, behold, ye would have had no imperfection in our record." (V. 33). It seems that the "reformed Egyptian" was not as precise a written language as Moroni would have liked, and those who kept the record were not able to express themselves as clearly using this vehicle as they would have preferred. Additionally, the Hebrew spoken by the Nephites had evolved over a thousand years into a dialect "that none other people knoweth." (V. 34).

Again, Moroni must have considered the record completed, because he ended this chapter with solemn formality. "And may the Lord Jesus Christ grant that (the prayers of the saints) may be answered according to their faith; and may God the Father remember the covenant which he hath made with the house of Israel; and may he bless them forever, through faith on the name of Jesus Christ, Amen." (V. 37).

Obviously, he later reconsidered, and gave us not only The Book of Moroni, but also The Book of Ether that he abridged from the 24 Gold Plates. Evidently, he wanted us to be familiar with the history of another people who were also destroyed because of unrighteousness.

The Book of Ether
The record of the Jaredites, taken from the twenty-four plates found by the people of Limhi in the days of King Mosiah.
2,200 B.C. to 261 - 121 B.C.

Ether
Chapter 1

In the 1879 Edition of The Book of Mormon, the "Book of Ether" was retitled with the following subscript added: "The record of the Jaredites, taken from the twenty-four plates found by the people of Limhi in the days of king Mosiah." This was done for clarification purposes.

The abridgment was most likely taken from Mosiah's earlier translation. (See Mosiah 28:1-10, & Moroni 1:1). If Moroni abridged The Book of Ether directly from the 24 Gold Plates, he would have had to first translate what would have amounted to +/- 1500 chapters, by the means of the Urim and Thummim, for he wrote: "And the hundredth part (of the record of Ether) I have not written." (Ether 15:33). This would have been an almost impossible task, considering the circumstances under which he had to labor. (See Ether 15:33)

In his work of abridgment, Moroni fulfilled the words of his father, who had promised when he was abridging the record of Mosiah that this account would be given later. (See Mosiah 28:19). The abridgment came "from the twenty and four plates which were found by the people of Limhi" about 121 B.C. (V. 2, see Mosiah 8:9).

Moroni indicated that the first part of The Book of Ether contained specific information "concerning the creation of the world, and also of Adam, and an account from that time even to the great tower." (V. 3). Since this information was readily available, or was "had among the Jews," Moroni chose not to duplicate the narrative. Actually, only a sketchy account of the creation and of the ancient patriarchs has survived to our day, since many of the plain and precious things have been taken from our Bible. (See 1 Nephi 13:26).

Moroni wrote, however, that Joseph Smith would "have power that he may get the full account." (V. 4). This may refer to the fact that Joseph Smith, through inspiration, was able to correct many passages in the Joseph Smith Translation of the Bible. Certainly, Joseph had a clear understanding of the creation and of the activities of the ancients because of the revelations that he regularly received from the Lord. (See J.S.H. 1:41 & 54).

Verse 4 might also refer to the fact that Joseph Smith would use the Urim and Thummim, the instrument provided by God and so appropriately called in the Hebrew "Lights and Perfections," to translate the inspired record contained on the plates entrusted to his care. It may well be that it will again be the Urim and Thummim that will be employed at some time in the future to reveal the sealed portion of the plates. At any rate, Moroni wrote that he would not give that full account of the Jaredites in his abridgment, but only that part "from the tower down until they were destroyed." (V. 5).

Moroni then gave a brief genealogy of Jared and his descendants. (V. 6-33). These verses document 29 generations from Jared to Ether. We know that the Tower episode occurred about 2,200 B.C. Omni 1:21 reports that Coriantumr lived among the People of Zarahemla, who descended from those Jews who came out from Jerusalem with Mulek, son of Zedekiah, sometime after 590 B.C. Therefore, the history of the Jaredites spans some 1,600 years.

If 25 years is accepted as one representative generation, there must have been some 64 generations during that 1,600-year period. One way to reconcile the apparent discrepancy in the text of The Book of Ether is by a proper understanding of the term "ben" in the Hebrew. This word can be translated as "son" or as "descendant," depending entirely upon the discretion of the translator.

Ether 1:6 states that Ether was a descendant of Coriantor; then Ether 11:23 clarifies that Ether was the son of Coriantor. Ether 1:15 states that Aaron was a descendant of Heth; then Ether 10:31 clarifies that Aaron was the son of Heth. Only in Ether 1:23 does it state that Morianton was a descendant of Riplakish, and later, in Ether 10:9, the term "descendant" is repeated. Perhaps it is at this point in the genealogical record that we encounter the required gap of some 35 generations.

The record of the Jaredites takes us back to the years just after the Flood, when "the whole earth was of one language, and of one speech." At that time, the people said: "Let us build us a city and a tower, whose top may reach unto heaven." (Genesis 11:1 & 4). The first acts of recorded history show people everywhere building towers, or ziggurats, to get to heaven. A good example is the Step Pyramid in Egypt, the oldest free-standing structure on earth. To the Babylonians, the tower was the binding place of heaven and earth, and the one sacred location where man could establish communion with God. In reality, it was a secularization of the House of The Lord, that most magnificent earthly construction, where alone we get our bearings on eternity.

The Lord saw fit to "confound the language of all the earth; and from thence did the Lord scatter them abroad upon the face of all the earth." (Genesis 11:9, see Ether 1:33). The word "confound" means one of two things, either "to confuse," so that the speech of one individual would be unintelligible to every other individual, or "to mix up" in the sense that there would be linguistic differences among different groups. (See Ether 13:8). Certainly, the latter definition would be appropriate to the confounding of languages at the Tower of Babel.

Verse 34 introduces us to "The Brother of Jared." He was "a large and mighty man, and a man highly favored of the Lord." The question has been asked: "Why did Ether refer to this special person as the brother of a man who was himself of lesser historical importance in the record?" The answer may be because the Brother of Jared omitted his name out of modesty, as "the disciple whom Jesus loved" omitted his name in the New Testament record. (See John 13:23). Or, it may be due to the nature of The Book of Ether, which is a family record of Jared, and not of his brother. Ether, a descendant of Jared, would naturally be inclined to give emphasis to the name of his direct line ancestor. A third explanation is that Moroni, when abridging the record, found the name of the Brother of Jared too cumbersome and awkward to deal with repetitively, and so chose not to translate it directly.

The name of the Brother of Jared is not mentioned in any of the Standard Works, or in the seven volume History of The Church, but many Latter-day Saints believe that it was revealed to Joseph Smith under the following circumstances: "While residing in Kirtland, Reynolds Cahoon had a son born to him. One day, when Joseph Smith was passing his door he called the Prophet in and asked him to bless and name the baby. Joseph did so and gave the boy the name Mahonri Moriancumer. When he had finished the blessing, he laid the child on the bed, and turning to Brother Cahoon he said: 'The name I have given your son is the name of the Brother of Jared. The Lord has just shown (or revealed) it to me.' William F. Cahoon, who was standing near, heard the Prophet make this statement to his father; and this was the first time the name of the Brother of Jared was known in the Church in this dispensation." ("The Juvenile Instructor," 27:282, & "Improvement Era," 8:705).

It is also interesting to note that a place of encampment of the Jaredites, where they "dwelt in tents upon the seashore for the space of four years," was called "Moriancumer." (Ether 2:13). "It was the custom of the people of Nephi to call their lands, and their cities, and their villages, yea, even all their small villages, after the name of him who first possessed them." (Alma 8:7). Evidently, this custom was also practiced among the Jaredites two millennia earlier.

One other point on the subject of this peculiar name deserves recognition. It may be coincidence, or it may have more to do with the ancients' fascination with metonymy, to recognize in the name Moriancumer the roots of two of the most significant hills in religious history: Mount Moriah, and the Hill Cumorah.

Because of his special status with God, the Brother of Jared was asked: "Cry unto the Lord, that he will not confound us that we may not understand our words." (V. 34). Because the Lord had compassion on Jared, "therefore, he did not confound the language of Jared." (V. 35). This means one of two things. Either the Lord did not "change" the language of the Jaredites, and so they continued to speak the Adamic tongue, or He changed their language uniformly, so that they could continue to communicate with each other.

Incidentally, within the circle of the Jaredites were Jared and his brother, and "their friends and their families." (V. 37, See, v. 41). Unlike that of Lehi, this party was not formed on the basis of blood relationships. Friends were counted among their people.

After receiving assurances that their language would not be confounded, Jared asked his brother to inquire of the Lord once more, concerning the anticipated scattering of the people from the land in the vicinity of the Tower. (V. 38). As the Bible records, after the confounding of languages at the Tower of Babel, "from thence did the Lord scatter them abroad upon the face of all the earth." (Genesis 11:9).

In Hebrew, the word for "earth" and "land" is the same: "eretz." Save by means of the context in which this Hebrew word is found, translators have no way of knowing the sense in which it is to be understood. (See Ether 13:17). It is important, when reading the Hebrew scriptures, to ponder those passages where "earth" and "land" are prominently mentioned, and to discern their true meaning by the power of the Spirit. (See Commentary References to Alma 24:19, Ether 1:6 & 1:38, & Commentary Reference to Ether 13:2).

In any event, the scattering of the people of the "earth" was not due, as one might suspect, to the confusion of tongues. After the Brother of Jared had been assured that the language of his people would not be confounded, the question of whether they would still be driven out of the land remained unanswered. The language they spoke had little to do with the act of driving them out of the land.

In these verses, the concept of a Promised Land for the Jaredites is introduced. The story of how these people responded to the Lord's invitation to gather to a Promised Land is strikingly different from the familiar scenario in Lehi's day, where the reader is provided with a narrative that is rich in detail. (V. 41-43, see Commentary Reference to Ether 9:31).

"And now I, Moroni, proceed to give an account of those ancient inhabitants who were destroyed by the hand of the Lord upon the face of this north country. And I take mine account from the twenty and four plates which were found by the people of Limhi, which is called the Book of Ether." (Ether 1:1-2).

Ether
Chapter 2

Moroni recorded that the Jaredites "went down into the valley which was northward, and the name of the valley was Nimrod, being called after the mighty hunter." (V. 1). This was probably the great valley system lying north of Mesopotamia and the Fertile Crescent.

Nimrod was the great grandson of Noah, through Ham and Cush. There is an ancient tradition that he obtained the stolen garment of Noah. With it, he became a powerful hunter, inasmuch as the beasts of the forests and plains recognized and subjected themselves to the emblem of authority represented by the garment of the priesthood. According to the Talmud, Nimrod's great success in hunting was due to the fact that he wore the coat of skins that had been made by God for Adam and Eve. Another tradition asserts that the garment, that was such a great asset to the hunter, was ultimately obtained by Esau, and was nothing less than his birthright, which he sold to Jacob for a mess of pottage.

The symbol of the priesthood vested in the garment also manifest itself in ancient Egypt. Pharaoh was of the lineage of Ham, and so was related to Nimrod, as well. The scriptures state that Pharaoh "was blessed as to the kingship, but cursed as to the priesthood." (Abraham 1:26-27). He offered Abraham the privilege of wearing his own royal insignia in the hope that Abraham would return the compliment by allowing Pharaoh to wear his priestly robes.

These ancient traditions, while directly related to the scriptural records, nevertheless create a broad tapestry of the types of things that could have happened thousands of years ago. The depth and breadth of the traditions that are generally supportive of the scriptures make a powerful case for The Book of Ether, precisely because of their universal applicability.

We see a vision of a great company traveling across the wind-swept steppes of Central Asia, whose weather has been one of the great driving forces in world history. A careful reading of the scriptures, for example, seems to indicate that it was not the confounding of languages at the Tower of Babel that drove the Jaredites out of the land, but rather conditions of climate.

The Jaredite caravan moved along, probably utilizing the great wagons familiar to students of ancient Asian history and culture. We know that the company had vehicles of sufficient size to even carry fish tanks. "And they did also prepare a vessel, in which they did carry with them the fish of the waters." (V. 2). They also carried "deseret, which, by interpretation, is a honeybee." (V. 3). This is the sole reference in The Book of Mormon to "deseret." The name is transliterated from the original record. It is one of the few Jaredite words in The Book of Mormon. (See Commentary

References to Ether 9:17-19 & 10:31-32). A related term, DSRT enjoyed a position of ritual prominence among the founders of the classical Egyptian civilization, who associated it very closely with the symbol of the bee. (See Hugh Nibley, "Lehi in The Desert," p. 184 & 188).

There are seven references in The Book of Mormon to bees or to honey, and all of them are associated with the Old World. Nowhere does The Book of Mormon mention honey or bees in a New World setting. As a matter of fact, entomologists believe that European colonists introduced bees to the New World only in the Seventeenth Century. Ether 6:7 reveals no mention of bees in the cargo taken aboard the Jaredite barges for the trans-oceanic crossing.

At the command of the Lord, the Jaredites moved "into the wilderness, yea, into that quarter where there never had man been." (V. 5). Whereas Lehi had the Liahona to direct his party, the Jaredites were guided by the Lord Himself, Who "did go before them, and did talk with them as he stood in a cloud, and gave directions whither they should travel." (V. 5).

Verse 6 goes so far as to say that they were "directed continually by the hand of the Lord." Is it so very different in the case of Latter-day Israel? "Some people might ask why did we stop with 136 revelations in the Doctrine & Covenants? Where is the 137th section? Why did we stop in 1847? I would like to share with you today the fact that revelation has not stopped. It is going on, on a daily basis, and visions and inspiration and revelation are such a part of this Church that you could hardly believe." (Robert L. Simpson).

So, too, do worthy individual members of the Church receive guidance. But "Road to Damascus" experiences are not typical of the way God communicates with His children. As Spencer W. Kimball said: "Looking for the spectacular, we often miss the constant flow of revealed communication that comes." (C.R., 4/1964).

The Jaredites encountered inland seas on the Asian Steppes, and built barges to cross them. These were not ships in the traditional sense, but were very special vessels whose construction specifications were given by the Lord. (V. 6, see v. 16). The "sea in the wilderness" mentioned in verse 7 was evidently the most formidable of these water barriers.

At this point in the abridgment, and in the best tradition of his father, Moroni made a brief editorial observation regarding the New World Land of Promise toward which the Jaredites were traveling. He wrote "And now we can behold the decrees of God concerning this land, that it is a land of promise; and whatsoever nation shall possess it shall serve God, or they shall be swept off when the fulness of his wrath shall come upon them. And the fulness of his wrath cometh upon them when they are ripened in iniquity." (V. 9, see v. 10-12).

Ezra Taft Benson declared of this land of promise that "the solution is not more wealth, more food, more technology, more government, or instruments of destruction. The solution is personal and national reformation. In short, it is to bring our national character ahead of our technological and material advances. Repentance is the sovereign remedy to our problems." ("Teachings of Ezra Taft Benson," p. 569 & 580).

Verse 13 records that the party "dwelt in tents upon the seashore for the space of four years" at a place they named Moriancumer. Mormon had earlier reported that among the Nephites "it was the custom of the people ... to call their lands, and their cities, and their villages, yea, even all their small villages, after the name of him who first possessed them." (Alma 8:7). Perhaps the Nephites adopted this practice from the Jaredites. If this is true, it would suggest that "Moriancumer" was a prominent name among these people.

Ether 3:3 says of the Jaredites: "For these many years we have been in the wilderness." During that period of time, the

Brother of Jared evidently "remembered not to call upon the name of the Lord" as fervently as he ought to have done, and the Lord chastened him for his neglect. (V. 14).

We need not suppose that the Brother of Jared was unworthy to enjoy the Second Comforter, for that was exactly his privilege as soon as he had "repented of the evil which he had done." (V. 15). In much the same way, young Joseph Smith neglected his responsibilities after the First Vision. His History records: "I continued to pursue my common vocations in life ... I was left to all kinds of temptations; and, mingling with all kinds of society, I frequently fell into many foolish errors, and displayed the weakness of youth, and the foibles of human nature, which, I am sorry to say, led me into divers temptations, offensive in the sight of God ... I was guilty of levity, and sometimes associated with jovial company, etc., not consistent with that character which ought to be maintained by one who was called of God, as I had been." (J.S.H. 2:27-28).

Aside from gleaning an insight into the human nature of both the Brother of Jared and of Joseph Smith, these verses from the records of their lives are instructive particularly for those who hold the priesthood in the Last Days. The operative words in Joseph's History are that his behavior was "not consistent with that character which ought to be maintained by one who was called of God." The manner of Joseph's calling was unique, and although the Brother of Jared enjoyed a similarly special relationship with the Lord, as David O. McKay declared at the close of a General Conference of the Church: "If we could be obedient to the counsel of the General Authorities that we have heard in this Conference, it would be sufficient to bring us into the presence of God." On an earlier occasion, Wilford Woodruff made this statement: "If anything under the heavens should humble men before the Lord and before one another, it should be the fact that we have been called of God." (Daniel Ludlow, "Latter-day Prophets Speak," p. 153).

The Lord said to the Brother of Jared: "I will forgive thee and thy brethren of their sins; but thou shalt not sin any more." (V. 15). In this series of verses, we are given an unusual opportunity to know the mind of the Lord concerning the relationship of the people to the Land of Promise. For he said: "These are my thoughts upon the land which I shall give you for your inheritance." (V. 15). "And (then) the Lord said: Go to work." (V. 16). This verse illustrates the principle that we must not rest on our laurels, or pause for too long on a plateau, when we need to be moving onward and upward. Eternal progression is a path, and not a point.

In New Testament times, there was to be no "Book of The Resolutions of The Apostles," but only the "Book of The Acts of The Apostles." Good intentions may be noble, but achievement is the hallmark of progress. Harold B. Lee was fond of saying: "Work without vision is drudgery, and vision without work is dreamery, but work with vision is destiny!" It was the destiny of the Jaredites to prosper in a land of promise, but only if they would keep the commandments of the Lord.

Spencer W. Kimball told a group of mission presidents: "So much depends upon our willingness to make up our minds, both individually and collectively, that present levels of performance are not acceptable, either to ourselves or to the Lord. In saying that, I am not calling for flashy, temporary differences in our performance levels, but (for) a quiet resolve to lengthen our stride." ("Church News," 3/22/1975). On another occasion, he said: "We have paused on some plateaus long enough. Let us resume our journey forward and upward. Let us quietly end our reluctance to reach out to others, whether in our own families, wards, or neighborhoods. We have been diverted, at times, from fundamentals upon which we must now focus in order to move forward as a person or as a people." (C.R., 4/1979).

When Joseph Smith was visited by the resurrected Angel Moroni, he reported: "(I) received instruction and intelligence from him at each of our interviews, respecting what the Lord was going to do, and how and in what manner his kingdom was to be conducted in the last days." (J.S.H. 2:54). Just so, Moroni reported that the Brother of Jared did go to work as the Lord had directed, and built the barges "according to the instructions of the Lord." (V. 16).

Special guidance concerning construction was necessary because the Lord was about to loose winds of incredible violence upon the seas that would make the ocean crossing extremely hazardous. (V. 16-20, see Ether 6:8). In every needful way, God prepared the Jaredites for a Noah-like water ordeal by giving them the skills necessary to build eight barge-like craft, and by reassuring them that He would save them in their hour of need from the watery depths. (V. 24-25, see Ether 3:1).

The barges were to be "exceedingly tight" (V. 17), and capable of submersion. (V. 24, see Ether 6:7). Special provision was made for those on board to breathe, as well: "And the Lord said unto the Brother of Jared: Behold, thou shalt make a hole in the top (thereof), and also in the bottom (thereof); and when thou shalt suffer for air thou shalt unstop the hole (thereof) and receive air." (V. 20).

In the First Edition of The Book of Mormon, the word "thereof" was included in verse 20, but it was deleted in all later editions, as it was thought to be superfluous. When critically examining this verse, however, the terms "in the top" and "in the bottom" do not seem to refer to the barge itself, but to the top and bottom of some other device that was used to admit air. Perhaps this was a chamber or cylinder of some kind that ran through the barge, and was designated in our text as "thereof." It could have been used to admit air at appropriate times, as well as to eliminate waste from the living quarters of the barges.

There was one additional problem to be addressed in the design of the barges. The Lord helped the Brother of Jared to overcome this difficulty by asking him the leading question: "What will ye that I should do that ye may have light in your vessels?" (V. 23). Windows (of glass) were out of the question, because they would "be dashed in pieces." (V. 23). Fire was not an option, either, because of the close quarters and lack of adequate ventilation.

The Lord reminded the Brother of Jared that his vessel would be "as a whale in the midst of the sea; for the mountain waves shall dash upon you." But He gave the assurance: "I will bring you up again out of the depths." (V. 24). "Therefore, what will ye that I should prepare for you, that ye may have light when ye are swallowed up in the depths of the sea?" (V. 25). Again, the Lord was teaching the Brother of Jared a great principle: Take a bold step when one is indicated. You cannot cross a chasm in two small bounds. In Chapter 3 we will learn how the Brother of Jared handled this challenge.

Ether
Chapter 3

When eight water-tight barges had been built for the voyage, the Brother of Jared climbed a mountain that the party called Shelem. (V. 1, see Commentary Reference to Ether 9:17-19). This suggests a Pacific crossing for the Jaredites, since no mountain "of exceeding height" exists on the European coastline of the Atlantic Ocean. There he "did molten out of a rock sixteen small stones; and they were white and clear, even as transparent glass." (V. 1.) There were to be two stones for each craft. He set the stones before him upon the top of the mount, and acknowledged his utter dependence upon God, even declaring: "Because of the fall our natures have become evil continually." (V. 2). These are not the words of an apostate, however, but of a humble servant of God.

In much the same way, "Moses was caught up into an exceedingly high mountain, and he saw God face to face, and he talked with him, and the glory of God was upon Moses; therefore, Moses could endure his presence." (Moses 1:1). After this experience, "Moses did again receive his natural strength like unto man ...(and) said unto himself: Now, for this cause I know that man is nothing, which thing I never had supposed." (Moses 1:10).

In other words, we are utterly dependent upon God, "for in him we live, and move, and have our being." (Acts 17:28). As King Benjamin taught: "And now I ask, can ye say aught of yourselves? I answer you, Nay. Ye cannot say that ye are even as much as the dust of the earth; yet ye were created of the dust of the earth; but behold, it belongeth to him who created you." (Mosiah 2:25).

The Brother of Jared realized that "because of the fall our natures have become evil continually." (V. 2). He recognized that it is necessary to be born again. (See Mosiah 5:7). It is not a question of development or of maturation, but rather of generation. One of the most emotional, miraculous, and awe-inspiring events of mortality is birth. It would be difficult to more dramatically conceptualize in metaphor the process of kindling the divine spark, of awakening the celestial potential, or of igniting the spirit lying dormant within the God in embryo, than to say that one must be born again in order to inherit eternal life.

And so, the Brother of Jared acknowledged the Fall of Adam in order to emphasize the transcendent event of all time, the Atonement of Christ. "To teach atonement without teaching fall is to relegate Jesus to no more than a guide, a great teacher, a coach, or an inspiring cheerleader." (Robert L. Millet, "Doctrinal Commentary on The Book of Mormon," 4:272). The Fall made possible our opportunity to be born again, and to bring to pass our immortality and eternal life. (See Moses 1:39). As Lehi taught: "Adam fell that men might be; and men are, that they might have joy." (2 Nephi 2:25).

It is remarkable that our opportunity for happiness is a gift from God. "It is by grace that we are saved, after all we can do." (2 Nephi 25:23). Brigham Young rightly observed: "There is no man who ever made a sacrifice on this earth for the kingdom of heaven except the Savior. I would not give the ashes of a rye straw for that man who feels he is making sacrifices for God. We are doing this for our own happiness, welfare, and exaltation, and for nobody else's. What we do, we do for the salvation of the inhabitants of the earth, not for the salvation of the heavens, the angels, or God." (J.D., 16:114, see Commentary Reference to 3 Nephi 15:1).).

The Brother of Jared said: "For these many years we have been in the wilderness." (V. 3). They had been passing through the refiner's fire, and the Lord had been merciful to them. The great expanse of the Asian Steppes would have swallowed up a party the size of the Jaredites for "many years."

On the mountain, the Brother of Jared eased up to the request that the Lord Himself had encouraged. (See Ether 2:25). Finally, he asked the question, that in Moroni's translation takes the form of a statement of fact: "Therefore touch these stones O Lord, with thy finger, and prepare them that they may shine forth in darkness; and they shall shine forth unto us in the vessels which we have prepared, that we may have light while we shall cross the sea. Behold, O Lord, thou canst do this. We know that thou art able to show forth great power, which looks small unto the understanding of men," that is to say, which men cannot comprehend or appreciate. (V. 4-5).

Perhaps, the Brother of Jared was familiar with similar circumstances on the Ark, for there are rabbinic legends that Noah had obtained light from shining stones given to him by God. (See Hugh Nibley, "An Approach to The Book of Mormon," Chapter 25: "Strange Ships and Shining Stones"). In any event, he received a most dramatic and physically direct answer to his request. "Behold, the Lord stretched forth his hand and touched the stones one by one with his finger." (V. 6). Then, "after the Lord had prepared the stones which the Brother of Jared had carried up into the mount, the Brother of Jared came down out of the mount, and he did put forth the stones into the vessels which were prepared, one in each end thereof; and behold, they did give light unto the vessels." Moroni's editorial observation is insightful for its duality: "And thus the Lord caused stones to shine in darkness, to give light unto men, women, and children, that they might not cross the great waters in darkness." (Ether 6:2-3).

When he saw His finger, "the Brother of Jared fell down before the Lord, for he was struck with fear." (V. 6). He was certain that he would die. The ancients understood that only under special circumstances could they endure the presence of God. As Moses wrote: "But now mine own eyes have beheld God; but not my natural, but my spiritual eyes, for my natural eyes could not have beheld; for I should have withered and died in his presence." (Moses 1:11).

The Lord explained to the Brother of Jared that it was because of his great faith that he had been permitted to see that the Lord should take upon Himself flesh and blood. "And the Lord said unto him: Because of thy faith thou hast seen that I shall take upon me flesh and blood; and never has man come before me with such exceeding faith as thou hast; for were it not so ye could not have seen my finger." (V. 9). He was entitled to receive the Second Comforter, for the Lord explained to him: "Because thou knowest these things, ye are redeemed from the fall; therefore, ye are brought back into my presence; therefore, I show myself unto you." (V. 13).

The Lord made a similar promise to the Latter-day Saints, when He said: "It is your privilege, and a promise I give unto you that have been ordained unto this ministry, that inasmuch as you strip yourselves from jealousies, and fears, and humble yourselves before me ... the veil shall be rent, and you shall see me and know that I am." (D&C 67:10). This privilege is not reserved for prophets alone, but is available to any person willing to pay the price in personal righteousness. (See D&C 93:1).

The Lord went on to identify Himself, saying, I am "he who was prepared from the foundation of the world to redeem my people. Behold, I am Jesus Christ. I am the Father and the Son. In me shall all mankind have life, and that eternally, even they who shall believe on my name, and they shall become my sons and my daughters." (V. 14).

Peter wrote that Christ "was foreordained before the foundation of the world." (1 Peter 1:20). John declared that He was "the Lamb slain from the foundation of the world." (Revelation 13:8). Both Moses and Abraham also taught of Christ's foreordination. "Behold, my Beloved and Chosen from the beginning" wrote Moses. (Moses 4:2). "And the Lord (God) said: Whom shall I send? And one answered like unto the Son of Man: Here am I, send me." (Abraham 3:27).

Jesus Christ is the Father, and we are His sons and daughters, in the sense that He united our bodies and spirits through the work that He was foreordained to do from the foundation of the world, namely atonement for sin and the resurrection of the physical body from death. Spiritually and physically, then, the faithful are begotten of Him. In a very special sense, He is our Father.

The Light of Christ nurtures each of us from our infancy and provides the opportunity for us to grow to the full extent of our spiritual stature as we pattern our lives after the Savior. King Benjamin identified the relationship that is reserved for those who join the family of Christ and abide by its rules of conduct. "And now, because of the covenant which ye have made, ye shall be called the children of Christ, his sons, and his daughters; for behold, this day he hath spiritually begotten you; for ye say that your hearts are changed through faith on his name; therefore, ye are born of him and have become his sons and his daughters." (Mosiah 5:7).

This relationship with Christ acknowledges that we are the spirit children of our Heavenly Father. By divine investiture of authority, our Father delegated to His Son all of the responsibilities associated with our mortal experience. In complete harmony with the will of the Father, His Son has faithfully carried out every duty related to the Plan of Salvation. His earthly mission was one of these responsibilities.

As the Savior taught: "He that believeth on me, believeth not on me, but on him that sent me. And he that seeth me seeth him that sent me." (John 12:44-45). The will of God the Father and of God the Son are in total harmony. Whatever His Son does, it is exactly as His Father would do in similar circumstances. We can accept the delegated activities of His Son, just as we would, had our Father performed them. Therefore, when Christ operates by divine investiture of authority, He may call Himself by either or both of the Holy titles of the Father or Son. In Him, eternal life fully vested. It is He to whom we look for our salvation.

In the next verse, the Lord made a very interesting statement. "And never have I showed myself unto man whom I have created." (V. 15). First, we know that it is the Father who created each of us, so His Son must again be speaking by divine investiture of authority when He refers to Himself as our Creator. But since Moses 7:4 and Doctrine & Covenants 107:53-54 clearly speak of personal visits of the Lord to those who lived before 2,200 B.C., He must have been referring in some special sense to His physical manifestation to the Brother of Jared.

Moses 7:4 reads as follows: "And I (Enoch) saw the Lord; and he stood before my face, and he talked with me, even as a man talketh one with another, face to face." The Prophet Joseph Smith taught: "Three years previous to the death of Adam, he called Seth, Enos, Cainan, Mahalaleel, Jared, Enoch, and Methuselah, who were all high priests, with the residue of his posterity who were righteous, into the valley of Adam-ondi-Ahman, and there bestowed upon them his last blessing. And the Lord appeared unto them, and they rose up and blessed Adam, and called him Michael, the prince, the archangel." (D&C 107:53-54).

Why then, did the Lord tell the Brother of Jared, that he had never before shown Himself unto man? It might be that the "Lord" identified in these verses is God the Father, but if not, then perhaps explanatory verses in Moroni's abridgment of Ether's record will reveal the answer. He wrote: "I could not make a full account of these things which are written, therefore it sufficeth me to say that Jesus showed himself unto this man in the spirit, even after the manner and in the likeness of the same body even as he showed himself unto the Nephites." (V. 17). Christ told the Brother of Jared: "Even as I appear unto thee to be in the spirit will I appear unto my people in the flesh." (V. 16). Perhaps the Savior was saying: "And never before have I revealed to man the image of my mortal body yet to come." Perhaps He was saying: "This is the first occasion when I have revealed Myself to man as the Son of God."

Verses 9, 19-20, and 26 clearly teach that the Brother of Jared came to the Lord with greater faith than had any other man before him. "And never has man come before me with such exceeding faith as thou hast." (V. 9). Therefore, a more complete translation of verse 15 might read: "And never have I showed myself unto a man with greater faith ... for never has man believed in me as thou hast." In this vein, then, the Lord made a distinction between believing and unbelieving men, when He said that He had never shown Himself to man. If this is the case, verse 15 would read: "And never have I showed myself to unbelieving man whom I have created, for never has man believed in me as thou hast."

One or more of these explanations may be correct. In any event, verse 15 continues: "Seest thou that ye are created after mine own image?" This clarifies Genesis 1:27, that reads: "So God created man in his own image." "God" must refer to Jesus Christ, and "image" to His pre-earthly spiritual body. This and other scriptures are better understood when we comprehend the concept of divine investiture of authority. For example, Moses 1:1-8 speaks of the creative endeavors of the Son, as if He were God the Father.

Moroni wrote: "Because of the knowledge of this man, he could not be kept from beholding within the veil; and he saw the finger of Jesus, which, when he saw, he fell with fear; for he knew that it was the finger of the Lord; and he had (faltering) faith no longer for he knew, nothing doubting. Wherefore, having this perfect knowledge of God, he could not be kept from within the veil." (V. 19-20).

Later in his abridgment of The Book of Ether, Moroni wrote: "So great was his faith in God, that when God put forth his finger he could not hide it from the sight of the Brother of Jared." (Ether 12:20). Faith is a principle of power possessed by God. By His faith, the worlds were made. (See Hebrews 11:3, Joseph Smith, "1st and 2nd Lectures on Faith"). His faith embraces within itself the knowledge of all things.

In contrast to God's perfect faith, our faith grows by degrees. Our struggling convictions are based on our developing knowledge of the truth. (See Alma 32:21). In a sense, when we gain a perfect knowledge of one of the principles of perfection, the faith required to master the principle becomes dormant, allowing us to focus our attention on another area of improvement. We may then nurture our confidence in that principle, as well, until, in our expanding arsenal of faith, it too becomes a powerful motivator of purposeful action. After the resurrection, those who by faith have attained the stature of God will possess all knowledge, and all faith. They will be full of faith, or faithful. Their perfect faith will have become the principle by which their application of knowledge is transformed into the power of Deity.

The Brother of Jared had spiritual experiences that set him apart from others. At the valley of Adam-ondi-Ahman, or "The Valley of God where Adam Dwelt," Adam's posterity had experiences of the same magnitude. Enoch's was such that he "and all his people walked with God, and he dwelt in the midst of Zion; and it came to pass that Zion was not, for God received it up into his own bosom; and from thence went forth the saying, Zion is Fled." (Moses 7:69).

The Lord told the Brother of Jared to write of the things that he had experienced, and to do so in the Adamic tongue: "For ye shall write them in a language that they cannot be read." (V. 22). Sacred experiences were to be recorded in the pure and undefiled language of heaven. Means would later be provided by God to interpret the record. The Urim and Thummim would be the bridge between sacred records and heavenly understanding. "I will cause in my own due time that these stones (comprising the Urim and Thummim) shall magnify (or make clear) to the eyes of men these things which ye shall write." (V. 24).

The Lord said: "I will show them in mine own due time unto the children of men." (V. 27). Nephi explained: "The day cometh that the words of the book which were sealed shall be read upon the house tops; and they shall be read by the power of Christ; and all things shall be revealed unto the children of men which ever have been among the children of men, and which ever will be even unto the end of the earth." (2 Nephi 27:11, see Alma 26:22, D&C 42:61, 88:67, 93:28, 101:32-34 & 121:26-32).

Then the Lord commanded the Brother of Jared: "Seal up the two stones which he had received, and show them not, until the Lord should show them unto the children of men." Mosiah may have used these same interpreters when he was asked by King Limhi to translate the 24 gold plates that had been found by his people. Ammon told Limhi: "I can assuredly tell thee, O king, of a man that can translate the records; for he has wherewith that he can look, and translate all records that are of ancient date; and it is a gift from God. And the things are called interpreters, and no man can look in them except he be commanded, lest he should look for that he ought not, and he should perish." (Mosiah 8:13).

Joseph Smith also had the opportunity to use the Urim and Thummim as an aid in his translation of The Book of Mormon, and as he later received revelations, such as Doctrine & Covenants Sections 3, 6, 7, 10, 11, 14, 15, 16, & 17. As he recorded in his History: "There were two stones in silver bows - and these stones, fastened to a breastplate, constituted what is called the Urim and Thummim - deposited with the plates; and the possession and use of these stones were what constituted "seers" in ancient or former times; and ... God had prepared them for the purpose of translating the book." (J.S.H. 2:35).

At some future time, these same interpreters will be used to translate the sealed portion of The Book of Mormon, in a day of consummate righteousness. "For the Lord said unto me: They shall not go forth unto the Gentiles until the day that they shall repent of their iniquity, and become clean before the Lord. And in that day that they shall exercise faith in me, saith the Lord, even as the Brother of Jared did, that they may become sanctified in me, then will I manifest unto them the things which the Brother of Jared saw, even to the unfolding unto them all my revelations, saith Jesus Christ, the Son of God, the Father of the heavens and of the earth, and all things that in them are." (Ether 4:6-7).

"The brother of Jared ... went forth unto the mount ... and did molten out of a rock sixteen small stones; and they were white and clear, even as transparent glass."
(Ether 3:1).

Ether
Chapter 4

Moroni reported that the Brother of Jared came down from the mount and recorded his experiences, and that, when he did so, he was "mighty in writing ... unto the overpowering of man to read them." (V. 1, see Ether 12:24). The Nephites were to have this record available to them for their edification only after Christ's ministry among them. (V. 2, see Ether 3:21).

The Book of Ether could have been a "Book of Mormon" for the Nephites who lived after the ministry of Christ. It could have served as their blueprint for survival, extending the invitation that all the blessings promised by the Lord could still have been theirs if they would have kept the commandments. But Moroni reported that his people had forfeit these potential blessings. "They have all dwindled in unbelief; and there is none save it be the Lamanites, and they have rejected the gospel of Christ; therefore, I am commanded that I should hide them up again in the earth." (V. 3). These records would lie in the dust for 1,400 years before they would again see the light of day to persuade mankind to turn from its self-destructive course. Therefore, Mormon commanded his son to make an abridgment of the 24 gold plates of Ether and deposit them with the other records, in the hope that they would be of benefit to his remnant in the Last Days. (See Mosiah 28:19).

Moroni testified that the things he wrote in his abridgment were "the very things which the Brother of Jared saw; and there never were greater things made manifest than those which were made manifest unto the Brother of Jared." (V. 4). The veil had been rent, and he had been permitted a glimpse of heaven itself. (See Commentary References to Ether 3:9 & 12:19-21).

Much of what had been revealed to the Brother of Jared was sealed by Moroni. "Wherefore the Lord hath commanded me to write them, and I have written them," Moroni explained. "And he commanded me that I should seal them up; and he also hath commanded that I should seal up the interpretation thereof; wherefore I have sealed up the interpreters, according to the commandment of the Lord." (V. 5).

That is to say, a portion of that which had been abridged from the 24 Gold Plates of Ether ("the very things which the Brother of Jared saw") was to remain untranslated by Joseph Smith "until the day that (the Gentiles should) repent of their iniquity, and become clean before the Lord." (V. 4 & 6). The "interpreters" or Urim and Thummim that were sealed up along with these records will be the means of their interpretation. (V. 5). When the time comes for these records to be received by the Church, the Prophet, Seer, and Revelator will use these interpreters to accomplish the task.

How much of the abridgment upon The Plates of Mormon was sealed is uncertain. Joseph Smith said only that "the volume was something near six inches in thickness, a part of which was sealed." (H.C., 4:537). Perhaps the sealed portion will not come forth until the Millennium, for verse 7 states that it will be in a day of consummate righteousness that "they shall exercise faith in me, saith the Lord, even as the Brother of Jared did, that they may become sanctified in me. Then will I manifest unto them the things which the Brother of Jared saw, even to the unfolding unto them all my revelations, saith Jesus Christ, the Son of God, the Father of the heavens and of the earth, and all things that in them are." (See Commentary Reference to Ether 3:14).

After so powerfully introducing Himself as the Author of the revelations recorded in the scriptures, Jesus Christ went on to issue a stern warning. "He that will contend against the word of the Lord, let him be accursed; and he that shall deny these things, let him be accursed; for unto them will I show no greater things, saith Jesus Christ; for I am he who speaketh." (V. 8). Their minds would be closed to further enlightenment, for pearls would not be cast before swine. (See Matthew 7:6).

This warning was accompanied by His declaration that He holds the destiny of men and nations in His hands. "And at my command, the heavens are opened and are shut; and at my word, the earth shall shake; and at my command, the inhabitants thereof shall pass away, even so as by fire." (V. 9). Nephi had understood that at the Lord's command, He could open the heavens and reveal Himself in The Book of Mormon. He prophesied: "The day cometh that the words of the book which were sealed shall be read upon the house tops; and they shall be read by the power of Christ; and all things shall be revealed unto the children of men which ever have been among the children of men, and which ever will be even unto the end of the earth." (2 Nephi 27:11).

The Lord declared: "These words are not of men nor of man, but of me; wherefore, you shall testify they are of me and not of man. For it is my voice which speaketh them unto you; for they are given by my Spirit unto you, and by my power you can read them one to another; and save it were by my power you could not have them. Wherefore, you can testify that you have heard my voice, and know my words." (D&C 18:34-36). This scripture makes Moroni's restatement of the Lord's warning all the more significant.

To Moroni, the Lord said: "He that believeth not my words believeth not my disciples ... But he that believeth these things which I have spoken, him will I visit with the manifestation of my Spirit, and he shall know and bear record ... And whatsoever thing persuadeth men to do good is of me; for good cometh of none save it be of me. (V. 10-12, see Moroni 7:16). It might seem obvious, but the key to an understanding of the things of the Spirit is to keep the Light of Christ working in our lives. God is no respecter of persons, and sufficient light is given to guide us to enjoy His Divine Nature. The Tree of Life that stands before us is far more impressive than is the great and spacious building surrounded, as it is, by swirling mists of darkness.

There is a divine spark within each of us that may only be dimmed by the ashes of transgression, but it is never completely snuffed out. Sometimes, we do not recognize the light for what it is. "In the dark recesses of memory, in unbidden suggestions, in trains of thought unwittingly pursued, in multiplied waves and currents all at once flashing and rushing, in dreams that cannot be dismissed, in the force of instinct, in the obscure, but certain intuitions of the spiritual life, we have glimpses of a great tide of life ebbing and flowing, rippling and rolling and beating about where we cannot see it." (E.S. Dallas). Job wrote: "For God speaketh once, yea twice, yet man perceiveth it not. In a dream, in a vision of the night, when deep sleep falleth upon men, in slumberings upon the bed; then he openeth the ears of men, and sealeth their instruction." (Job 33:14-16).

The Savior said to Moroni: "I am the same that leadeth men to all good. I am the Father, I am the light, and the life, and the truth of the world." (V. 12). The Spirit that lights our lives is a gift of God, and is a land unpromised and unearned. "It is a realm of spirit, of sensory delight, of fragrance, sound, form, and color. It is the realm of human associations, of gratitude, loyalty, and appreciation, of selflessness, helpfulness, and forgiveness; of friendship, love and compassion. It is the realm of human growth and transcendence, of truth discovered and accepted, of beauty created and enjoyed, of goodness deepened and made manifest in life. None of us is a stranger to these realms of spirit. We have sensed the world about us, smelled its fragrance, heard its sounds, glimpsed its forms and colors. We have warmed our souls in the glow of human associations; have had our moments of selflessness and gratitude, love, and forgiveness. We have felt an upward reach within us when made suddenly aware of a truth, a beauty, and goodness above and beyond our own attainment. But few of us know these realms as our natural habitat, as the normal residence of our spirits. We are more at home, more at ease, in the world of things, in the world of getting and spending. So, when conflicts arise between our spiritual and our material worlds, as they inevitably do, it is usually our spiritual world that suffers, and suffers tragically." (P.A. Christensen, "A Land Unpromised and Unearned," BYU Studies, 16:1). It is the challenge of every member of the Church to gain fluency in the language of the Spirit, for it is our tendency "to fill space, as if what we have, what we are, is not enough. Being affluent, we strangle ourselves with what we can buy, things whose opacity obstructs our ability to see what is really there." (Gretel Erlich).

From the pages of The Book of Ether, comes the Savior's invitation to both Jew and Gentile: "Come unto me ... and I will show unto you the greater things ... and it shall be made manifest unto you how great things the Father hath laid up for you." (V. 13-14). As Helen Keller observed from her unique perspective: "Why cannot the soul discard the poor lenses of the body, and peer through the telescope of truth into the infinite reaches of immortality?"

In chapter 3, Moroni had related the experience of the Brother of Jared before the veil of the Lord. Now he wrote the words of the Savior to the house of Israel in the Last Days: "When ye shall rend that veil of unbelief which doth cause you to remain in your awful state of wickedness ... then shall ye know that the Father hath remembered the covenant which he made unto your fathers." (V. 15). But these blessings will only come in a day when Israel calls "upon the Father in (the name of Christ), with a broken heart and a contrite spirit." (V. 15). They will come in a day when additional revelations of the Apostle John will be revealed. "And then shall my revelations which I have caused to be written by my servant John be unfolded in the eyes of all the people." (V. 16, see D&C 93:16-18).

Finally, the Lord commanded Moroni to cry repentance to all the "ends of the earth, and come unto me, and believe in my gospel, and be baptized in my name; for he that believeth and is baptized shall be saved; but he that believeth not shall be damned; and signs shall follow them that believe in my name. And blessed is he that is found faithful unto my name at the last day, for he shall be lifted up to dwell in the kingdom prepared for him from the foundation of the world. And behold, it is I that hath spoken it. Amen." (V. 18-19).

In a very revealing statement, Moroni added: "And now I, Moroni, have written the words which were commanded me, according to my memory." (Ether 5:1). Some have wondered why some scriptures reflect the grammatical style of other passages, or why some prophets echo the words of others, or why the Savior's teachings to one people mirror His teachings to others. The Book of Mormon prophets, who not only had access to many records, but also to the impressions of the Holy Ghost, may have relied to a significant extent on their memories to convey their messages. The process of transforming the "reformed Egyptian" into English, Joseph Smith suggested, was more a recording of his impressions that it was a direct word for word translation in the familiar and more profane sense. Certainly, these impressions would be flavored by Joseph's experience, and by his recollection of his favorite passages from the scriptures.

"I am the light,
and the life, and the
truth of the world."
(Ether 4:12).

Ether

Chapter 5

Moroni was familiar with the manner in which The Book of Mormon would come to the world in the Last Days, and so after reporting that he had written the words of Ether according to his memory, he charged Joseph Smith not to touch or translate the sealed portion of the record, "except by and by it shall be wisdom in God." (V. 1). However, Joseph was told that he could "show the plates unto those who (would) assist to bring forth this work." (V. 2). Specifically, the plates were to be shown unto three, who would receive the testimony of "the Father, also the Son, and the Holy Ghost." (V. 4). These witnesses were given the following charge: "And ye shall testify that you have seen them, even as my servant Joseph Smith, Jun., has seen them." (D&C 17:5, see D&C 5:12).

True to their mandate, these Three Witnesses (Oliver Cowdery, David Whitmer, and Martin Harris) bore record that they had "seen the plates which contain this record" which had "been translated by the gift and power of God, for His voice hath declared it unto us." ("The Testimony of The Three Witnesses"). These men were true to their testimony until the ends of their lives.

These independent witnesses were obedient to the express command of God, and their words will "stand as a testimony against the world at the last day." (V. 4). The Book of Mormon is not just another book about religion, because the eternal welfare of its readers is at stake. Christ Himself felt it necessary to add His own witness to the work, when He told these three witnesses, through Joseph Smith: "And (Joseph) has translated the book, even that part which I have commanded him, and as your Lord and your God liveth, it is true." (D&C 17:6). Even the text itself stands as a witness of its validity. "And in the mouths of three witnesses shall these things be established; and the testimony of three, and this work, in the which shall be shown forth the power of God and also his word, of which the Father, and the Son, and the Holy Ghost bear record - and all this shall stand as a testimony against the world at the last day." (V. 4). Joseph Smith recorded in his History, that when the angel of God visited the Three Witnesses, he said to them: "These plates have been revealed by the power of God. The translation which you have seen of them is correct, and I command you to bear record of what you now see and hear." (D.H.C., 1:54-55).

The external evidence that will prove or disprove The Book of Mormon does not exist. "When, indeed, is a thing proven? Only when an individual has accumulated in his own consciousness enough observations, impressions, reasonings, and feelings to satisfy him personally that it is so. The same evidence that convinces one expert may leave another completely unsatisfied. The impressions that build up the definite proof are themselves nontransferable." (Hugh Nibley, "Since Cumorah," p. viii).

Benjamin had declared of the plates: "We can know of their surety because we have them before our eyes." (Mosiah

1:6). But in our day, we can have that same witness, through Joseph Smith's translation. To him, the Lord said: "This generation shall have my word through you." (D&C 5:10). For us, "the presence of the plates would only prove that there are plates, no more. It would not prove that Nephites wrote them, or that an angel brought them, or that they had been translated by the gift and power of God. A far more impressive claim is put forth when the whole work is given to the world as a divinely inspired translation." (Hugh Nibley, "An Approach to The Book of Mormon," p. 17-18, see Commentary Reference to Mosiah 1:6).

The only condition placed on individuals when they are exposed to The Book of Mormon and its teachings, and who then receive a confirmation by the Spirit that they are true, is that they then "repent and come unto the Father in the name of Jesus" in order to be "received into the kingdom of God." (V. 5).

Moroni suggested that resolving the issue of the divine authenticity of The Book of Mormon rests in the hands of those who read his words. He said, "If I have no authority for these things, judge ye." (V. 6). On every issue, then, there are three votes cast. Heavenly Father casts His vote in favor of us, and Satan casts his against us. We cast the deciding vote, and all eternity hangs in the balance. One vote really does count. When we stand before God at the last day, and Moroni is there, we will recognize and acknowledge his authority to have made these bold declarations. (V. 6, see Moroni 10:34).

Ether
Chapter 6

After the digression in chapter 5, Moroni explained that he would now proceed with "the record of Jared and his brother." (V. 1). We sense in this verse that Moroni was not as concerned as was Ether that the 24 gold plates be regarded as a history primarily of the Brother of Jared. Instead, he focused his abridgement efforts on the principles contained in the record..

With the 16 shining stones "to give light unto men, women, and children, that they might not cross the great waters in darkness," the party was ready to make final preparations for their voyage of discovery. (V. 2-3). They now had the light of the Lord to illuminate their way. No longer would the terrors of the unknown or mists of darkness be allowed to deter them from their course.

They gathered together "all manner of food, that thereby they might subsist upon the water, and also food for their flocks and herds, and whatsoever beast or animal or fowl that they should carry with them." (V. 4). Interestingly, there is no mention in the cargo of bees or hives. Naturalists believe that bees were unknown in the New World until the Seventeenth Century, when European immigrants introduced them. (See Commentary Reference to Ether 2:3). Also, when we visualize in our mind's eye these heavily laden barges, the necessity of an efficient refuse disposal system becomes obvious. The ingenious method casually mentioned by Moroni in his abridgment was surely sufficient to the task. (See Commentary Reference to Ether 2:20).

No sooner had the party set forth upon the ocean, than "the Lord God caused that there should be a furious wind blow upon the face of the waters, towards the promised land, and thus they were tossed upon the waves of the sea before the wind. And it came to pass that they were many times buried in the depths of the sea, because of the mountain waves which broke upon them, and also the great and terrible tempests which were caused by the fierceness of the wind. And it came to pass that the wind never did cease to blow towards the promised land while they were upon the waters. And thus, they were driven forth, three hundred and forty and four days upon the water." (V. 5, 6, 8 & 11).

Moroni described a passage over the ocean of almost incredible dimension, unique in the annals of seafarers. Only because the Jaredites had followed the Lord's prescribed plan with exactness were they able to endure such an ordeal. Perhaps there is a type in this experience and a lesson to be learned. The wind and the waves are always on the side of the ablest navigator who sets his course by the standard of the Gospel of Jesus Christ. When our hearts are right, no wind can blow except to fill our sails. A good mariner can read the weather like a book, and can use his skills and equipment to set a course that will lead unerringly to his destination. The same wind that might cause a less seaworthy craft to founder, fills the sails of that vessel whose helmsman is a skilled seafarer.

During the voyage, navigators cannot necessarily see the port that is their destination. Sometimes, it is over the horizon of their vision, and sometimes, the tack appears to be taking the ship away from, rather than toward, a safe harbor. But if correct principles are followed, the landfall is always sure. The best Mariner of all was the Savior Jesus Christ. The scriptures tell us: "When he was entered into a ship, his disciples followed him. And, behold, there arose a great tempest in the sea, insomuch that the ship was covered with the waves: but he was asleep. And his disciples came to him, and awoke him, saying, Lord, save us: we perish. And he saith unto them, Why are ye fearful, O ye of little faith? Then he arose, and rebuked the winds and the sea; and there was a great calm. But the men marvelled, saying, What manner of man is this, that even the winds and the sea obey him!" (Matthew 8:23-27).

The water ordeal of the Jaredites took place during 344 long days and nights on the ocean. If it were necessary for us to similarly have our faith tried, or to be tested by walking barefoot and destitute across the Great Plains with the Pioneer Saints, Heavenly Father could have easily arranged for us to have been born into circumstances that would have accommodated that need. In fact, the trials we face today are the very ones that are tailored to test our faith. Wilford Woodruff, who walked with Zion's Camp to Missouri from Kirtland, Ohio, said: "We gained an experience that we never could have gained in any other way. We had the privilege of traveling one thousand miles with (the Prophet Joseph Smith), and seeing the workings of the Spirit of God with him, and the revelations of Jesus Christ unto him, and the fulfilment of those revelations. Had I not gone up with Zion's Camp, I should not have been here today." (J.D.,, 13:158).

Once the feet of the Jaredites were upon the dry ground of the promised land, "they bowed themselves down upon the face of the land, and did humble themselves before the Lord, and did shed tears of joy before the Lord, because of the multitude of his tender mercies over them." (V. 12, see Psalms 145:9, 51:1, 77:8 & 103:4, & 1 Nephi 8:8). They recognized the protective hand of the Lord over them. After all, He had promised: "I will go before thee into a land which is choice above all the lands of the earth." (Ether 1:42, see 1 Nephi 2:20).

It was a "choice" land because it had been the location of the Garden of Eden and the Valley of Adam Ondi Ahman, and it would be the land where Christ would come to personally minister among the Nephites. Also, it would be the land of Zion, the New Jerusalem, that would be one of the seats of government during the Millennial Reign of Christ. Truly, the Jaredites were greatly blessed and privileged to come to such a choice land.

The population of the Jaredite colony at this time was something above 30 individuals. (V. 14-16). This included the families of Jared, his brother, and their friends. This gene pool would be relatively heterogeneous, and multiplying arithmetically for even a few generations, a population in the millions would be possible. The record only says of these people: "Therefore, they began to be many" and "they began to spread upon the face of the land." (V. 16 & 18).

An assembly and a census of the entire nation formally inaugurated Jaredite history in the New World. "Accordingly, the people were gathered together." (V. 20). Jared had 4 sons and eight daughters, and his brother had 22 sons and daughters. (V. 20). These numbers of offspring suggest that the at least some of the Jaredites practiced plural marriage, but the record is silent on the subject. (See Ether 2:1-2).

Jared and his brother advanced in years, and were soon to go "down to their graves." (V. 21). Their people desired "that they should anoint one of their sons to be a king over them." (V. 22). Neither Jared nor his brother thought this was a good idea, because they felt that it would lead to the captivity of the people. Nevertheless, they granted the request, but only under pressure. "And Orihah," one of the sons of Jared, "was anointed to be a king over the people." (V. 27, see Commentary References to Mosiah 29). Luckily, Orihah "did walk humbly before the Lord, and did remember how great things the Lord had done for his father, and also taught his people how great things the Lord had done for their fathers." (V. 30).

Only because the Jaredites had followed the Lord's prescribed plan with exactness had they been able to endure such an ordeal as they had experienced. Perhaps there is a type in this experience, and a lesson to be learned. The wind and the waves are always on the side of the ablest navigator who sets his course by the standard of the Gospel of Jesus Christ.

"And when they had
set their feet upon the shores
of the promised land, they bowed
themselves down upon the face of the
land, and did humble themselves before
the Lord, and did shed tears of joy before the
Lord, because of the multitude of his tender
mercies over them." (Ether 6:12).

Ether
Chapter 7

Of the Jaredites, Hugh Nibley wrote: "Their whole history is the tale of a fierce and unrelenting struggle for power. The Book of Ether is a typical ancient chronicle, a military and political history related by casual reference to the wealth and splendor of kings." ("The World of The Jaredites," p. 192).

Their first king, Orihah, lived to a great age, and "begat sons and daughters; yea, he begat thirty and one." (V. 1-2). A son named Kib was even born "in (Orihah's) old age." (V. 3). These references to the fruitful posterity of the king, and to his advanced age when still fathering children, suggest that plural marriage was practiced by the Jaredites. (See Ether 1:20, 7:26, 9:14, 9:21, 9:23, 10:4 & 10:13).

Only one reference is made by Moroni, in Ether 9:24, regarding the age of an elderly companion queen who remains unnamed. In that verse, the record states that the king had no children "even until he was exceedingly old. And it came to pass that his wife died, being an hundred and two years old." (Ether 9:23-24). When she died, the king "took to wife, in his old age, a young maid, and begat sons and daughters." (Ether 9:24). This would suggest a monogamous relationship with his wife throughout the life of this particular king. (See Commentary Reference to Ether 6:20).

In any case, Orihah's grandson named Corihor became disenchanted with his father Kib, left home to seek his fortune, and "drew away many people after him." (V. 4). Thus, began "the peculiar warfare of the Jaredites, a war of motion with no set frontiers, great armies, sweeping over the (land) in flight or pursuit, making the most of space by falling back on this or that wilderness, setting up rival camps for a year or two, while dissenting groups or individuals join themselves to one army or another. It is Asia all over again." (Hugh Nibley, "The World of The Jaredites," p. 224). Corihor "gathered together an army (to come) up into the land of Moron where the king dwelt." (V. 5). The fugitive who draws off people from his rivals and gathers his forces in the wilderness is a conventional figure of the Asiatic Steppes. (See "World of The Jaredites," P. 194).

When Corihor took his father Kib captive, he "brought to pass the saying of the Brother of Jared that they would be brought into captivity." (V. 5). Also, Corihor acted out the drama in the Asiatic custom, where a king would frequently be held in captivity for many years, even for all the remainder of his days, where he might have children who would some day seek revenge for their family, and power for themselves. (See V. 7-22). All these events took place in the Land of Moron, which "was near the land which is called Desolation by the Nephites." (V. 6). This was north of the narrow neck of land, beyond Bountiful, in the land of Mormon's nativity.

In his old age, while Kib dwelt in captivity, a son named Shule was born to him. (V. 7). Through the efforts of Shule, Corihor repented of his evil ways and the kingdom was restored to Kib, who gratefully bestowed his powers of office upon Shule. (V. 8-10). The young king executed "judgment in righteousness." (V. 11). "And also, in the reign of Shule there came prophets among the people, who were sent from the Lord, prophesying that the wickedness and idolatry of the people was bringing a curse upon the land, and that they should be destroyed if they did not repent." (V. 23). But, in typical fashion, "the people did revile against the prophets, and did mock them." (V. 24). By Shule's authority, however, laws were passed giving these prophets the freedom of speech and due process, "and by this cause the people were brought unto repentance." (V. 24-25, see Mosiah 27:2, Alma 1:21 & 4:8).

In the days of Alma the Younger, the same conditions had existed in Zarahemla. Alma had been commissioned by the Lord to "go forth among his people, or among the people of Nephi, that he might preach the word of God unto them, to stir them up in remembrance of their duty, that he might pull down, by the word of God, all the pride and craftiness and all the contentions which were among his people, seeing no way that he might reclaim them save it were in bearing down in pure testimony against them." (Alma 4:19). He had been successful among the people of the City of Zarahemla, where he was allowed a forum. But in Ammonihah, the people had "withstood all his words, and reviled him, and spit upon him, and caused that he should be cast out of their city." (Alma 8:13, see Alma 14:7). The natural consequence of these people rejecting the words of the prophets was their physical and spiritual destruction. Mormon later reported: "Every living soul of the Ammonihahites was destroyed, and also their great city." (Alma 16:9).

Under the reign of Shule and the influence of the holy prophets sent by the Lord, however, "the people did repent of their iniquities and idolatries (and) the Lord did spare them, and they began to prosper again in the land." (V. 26). "And there were no more wars in the days of Shule; and he remembered the great things that the Lord had done for his fathers in bringing them across the great deep into the promised land; wherefore he did execute judgment in righteousness all his days." (V. 27).

Ether
Chapter 8

In this chapter we are introduced to the story of the "dancing princess." This tale of intrigue has widespread and ancient parallels, that consist of the strange traditions of throne succession. (See Hugh Nibley, "World of The Jaredites," p. 207-210). The descendants of Shared ruled their kingdoms with treachery and cunning, and obtained "an account concerning them of old, that they by their secret plans did obtain kingdoms and great glory." (V. 9). These dark secrets were the oaths and covenants that "had been handed down even from Cain, who was a murderer from the beginning." (V. 15).

One Akish was particularly manipulative, and gathered around him all those who would swear to him "by the God of heaven, and also by the heavens, and also by the earth, and by their heads, that whoso should vary from the assistance which Akish desired should lose his head; and whoso should divulge whatsoever thing Akish made known unto them, the same should lose his life." (V. 14). These adherents of the secret combinations were kept and maintained by oath. (See v. 17).

That these secret plans were even available testifies to the tremendous "power of the devil to administer these oaths unto the people, to keep them in darkness, to help such as sought power to gain power, and to murder, and to plunder, and to lie, and to commit all manner of wickedness and whoredoms." (V. 16). Joseph Fielding Smith, Jr. taught: "Satan has power to place thoughts in our minds and to whisper to us in unspoken impressions to entice us to satisfy our appetites or desires, and in other ways he plays upon our weakness and desires." ("1972-73 Melchizedek Priesthood Personal Study Guide," p. 298). However, he can only do this if we have previously dismissed the Spirit of Christ or the Holy Ghost by engaging in behavior that is inconsistent with their nature.

This is why King Benjamin cautioned his people: "But this much I can tell you, that if ye do not watch yourselves, and your thoughts, and your words, and your deeds, and observe the commandments of God, and continue in the faith of what ye have heard concerning the coming of our Lord, even unto the end of your lives, ye must perish. And now, O man, remember, and perish not." (Mosiah 4:30).

Akish and his fellow conspirators "formed a secret combination, even as they of old." (V. 18). It is one thing to worship idols, for men and women have always done this. In the Last Days, however, the Lord told Joseph Smith that those in the world "have strayed from mine ordinances, and have broken mine everlasting covenant. They seek not the Lord to establish his righteousness, but every man walketh in his own way, and after the image of his own God, whose image is in the likeness of the world, and whose substance is that of an idol." (D&C 1:15-16).

The problem with those who worship idols is that "the devil delighteth in them, and he rules in the earth" by the manipulation of such weak-willed individuals. (2 Nephi 9:37). Unprincipled and undisciplined minds are easily swayed by the siren song so seductively sent by Satan. Where this practice of idolatry is prevalent, the legitimate rule of priesthood authority is absent. It is this substitution of the sacred by the profane that is an abomination in the sight of God. Idol worship that is also accompanied by secret oaths and covenants that mock God is the epitome of taking His name in vain. It is blasphemy and is "most abominable and wicked of all, in the sight of God." (V. 18).

So dangerous were these oaths to the spiritual welfare of the people, that Moroni would not write them down in his abridgment of The Book of Ether. They were had among the Lamanites, and such was their power, wrote Moroni, that they "have caused the destruction of this people of whom I am now speaking, and also the destruction of the people of Nephi." (V. 20-21, see Helaman 2:13).

Moroni posted this dire warning because there is no reason to believe that Satan will not again put it into the hearts of men to form secret societies. He wrote: "And whatsoever nation shall uphold such secret combinations, to get power and gain, until they shall spread over the nation, behold, they shall be destroyed." (V. 22). "Wherefore, O ye Gentiles, it is wisdom in God that these things should be shown unto you, that thereby ye may repent of your sins, and suffer not that these murderous combinations shall get above you, which are built up to get power and gain - and the work, yea, even the work of destruction come upon you." (V. 23).

Moroni reiterated that it is Satan who is responsible for the formation of secret combinations, for it is he "who hath hardened the hearts of men that they have murdered the prophets, and stoned them, and cast them out from the beginning." (V. 25). Moroni had witnessed the tremendous power of the devil, that is unleashed when men and women renounce their allegiance to Christ and willfully rebel against the light. His father had abridged the record of Nephi, and had undoubtedly shared with Moroni the insights these scriptures provided. Nephi had recorded that, at the time of the crucifixion of Christ, there was in Zarahemla a "great mourning and howling and weeping among all the people continually." (3 Nephi 8:23). "They were heard to cry and mourn, saying: O that we had repented before this great and terrible day, and had not killed and stoned the prophets, and cast them out." (3 Nephi 8:25). In light of the Savior's later declaration to these people, that they were spared because they were more righteous than their brethren, it is reasonable to conclude that they had not literally done these terrible things. (See 3 Nephi 9:13).

Mormon reported that those who survived the destruction in the Land of Zarahemla were "they who received the prophets and stoned them not; and it was they who had not shed the blood of the saints." (3 Nephi 10:12). But perhaps, they had not been as valiant in the testimony of Jesus as they could have been. Perhaps, they had figuratively stoned the prophets by ignoring their counsel and denying their authority. That they were "more righteous than their brethren" may have been true but it might not be saying much, inasmuch as their brethren had been destroyed "because of their sins and their wickedness, which was above all the wickedness of the whole earth, because of their secret murders and combinations; for it was they that did destroy the peace of my people and the government of the land; therefore I did cause them to be burned, to destroy them from before my face, that the blood of the prophets and the saints should not come up unto me any more against them." (3 Nephi 9:9). "And thus were the howlings of the people great and terrible." (V. 25).

The lessons of both 3 Nephi and The Book of Ether provide invaluable voices of warning to help us understand how important it is to actively stand up against evil practices today. Moroni looked forward to the day when "Satan may have no power upon the hearts of the children of men, but that they may be persuaded to do good continually, that they may come unto the fountain of all righteousness and be saved." (V. 26).

Satan is powerless when the people are obedient to God's commandments. Nephi was speaking of the millennial reign of Christ, when he said that "because of the righteousness of his people, Satan has no power; wherefore, he cannot be loosed for the space of many years; for he hath no power over the hearts of the people, for they dwell in righteousness, and the Holy One of Israel reigneth." (See Commentary Reference to 1 Nephi 22:26, & to 2 Nephi 30:18).

But even amidst the tumult of the Last Days, the Saints of God can stand in holy places, and be not moved, if they dwell in righteousness and invite the Holy One of Israel to reign in their midst. (See D&C 45:32).

"And whatsoever nation shall uphold such secret combinations … shall be destroyed … Wherefore, O ye Gentiles, it is wisdom in God that these things should be shown unto you, that thereby ye may repent of your sins, and suffer not that these murderous combinations shall get above you, which are built up to get power and gain."
(Ether 8:22-23).

Ether
Chapter 9

After his aside at the end of Chapter 8, when he cautioned those living in the Last Days about secret combinations, Moroni once again returned to his abridgment of the 24 Gold Plates of Ether. "And now I, Moroni, proceed with my record." (V. 1).

Akish continued to wreak havoc among the Jaredites, "and he applied unto those whom he had sworn by the oath of the ancients." (V. 5). "For so great had been the spreading of this wicked and secret society, that it had corrupted the hearts of all the people." (V. 6). Akish was prominent among those who followed Satan, even starving to death one of his own sons, because he feared his potential challenge. (V. 7).

Satan's Golden Question has always been: "Have you any money?" His philosophy is that everything in the world has its price. "The people of Akish were desirous for gain, even as Akish was desirous for power; wherefore (other) sons of Akish did offer them money, by which means they drew away the more part of the people after them." (V. 11). How cheaply do most of us sell that which is most dear! "That for which all virtue is sold, and almost any vice - Almighty Gold!" (Ben Jonson). The irony is that it was all for nothing, for the result of their passion for telestial treasures and of their fratricidal bickering was "the destruction of nearly all the people of the kingdom." (V. 12).

After the inevitable execution of the judgments of God against these wicked people, the pendulum once again swung the other way. Emer was anointed king, and he "did execute judgment in righteousness all his days." (V. 21). "And thus, the Lord did pour out his blessings upon this land, which was choice above all other lands; and he commanded that whoso should possess the land should possess it unto the Lord, or they should be destroyed when they were ripened in iniquity; for upon such, saith the Lord, I will pour out the fulness of my wrath." (V. 20).

The land was blessed with "all manner of fruit, and of grain, and of silks, and of fine linen, and of gold, and of silver, and of precious things. And also, all manner of cattle, of oxen, and cows, and of sheep, and of swine, and of goats, and also many other kinds of animals which were useful for the food of man. And they also had horses, and asses, and there were elephants and cureloms and cumoms." (V. 17-19, see V. 32, & 10:19, 3 Nephi 4:4, & Commentary Reference to 3 Nephi 4:4).

Cureloms and cumoms deserve our attention, because these strange animals evidently were foreign to Moroni's experience. He could find no words to adequately describe them, and so used the original Jaredite terms in his abridgment. It is fortunate that he did so, however, because they are the only Jaredite common nouns known to us,

253

with the exception of "deseret," that by interpretation, means "honeybee," and possibly "Shelem," that characterized the height of the mount upon which the Brother of Jared had obtained his sixteen shining stones. (See Ether 2:3, and 3:1).

The Jaredite and Nephite languages were entirely different, and these words have a ring all their own. "Their most characteristic feature is their ending in "m." This is called "mimation" and is actually found among the most ancient languages of the Near East, where it was followed by the later "nunation" or ending in "n," the most characteristic feature of classical Arabic and also of Nephite proper names. The correct use and sequence of mimation and nunation in The Book of Mormon speaks strongly for the authenticity of the record, for the principle is a relatively recent philological discovery." (High Nibley, "The World of The Jaredites," p. 243).

The reign of Emer was characterized by those qualities that are the natural result of obedience to the laws of God. As a matter of fact, "he saw peace in the land; yea, and he even saw the Son of Righteousness, and did rejoice and glory in his day; and he died in peace" at the ripe old age of 142. (V. 22 & 24). As a result of his faith, he was able to live long and prosper.

Then the pendulum lost its forward momentum, and as it faltered, the people "began to embrace the secret plans again of old." (V. 26). To counterbalance the negative effect of the secret societies, "there came prophets in the land again, crying repentance." (V. 28). By the authority of the priesthood, these servants of God pronounced a curse upon the land, except the people should repent. (V. 28). But, in typical fashion, "the people believed not the words of the prophets, but they cast them out." (V. 29). The people of Ammonihah would do the same thing to Alma and Amulek, before their destruction around 80 B.C.

Only after severe hardship, including a prolonged drought and the introduction of poisonous serpents to the land, that were the fulfilment of the curse that had been decreed by God, did the people begin to "repent of their iniquities and cry unto the Lord." (V. 30-34). Moroni indicated in his abridgment that the flocks of the people fled before these snakes "toward the land southward, which was called by the Nephites Zarahemla." (V. 31). Although "there were many of (these animals) which did perish by the way; nevertheless, there were some which fled into the land southward." (V. 32).

When Lehi's party embarked from Bountiful on the ship they had constructed, they took with them only those things that the Lord had commanded them to bring. The only provisions identified by name included fruits, meat, honey, and seeds. (See 1 Nephi 18:6 & 24). Animals were conspicuously absent. Nevertheless, when they arrived in the promised land, they discovered "that there were beasts in the forest of every kind, both the cow and the ox, and the ass and the horse, and the goat and the wild goat, and all manner of wild animals, which were for the use of men." (1 Nephi 18:25). It is likely that these animals, discovered by Lehi's party in the land of their first inheritance, were descended from those very animals that had been driven by the hand of the Lord from the north countries, into the land southward.

When the Jaredites finally "had humbled themselves sufficiently before the Lord, he did send rain upon the face of the earth." (V. 35). This manifestation of power was enough to influence the people in general to fear God and to observe His statutes. The purpose of chastisement has always been to bring God's children to repentance, and once again His correction was effective in doing so.

Ether
Chapter 10

As much as a third of Jaredite history may be covered in this one chapter. Unlike the Nephites, we have seen that the Jaredites were committed monarchists. (See Commentary Reference to Mosiah 29:2). In the four verses describing the reign of Riplakish, for example, we are provided with every detail of the portrait of an Asiatic overlord. The Book of Ether paints a picture that is completely alien to Western experience, and certainly to Joseph Smith or even to his more learned contemporaries living on the frontier of Western New York in the 1820s.

Riplakish had "many wives and concubines," and Moroni condemned him for his "whoredoms and abominations." (V. 5 & 7). Throughout The Book of Mormon, it is always apostate Nephites or Lamanites who embark upon ambitious building programs, single-mindedly constructing monuments of stone in attempts to validate and to commemorate their significance, while taxing the people beyond their ability to bear the burden. Here, we find Riplakish doing the same thing in the north countries. He "did build many spacious buildings" and "all manner of fine workmanship he did cause to be wrought." (V. 5 & 7).

We are reminded of Shelley's Ozymandias: "I met a traveler from an antique land, who said Two vast and trunkless legs of stone stand in the desert. Near them, on the sand, half sunk, a shattered visage lies, whose frown and wrinkled lip, and sneer of cold command, tell that its sculptor well those passions read which yet survive stamped on these lifeless things, the hand that mocked them, and the heart that fed; and on the pedestal these words appear: "My name is Ozymandias, King of Kings: Look on my works, ye mighty, and despair!" Nothing beside remains. Round the decay of that colossal wreck, boundless and bare the lone and level sand stretches far away."

In verse 19, we learn that after many generations, "the poisonous serpents were destroyed" that had prevented the excursion of the people into the land south of the narrow neck. "Wherefore, they did go into the land southward, to hunt food for the people of the land," who must have by this time become quite numerous, "for the land was covered with animals of the forest." Because of the abundance of game there, this land was maintained by the Jaredites as a hunting park in the best Asiatic tradition. "And they did preserve the land southward for a wilderness, to get game. And the whole face of the land northward was covered with inhabitants." (V. 21).

This would explain why there were no traces of civilization in the Land Southward when the People of Zarahemla established their colony there, or when the Nephites immigrants arrived. It was only when the People of Limhi sent out an expedition from the Land of Nephi in search of Zarahemla that the Land of Desolation north of the narrow neck was discovered by them.

The record states that the Jaredites had "silks, and fine-twined linen; and they did work all manner of cloth." (V. 24). The Chinese were working with silk about 2,500 B.C., and in India as early as 4,000 B.C. (See Commentary Reference to Alma 4:6). That the Jaredites knew about silk production suggests that their wandering took them across Asia before they embarked from a Pacific shore on their journey to the New World. Silkworms must have been a valued part of the cargo taken aboard their barges.

Moroni identified a Jaredite king by the name of Hearthom, who lost his kingdom and was thrown into prison, where he lived for the rest of his life. (V. 30). Then, his son Heth, his grandson Aaron, his great-grandson Amnigaddah, and his great-great grandson Coriantum likewise lived in captivity for all their lives. (V. 31). Once again, we are introduced to a pattern completely alien and shocking to the Western mind, but normal to those familiar with ancient Asiatic practices.

Com, who was the son of Coriantum, managed to obtain his own freedom, and then to draw away half of the kingdom. (V. 31-32). He opposed the king, a man by the name of Amgid, "and they fought for the space of many years, during which time Com gained power over Amgid, and obtained power over the remainder of his kingdom." (V. 32). But his greater challenge was the presence of "robbers in the land (who) adopted the old plans, and administered oaths after the manner of the ancients, and sought again to destroy the kingdom." (V. 33).

As we encounter more kings in The Book of Ether, we might pause to ask why it is that Jaredite names pop up in the Nephite records. After all, Moroni had reported in the opening verse of his abridgment of the 24 Gold Plates of Ether that these "ancient inhabitants (of the land) were destroyed by the hand of the Lord upon the face of this north country." How could there have been communication between these two civilizations?

We must remember that the Jaredite and Mulekite culture overlapped by at least 9 months, and perhaps for a much greater period of time. (See Omni 1:21). "At any rate, we have proof that the Jaredites made a permanent cultural impression on the Nephites through Mulek, for centuries after the destruction of the Jaredite nation, we find a Nephite bearing the name of Coriantumr, (Helaman 1) and learn that this man was a descendant of Zarahemla, the illustrious leader of the Mulekites. This shows the Jaredite influence reaching the Nephites through Mulekite channels, which is exactly what one would expect." (Hugh Nibley, "The World of The Jaredites," p. 244-245).

Interestingly, the name "Moroni" itself has Jaredite roots, inasmuch as the land first settled by the Jaredites was called Moron. "Moroni" means "belonging to Moron," or "of Moron." When Mormon was eleven years old, he was carried by his father "into the land southward, even to the land of Zarahemla." (Mormon 1:6). This suggests that the land of Mormon's birth was in the Land Northward, perhaps in Moron itself. It would be natural for the father to name his son after the land of his own nativity. If they do nothing else, these interesting word associations invite further study into the less obvious currents flowing through The Book of Mormon that give credence to its authenticity.

Ether
Chapter 11

Once again, prophets were sent into the land to cry repentance, but these "were rejected by the people" who "sought to destroy them." (V. 1 & 2). These priesthood servants of God were protected, thanks to the enlightened leadership of Com, but after his death they were once again vulnerable to the wicked designs of his nephew, who was associated with the secret combinations. (V. 2-4, see V. 7).

Consequently, "all the prophets who prophesied of the destruction of the people (were) put to death." (V. 5). Before their martyrdom, however, "they had testified that a great curse should come upon the land, and also upon the people, and that there should be a great destruction among them, such as one as never had been upon the face of the earth, and their bones should become as heaps of earth upon the face of the land, except they should repent of their wickedness." (V. 6).

When wars, contentions, famines, and pestilence followed, "such as one as never had been known upon the face of the earth" (V. 7), "the people began to repent of their iniquity; and inasmuch as they did, the Lord did have mercy on them." (V. 8). Unfortunately, it only took another generation or two for the people to slide back into apostasy. This prompted the Lord to again send "many prophets" into the land who testified, "the Lord would utterly destroy them from off the face of the earth except they repented of their iniquities." (V. 12). "And it came to pass that the people hardened their hearts, and would not hearken unto their words; and the prophets mourned, and withdrew from among the people." (V. 13, see Moroni 9:20).

Two generations passed, but the situation did not improve. Again, the Lord sent "many prophets (who) prophesied of great and marvelous things, and cried repentance unto the people, and except they should repent. the Lord God would execute judgment against them to their utter destruction." (V. 20, see V. 14 & 18).

Allusion was made to the Nephites and the People of Zarahemla, who possibly already inhabited the Land Southward. These prophets warned that "the Lord God would send or bring forth another people to possess the land," should the Jaredites not repent. (V. 21). But Satan had such a grip on the people, that "they did reject all the words of the prophets, because of their secret society and wicked abominations." (V. 22).

Moron, who had been king of the Jaredite nation, was overthrown and spent the rest of his life in captivity. (V. 18). While in prison, Coriantor was born. (V. 18). Unfortunately, he too "dwelt in captivity all his days." (V. 19). The Prophet Ether, the son of Coriantor, was born in these circumstances in a Jaredite prison. And it came to pass that Coriantor begat Ether, and he died, having dwelt in captivity all his days." (V. 23). Ether would have been king of the land, with power and authority to execute righteous leadership, had the situation been different. As it turned out, he was able to break the pattern of captivity of his fathers.

"And they hearkened not unto the voice of the Lord, because of their wicked combinations; wherefore, there began to be wars and contentions in all the land, and also many famines and pestilences, insomuch that there was a great destruction."
(Ether 11:7).

Ether
Chapter 12

It is only in this chapter, that we are introduced to the prophet Ether who "came forth in the days of Coriantumr, and began to prophesy unto the people, for he could not be restrained because of the Spirit of the Lord which was in him." (V. 2). In Ether's day, "Coriantumr was king over all the land." (V. 1). It was he who later wandered into the Land of Zarahemla, sometime between 279 B.C. and 130 B.C., after the last great battles of the Jaredite people. (See Omni 1:21, & Ether 13:21).

Ether took his ecclesiastical responsibilities very seriously, "for he did cry from the morning, even until the going down of the sun, exhorting the people to believe in God unto repentance, lest they should be destroyed." (V. 3). This is the same familiar message of the prophets in all ages. (See Ether 7:23, 9:28 & 11:1). When the people fail to repent, they forfeit the assurance of peace in this life and of eternal life in the resurrection. Their present and future happiness is first jeopardized, and then destroyed.

But those who believe in God and are obedient to His will that is fully explained by the Plan of Salvation "hope for a better world, yea, even a place at the right hand of God, which hope cometh of faith, maketh an anchor to the souls of men, which would make them sure and steadfast, always abounding in good works, being led to glorify God." (V. 4). This tremendous promise is all the more powerful because of its brevity. In only a few words, it defines the Plan of the Father and harmonizes beautifully with His Own "mission statement", which is to bring to pass the immortality and eternal life of His children. (See Moses 1:39).

Although these principles were "great and marvelous," Ether's contemporaries "did not believe, because they saw them not." (V. 5, see Commentary Reference to Ether 12:19). They could not "see" that Ether's message was essential to their salvation. Their spiritual blindness prevented them from catching the vision of what he said. The standard of the world is: "Seeing is believing." But seeing is not only irrelevant to the acquisition of faith, it often focuses our attention on the wrong message. The example of Madison Avenue's marketing materials testifies that this is true. Instead, as Harold B. Lee taught: "You must learn to walk to the edge of the light, and then a few steps into the darkness; then the light will appear and show the way before you." ("The Edge of the Light," BYU Today, 3/1991, 22-23). This is the way faith is developed and strengthened.

Moroni took the opportunity, at this point in his abridgment, to "speak somewhat concerning these things." (V. 6). There are probably three classic definitions of faith in the scriptures. They are:

One: "Faith is not to have a perfect knowledge of things; therefore, if ye have faith ye hope for things which are not seen, which are true." (Alma 32:21). This is correct in the ultimate sense. In Alma's usage, the verse might more clearly read: "Faith is not to have a perfect knowledge of things gained through one's own experiences." In the context in which Alma taught this principle to his Zoramite audience, it is important to remember that Korihor's demand for a sign had been the condition for his faith, since he trusted only his physical senses. The rational approach is the enemy of faith. Some things need to be believed to be seen. (See Commentary Reference to Alma Chapter 32).

Two: "Now faith is the substance of things hoped for, the evidence of things not seen." (Hebrews 11:1). In this context, faith is not developed by receiving signs from heaven. As Alma told the Zoramites, "If a man knoweth a thing, he hath no cause to believe, for he knoweth it." (Alma 32:18). No expenditure of faith is necessary to receive signs. When the sign is given, we might have a sure knowledge of the event, but no exercise of faith has been made to produce it. Under proper circumstances, however, "by doing our duty, faith increases until it becomes perfect knowledge." (Heber J. Grant, C.R., 4/1934). Initially, faith is to believe what we do not see, and the reward of faith is to see what we believe.

Three: "Faith is things which are hoped for and not seen; wherefore, dispute not because ye see not, for ye receive no witness until after the trial of your faith." (V. 6). It is important to remember that in matters of faith the Lord is not on trial. At the Bar of Justice, the Judge will review the evidence, and our previous acceptance or rejection of that evidence will determine our reward or punishment. The trial that we call the mortal experience is eminently fair.

This definition given by Moroni served as his opportunity to show us how we might develop more justifiable faith. (See Alma Chapter 32, Moses 6:60, & Commentary Reference to V. 18). In verses 7-22 Moroni taught that the miracles from the scriptures with which we are familiar were only made possible by the exercise of faith, and that each of us has the power to develop that same intensity of understanding.

It was by faith that Christ appeared to many after His resurrection. (V. 7). When we read in the sacred records of these experiences, a way is prepared that we, too, might be "partakers of the heavenly gift, that (we) might hope for those things which (we) have not seen." (V. 8). It becomes possible for us to immerse ourselves in the emotion of the two disciples on the Road to Emmaus, who, after communing with the Resurrected Lord, declared: "Did not our heart burn within us, while he talked with us by the way, and while he opened to us the scriptures?" (Luke 24:32).

"It was by faith that they of old were called after the holy order of God." (V. 10). The exercise of priesthood power is based solely upon the principles of faith and righteousness. If, in the exercise of these responsibilities, we "undertake to cover our sins, or to gratify our pride, our vain ambition, or to exercise control or dominion or compulsion upon the souls of the children of men, in any degree of unrighteousness," our authority is taken from us. (D&C 121:34-37).

Therefore, priesthood can have real meaning only to those disciples who have developed saving faith, who know Heavenly Father and have accepted Jesus Christ as their Savior, and who have entered the fold through the covenant symbolized by baptism. "And again, by way of commandment to the church concerning the manner of baptism - All those who humble themselves before God, and desire to be baptized, and come forth with broken hearts and contrite spirits, and witness before the church that they have truly repented of al their sins, and are willing to take upon them the name of Jesus Christ, having a determination to serve him to the end, and truly manifest by their works that they have received of the Spirit of Christ unto the remission of their sins, shall be received by baptism into his church." (D&C 20:37, see Moroni 6:1-3).

The Law of Moses, Moroni pointed out, was given because it was tailored to meet the needs of Israel at the time. "But in the gift of his Son hath God prepared a more excellent way; and it is by faith that it hath been fulfilled." (V. 11, see 1 Corinthians. 12:31). Faith is the driving force that propels us toward our eternal destiny. Without it, God's work is frustrated. "For if there be no faith among the children of men God can do no miracle among them; wherefore he showeth not himself until after their faith." (V. 12, see V. 30).

The stories from the scriptures are inspiring because they demonstrate the great faith of those who have played roles in the drama. (See V. 16). "It was the faith of Alma and Amulek that caused the prison to tumble to the earth." (V. 13). "It was the faith of Nephi and Lehi that wrought the change upon the Lamanites, that they were baptized with fire and with the Holy Ghost." (V. 14). "It was the faith of Ammon and his brethren which wrought so great a miracle among the Lamanites." (V. 15). "It was by faith that the three disciples obtained a promise that they should not taste of death." (V. 17).

Moroni taught that the essential ingredient of saving faith is to first believe in the Son of God. (V. 18). Every discussion of faith must distinguish it from its caricatures. It is not credulity. It is not belief, which is knowledge without a moral element of responsibility. It is not a formula to get the world to do your bidding. It is antithetical to cynicism and pessimism. Instead, faith inspires confidence that life is a school of discipline whose Author and Teacher is God.

Truth is at the very foundation of faith. Heavenly Father will not cause a person to have faith in that which is false. Justifiable faith is faith with sufficient evidence. It is faith in action, supported by good works that are motivated by the Holy Ghost. It is faith of such quality that at the Bar of Justice the Holy Ghost will stand beside us and argue in our behalf that the power of the Atonement must raise us to a resurrection of glory and eternal life.

Heavenly Father does not expect us to exercise faith in those things for which there is insufficient evidence. The key to liberation from enslavement to apostate religious dogma is saving faith in the divine mission of the Son of God. Many who lived before the mortal ministry of the Savior had such faith that they received the Second Comforter, the personal ministry of Jesus Christ, and "they truly saw with their eyes the things which they had beheld with an eye of faith, and they were glad." (V. 19). Even as Moroni taught that "if there be no faith among the children of men, God can do no miracle among them" (V. 12), he explained that the opposite is also true. Our faith in God may become so great that we cannot "be kept without the veil." (V. 21). When we reach that point in our spiritual development, "the veil shall be rent," promised the Lord, "and you shall see me and know that I am." (D&C 67:10).

Moroni explained that even his abridgment of the sacred records that would come to the Gentiles in the Last Days was the product of the faith of his fathers. (V. 22). Even though he was, at times, discouraged with his efforts, the Lord commanded him to persevere. He said: "Lord, the Gentiles will mock at these things, because of our weakness in writing ... And thou hast made us that we could write but little, because of the awkwardness of our hands ... Wherefore, when we write we behold our weakness, and stumble because of the placing of our words; and I fear lest the Gentiles shall mock at our words." (V. 23-25, see Commentary Reference to Alma 24:19).

The Lord's response to Moroni's concern is a classic passages of scripture. He said: "Fools mock, but they shall mourn; and my grace is sufficient for the meek, that they shall take no advantage of your weakness; And if men come unto me I will show unto them their weakness. I give unto men weakness that they may be humble; and my grace is sufficient for all men that humble themselves before me; for if they humble themselves before me, and have faith in me, then will I make weak things become strong unto them." (V. 26-27).

These verses can be better understood because of Moroni's editorial insertion of his discourse on faith in the preceding verses. When the Lord told him that He would show the Gentiles that the way to perfection is the development of "faith, hope, and charity," Moroni was comforted, and his personal testimony of faith as a principle of perfection was validated. (V. 28-29).

He used the experiences of the Brother of Jared as examples of the powerful effect of faith: "For (he) said unto the mountain Zerin, remove - and it was removed." (V. 30). Many have assumed that the Savior was only giving a dramatic illustration of the power of faith when he said: "If ye have faith as a grain of mustard seed, ye shall say unto this mountain, Remove hence to yonder place; and it shall remove." (Matthew 17:20). However, Moroni's record tells us that the basis for His illustration may have been an actual event from antiquity.

So too, was Enoch a faithful servant of the Lord. "And so great was the faith of Enoch that he led the people of God, and their enemies came to battle against them; and he spake the word of the Lord, and the earth trembled, and the mountains fled, even according to his command; and the rivers of water were turned out of their course; and the roar of the lions was heard out of the wilderness; and all nations feared greatly, so powerful was the word of Enoch, and so great was the power of the language which God had given him." (Moses 7:13, see J.S.T. Genesis 14:25-40).

Moroni understood that "man must hope, or he cannot receive an inheritance in the place which (God has) prepared." (V. 32). Hope in Christ, born of faith, is essential to securing eternal life. Mormon had taught in the synagogue "concerning hope. How is it (he had asked) that ye can attain unto faith, save ye shall have hope? And what is it that ye shall hope for? Behold I say unto you that ye shall have hope through the atonement of Christ and the power of his resurrection, to be raised unto life eternal, and this because of your faith in him according to the promise. Wherefore, if a man have faith, he must needs have hope; for without faith there cannot be any hope." (Moroni 7:40-42).

Moroni also understood that "except men shall have charity, they cannot inherit that place" that has been prepared for them in the mansions of heaven. (V. 34). Charity is the quality of love possessed by the Savior. But 1 John 4:19 says: "We love him, because he first loved us." In other words, charity works both ways. Charity is the pure love of Christ, in the sense that it defines not only how He loves us, but also how we love Him.

Moroni's father had also taught the people concerning charity. Mormon said that we "cannot have faith and hope, save (we are) meek, and lowly of heart. If so, our faith and hope is in vain," but if a man possesses these qualities, "and confesses by the power of the Holy Ghost that Jesus is the Christ, he must needs have charity." (Moroni 7:43-44).

Christ assured Moroni that because he had been faithful throughout his life, his garments had been washed clean in the redeeming blood of Christ and he would receive his inheritance in the Celestial Kingdom of God. (V. 37). Surely this knowledge sustained him through the difficult years after Cumorah. Not long before he succumbed to brain cancer, Wes Belknap, the Dean of the College of Religious Instruction at Brigham Young University, said: "Brethren, we are taught that Christ endured afflictions of every kind. If he only endured my kind, the kind I have known in the hospital these past months, he loves us much more than we can comprehend".

Charity, the pure love of Christ, more than counterbalances the evil influences that sometimes seem to prevail in the world. "Two forces are operating, two voices are calling, one coming out from the swamps of selfishness and force, where success means death, and the other from the hilltops of justice and progress, where even failure brings glory. Two lights are seen on our horizon, one, the last fading marsh light of power, and the other the slowly rising sun of human brotherhood. Two ways lie open for us, one leading to an ever lower and lower plane, where are heard the cries of despair and the curses of the poor, where manhood shrivels and possessions rot down the possessor, and the other leading to the highlands of the morning, where are heard the glad shouts of humanity, and where honest effort is rewarded with immortality." (John P. Altgeld).

Perhaps Moroni thought that he would be unable to finish the abridgment of The Book of Ether, because the last verses of this chapter is a farewell to the Gentiles. (V. 38-41). It was also to be his farewell, he said, to "my brethren whom I love." Incidentally, these verses were also the last scriptures that Hyrum Smith read, before going to his martyrdom at Carthage Jail.

Moroni bore a special testimony of the Savior. He wrote that at the Judgment Seat of Christ: "Ye shall know that I have seen Jesus, and that he hath talked with me face to face." (V. 39). Each of the four principal authors of The Book of Mormon testified that they had seen the Savior and visited with Him. These were Nephi (2 Nephi 11:2), Jacob (2 Nephi 11:3), Mormon (Mormon 1:15), and Moroni. (Ether 12:39).

In closing, he wrote: "And now, I would commend you to seek this Jesus of whom the prophets and apostles have written, that the grace of God the Father, and also the Lord Jesus Christ, and the Holy Ghost, which beareth record of them, may be and abide in you forever. Amen." (V. 41). We might well ask ourselves: "How ought we to seek Jesus?" One way is by reading and studying The Book of Mormon, whose pages are literally filled with references to Christ by name or inference. Some form of His name is mentioned an average of every 1.7 verses in the text. Within its pages, He is identified by 88 name titles, 23 in The First Book of Nephi alone. Of the 239 chapters in The Book of Mormon, 233 have references to Christ. (Only Mosiah 9 & 22, Alma 51 & 52, and Helaman 1 & 2 do not.).

In The Book of Mormon: "We talk of Christ, we rejoice in Christ, we preach of Christ, according to our prophecies, that our children may know to what source they may look for a remission of their sins." (2 Nephi 25:26). As we read The Book of Mormon, we "press forward with a steadfastness in Christ, having a perfect brightness of hope, and a love of God and of all men. (We) press forward, feasting upon the word of Christ, and endure to the end." When we do this, "behold, thus saith the Father: Ye shall have eternal life." (2 Nephi 31:20). This focus on purpose and action perfectly describes Moroni. How appropriate it is that Heavenly Father should have chosen him to announce to Joseph Smith the Restoration of the Gospel in the Last Days. "And I saw another angel fly in the midst of heaven, having the everlasting gospel to preach unto them that dwell on the earth, and to every nation, and kindred, and tongue, and people, Saying with a loud voice, Fear God, and give glory to him; for the hour of his judgment is come; and worship him that made heaven, and earth, and the sea, and the fountains of waters." (Revelation 14:6-7).

"I give unto men weakness
that they may be humble; and my grace
is sufficient for all men that humble themselves
before me; for if they humble themselves before me,
and have faith in me, then will I make weak
things become strong unto them."
(Ether 12:27).

Ether
Chapter 13

However, Moroni was given more time to complete his abridgment of The Book of Ether. (V. 1). He indicated that Ether was a great prophet, and that he had told his brethren the Jaredites "of all things, from the beginning of man." (V. 2). This verse indicates that Ether had knowledge of the Flood, and "that after the waters had receded from off the face of this land it became a choice land above all other lands." (V. 2). After all, Jared and his brother lived only 200 years after the great Flood in the time of Noah. Moses quite specifically chronicled the time of the Flood, that occurred "in the six hundredth year of Noah's life, in the second month, the seventeenth day of the month". (Genesis 7:11). This would place it around 2,400 B.C.

"And the waters prevailed exceedingly upon the earth; ("eretz") and all the high hills, that were under the whole heaven, were covered. And every living substance was destroyed which was upon the face of the ground, both man, and cattle, and the creeping things, and the fowl of the heaven; and they were destroyed from the earth: and Noah only remained alive, and they that were with him in the ark." (Genesis 7:19 & 23).

The prophets have always taught of the universality of the Flood, over all the "earth." However, in Hebrew, the words "earth" and "land" are derived from the same word: "eretz." The way this word is translated depends entirely upon the context in which it is given, and it is up to the translator to make the correct determination. (See Commentary References to Alma 24:19 & Ether 1:6, 1:35, 1:38 & 13:2).

Joseph Fielding Smith, Jr. wrote: "Now, when Christ comes, we will get a new heaven and a new earth, and all of these corruptible things will be removed. They will be consumed by fire; and somebody said, 'Brother Smith, do you mean to say that it is going to be literal fire?' I said, 'Oh, no, it will not be literal fire any more than it was literal water that covered the Earth in the flood." ("The Signs of the Times, p. 41). It is not within the scope of this Commentary to address the question of the universality of the Flood, but it is interesting to be aware of the existence of different perspectives by authoritative priesthood sources on the issue.

Enoch, who lived about 3,000 B.C., "looked upon the earth; and he heard a voice from the bowels thereof, saying: Wo, wo is me, the mother of men; I am pained, I am weary, because of the wickedness of my children. When shall I rest, and be cleansed from the filthiness which is gone forth out of me: when will my Creator sanctify me, that I may rest, and righteousness for a season abide upon my face?" (Moses 7:48).

One of the purposes of the Flood was to cleanse the earth, that a place might be prepared where the righteous could live in "a chosen land of the Lord; wherefore the Lord would have that all men should serve him who dwell upon the face thereof." (V. 2). Moroni understood that the Flood might be a symbolical representation of the sanctification the earth, and that man in general and the Jaredites in particular might once again have an opportunity to exercise a righteous stewardship over it.

Moroni realized that because the Jaredites had polluted their inheritance, they had been literally destroyed from off the face of the earth. The words of the Prophet Ether had fallen upon deaf ears. His people would not understand that their land was to be "the place of the New Jerusalem, which should come down out of heaven, and the holy sanctuary of the Lord." (V. 3). Built upon celestial principles, this city would be "a holy city unto the Lord," and joining it would be the translated City of Enoch. (V. 5, see Moses 7:13-21).

Ether had a clear vision of both of the millennial cities: The New Jerusalem in the Western Hemisphere, and the Old Jerusalem in the Eastern Hemisphere. (V. 5-11). They will be built in a day when there should be "a new heaven and a new earth; and they shall be like unto the old, save the old have passed away, and all things have become new." (V. 9).

Their inhabitants will be holy, "and blessed are they who dwell therein, for it is they whose garments are white through the blood of the Lamb." (V. 10). Ether's people, however, could not conform the conduct of their lives to a standard of behavior in harmony with these prophecies. When they were past feeling, that the spirit could no longer strive with them, they were destroyed. (See Moroni 9:20, Ether 11:13 & 15:19). "For behold, this is a land which is choice above all other lands; wherefore he that doth possess it shall serve God or shall be swept off; for it is the everlasting decree of God. And it is not until the fulness of iniquity among the children of the land, that they are swept off." (Ether 2:10).

Moroni was about to write more, but then he was forbidden to do so. Nevertheless, "great and marvelous were the prophecies of Ether; but (his people) esteemed them as naught, and cast him out." (V. 13). The same conditions exist today. When the prophets speak, they are often either ridiculed or ignored, and their counsel is cast aside and dismissed as irrelevant nonsense.

When Mormon recorded the events of the ministry of Jesus among the Nephites, he wrote that those in the Last Days would receive The Book of Mormon "to try their faith, and if it shall so be that they shall believe these things, then shall the greater things be made manifest unto them. And if it so be that they will not believe these things, then shall the greater things be withheld from them, unto their condemnation." (3 Nephi 26:9-10). We are on "scripture probation", as it were, to see if we will accept and utilize that which we already have. We are a scripture possessing people, but we need to be scripture reading, scripture literate, and scripture obedient, as well.

After Ether was cast out from among his people, he hid "in the cavity of a rock (and) made the remainder of this record, viewing the destruction which came upon the people." (V. 14). The final conflict among the Jaredites commenced, with Coriantumr on one side, and those who employed "the secret plans of wickedness, of which hath been spoken" on the other. (V. 15). The oaths and covenants of the secret society of the devil bound the people who had renounced their agency and left them defenseless. His strong cords would soon drag them kicking and screaming down to hell. (See 2 Nephi 28:19-23).

The fatal flaw of the Jaredites was that "there were none of the fair sons and daughters upon the face of the whole earth who repented of their sins." (V. 17). Consequently, "there were many people who were slain by the sword of those secret combinations, (who were) fighting against Coriantumr that they might obtain the kingdom." (V. 18).

If anything can be said of the nature of God in this circumstance, it is that He is consistently patient and long suffering with his people. We might not think the Jaredites deserved such consideration, but "the word of the Lord came to Ether, that he should go and prophesy unto Coriantumr that, if he would repent, and all his household, the Lord would give unto him his kingdom and spare the people." (V. 20).

We are reminded of the mission of Jonah to the inhabitants of the wicked city of Nineveh. So frightened was Jonah when commanded by the Lord to preach repentance to these people, that he headed in the opposite direction. After a detour through Tarshish, aboard ship, and then in the alimentary canal of a great fish, he finally delivered the word of the Lord, and "the people of Nineveh believed God, and proclaimed a fast, and put on sackcloth, from the greatest of them even to the least of them. And God saw their works, that they turned from their evil way; and God repented of the evil, that he had said that he would do unto them; and he did it not." (Jonah 3:5 & 10). The Joseph Smith Translation of this verse reads: "And God saw their works, that they turned from their evil way and repented; and God turned away the evil that he had said he would bring upon them." (J.S.T. Jonah 3:10). The J.S.T. certainly clarifies biblical passages that otherwise contradict established principles.

But, in this case, neither Coriantumr nor his people would repent, "and the wars ceased not, and they sought to kill Ether." (V. 22). Now, the decree of God was unalterable. The people of Coriantumr would "be destroyed, and all his household save it were himself. And he should only live to see the fulfilling of the prophecies which had been spoken concerning another people receiving the land for their inheritance; and Coriantumr should receive a burial by them; and every soul should be destroyed save it were Coriantumr." (V. 21). Every element of this prophecy would be fulfilled, as is attested elsewhere in The Book of Mormon. (See Omni 1:21, Ether 15:23 & 32).

All the grim ferocity with which the ruler concentrates his energy against the person of a rival king was illustrated in the struggles of Coriantumr against Shared, Lib, and Shiz. "And it came to pass that Coriantumr was exceedingly angry with Shared, and he went against him with his armies to battle." (V. 27). "And all the people upon the face of the land were shedding blood, and there was none to restrain them." (V. 31).

"This land (is destined to become) a choice land above all other lands, a chosen land of the Lord; wherefore the Lord would have that all men should serve him who dwell upon the face thereof; and it (will be) the place of the New Jerusalem, which should come down out of heaven, and the holy sanctuary of the Lord."
(Ether 13:2-3).

Ether
Chapter 14

As in the days of Mormon, there was "a great curse upon all the land because of the iniquity of the people." (V. 1, see Mormon 1:17-19). No-one's property was safe unless it was under the direct control of its owner, "and every man kept the hilt of his sword in his right hand, in the defence of his property and his own life and of his wives and children." (V. 2). Verse 2 suggests the Jaredites practiced polygamy, but if they did, we have no way of knowing whether or not it was approved by the Lord. The Brother of Jared had 22 sons and daughters (Ether 6:20), and Orihah had 31. (See Ether 7:2). Riplakish had many wives. (Ether 10:5). He was condemned for wickedness, but not necessarily because he had many wives. (See Commentary Reference to Ether 7:3).

The battles between Coriantumr and Shared, Gilead, Lib, and Shiz, that are chronicled in this chapter, were fought with frenzy on a number of fronts. (V. 3-16). Shiz, who was particularly bloodthirsty, "did slay both women and children. And there went a fear of Shiz throughout all the land; yea, a cry went forth throughout the land - Who can stand before the army of Shiz? And so great and lasting had been the war, and so long had been the scene of bloodshed and carnage, that the whole face of the land was covered with the bodies of the dead." (V. 17-18 & 21, see Omni 1:22). "So swift and speedy was the war, that there was none left to bury the dead," and the decimated armies marched from battle to battle "leaving the bodies of both men, women, and children strewed upon the face of the land, to become a prey to the worms of the flesh." (V. 22).

"And thus, we see," wrote Moroni, "their wickedness and abominations had prepared a way for their everlasting destruction." (V. 25). The pain and suffering of the spiritually dead Jaredites was the product of the cruelty that consumed them. Truly, "it is by the wicked that the wicked are punished; for it is the wicked that stir up the hearts of the children of men unto bloodshed." (Mormon 4:5).

Moroni ended his abridgement of this chapter with Coriantumr and Shiz personally leading their armies into hand-to-hand combat. (V. 26-31).

"Now there began to be
a great curse upon all the land
because of the iniquity of the people,
in which, if a man should lay his tool
or his sword upon his shelf, or upon the place
whither he would keep it, behold, upon the morrow,
he could not find it, so great was the curse upon the
land. Wherefore every man did cleave to that which was
his own, with his hands, and would not borrow neither
would he lend; and every man kept the hilt of his
sword in his right hand, in the defense of his
property and his own life and of his
wives and children."
(Ether 14:1-2).

Ether
Chapter 15

"Wars of extermination are a standard institution in the history of Asia" and the last battles of the Jaredites followed this pattern exactly. (Hugh Nibley, "The World of The Jaredites," p. 235). Coriantumr saw that "there had been slain two millions of mighty men, and also their wives and their children" in probably the bloodiest conflict ever fought in the Americas. (V. 2).

To cite a few examples from the Old World, though, when Jenghiz Kahn overcame the great Merkit nation, he left only one man alive. It is estimated that 40 million died in the wars of the great Kahn. The Assyrian kings would systematically annihilate every living thing in the lands they had conquered, sowing fields with salt, and flooding the sites of the cities they had destroyed, in order to convert them into inhospitable and uninhabitable wastelands. In cities of a million inhabitants, the Mongols left not even a dog or a cat alive, and they converted vast provinces into complete deserts. The mutual suicide of nations was not uncommon. (See Hugh Nibley, "The World of The Jaredites," p. 236).

Coriantumr began to realize that Ether was right. At least, he recognized the accuracy of his prophecies, and "he began to repent of the evil which he had done." (V. 3). But it was too late in the day. His people had a bloodthirst and would not repent, for they "were stirred up to anger against the people of Shiz." (V. 6).

"And it came to pass that the army of Coriantumr did pitch their tents by the hill Ramah; and it was that same hill where ... Mormon did hide up the records unto the Lord, which were sacred." (V. 11). The hill Ramah is identified in Mormon 6:6 as the hill Cumorah. We don't know if this hill had any particular significance for the Jaredites, but it is possible that it was there that Ether hid his records "in a manner that the people of Limhi did find them." (V. 33).

Just as Mormon would later witness the final destruction of the Nephites from the hill Cumorah, "it came to pass that Ether did behold all the doings of the people" from that vantage point. (V. 13). For four years, the people gathered either to the army of Coriantumr or to the army of Shiz (V. 14), "both men, women and children being armed with weapons of war, having shields, and breastplates, and head-plates, and being clothed after the manner of war." (V. 15).

The final battle commenced under the most terrible of circumstances, for "the Spirit of the Lord had ceased striving with them, and Satan had full power over the hearts of the people" who "were drunken with anger. (V. 19 & 22). "Their cries, and their howlings, and their mournings, for the loss of the slain of their people" filled the air. (V. 17).

Finally, only 121 combatants were left on the field of battle. (V. 23). These fought all the next day, and when the sun went down, there were only 59 left. (V. 25). Though few in number, they nevertheless formed a "shield wall" designed to protect the king. Here is another description of Asiatic warfare, in the best tradition.

"When they had all fallen by the sword, save it were Coriantumr and Shiz, behold Shiz had fainted with the loss of blood." (V. 29). For his part, Coriantumr was so fatigued that he had to lean on his sword for a while just to regain enough strength to raise it and swing it hard enough to smite off the head of Shiz. (V. 29-30). With this last burst of energy, Coriantumr "fell to the earth, and became as if he had no life." (V. 32). Of course, we know from The Book of Mormon record that, just as Ether had prophesied, he did survive the battle and wandered to the Land of Zarahemla to the south, where the People of Zarahemla found him. He lived with them for nine months, before succumbing to his wounds. (See Omni 1:21-22, Ether 13:21, & Commentary Reference following Ether 10:33).

Ether left his hiding place and "beheld that the words of the Lord had all been fulfilled; and he finished his record ... and he hid them in a manner that the people of Limhi did find them." (V. 33). "Now the last words which are written by Ether are these: Whether the Lord will that I be translated, or that I suffer the will of the Lord in the flesh, it mattereth not, if it so be that I am saved in the kingdom of God. Amen." (V. 34).

Moroni must have felt a strong bond with Ether. Each was the last righteous survivor of a doomed civilization, and both had been rejected by their people. Although their fates were uncertain, they had unswerving faith in the goodness of God.

The Book of Moroni
400 A.D. - 421 A.D.

Moroni
Chapter 1

Moroni's contributions to The Book of Mormon include Mormon chapters 8-9, his abridgment of The Book of Ether, and The Book of Moroni chapters 1-6 & 10. Unlike The Book of Ether, The Book of Moroni contains virtually no narrative, but instead consists of a series of small appendices to The Book of Mormon itself, teachings of his father Mormon, and a final testimony and exhortation by Moroni. It is noteworthy that its literary style is entirely different from The Book of Ether. For example, the term "and it came to pass" is found no less than 117 times in The Book of Ether, but not once in The Book of Moroni.

"This last edition to the writings of Moroni is in some ways unsurpassed. It is choice, containing in its short compass a number of elements that are brought together only by virtue of the fact that they are timely and good. They appear like extremely valuable fillers. They lack something in connection or continuity, and are obviously end materials." (Daniel H. Ludlow, "Companion to Your Study of The Book of Mormon," p. 330).

After making the abridgment of The Plates of Ether to satisfy the command of his father, Moroni had thought that his record was complete. He wrote: Now I, Moroni, after having made an end of abridging the account of the people of Jared, I had supposed not to have written more." (V. 1, see Ether 15:34). But sometime between 400 and 421 A.D., Moroni found the time and energy to add to The Plates of Mormon.

During those years, he continually hid from the Lamanites, whose fratricidal conflicts continued to rage unabated. In 401 A.D., 15 years after the final battle at Cumorah, Moroni had observed: "The whole face of this land is one continual round of murder and bloodshed; and no one knoweth the end of the war." (Mormon 8:8). Now he wrote: "Their wars (continued to be) exceedingly fierce among themselves." (V. 1).

Like mad dogs, the Lamanites lashed out indiscriminately, "and because of their hatred they put to death every Nephite that (would) not deny the Christ." (V. 2). This verse, written at least 15 years after the destruction of the Nephite nation, confirms that there were still Nephites living in the land. Some had surely apostatized and had become Lamanites, but others continued to die as martyrs to their faith. For his part, Moroni declared that he would not deny the Christ. He would not apostatize and become a "Lamanite," nor would he renounce the faith just to save his life. "Wherefore," he said, "I wander whithersoever I can for the safety of mine own life." (V. 3). He was given the time to "write a few more things, that perhaps they (might) be of worth" to the Lamanites in a future day. (V. 4).

"Now I, Moroni, after having made an end of abridging the account of the people of Jared, I had supposed not to have written more, but I have not as yet perished ... Wherefore, I write a few more things, contrary to that which I had supposed." (Moroni 1:1 & 4).

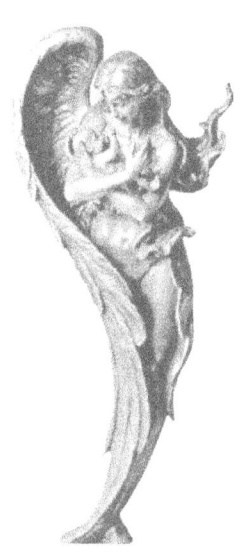

Moroni
Chapter 2

Chapters 2-5 of The Book of Moroni consist of Moroni's appendices to the text that carefully document essential basic ordinances of the Gospel. The fact that these were recorded at all attests to the necessity of a formal Church organization among a righteous people, even though in The Book of Mormon very little is written about such a body.

"These ordinances are not empty, passive rituals; rather, they bind us to receive the promises and blessings of the Gospel by means of a covenant of action between ourselves and the Lord." (Robert L. Millett, "Doctrinal Commentary on The Book of Mormon," 4:319). Having experienced the drama found within the pages of The Book of Mormon in the accounts of Nephi, Jacob, Benjamin, Mosiah, Abinadi, Alma, and of all its other historical figures, it is appropriate that in the final chapters of the text we are introduced to a few of the ordinances that bridge the gulf between earth and heaven. These ordinances also attest to the nature of God, and confirm that His Church is founded on unchanging principles and that the requirements for obtaining salvation are unchanging and are the same for all.

It is appropriate that Moroni first illustrated the manner of bestowal of the Holy Ghost. Its receipt is basic to the administration of all priesthood ordinances, and to the operation of the Church. Mormon had recorded how the Lord had "touched with his hand the disciples whom he had chosen, one by one, even until he had touched them all, and spake unto them as he touched them. And the multitude heard not the words which he spake, therefore they did not bear record; but the disciples bare record that he gave them power to give the Holy Ghost. And I will show unto you hereafter that this record is true." (3 Nephi 18:36-37). In this chapter, the promised explanation is given. Here, we receive "the words of Christ, which he spake unto his disciples, the twelve whom he had chosen, as he laid his hands upon them." (V. 1).

After Jesus had laid his hands upon the Twelve, "there came a cloud" that is symbolic of the presence of the Lord, that "overshadowed the multitude that they could not see Jesus." (3 Nephi 18:38, see Exodus 19:9). Within that cloud, Jesus had called each by name and taught them: "Ye shall call on the Father in my name, in mighty prayer; and after ye have done this, ye shall have power." (V. 2). The power to confer the Holy Ghost has to be earned and then retained through continuing personal righteousness. Joseph Smith taught the same principle, when he wrote: "Many are called but few are chosen," and it is critical to "learn this one lesson - that the rights of the priesthood are inseparably connected with the powers of heaven, and that the powers of heaven cannot be controlled nor handled only upon the principles of righteousness." (D&C 121:34-36).

The Savior verified that the manner in which he had instructed the Twelve to confer the Holy Ghost was procedurally correct, when He said: "For thus do mine apostles." (V. 2). This is the only instance in The Book of Mormon where the term "apostle" is used in such a context that it could refer to the Nephite Twelve and to an office within the Melchizedek Priesthood. Clearly, they held the Melchizedek Priesthood, for it is by this authority that this ordinance of the Gospel is administered. (See Commentary References to Moroni Chapter 3).

Moroni
Chapter 3

This chapter comprises another appendix to The Book of Mormon. Following an explanation of the process by which the Holy Ghost is conferred, it was natural that Moroni would next focus on the manner of ordination to the offices within the priesthood, when he wrote: "They ordained them by the power of the Holy Ghost, which was in them." (V. 4). The pattern, outlined in verse 2, is to pray to the Father in the name of Jesus Christ, state the office to which the individual is to be ordained, give an appropriate blessing, and close with "Amen." The offices mentioned in this verse include those of "elder" from the Melchizedek Priesthood and "priest" and "teacher" from the Aaronic Priesthood.

"In earlier Nephite times, priests and teachers were called to service in the kingdom. These were not officers in the Aaronic Priesthood as we know it today. They were priests and teachers in the general sense that they were Melchizedek Priesthood servants who ministered to the people and taught the Gospel." (Robert Millet, "Doctrinal Commentary on The Book of Mormon," 4:323-324).

"When the Savior came to the Nephites, he established the Church in its fulness among them, and he informed them that former things had passed away, for they were all fulfilled in him. He gave the Nephites all the authority of the priesthood that we exercise today. Therefore, we are justified in the belief that not only was the fulness of the Melchizedek Priesthood conferred, but also the Aaronic, just as we have it in the Church today; and this Aaronic Priesthood remained with them from this time until, through wickedness, all priesthood ceased. We may be assured that in the days of Moroni the Nephites did ordain teachers and priests in the Aaronic Priesthood; but before the visit of the Savior, they officiated by the authority of the Melchizedek Priesthood." (Joseph Fielding Smith, Jr., "Answers to Gospel Questions," 1:124 & 126).

When Christ personally established His Church among the Nephites, He ordained worthy individuals to offices in both the Aaronic and the Melchizedek Priesthood. His organization of the Church in the Last Days, through His prophet, is illustrative of the way it was likely formerly organized among the Nephites.

Part of the instruction Joseph Smith received from heavenly messengers pertained to the organization of the Church. This was done between the time the Witnesses viewed the ancient record and April 6, 1830. That instruction included ordination to the Aaronic and Melchizedek Priesthood by authorized servants sent from the presence of God. As the Doctrine and Covenants clearly teaches: "There are, in the church, two priesthoods, namely, the Melchizedek and Aaronic, including the Levitical Priesthood." These comprise "two divisions or grand heads." (D&C 107:1 & 6).

It is clear that the Lord intends that the government of the Church be presided over by those holding the Melchizedek

Priesthood, that "holds the right of presidency, and has power and authority over all the offices in the church in all ages of the world, to administer in spiritual things." (D&C 107:8). "The power and authority of the higher, or Melchizedek Priesthood is to hold the keys of all the spiritual blessings of the church - to have the privilege of receiving the mysteries of the kingdom of heaven, to have the heavens opened unto them, to commune with the general assembly and church of the Firstborn, and to enjoy the communion and presence of God the Father, and Jesus the mediator of the new covenant." (D&C 107:18-19).

It is equally clear that the Lord intends that the Aaronic Priesthood fully function when the government of the kingdom is complete. "The power and authority of the lesser, or Aaronic Priesthood, is to hold the keys of the ministering of angels, and to administer in outward ordinances, the letter of the gospel, the baptism of repentance for the remission of sins, agreeable to the covenants and commandments." (D&C 107:20).

When we understand the government of the Church as we read the Lord's Revelation on Priesthood, (D&C 84), we can better understand why it was procedurally correct to bestow the Aaronic Priesthood upon the Nephites at the time the Church was established among them, even though for 600 years they had already governed the Church by the authority of the Melchizedek Priesthood. It might even be argued that the Church was never perfectly organized until both the Aaronic and Melchizedek Priesthood governed it. As the Lord said, "Wherefore, now let every man learn his duty, and act in the office in which he is appointed, in all diligence." (D&C 107:99). The Church has always required faithful service from the brethren of the Church, and the priesthood has always been a robe of responsibility to those who bear it.

Moroni
Chapter 4

This third appendix deals with the Sacramental Prayer that is offered over emblems representing the "flesh and blood of Christ." (V. 1). The order in which these appendices were given is significant. First was instruction concerning the bestowal of the Holy Ghost. Second was the process of ordination to the various offices within the Priesthood, by the power of God and under the inspiration of the Holy Ghost. Third was instruction concerning the specific manner in which Priesthood responsibilities should be carried out in order to benefit the congregations of the faithful. Officiating at the Sacrament table are elders or priests who "kneel down with the church, and pray to the Father in the name of Christ." (V. 2).

The Gospel of Mark records the administration of the Sacrament at the Lord's Last Supper: "And as they did eat, Jesus took bread, and blessed, and brake it, and gave to them, and said, Take, eat. This is my body. And he took the cup, and when he had given thanks, he gave it to them: and they all drank of it. And he said unto them, This is my blood of the new testament, which is shed for many. Verily I say unto you, I will drink no more of the fruit of the vine, until that day that I drink it new in the kingdom of God." (Mark 14:22-25).

The Joseph Smith Translation of the Bible renders these verses as follows: "And as they did eat, Jesus took bread and blessed it, and brake, and gave to them, and said, <u>Take it</u>, and eat. <u>Behold, this is for you to do in remembrance of my body; for as oft as ye do this ye will remember this hour that I was with you</u>. And he took the cup, and when he had given thanks, he gave it to them; and they all drank of it. And he said unto them, <u>This is in remembrance</u> of my blood <u>which is shed for many, and</u> the new testament <u>which I give unto you; for of me ye shall bear record unto all the world. And as oft as ye do this ordinance, ye will remember me in this hour that I was with you and drank with you of this cup, even the last time in my ministry</u>. Verily I say unto you, <u>of this ye shall bear record; for</u> I will no more drink of the fruit of the vine with you, until that day that I drink it new in the kingdom of God." (J.S.T. Mark 14:20-25, differences from the K.J.T. underlined).

The Gospel of St. Matthew renders the relevant verses as follows: "And as they were eating, Jesus took bread, and blessed it, and <u>broke</u> it, and gave it to <u>the disciples</u>, and said, Take, eat; this is my body. And he took the cup, and <u>gave</u> thanks, and <u>gave</u> it to them, <u>saying, Drink ye all</u> of it; For this is my blood of the New Testament, which is shed for many for <u>the remission of sins</u>. <u>But</u> I say unto you, I will not drink <u>henceforth</u> of this fruit of the vine, until that day when I drink it new with you in <u>my Father's</u> kingdom." (Matthew 26:26-29, differences from the K.J.T. of Mark underlined).

The Joseph Smith Translation of the same verses in Matthew gives the following clarification: "And as they were eating, Jesus took bread and <u>brake it</u>, and blessed it, and gave to his disciples, and said, Take, eat; this is <u>in remembrance of</u> my body <u>which I give a ransom for you</u>. And he took the cup, and gave thanks, and gave it to them, saying, Drink ye all of it. For this is <u>in remembrance of</u> my blood of the new testament, which is shed for <u>as many as shall believe on my name</u>, for the remission of <u>their</u> sins. <u>And I give unto you a commandment, that ye shall observe to do the things which ye have seen me do, and bear record of me even unto the end</u>. But I say unto you, I will not drink henceforth of this fruit of the vine, until that day when I <u>shall come and</u> drink it new with you in my Father's kingdom." (J.S.T. Matthew 26:22-26, differences from the K.J.T. of Matthew underlined).

The Joseph Smith Translation of these verses removes all doubt as to their meaning, and is in complete harmony with the words of the covenant as it is contained in Doctrine and Covenants Section 20 and in The Book of Moroni Chapters 4 & 5, that clearly teach the symbolism of Christ's sacrifice within the emblems of the Sacrament.

Some have wondered why the congregation does not kneel during the sacramental prayers, since the instruction given in both The Book of Moroni and the Doctrine and Covenants reads: "And the elder or priest shall administer it; and after this manner shall he administer it - he shall kneel with the church." (D&C 20:76 & Moroni 4:2). These verses should be interpreted to mean that the priesthood bearers who administer the sacrament kneel "in the presence of the church." If it were necessary for the congregation to kneel with the officiator, we can be sure that priesthood leaders of the Church would have given that instruction as a clarification of the scriptures. It seems clear that it is really only the words of the prayer itself that are critical to the covenant, as the body of the Church participates in this ordinance of the Gospel.

Moroni's prayer reads as follows: "O God, the Eternal Father, we ask thee in the name of thy Son, Jesus Christ, to bless and sanctify this bread to the souls of all those who partake of it; that they may eat in remembrance of the body of thy Son, and witness unto thee, O God, the Eternal Father, that they are willing to take upon them the name of thy Son, and always remember him, and keep his commandments which he hath ("has" in the Doctrine & Covenants) given them, that they may always have his Spirit to be with them. Amen." (V. 3, see D&C 20:77).

When we "witness" before God as we participate in the ordinance, we covenant to take upon ourselves the name of Christ, remember Him, and keep His commandments. God's part of the covenant is to grant us the Holy Ghost to help us to do our duty. As baptized members of the Church, we receive the greater light of the Holy Ghost, because we have greater responsibilities to be true to our baptismal covenants. "For of him unto whom much is given much is required; and he who sins against the greater light shall receive the greater condemnation." (D&C 82:3). Since we will be judged by the laws to which we have been responsible while on the earth, we will vary in the exactness with which we will be required to account for our deeds. As the Savior said: "And that servant, which knew his lord's will, and prepared not himself, neither did according to his will, shall be beaten with many stripes. But he that knew not, and did commit things worthy of stripes, shall be beaten with few stripes. For unto whomsoever much is given, of him shall much be required." (Luke 12:47-48).

This may also explain why it is the practice of the Church that only worthy members partake of the Sacrament. Of non-members it is not required, because partaking of the emblems of Christ involves a promise to renew the covenant of baptism, to take upon themselves the name of Christ, to always remember Him, and to keep His commandments, so that they may have his Spirit to be with them, which strengthens them and prompts them to do that which is right in the sight of God.

Moroni
Chapter 5

This fourth appendix also deals with the Sacramental Prayer, specifically with "the manner of administering the wine." (V. 1). Moroni was familiar with his father's abridgment of Third Nephi - The Book of Nephi, and knew that the words of the covenant prayer had not been included, and so he appended it here, on the final leaves of The Plates of Mormon. (See 3 Nephi 18).

Some ask: "What was the nature of the 'wine' spoken of in these verses?" There is little doubt that Jesus and His disciples drank fermented wine, and not "new wine" as so many Latter-day Saints would like to believe. There is nothing inherently wrong with drinking wine; the Word of Wisdom was only given "in consequence of the evils and designs which do and will exist in the hearts of conspiring men in the last days," who would subvert the drinking of spirits to suit the wicked purposes of the adversary. (D&C 89:4). So observed Hartman Rector, Jr., in July 1986, in a personal conversation with the author.

Nevertheless, the Prophet Joseph Smith received a revelation in August 1830, regarding the use of wine in the Sacrament. He later recalled: "Early in the month of August Newel Knight and his wife paid us a visit at my place in Harmony, Pennsylvania; and as neither his wife nor mine had been as yet confirmed, it was proposed that we should confirm them, and partake together of the Sacrament, before he and his wife should leave us. In order to prepare for this, I set out to procure some wine for the occasion, but had gone only a short distance when I was met by a heavenly messenger, and received the following revelation, the first four paragraphs of which were written at this time." (H.C., 1:106).

"Listen to the voice of Jesus Christ, your Lord, your God, and your Redeemer, whose word is quick and powerful. For, behold, I say unto you, that it mattereth not what ye shall eat or what ye shall drink when ye partake of the sacrament, if it so be that ye do it with an eye single to my glory - remembering unto the Father my body which was laid down for you, and my blood which was shed for the remission of your sins. Wherefore, a commandment I give unto you, that you shall not purchase wine neither strong drink of your enemies; Wherefore, you shall partake of none except it is made new among you; yea, in this my Father's kingdom which shall be built up on the earth." (D&C 27:1-4).

In this revelation, the Lord bore witness of the simplicity of the ordinance of the Sacrament, emphasizing that it is does not matter what we drink, as long as we do it in sincerity with an eye single to the glory of God. It is important to remember that the water, or the wine, is only symbolical of the redeeming blood of Christ. It does not become His blood through some mystical transformation, as many would believe. The doctrine of transubstantiation is false. The emblems of the Sacrament simply serve to focus our attention where it belongs: on the Son of God and His sacrifice for us, and on the covenants we have previously made with him at the waters of baptism.

The revelation recorded in D&C Section 27 was given some two and a half years before the revelation known as The Word of Wisdom was received. The Church did not adopt the practice of using water in place of wine because of that revelation, although the two are loosely connected. In each case, intervention by the Lord was prompted by the evil designs of conspiring men who would go to any length to destroy the order of the Church.

The Sacramental Prayer recorded by Moroni reads as follows: "O God, the Eternal Father, we ask thee, in the name of thy Son, Jesus Christ, to bless and sanctify this wine to the souls of all those who drink of it, that they may do it in remembrance of the blood of thy Son, which was shed for them; that they may witness unto thee, O God, the Eternal Father, that they do always remember him, that they may have his Spirit to be with them. Amen." (V. 2). This prayer is identical to that received by Joseph Smith and recorded as Doctrine & Covenants 20:78-79, that was received in April 1830.

The Lord taught the Nephites: "Ye shall not suffer any one knowingly to partake of my flesh and blood unworthily, when ye shall minister it. For whoso eateth and drinketh my flesh and blood unworthily eateth and drinketh damnation to his soul; therefore, if ye know that a man is unworthy to eat and drink of my flesh and blood ye shall forbid him." (3 Nephi 18:28-29). These verses suggest that it is not the purpose of the Sacrament to obtain a remission of sins, but rather to recommit oneself to the covenant of baptism, and to receive by an additional covenant the Spirit of God so that one might more surely hold fast to the iron rod. If the purpose of the Sacrament were to obtain a remission of sins, it would not be forbidden to those in greatest need.

The reason that those who partake without proper preparation drink damnation to their souls is that such an action blocks the channels through which spiritual power flows. It is the halt in progression that is damning to the soul. Conversely, this is also why partaking of the Sacrament in worthiness endows the individual with great power. Heavenly Father blessed us with the covenant so that when we approach Him through this ordinance, His promises to us might be freely fulfilled. Through Joseph Smith, He said: "Let thy bowels also be full of charity towards all men, and to the household of faith, and let virtue garnish thy thoughts unceasingly; then shall thy confidence wax strong in the presence of God; and the doctrine of the priesthood shall distill upon thy soul as the dews from heaven. The Holy Ghost shall be thy constant companion, and thy scepter an unchanging scepter of righteousness and truth; and thy dominion shall be an everlasting dominion, and without compulsory means it shall flow unto thee forever and ever." (Doctrine & Covenants 121:45-46).

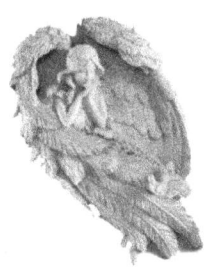

Moroni
Chapter 6

Following his instruction concerning the Holy Ghost, the Priesthood, and the Sacrament, Moroni turned his attention to the manner of baptism in the Church. He wrote of the qualifications for baptism, that none were "baptized save they brought forth fruit meet that they were worthy of it. Neither did they receive any unto baptism save they came forth with a broken heart and a contrite spirit, and witnessed unto the church that they truly repented of all their sins. And none were received unto baptism save they took upon them the name of Christ, having a determination to serve him to the end." (V. 1-3, see Commentary Reference to Mosiah 18:8-10).

It goes without saying that the requirements articulated by Moroni presuppose that the applicant has reached the age of accountability. Almost a year before the formal organization of the Church, the Lord taught Joseph Smith that "all men must repent and be baptized, and not only men, but women, and children who have arrived at the years of accountability." (D&C 18:42). Elsewhere in the Doctrine & Covenants, the Lord specifies the age of accountability as eight years. (See D&C 68:27).

There is also a "worthiness component" to baptism. Moroni said that none were baptized unless they "brought forth fruit," or demonstrated by their good works that the conduct of their lives had been brought into harmony with Gospel principles. As our faith convicts us of our sins, it propels us on the path toward perfection by motivating us to good works.

The account from the ministry of Alma offers plain counsel concerning the proper attitude of those who desire baptism, and it should be studied by all those who desire to take upon themselves the name of Christ. "And it came to pass that he said unto them: Behold, here are the waters of Mormon (for thus were they called) and now, as ye are desirous to come into the fold of God, and to be called his people, and are willing to bear one another's burdens, that they may be light; Yea, and are willing to mourn with those that mourn; yea, and comfort those that stand in need of comfort, and to stand as witnesses of God at all times and in all things, and in all places that ye may be in, even until death, that ye maybe redeemed of God, and be numbered with those of the first resurrection, that ye may have eternal life - Now I say unto you, if this be the desire of your hearts, what have you against being baptized in the name of the Lord, as a witness before him that ye have entered into a covenant with him, that ye will serve him, and keep his commandments, that he may pour out his Spirit more abundantly upon you?" (Alma 18:8-10).

The "broken heart" to which Moroni referred in verse 2 is teachable because it is softened to receive the things of the Spirit. It is "to be broken down with deep sorrow for sin, to be humble and thoroughly penitent, to have attained sincere and purposeful repentance." (Bruce R. McConkie, "Mormon Doctrine," p. 161, see Mosiah 5:2). A "contrite spirit" is to be "bruised in heart, sorrow, or affliction of mind for some fault or injury done. It is penitence for sin." (O.E.D.). When one has a contrite spirit, one is crushed or broken in spirit by a sense of sin, and is so brought to complete repentance. (See 2 Nephi 4:32).

At this level of spiritual preparation, we are prepared to ask, as did those on the Day of Pentecost: "What shall we do?" The answer is straightforward: "Repent and be baptized every one of you in the name of Jesus Christ for the remission of sins." (Acts 2:37-38). Wherever the authority of the Priesthood rests with righteous individuals, those who are received unto baptism take upon them "the name of Jesus Christ, having a determination to serve him to the end." (V. 3). Joseph Smith taught: "In the former ages of the world, before the Saviour came in the flesh, the 'saints' were baptized in the name of Jesus Christ to come, because there never was any other name whereby men could be saved." ("Teachings," p. 266). Throughout The Book of Mormon, this principle is consistently reinforced. (See Mosiah 18:8-10).

Joseph Fielding Smith, Jr. taught: "Baptism for the remission of sins is an ordinance of the gospel which has been required of all who seek the kingdom of God since the transgression of Adam. In fact, each principle and ordinance of the gospel has always been required for the salvation of mortal man." ("1971-72 Melchizedek Priesthood Manual," p. 158). The Pseudepigraphic Book of Adam and Eve records: "Adam came to Jordan and he entered into the water, and he plunged himself altogether into the flood, even to the hairs of his head, while he made supplication to God and sent up prayers to him." (Quoted in "Christ's Eternal Gospel," p. 118-119). There seems to have been Pre-Christian Baptism at Qumran as well. From "The Manual of Discipline," or "The Serek Scroll," we read: "His sin is forgiven him and in the humility of his soul he is for all the Laws of God; his flesh is cleansed shining bright in the waters of purification, even in the waters of baptism, and he shall be given a new name in due time to walk perfect in all the ways of God." (Hugh Nibley, "An Approach to The Book of Mormon," p. 149).

"The place of baptism," El Maghtas in Arabic, is reputedly the site of Christ's baptism. It is here that numerous pilgrims come each year for the feast of Epiphany, on January 6, to immerse their bodies in the sacred waters. (See Emmanuel Dehan, "And the Walls Came Tumbling Down," p. 28-29). It is interesting that this site, on the banks of the Jordan River, marks the lowest body of fresh water upon the face of the earth. When Jesus was baptized there, He physically and symbolically descended beneath us all. (See D&C 88:6 & 122:8).

Moroni reported that after their baptism of water, the people only became members of the Church when they had received the Holy Ghost. When they "were wrought upon and cleansed by the power of the Holy Ghost, they were numbered among the people of the church of Christ." (V. 4). The scriptures repeatedly speak of "the baptism of fire and the Holy Ghost." (See D&C 19:31, 20:4, Matthew 3:11, 2 Nephi 31:11, 13 §17, Mosiah 27:24-26, 3 Nephi 12:1 & 27:20). Joseph Smith taught: "You might as well baptize a bag of sand as a man if not done in view of the remission of sins and getting the Holy Ghost. Baptism by water is but half a baptism, and is good for nothing without the other half, that is, baptism of the Holy Ghost." ("Teachings," p. 314). "For by the water ye keep the commandment; by the Spirit ye are justified, and by the blood ye are sanctified." (Moses 6:60). Nephi taught: "The gate by which ye should enter is repentance and baptism by water; and then cometh a remission of your sins by fire and by the Holy Ghost." (2 Nephi 31:17). The presence of the Holy Ghost purges the effects of sin, while the blood of Jesus purifies our tainted souls. Through the miracle of His Atonement, one more repentant sinner is thus added to the membership rolls of Christ's Church.

After their confirmation as members of the Church, Moroni reported: "Their names were taken, that they might be remembered and nourished by the good word of God, to keep them in the right way, to keep them continually watchful unto prayer." (V. 4). It sounds as if, even in the Primitive Church, there was a ministering organization established to assist the members. In the Restored Church, it is the teacher's duty "to watch over the church always, and be with and strengthen them; and see that there is no iniquity in the church, neither hardness with each other, neither lying, backbiting, nor evil speaking; and see that the church meet together often, and also see that all the members do their duty." (D&C 20:53-55). Moroni wrote that it had been important for the new members to rely "alone upon the merits of Christ, who was the author and the finisher of their faith." (V. 4, see Hebrews 5:9 & 12:2). In reality, God our Father is the Author of the Plan of Salvation. But the Son of God, by divine investiture of authority, carried out the Plan and the will of His Father.

The Nephite Saints had always been clearly taught to Whom they should look for salvation. Jacob recorded: "For this intent have we written these things, that they may know that we knew of Christ, and we had a hope of his glory many hundred years before his coming; and not only we ourselves had a hope of his glory, but also all the holy prophets which were before us." (Jacob 4:4). Nephi said: "We talk of Christ, we rejoice in Christ, we preach of Christ, we prophesy of Christ, and we write according to our prophecies, that our children may know to what source they may look for a remission of their sins." (2 Nephi 25:26).

Moroni must have remembered that his father had told him that the Nephite Church had met together often "to speak one with another concerning the welfare of their souls." (V. 5). They had sought regular spiritually aerobic exercise in order to keep fit. The Lord counseled Joseph Smith: "That thou mayest more fully keep thyself unspotted from the world, thou shalt go to the house of prayer and offer up thy sacraments upon my holy day. For verily this is a day appointed unto you to rest from your labors, and to pay thy devotions unto the Most High." (D&C 59:9-10). In his second epistle to Timothy, the Apostle Paul urged the faithful to strengthen each other with the following counsel: "And the things that thou hast heard of me among many witnesses, the same commit thou to faithful men, who shall be able to teach others also." (2 Timothy 2:2, see D&C 84:78-80).

On another occasion, Paul wrote: "When for the time ye ought to be teachers, ye have need that one teach you again which be the first principles of the oracles of God; and are become such as have need of milk, and not of strong meat." (Hebrews 5:12). In other words, new members of the Church were to be taught the first principles and doctrine of Christ in order to strengthen their faith and testimonies leading to purposeful conversion. The question that should always be on the minds of those to whom this stewardship responsibility falls is: "Are we giving converts skim milk, or 2% milk, or are we giving them rich, whole, fresh, fortified, organically produced milk that is free of genetically modified organisms?"

Moroni wistfully reported that, in the days when his people had been more obedient, "the church did meet together oft, to fast and to pray, and to speak one with another concerning the welfare of their souls." (V. 5). We sense that he was fondly reminiscing about those former days when he had enjoyed the companionship of faithful members of the Church, who regularly reviewed and renewed their covenants with the Lord. (See Commentary Reference to Mosiah 5:2). Later, the Apostle Paul would write of Church members from diverse backgrounds, that they were "no more strangers and foreigners, but fellowcitizens with the saints and of the household of God." (Ephesians 2:19).

Today, fellowship is equally important to the welfare of our souls. Too often, however, our services "are vulgar and profane, and demeaning to the character of those who would call themselves the Saints of The Most High God, and it is altogether out of place on such occasions to hear people talk about secular things." (John Taylor, J.D., 22:226). When we secularize the sacred, unconsciously trivializing the celestial, we render it telestial.

Melvin J. Ballard counseled: "The road to the Sacrament table is the path of safety for the Latter-day Saints." (C.R., 4/1915). We must recognize the truth in that statement, for Satan surely does. If he can convince us that the ordinance of the Sacrament is not essential to our spiritual well-being, or that it is foolish, or if we have lost the sense of its powerful effect on us and its importance to our spiritual well being, he will have won a major victory. "And others will he pacify, and lull them away into carnal security, that they will say: All is well in Zion; yea, Zion prospereth, all is well - and thus the devil cheateth their souls, and leadeth them away carefully down to hell." (2 Nephi 28:21). Satan stealthily tries to move us from white, through every subtle shade of grey, to black. He tries to make us believe we are gaining something, when we are really losing everything.

Perhaps, it is because it is easy to get out of focus, lose our grip on the rod of iron, and wander from obedience to our covenants, that Moroni recorded that the Church had been "strict to observe that there should be no iniquity among them." (V. 7). Perhaps he lamented that, had they been more zealous, they would not have apostatized. Religious fanaticism and blind obedience have no place within the Church, and free will ought to rule supreme among its guiding principles, but there is something to be said for strict orthodoxy among its members.

Law rules the government of the Church, and the Savior is both its Author and its Judge. Only those who have not been born again feel restricted by the commandments, but it is because they have not experienced the freedom of submission to Gospel principles. For those who are obedient, the Gospel is the perfect law of liberty. (See James 1:25). "When obedience ceases to be an irritant and becomes our quest, in that moment God will endow us with power." (Ezra Taft Benson, C.R., 4/1988). "Stand fast therefore in the liberty wherewith Christ hath made us free, and be not entangled again with the yoke of bondage." (Galatians 5:1).

When members of the Church make a mistake, and sin, as they inevitably do, the Gospel provides the opportunity to recognize it, right the wrong if possible, refrain from repeating it, repent for having made it, receive forgiveness for the transgression, and then move on. Potential stumbling blocks then become stepping-stones, and mortality with all its potential pitfalls becomes the vital growth experience it was designed to be. As Moroni wrote: "And as oft as they repented and sought forgiveness, with real intent, they were forgiven." (V. 8).

The Atonement stipulates that we travel the Royal Road of Repentance. This Requires that we act with Responsibility, as we Recognize the Reality of our transgression and view it with Revulsion, and experience Remorse that drives us to our knees. In our heart-felt prayers, we Relate to our Heavenly Father how we feel, in a process of confession that is the most painful example of Revelation. This demands that we Renounce our self-defeating behaviors, make Restitution to injured parties where possible, and then do whatever is necessary, as the Spirit directs us, to submit ourselves to a Refiner's fire that will help us to Re-establish a Reconciliation with heaven and Regain the Rapport with Jesus Christ that had formerly been our hope and our joy. As we Renew our Resolve to Recommit ourselves to walk the covenant path, it will be through the miracle of the grace of Him Who is our Redeemer, that we will Receive a Remission of our sin. Only then, will it become possible to move forward with purpose toward our Reward in heaven.

Without repentance and the Atonement, mortality would be nothing more than a cruel joke. "For I, (said) the Lord, cannot look upon sin with the least degree of allowance." (D&C 1:31). No-one could measure up and Justice would require that we all stand condemned on Judgment Day. Even the Savior said: "There is none good, but God." But then He added the modifier that makes mortality a wonderful learning laboratory: "But if thou wilt enter into life, keep the commandments." (Matthew 19:17). There is no greater commandment than this: "Repent and be baptized, every one of you, for a remission of your sins;' yea, be baptized even by water, and then cometh the baptism of fire and of the Holy Ghost." (D&C 33:11).

With the slate wiped clean, Moroni remembered how his father had told him the Nephite Saints had enjoyed a beautiful spirit in their meetings, that "were conducted by the church after the manner of the workings of the Spirit, and by the power of the Holy Ghost; for as the power of the Holy Ghost led them whether to preach, or to exhort, or to pray, or to supplicate, or to sing, even so it was done." (V. 9, see D&C 20:42).

"The great objective of our work is to build character and build faith in the lives of those whom we serve. If one cannot accept ... the programs of the church in an orthodox way without reservation, he should not teach." (Spencer W. Kimball, C.R., 4/1948). As a matter of fact, without the Spirit, we cannot teach, for the Savior said: "If ye receive not the Spirit ye shall not teach." (D&C 42:14). The power to convey Gospel principles comes through the Spirit. It must reside in those who deliver the word and those who receive it. This is the beauty of Gospel instruction. It is a foolproof method for sharing the Good News. But it is a delicate process, and cannot be mishandled or misrepresented. It is no wonder that the Savior warned: "Be ye clean that bear the vessels of the Lord." (D&C 38:42, see D&C 133:5, Isaiah 52:11, 3 Nephi 20:41 & Commentary Reference to 2 Nephi 28:14).

.

"Their meetings were conducted
by the church after the manner of the
workings of the Spirit, and by the power
of the Holy Ghost; for, as the power of
the Holy Ghost led them whether to
preach, or to exhort, or to pray,
or to supplicate, or to sing,
even so, it was done."
(Moroni 6:9).

Moroni
Chapter 7

The next three chapters are the words of Mormon, included by Moroni in his book because he thought that they would be of value in the Last Days. First are the words "which he spake concerning faith, hope, and charity." (V. 1). These were given as he taught his people "in the synagogue which they had built for the place of worship." (V. 1).

Alma 16:13 reveals that "synagogues built after the manner of the Jews" were commonly used for worship by the Nephites. Today, Bible scholars believe that synagogues first arose as a principal place of worship during the Babylonian exile, in the absence of the temple. This would place their initial use at the time of Ezra, about 590 B.C. Consequently, the word "synagogue" occurs only once in the Old Testament, in Psalms 74:8, and yet it appears 26 times in The Book of Mormon.

Since the departure of Lehi from Jerusalem preceded the Babylonian exile, the frequent use of the term in The Book of Mormon before the visit of Christ to the Nephites invites misunderstanding, but can be explained in any of several ways. First, synagogue worship could have quite simply pre-dated the exile, and either Lehi's or Mulek's party could have brought with them the practice of synagogue worship. However, there is no mention of such worship in The Book of Mormon until Alma 16:13: "And Alma and Amulek went forth preaching repentance to the people in their temples and in their sanctuaries and also in their synagogues, which were built after the manner of the Jews" (2 Nephi 26:26 speaks of synagogue worship in the Last Days).

Secondly, it is possible that there were other groups of Israelite expatriates not identified in The Book of Mormon who wandered to the New World after the exile. These could have brought the concept of synagogue worship with them, and they could have introduced the practice to the Nephites, if they intermingled with them.

Thirdly, the Nephite word for "place of assembly" simply could have been reasonably and accurately translated by the power of the Spirit into the English language as "synagogue". This is quite intriguing, and makes another powerful statement in support of the authenticity of The Book of Mormon for the following reason. It consistently uses the term "synagogue," that is a Greek word, to designate early Jewish assemblies, and "church," from the Greek "ecclesia," to designate such assemblies only after they had become Christian. It is hard to think of more appropriate terms in the narrative, bearing in mind that this is a translation, and that the purpose of the words is not to convey what the Nephites actually called their communities, but only to craft a word portrait of these communities in our own minds.

Moroni 7:1 reveals that the people of Mormon's day had built a place of assembly, or a synagogue, where Mormon could then teach them the true principles of faith, hope, and charity. He did this just as Alma and Amulek had done when preaching the first principles to the inhabitants of the Land of Zarahemla surrounding the wasted city of Ammonihah. (See Alma Chapter 16).

Remember that in Mormon's day, great wickedness prevailed upon the whole face of the Land of Zarahemla, "and there were no gifts from the Lord, and the Holy Ghost did not come upon any, because of their wickedness and unbelief." (Mormon 1:14). Mormon was just 15 years of age, and had received the Second Comforter. (Mormon 1:15). But he was "forbidden (at that time) to preach unto (the Nephites) because of the hardness of their hearts." (Mormon 1:17).

In these circumstances, it is unclear when or to whom Mormon was addressing his remarks in Chapter 7 of The Book of Moroni, since he had passed away by the time this epistle was recorded by his son Moroni. Mormon had declared: "Because of the gift of his calling unto me ... I am permitted to speak unto you at this time." (V. 2). As he had reported in his Abridgement of 3 Nephi, he confirmed that he was "a disciple of Jesus Christ, the Son of God, (who had) been called of him to declare his word among his people, that they might have everlasting life." (3 Nephi 5:13).

Perhaps Moroni thought this counsel that had earlier been given by his father would be important for the few remaining believers left in the land who were among the Nephites who would not renounce their faith after the last great battle at Cumorah. (See Moroni 1:1). Perhaps it was they who were still the faithful members "of the Church, (who were) the peaceable followers of Christ, and (who had) obtained a sufficient hope by which (they could) enter into the rest of the Lord, from this time henceforth until (they would) rest with him in heaven." (V. 3). If these records had somehow become available to them, the words of their fallen prophet-leader would have been of great comfort in the days of their greatest temporal trials and persecutions.

Mormon spoke of their "peaceable walk with the children of men." (V. 4). In other words, as these disciples continued to strive to conduct their lives in holiness, they would obtain the peace that would bring them into a spiritual sanctuary from the cares of the world and into the Rest of the Lord. (See D&C 20:69). Even among those whose telestial lives were of the most carnal and sensual nature, these disciples would be able to taste of the goodness of God and experience the peace which surpasseth understanding. (See Philippians 4:7).

It was natural that Moroni would use the teachings of his father to introduce the subjects of faith, hope, and charity, by contrasting good and evil, examples of which were so strikingly prevalent in their day, and in every culture in the Last Days. (V. 5-24). Mormon declared: "God hath said a man being evil cannot do that which is good; for if he offereth a gift, or prayeth unto God, except he shall do it with real intent, it profiteth him nothing." (V. 6). Outwardly, at least, evil people can do good, but in the end their works are neither a blessing to themselves nor to those whom they pretend to serve. Their good deeds lack the power to enrich or transform lives, and "they are not counted unto (them) for righteousness." (V. 7, see v. 8-10). If we are servants of the devil, we cannot follow Christ; and if we follow Christ we cannot be servants of the devil. We cannot have it both ways. A house divided against itself cannot stand. (See Mark 3:25). Double mindedness creates behavioral indecision, emotional instability, and eventually, spiritual schizophrenia.

Mormon revealed the simple test by which we might gauge worth. He said: "That which is of God inviteth and enticeth to do good continually; wherefore, every thing which inviteth and enticeth to do good, and to love God, and to serve him, is inspired of God." (V. 13). Because Madison Avenue's manipulation of the media does an excellent job of confusing right from wrong, Mormon cautioned: "Wherefore, take heed, my beloved brethren, that ye do not judge that which is evil to be of God, or that which is good and of God to be of the devil." (V. 14).

There are no shades of grey for those who receive the ordinances of the Priesthood of God. Members of the Church have not only the Light of Christ, but also the greater illumination and knowledge given by the Holy Ghost. "For behold, my brethren, it is given unto you to judge, that ye may know good from evil; and the way to judge is as plain, that ye may know with a perfect knowledge, as the daylight is from the dark night." (V. 15). Note that J.S.T. Matthew 7:1-2 reads: "Now these are the words which Jesus taught his disciples, that they should say unto the people. Judge not unrighteously, that ye be not judged; but judge righteous judgement." (See also Alma 41:14-15, 3 Nephi 14:1, & D&C 11:2).

"The Spirit of Christ is given to (each one of us, that we) may know good from evil; wherefore, I show unto you the way to judge; for every thing which inviteth to do good, and to persuade to believe in Christ, is sent forth by the power and gift of Christ; wherefore ye may know with a perfect knowledge it is of God." (V. 16, see John 1:19). This is not the Holy Ghost, but rather the Light of Christ, that gives order even to the universe. (See D&C 88:6-13, & Essay: "The Light of Christ").

Moroni 2:2 confirms that if we respond to the Light of Christ, we will be led to the Holy Ghost, Who abides with us only when we are obedient to Gospel principles. He "is a personage in the Godhead, and is not that which lighteth every man that comes into the world, which is the Spirit of God which proceeds through Christ to the world, that enlightens every man that comes into the world, and that strives with the children of men until it brings them to a knowledge of the truth and the possession of the greater light and testimony of the Holy Ghost." (Joseph F. Smith, "Gospel Doctrine", p. 67-68.).

Considering the wicked state of the Nephite nation at the time that Mormon had been addressing a congregation in the synagogue, it is likely that the Light of Christ would have been the sole source of their spiritual guidance. In verse 9, he said: "And now, my brethren, seeing that ye know the light by which ye may judge, which light is the light of Christ, see that ye do not judge wrongfully." (See J.S.T. Matthew 7:2, above). He continued: "I beseech of you, brethren, that ye should search diligently in the light of Christ that ye may know good from evil." (V. 19). He seems to have been speaking to those who had not received the Holy Ghost as their constant companion. Mormon further exhorted: "If ye will lay hold upon every good thing, and condemn it not, ye certainly will be a child of Christ." (V. 19).

King Benjamin had promised his subjects the same peace. The Nephites of that day were members of the Church who had not been unswervingly faithful to their covenants. At the conclusion of his reformatory address to the people of Zarahemla, he declared: "And now, because of the covenant which ye have made ye shall be called the Children of Christ." (Mosiah 5:7). It seems that Mormon was speaking to a congregation in the same set of spiritual circumstances who needed to be led by the hand along the strait and narrow way, because in the next verses he explained: "I will tell you the way whereby ye may hold on every good thing." (V. 21).

He taught that God the Father knows all things, "being from everlasting to everlasting." (V. 22). From our perspective, eternity spans the time from uncreated intelligence, through our spiritual development as children of our Heavenly Father, on into mortality, and finally to our reunion with Him in the resurrection. As far as we are concerned, God is our Companion every step of our journey: "And they shall call his name Emmanuel, which being interpreted is, God with us." (Matthew 1:23).

His faith, hope and charity define His attributes of perfection with absolute clarity. We model our behavior after His Son Jesus Christ, Who is One with the Father. In Him, "there should come every good thing." (V. 22). All principles and doctrines of any importance are connected to Christ, and most especially His Atonement. Without it, we are lost, or as Mormon put it: "All things which are good cometh of Christ; otherwise, men were fallen, and there could no good thing come unto them." (V. 24).

With this basis laid before the congregation in the synagogue, Mormon was ready to teach the foundation principles of faith, hope, and charity. (V. 25-48). God bestows his Spirit, that we might begin "to exercise faith in Christ" and thus lay hold upon every good thing. (V. 25). He does this by the ministering of angels and by providing the spoken and written word through His Priesthood servants.

Faith and repentance lead us to the strait gate of baptism. Those who pass through that narrow portal will obtain a remission of sins, gain membership in the Church, and clear the final hurdles standing in the way of their personal sanctification through repentance and receipt of the Holy Ghost. They will then find themselves squarely on the path of eternal progression leading to the Celestial Kingdom. The way is strait and narrow, and the Gospel standard is undeviating with no room for rationalization or compromise. There is no latitude in God's declaration that He "cannot look upon sin with the least degree of allowance." (D&C 1:31).

"This seems a harsh scripture, for it clearly states that God cannot tolerate sin or sinfulness in any degree. He can't wink at it, or ignore it, or turn and look the other way. He won't sweep it under the rug or say, 'Well, it's just a little sin. It'll be all right.' God's standard, the celestial standard, is absolute, and it allows no exceptions. There is no wiggle room. Many people seem to have the idea that the Judgment will somehow involve weighing or balancing, with their good deeds on one side of the scales and their bad deeds on the other. If their good deeds outweigh their bad, or if their hearts are basically good and outweigh their sins, then they can be admitted into the presence of God. This notion is false. God cannot, will not, allow moral or ethical imperfection in any degree whatsoever to dwell in his presence. He cannot tolerate sin 'with the least degree of allowance' (precisely and only because His Plan of Salvation is designed to save us all in His Celestial Kingdom. It is not a question of whether our good deeds outweigh our sins. If there is even one sin on our record, we are finished. The celestial standard is complete innocence, pure and simple, and nothing less than complete innocence will be tolerated in the kingdom of God." (Stephen Robinson, "Believing Christ," p. 1-2).

The beauty of the Plan is that the "children of men" receive by faith the power to "become the sons (and daughters) of God." (Moroni 7:24 & 26). These are they who "will cleave unto every good thing," as Mormon had taught them to do. (Moroni 7:28, see Moroni 7:5-24). As they do this, Christ "advocateth the cause of the children of men." (Moroni 7:28). His mission is one of building faith among the people. Angels, who are His servants, are commissioned to the work. "And the office of their ministry is to call men (and women) unto repentance, and to fulfil and to do the work of the covenants of the Father, which he hath made unto the children of men, to prepare the way among the children of men, by declaring the word of Christ unto the chosen vessels of the Lord, that they may bear testimony of him." (Moroni 7:31).

The Lord told Joseph Smith: "To some it is given by the Holy Ghost to know that Jesus Christ is the Son of God, and that he was crucified for the sins of the world. To others it is given to believe on their words, that they also might have eternal life if they continue faithful." (D&C 46:13-14). This would apply to all who listen to the General Authorities of the Church bear testimony. "And by doing so, the Lord God prepareth the way that the residue of men may have faith in Christ, that the Holy Ghost may have place in their hearts." (Moroni 7:32).

In our day, the Twelve Apostles and other General Authorities of the Church declare with boldness their witness of the truth, that faith might increase in the hearts of those who hear their testimony. Hence the following representative samplings of testimony: "I know Him. I testify that He is real. I testify as a witness." (Enzio Busche). "I know of the divinity of the Lord Jesus Christ, for it has been revealed to me in a most interesting, complete, and beautiful way." (L. Tom Perry). "I leave you with that special witness which is mine to bear, for I have witnessed it with my own eyes, and heard it with my own ears." (L. Tom Perry). "In a coming day I shall feel the nail marks in his hands and in his feet and shall wet his feet with my tears. But I shall not know any better then than I know now that he is God's

Almighty Son, that he is our Savior and Redeemer, and that salvation comes in and through his atoning blood and in no other way." (Bruce R. McConkie, C.R., 4/1985). And ultimately, "after the many testimonies which have been given of him, this is the testimony, last of all, which we give of him: That he lives! "For we saw him" (Joseph Smith & Sydney Rigdon, D&C 76:22-23).

As the sparks of faith struck off the Divine Anvil of God ignite the flame of our own testimonies, we develop the "power to do whatsoever thing is expedient" or right to do. That thing, said the Savior, is to "repent all ye ends of the earth, and come unto me, and be baptized in my name, and have (more) faith in me, that ye may be saved." (Moroni 7:34). This is the fruits of faith, to be saved in the Celestial Kingdom of God, and it is the very reason for the ministry of God and His chosen servants among the children of men.

God will continue His ministry, and work miracles among the children of men, as "long as time shall last, or the earth shall stand, or there shall be one man upon the face thereof to be saved." (Moroni 7:36, see Moses 1:39). In the deteriorating circumstances under which this sermon was delivered to the Nephites, Mormon condemned his people for their lack of faith. He said: "Wherefore, if these things have ceased, wo be unto the children of men, for it is because of unbelief, and all is vain." (Moroni 7:37). His congregation must have been beset by "sorceries, and witchcrafts, and magics, and the power of the evil one was wrought upon all the face of the land" because of the lack of faith of the people. (Mormon 1:19).

The fire of the Spirit in Mormon's day had been extinguished by sin, which led him to declare: "If these things have ceased, then has faith ceased also; and awful is the state of man, for they are as though there had been no redemption made." (Moroni 7:38). As Alma put it: "For behold, if ye have procrastinated the day of your repentance even until death (or if you have waited to develop saving faith until you were spiritually dead to the Light of Christ), behold, ye have become subjected to the spirit of the devil, and he doth seal you his (because you can no longer make the vital distinctions between good and evil or light and darkness); therefore, the Spirit of the Lord hath withdrawn from you, and hath no place in you, and the devil hath all power over you (for you have voluntarily surrendered your freedom to act independently), and this is the final state of the wicked (for there is no recovery, and because of the hardness of their hearts, it will be as if there had been no redemption made)." (Alma 34:35, see Mosiah 16:5, Alma 11:41 & 12:18, & Helaman 14:18).

Then, as his son Moroni recalled, Mormon had exhorted his congregation to rise to the occasion: "But behold, my beloved brethren, I judge better things of you, for I judge that ye (still) have faith in Christ because of your meekness; for if ye have not faith in him, then ye are not fit to be numbered among the people of his church." (Moroni 7:39). He was likewise old Tevya, in "The Fiddler on The Roof", who told his daughters: "In Anatevka, God knows who you are, and what you may become." (Joseph Stein).

Mormon's judgment that his people were capable of choosing the better part indicates that he believed they still had a hope in Christ. For "how is it that ye can attain unto faith, save ye shall have hope?" he asked. (Moroni 7:40). Later, Moroni would voice the same sentiment: "Wherefore, there must be faith; and if there must be faith, there must also be hope." (Moroni 10:20).

Hope in Christ is to have the assurance of peace, that the direction of our lives is on track, and that the Lord is pleased with our efforts. As Mormon said, hope is born of faith. "Behold, I say unto you that ye shall have hope through the atonement of Christ and the power of his resurrection, to be raised up unto life eternal, and this because of your faith in him according to the promise" that was made to each of us before the foundation of the world. (Moroni 7:41). Mormon's hope was not trust in a pipe dream, nor was it a high-stakes gamble. Rather, it was the inevitable result of well-founded faith, because he was "meek and lowly of heart." (Moroni 7:43).

upon his foundation of faith and hope, Mormon was ready to reveal how charity is the supreme characteristic of faithful disciples. (Moroni 7:44-48). He taught: "If a man be meek and lowly in heart, and confess by the power of the Holy Ghost that Jesus is the Christ," with a sure hope born of faith, "he must needs have charity." (Moroni 7:44, see 2 Nephi 33, & Ether 12:32). The similarity of these verses concerning charity to that given by the Apostle Paul and recorded in the New Testament (1 Corinthians 13:4-8) has raised a question in the minds of some sceptics as to the origin of the counsel. Perhaps, both Mormon and Paul had access to the same or similar ancient records dealing with faith, hope, and charity, or it may be that the Holy Ghost revealed the same ideas to each prophet in essentially the same language of the Spirit. Or, as Joseph Smith translated the record by the same power, impressions relating to the spirit of the message could have come to him in such a manner that he recorded his translation in familiar biblical language.

Moroni 7:45 reads: "And charity suffereth long (or is the quality of patience, from God's perspective, toward people and circumstances), and is kind (or is characterized by sensitivity toward others and is empathic), and envieth not (or is less concerned with telestial trivia and more focused on celestial sureties), and is not puffed up, seeketh not her own (or is selfless), is not easily provoked (but reflects poise under provocation), thinketh no evil (or has no hidden agenda to follow), and rejoiceth not in iniquity, (or is repulsed by sin), but rejoiceth in the truth, beareth all things, believeth all things, hopeth all things, endureth all things" (by being drawn toward the light, and remaining continually open to that which is good).

Paul's phraseology was: "Charity suffereth long, and is kind; charity envieth not; charity vaunteth not itself, is not puffed up, doth not behave itself unseemly, seeketh not her own, is not easily provoked, thinketh no evil; rejoiceth not in iniquity, but rejoiceth in the truth; beareth all things, believeth all things, hopeth all things, endureth all things. Charity never faileth." (1 Corinthians 13:4-8).

When God said: "Let us make man in our image, after our likeness," He meant that we should have the same physical characteristics as our heavenly parents, and their spiritual characteristics (faith, hope, and charity), as well. (See Moses 2:26). Without these God-like qualities, we are nothing, for our progression must stop. "If ye have not charity, ye are nothing, for charity never faileth. Wherefore, cleave unto charity, which is the greatest of all (spiritual gifts), for all things must fail (without it)." (V. 46). It is the greatest of all the noble characteristics of God. "Charity is the pure love of Christ, and it endureth forever, and whoso is found possessed of it at the last day, it shall be well with him." (V. 47, see Commentary Reference to Ether 12:34). At the very least, charity motivates us to Christian service, but at its best, it prepares us to be like God, so that in a coming day we will feel comfortable in His Presence. It is a gift of the Spirit that is bestowed upon the faithful by the matchless grace of God. (See 1 Nephi 17:29, Mosiah 2:11 & 4:6, Alma 9:11, & Helaman 4:25).

Only when we carefully and prayerfully read and ponder this masterful discourse on faith, hope, and charity, will we comprehend the summary statement by Mormon in verse 48. It is all the more meaningful when it is understood in the context of the turmoil existing in Zarahemla prior to 385 A.D. "Wherefore, my beloved brethren," urged Mormon, "pray unto the Father with all the energy of heart, that ye may be filled with this love, which he hath bestowed upon all who are true followers of his Son, Jesus Christ; that ye may become the sons (and daughters) of God; that when he shall appear we shall be like him, for we shall see him as he is; that we may have this hope; that we may be purified even as he is pure. Amen."

Moroni
Chapter 8

Chapters 8 and 9 were written by Mormon and were later included by his son in The Book of Moroni. It seems to be a fair exchange for the two chapters (Mormon Chapters 8 & 9) that were written by Moroni that he added to his father's book.

Verses 1-8 provide a historical context for the doctrinal discourse that follows. Moroni had been called to a position of significant priesthood responsibility, and his father had written to him to give him counsel relating to his stewardship. (V. 1-2). Very tenderly, Mormon expressed to him the sentiments characteristic of all priesthood leaders but particularly poignant inasmuch he was speaking to his own son. The way he opened his epistle must have been very comforting to Moroni. Mormon wrote: "My beloved son, Moroni, I rejoice exceedingly that our Lord Jesus Christ hath been mindful of you, and hath called you to his ministry, and to his holy work. I am mindful of you always in my prayers, continually praying unto God the Father in the name of his Holy Child, Jesus, that he, through his infinite goodness and grace, will keep you through the endurance of faith on his name to the end." (V. 2-3).

Characteristically, Mormon's thoughts were directed to another whose welfare was more important than his own. This time it was his own son, who would experience great spiritual and physical trials. There is sweetness in the way Mormon opened his epistle that draws us in to an attitude of complete trust and confidence. Mormon's description of Jesus as the Holy Child of God the Father suggests the intimacy of parents to their children, and gives us a glimpse of just how strong the relationship between Moroni and his father must have been.

Our goal is to discover the very personal levels of the experiences of the Savior, for when He speaks of "knowing Him," he must be referring to a special sense of the relationship. It is not enough that we know about Him by reading the Gospels or by listening to others speak of Him. We must know Him through the bonds of common experience and common feeling.

Melvin J. Ballard related an experience that might be shared by all those who have received the covenants and hope to enjoy the Second Comforter. He said: "I found myself one evening in the dreams of the night in the temple. After a season of prayer and rejoicing, I was informed that I should have the privilege of entering into a room to meet a glorious Personage, and, as I entered the door, I saw, seated on a raised platform, the most glorious Being my eyes have ever beheld or that I ever conceived existed in all the eternal worlds. As I approached to be introduced, he arose and stepped towards me with extended arms, and he smiled as he softly spoke my name. If I shall live to be a million years old, I shall never forget that smile. He took me in his arms and kissed me, pressed me to his bosom and blessed me, until the marrow of my bones seemed to melt. When he had finished, I fell at his feet, and as I bathed them with my tears and kisses, I saw the prints of the nails in the feet of the Redeemer of the world. The feeling that I had in the presence of Him who hath all things in his hands, to have his love, his affection and his blessing was such that if I ever can receive that of which I had but a foretaste, I would give all I am, all that I ever hope to be, to feel what I then felt." ("Sermons and Missionary Experiences of Melvin Joseph Ballard," p. 156).

As Job wrote: "For God speaketh once, yea twice, yet man perceiveth it not. In a dream, in a vision of the night, when deep sleep falleth upon men, in slumberings upon the bed; then he openeth the ears of men, and sealeth their instruction." (Job 33:14-16, & Commentary Reference to Ether 4:11-12). Mormon desired a similarly intimate relationship with the Savior for his own people, and so he found it necessary to speak to his son about a practice that had crept into the Church that grieved him tremendously. He had learned, he wrote, that "there have been disputations among you concerning the baptism of your little children." (V. 5).

There have always been such disagreements. The practice of infant baptism in various sects in the Last Days, and the differences of opinion regarding the correct method of baptism in Joseph Smith's day, in particular, made the Restoration of the Gospel necessary. It is critically important that the ordinance that admits us into the fold of the Good Shepherd be carried out according to His instruction, for there is only "one Lord, one faith, (and) one baptism." (Ephesians 4:5). "Except a man be born of water and of the Spirit," declared the Savior, "he cannot enter into the kingdom of God." (John 3:5).

Even in the days of the patriarchs, there was confusion among the ancients concerning the proper administration of the ordinance of baptism. "And it came to pass, that Abram fell on his face, and called upon the name of the Lord. And God talked with him, saying, My people have gone astray from my precepts, and have not kept mine ordinances, which I gave unto their fathers. And they have not observed mine anointing, and the burial, or baptism wherewith I commanded them; but have turned from the commandment, and taken unto themselves the washing of children, and the blood of sprinkling; And have said that the blood of the righteous Abel was shed for sins; and have not known wherein they are accountable before me." (J.S.T. Genesis 17:3-7).

Mormon considered the difference of opinion to be of such magnitude that immediately upon learning of it, he went and "inquired of the Lord concerning the matter." (V. 7). The ecclesiastical counsel that he subsequently gave to Moroni came by direct revelation from the Lord, "by the power of the Holy Ghost." (V. 7, see v. 16 & 21). The reason that a correct understanding of baptism is essential is that it is the foundation ordinance that lies at the very heart of the Gospel of Jesus Christ.

As the Savior taught the Nephites: "This is the gospel which I have given unto you - that I came into the world to do the will of my Father, because my Father sent me. And my Father sent me that I might be lifted up upon the cross; and after that I had been lifted up upon the cross, that I might draw all men unto me ... And it shall come to pass, that whoso repenteth and is baptized in my name shall be filled ... And he that endureth not unto the end, the same is he that is also hewn down and cast into the fire, from whence they can no more return, because of the justice of the Father." (3 Nephi 27:13-21).

Mormon had a correct understanding of the mission of the Redeemer, and knew that He had come "into the world not to call the righteous but sinners to repentance; the whole need no physician, but they that are sick; wherefore little children are whole, for they are not capable of committing sin." (V. 8). Therefore, he said, "it is solemn mockery before God, that ye should baptize little children," because to do so denies the power of the Atonement. (V. 9, see v. 23).

The doctrine of infant baptism rejects the doctrine that Jesus Christ atoned for the "original sin" of Adam and Eve, and refutes the concept of individual accountability. (See V. 20 & the 2nd Article of Faith). It demands that little children who die without baptism cannot enter heaven. But the Atonement did redeem them from the Fall. It is true that they are capable of actions that are inconsistent with obedience to Gospel principles, but they are not counted against them as sins. They are not culpable. They only "begin to become accountable" as they approach the age of eight. (D&C 29:47).

Rather, Mormon wrote: "This thing shall ye teach - repentance and baptism unto those who are accountable and capable of committing sin; yea, teach parents that they must repent and be baptized, and humble themselves as their little children, and they shall all be saved with their little children." (V. 10). Then, for added emphasis, he declared: "Little children need no repentance, neither baptism. Behold, baptism is unto repentance to the fulfilling the commandments unto the remission of sins. But little children are alive in Christ, even from the foundation of the world." (V. 11-12). It was an integral part of the Plan of Salvation, ordained in the Grand Council in Heaven before the world was, that little children who died before the age of accountability would be saved in the Celestial Kingdom by the infinite power of the Atonement. "If not so, God is a partial God, and also a changeable God, and a respecter of persons; for how many little children have died without baptism!" (V. 11). Another unusual exclamation point in the narrative of The Book of Mormon attests to the importance of this principle.)

Those who labor under the burden of a belief in infant baptism are "in the gall of bitterness," for how could a just and loving Father in Heaven consign so many of His innocent children to an eternal fate that, on their own merits, they did not deserve? (V. 14). They are "in the bonds of iniquity" as well, in the sense that they must experience despair, or a sense of hopelessness regarding their little ones who have died without baptism. (V. 14). "Despair cometh because of iniquity," because when sin clouds vision, unrepentant sinners can see no way out of their miserable situations. (Moroni 10:22). Apostate teachings leave no alternative but to suggest that "if little children could not be saved without baptism, these must have gone to an endless hell." (V. 13).

If people would follow the counsel given in Mormon's great discourse on faith, hope, and charity, preserved for us in Moroni Chapter 7, they would recognize the doctrine of infant baptism for the damnable heresy that it is. Those who persist in their adherence to this practice "must go down to hell." (V. 14). "For awful is the wickedness to suppose that God saveth one child because of baptism, and the other must perish because he hath no baptism. We be unto them that shall pervert the ways of the Lord after this manner, for (after they understand the role of accountability, its effects relating to the Fall of Adam, and the availability of redemption through the Atonement) they shall perish except they repent." (V. 15-16).

Whereas those who teach the doctrine of infant baptism believe that those children who die without the ordinance will go to hell, the truth is that "they (the professors of the doctrine are the ones who) are in danger of death, hell, and an endless torment." (V. 21). Mormon knew that he was speaking forthrightly, but God had commanded him to do so. Our eternal welfare depends upon our correct understanding of this doctrine. (V. 21).

To Mormon, it was perfectly clear. He spoke "with boldness, having authority from God." (V. 16). He was "filled with charity, which is everlasting love." (V. 17). Little wonder that he had characterized charity as the greatest of all the spiritual gifts of God, and had declared: "Charity never faileth." (Moroni 7:46). Perhaps Mormon was saying that if a person were filled with faith, hope, and charity, the doctrines related to the correct administration of priesthood ordinances would distill upon their souls as the dews from heaven. (See D&C 121:45).

Mormon explained that "little children cannot repent." (V. 19). They are not accountable, because the Plan ordained "that all little children are alive in Christ, and also all they that are without the law. (V. 22, see v. 12). Without sin, there is no need for repentance or for baptism. "For the power of redemption cometh on all them that have no law; wherefore, he that is not condemned, or he that is under no condemnation, cannot repent; and unto such baptism availeth nothing." (V. 22).

2 Nephi 9:25-26 teaches that the Law of Mercy satisfies the demands of Justice for those who did not have knowledge of God's laws. Nevertheless, all those who have reached the age of accountability have the light of Christ and a foundation of knowledge of what is good and what is evil. Because of the Atonement, all have equal opportunity before the Lord, and "the privilege, living or dead, of accepting the conditions of the great Plan of Redemption provided by the Father, through the Son, before the world was." (John Taylor, "Mediation and Atonement," p. 181). But "wo" unto those who have the law, if they transgress. "Wo" is a condition of deep suffering from misfortune and affliction, or grief and calamity. Our lives are days of probation, a time of testing, or of putting to the proof our declared values. "Repentance is (always available) unto them that are under condemnation and under the curse of a broken law." (V. 24).

Then, in a grand summary statement, Mormon concluded: "The first fruits of repentance is baptism; and baptism cometh by faith unto the fulfilling the commandments; and the fulfilling the commandments bringeth remission of sins; and the remission of sins bringeth meekness, and lowliness of heart; and because of meekness and lowliness of heart cometh the visitation of the Holy Ghost, which Comforter filleth with hope and perfect love, which love endureth by diligence unto prayer, until the end shall come, when all the saints shall dwell with God." (V. 25-26).

As a postscript, Mormon revealed to his son that things were not going well for the Nephites at the time he wrote his epistle. He indicated that his responsibilities as the military commander might require that he lead his army against the Lamanites. (V. 27, see Mormon 6:7). If that were to be the case, he feared that he might not be able write again. In fact, he was able to send just one last letter, that has been preserved for us as Moroni Chapter 9.

Mormon's concern for the Nephites was profound. He wrote: "I fear lest the Spirit hath ceased striving with them; and in this part of the land, they are also seeking to put down all power and authority which cometh from God; and they are denying the Holy Ghost." (V. 28). They were willfully rebellious. (See Mormon 1:16, & Moroni 9:23). Mormon concluded with the pessimistic assessment: "They must perish soon," for they were ripened in iniquity. (V. 29).

Mormon bid farewell to his son, until he should have the opportunity to write to him or meet him again. (V. 30). Likely, they got to see each other, although the circumstances were not pleasant. It would have been on the field of battle at Cumorah, when Mormon "beheld the ten thousand of (his) people who were led by (his) son Moroni." (Mormon 6:12). After the slaughter, which had spared only 25 Nephites, Mormon and Moroni might have been among those who had attempted an escape into the south countries. (Mormon 6:15). Perhaps, it was in the confusion of this flight that Mormon, who had been wounded (Mormon 6:10), was overtaken and slain by the Lamanites. (Mormon 8:2). Moroni did not report the details. He only wrote: And my father also was killed by them, and I even remain alone to write the sad tale of the destruction of my people. But behold, they are gone." (Mormon 8:3).

Moroni
Chapter 9

Although the chronological footnotes to The Book of Mormon indicate that Moroni made this record some time between 400 and 421 A.D., clearly the epistles of Mormon in Chapters 8 and 9 of The Book of Moroni were written some time around 385 A.D., when the last battle at Cumorah was fought.

This second epistle is his farewell to his son. Mormon 7:3 gives the impression that Mormon did not have the chance to say good-bye to Moroni. It would be truly heartbreaking if that had been the case. In this chapter, Mormon revealed that he was given the opportunity to bid his son a tender farewell. Perhaps, he was even able to see Moroni, embrace him, and entrust to his care the sacred records of their people. (See V. 24). Mormon had earlier written: "I, Mormon, began to be old; and knowing it to be the last struggle of my people, and having been commanded of the Lord that I should not suffer the records which had been handed down by our fathers, which were sacred, to fall into the hands of the Lamanites, (for the Lamanites would destroy them) therefore I made this record out of the plates of Nephi, and hid up in the hill Cumorah all the records which had been entrusted to me by the hand of the Lord, save it were these few plates which I gave unto my son Moroni." (Mormon 6:6).

Mormon reported to his son that a great number of choice men had fallen by the sword. (V. 2). Evidently, among the Nephites there were still those who were faithful to their covenants. Abraham had begged the Lord to spare the wicked city of Sodom if just ten righteous individuals could be found there. "And (the Lord) said, I will not destroy it for ten's sake." (Genesis 18:32-33). In our day, Joseph Fielding Smith declared: "I believe there has never been a moment of time since the creation but what there has been someone holding the priesthood on the earth to hold Satan in check." ("The Place of The Living Prophet, Seer, and Revelator").

But the Nephites were running out of time, as well as worthy bearers of the priesthood. Their righteous brethren were dwindling in numbers through attrition, and Mormon said: "I fear lest the Lamanites shall destroy this people; for they do not repent, and Satan stirreth them up continually to anger." (V. 3). He went on: "I am laboring with them continually; and when I speak the word of God with sharpness they tremble and anger against me; and when I use no sharpness, they harden their hearts against it; wherefore, I fear lest the Spirit of the Lord hath ceased striving with them." (V. 4, see 1 Nephi 18:20, Enos 1:23, & Ether 15:19-20). Their spiritual depravity was nearing critical mass, when the Spirit would be withdrawn, leaving their lives in chaos and ruin.

Nevertheless, in the hope that the priesthood might yet stave off impending pandemonium, Mormon urged Moroni to labor diligently, that they might "conquer the enemy of all righteousness." (V. 6). We have read in Mormon 3:11 that Mormon refused to be the leader of the Nephite armies, but Mormon 5:1 tells us that he relented, and once again assumed command. Perhaps, he did so because of the horrible atrocities committed by the Lamanites against his people that are documented in Mormon 5:8. "And now behold, I, Mormon, do not desire to harrow up the souls of men in casting before them such an awful scene of blood and carnage as was laid before mine eyes."

As terribly as the Lamanites treated them, the Nephites reciprocated in kind. (V. 9-10). Mormon lamented that such a people could not hope to avoid the judgment of God. (V. 11-14). He wrote: "O the depravity of my people! They are without order and without mercy." (V. 18). "The tragedy of the Nephites who brought destruction by war upon their own heads, was not what became of them, but what they themselves became." (Hugh Nibley, "Since Cumorah," p. 425). "They have become strong in their perversion," reported Moroni, "and they are alike brutal, sparing none, neither old nor young; and they delight in everything save that which is good; and the suffering of our women and our children upon all the face of this land doth exceed everything; yea, tongue cannot tell, neither can it be written." (V. 19). Mormon no longer had anything positive to report concerning his Nephite brethren. He did suggest, however, that perhaps at least some of the women and children were less culpable. (See Jacob 2:9).

Moroni was well acquainted with the character of his people. He knew they were "without principle," past feeling, and that their wickedness exceeded even that of the Lamanites. (V. 20, see V. 4, & Ether 11:3). Unlike Father Abraham, who interceded for the inhabitants of Sodom, Mormon could not "recommend them unto God lest he should smite (him)." (V. 21). It would have been morally indefensible to do so.

However, Mormon tenderly consoled his son by assuring him that he was continually in his prayers. (V. 22). There was wholesale apostasy among the Nephites, and Mormon reluctantly reported: "Many of our brethren have deserted over unto the Lamanites, and many more will also desert over unto them." (V. 24). Perhaps, there is in this passage an intended lesson for our day. As our leaders exhort us, so too did Mormon urge his own son: "Be faithful in Christ; and may not the things which I have written grieve thee, to weigh thee down unto death; but may Christ lift thee up, and may his sufferings and death, and the showing his body unto our fathers, and his mercy and long-suffering, and the hope of his glory and of eternal life, rest in your mind forever. And may the grace of God the Father, whose throne is high in the heavens, and our Lord Jesus Christ, who sitteth on the right hand of his power, until all things shall become subject unto him, be, and abide with you forever. Amen." (V. 25-26).

These last words of Mormon in The Book of Mormon are as applicable today as they were in 400 A.D. The war is even now raging in the hearts of men and women. Truly did Neal A. Maxwell predict that in the Last Days, discipleship would be lived in crescendo, as the adversaries gathered in diametrically opposing ideological camps. To reinforce the regiments of the righteous, God would send His "children, coming down like gentle rain through darkened skies, with glory trailing from their feet, and endless promise in their eyes. His young ones would grow tall and strong, like silver trees against the storm. They would not bend with the wind or the change, but stand to fight the world alone. These warriors will be the few, saved for Saturday; to come the last day of the world. They will rise in their might to win the battle raging in the hearts of men, on Saturday, even though they are strangers from a realm of light, who have forgotten all, the memory of their former life and the purpose of their call. Over time, they will learn why they're here, and who they really are." (Doug Stewart, adapted from "Saturday's Warrior").

Aptly did Josiah Gilbert Holland pray for deliverance by men sent from God, like Mormon and Moroni. "God, give us men and women with strong minds, great hearts, true faith and ready hands, whom the lust of office does not kill, and whom the spoils of office cannot buy; Men and women who possess opinions and a will, who have honor, and who will not lie. Men and women who can stand before demagogues and damn their treacherous flatteries without winking. Tall men and women, sun-crowned, who live above the fog in public duty and in private thinking. For while the rabble, with their thumb-worn creeds, their large professions and their little deeds, mingle in selfish strife, Lo! Freedom weeps, Wrong rules the land, and Justice sleeps." (Adapted).

Moroni
Chapter 10

Herein is Moroni's best writing. He was obviously full of the Spirit, and was no longer concerned about perceived inadequacies in his writing style. Possibly, some time had passed since he had last engraven upon the plates. This last chapter was written about 421 A.D. when he was about to seal up the records. But before doing so, he wanted to speak "a few words by way of exhortation" to Latter-day Israel. (V. 1-2).

He first urged those who would read The Book of Mormon to recognize how merciful God has been to His children from the time of Adam to the present day, and that He has given us "a marvelous work and a wonder" as a companion body of scripture to the Bible, to testify independently that Jesus is the Christ, the Savior of the World. (V. 3, see 2 Nephi 25:17, 27:26, Helaman 3:13-16, 3 Nephi 5:8, 20:8 & 21:9, Mormon 7:9, D&C 4:1, & Isaiah 29:14).

Moroni next described a simple, uncomplicated, and yet ingenious way in which The Book of Mormon can be put to the test. The way of the world is to scrutinize and analyze data, compile reports, develop hypotheses, construct paradigms, reach compromise, forge consensus, and finally publish conclusions, leaving the way open for debate in academic circles. But "O that cunning plan of the evil one! O the vainness, and the frailties, and the foolishness of men! (Two more exclamation points!!) When they are learned they think they are wise, and they hearken not unto the counsel of God, for they set it aside, supposing they know of themselves, wherefore, their wisdom is foolishness and it profiteth them not. And they shall perish. But to be learned is good if they hearken unto the counsels of God." (2 Nephi 9:29-30, see 3 Nephi 30:6-7, & Moroni 8:11-12,).

An appeal to vanity is Satan's way of turning our minds against the Plan of Salvation. (See 2 Nephi 14:22, 28:4 & 14). "I" and "Mine" are usually accompanied by an unbended knee. Neal Maxwell wrote: "To the humble, the simpleness and the easiness of the way are glad realities; to the crowded, ego filled minds of proud men, the sudden burst of light from a spiritual sunrise is irritating rather than awesome, and causes them to blink rather than to stare in reverent awe." ("That My Family Should Partake," p. 82).

Moroni suggested that behavioral characteristics, and not the principles of the scientific method, are necessary to come to the knowledge of eternal principles. He described meekness, lowliness of heart, and humility as the traits that lead to illumination by truth. The two greatest minds in mathematics and physics in the history of the world revealed the following about the role these qualities played as they reached the pinnacles of individual accomplishment:

Sir Isaac Newton wrote: "I do not know what I may appear to the world, but to myself I seem to have been only like a boy playing on the seashore, and diverting myself now and then in finding a smoother pebble or a prettier shell than ordinary, while the great ocean of truth lay all undiscovered before me." (Quoted by Jacob Bronowski, in "The Ascent of Man," p. 236). Albert Einstein wrote: "Many times a day I realize how much my own life is built upon the labors of my fellow men, both living and dead, and how earnestly I must exert myself in order to give in return as much as I have received. My peace of mind is often troubled by the depressing sense that I have borrowed too heavily from the work of others."

The inspired formula suggested by Moroni is revealed in verses 4 and 5: "And when ye shall receive these things, I would exhort you that ye would ask God, the Eternal Father, in the name of Christ, if these things are not true; and if ye shall ask with a sincere heart, with real intent, having faith in Christ, he will manifest the truth of it unto you, by the power of the Holy Ghost. And by the power of the Holy Ghost ye may know the truth of all things." (See Commentary Reference to Ether 5:4). He firmly believed that the power of God works miracles in our lives. He knew that the Light of Christ, sometimes called the Spirit of God or the Holy Spirit, as well as the Holy Ghost, ignite us to allow religious recognition and conversion to take place. Therefore, he urged those in the Last Days: "Deny not the gifts of God, for they are many." (V. 8). All these gifts, he said, "are given by the manifestations of the Spirit of God unto men, to profit them." (V. 8).

Moroni then identified a number of these spiritual gifts. He wrote that "to one is given by the Spirit of God, that he may teach the word of wisdom." (V. 9). The Lord instructed Joseph Smith: "Teach one another the doctrine of the kingdom," to the end that all might be edified in Christ. (D&C 88:77). Perhaps the most dramatic spiritual manifestation resulting from seeking wisdom from God was that received by Joseph Smith, who had read in James 1:5-6: "If any of you lack wisdom, let him ask God, that giveth to all men liberally, and upbraideth not; and it shall be given him. But let him ask in faith, nothing wavering." When he put that injunction to the test, he learned and never forgot the powerful lesson that wisdom leading to salvation comes from God by revelation.

Chauncy Riddle described his receipt of revelation. "He said he felt he had received some revelation before. However, he saw that random revelation was not sufficient. To be a rock, a bastion of surety, he knew that revelation must be something upon which he could count and receive on every occasion of real need. So, he began to seek it actively. He prayed, fasted, and lived the Gospel as best He knew. He was faithful in his Church duties, and tried to live up to every scruple which his conscience enjoined upon him. Then, revelation did come. Intermittently, haltingly at first, then steadily, over some years, it finally came to be a mighty stream of experience. He came to know that at any time of day or night, in any circumstance, for any real need, he could get help. That help came in the form of feelings of encouragement when things seemed hopeless. It came in ideas to unravel puzzles that blocked his accomplishment. It came in priesthood blessings that were fully realized. It came in whisperings of prophecy that were fulfilled. It came in support and even anticipation of what the General Authorities of the Church would say and do in General Conference. It came in the gifts of the Spirit, as the wonders of eternity were opened to the eyes of his understanding. That stream of spiritual experience became a river of living water that nourished his soul in every situation. It became the most important factor of his life. It became the basis of his love, life, understanding, hope, and progress. He so lived that he realized that if it were taken away, all that he had become would be dust and ashes. His only regret was that he was not yet able to take full advantage of it. His life did not yet conform to all that he knew. But he knew and did not just believe." ("Pillars of My Faith – What A Privilege To Believe!" "Sunstone Magazine", 5/1988).

Moroni wrote: "To another (it is given) that he may teach the word of knowledge by the same Spirit." (V. 10, see 1 Corinthians 12:8). Joseph Smith taught: "It is impossible for a man to be saved in ignorance" of the saving principles of the Gospel." (D&C 131:6) We must have knowledge of them and of our Heavenly Father, for Jesus unequivocally taught: "This is life eternal, that they might know thee the only true God, and Jesus Christ, whom thou hast sent." (John 17:3). Any knowledge that we do have of Them is a gift of the Spirit. (See Essay: "Gifts of The Spirit").

The word and the will of the Lord that came to the Saints through Brigham Young was: "Let him that is ignorant learn wisdom by humbling himself and calling upon the Lord his God, that his eyes may be opened that he may see, and his ears opened that he may hear. For my Spirit is sent forth into the world to enlighten the humble and contrite." (D&C 136:32-33).

Other spiritual gifts mentioned by Moroni include faith, healing, the working of miracles, and prophesying. (V. 11-12). Because miracles are manifestations of the power of God, they remain incomprehensible to the world. For "the natural man receiveth not the things of the Spirit of God: for they are foolishness unto him: neither can he know them, because they are spiritually discerned." (1 Corinthians 2:14). Since "the testimony of Jesus is the spirit of prophecy" (Revelation 19:10), it follows that any person who has received this gift is a prophet, since a testimony can only be received by revelation from the Holy Ghost, and since prophecy consists of what holy men speak when they are moved upon by the Spirit.

Moroni finally mentioned the ministering of angels that accompanies the Aaronic Priesthood (V. 14, see D&C 13 & 84:26), and the gift of tongues and interpretation of tongues. (V. 15-16). Every gift, he wrote, comes "by the Spirit of Christ." (V. 17, see v. 18). That Spirit is the vehicle that unlocks the door to communication from heaven, and the recipient is quickened by the purifying influence of the Holy Ghost.

In verse 3, Moroni had urged those who read The Book of Mormon to ponder in their hearts just how merciful God has been to His children. Now he asked that we might remember how anxious Heavenly Father is to bestow these spiritual gifts upon us. Nothing except our unbelief will stand in the way. (V. 19). "Wherefore, there must be faith, and if there must be faith there must also be hope; and if there must be hope there must also be charity." (V. 20). In these verses, we begin to understand why Moroni recorded his father's sermon in Moroni Chapter 7. We can visualize Moroni furtively reading and re-reading this account in the lonely days following Cumorah. He thought the principles were important enough to re-emphasize them here in his own farewell: "Except ye have charity, ye can in nowise be saved in the kingdom of God; neither can ye be saved in the kingdom of God if ye have not faith; neither can ye if ye have no hope. And if ye have no hope ye must needs be in despair; and despair cometh because of iniquity." (V. 21-22, see Alma 41:10).

Next, Moroni warned that when the power and gifts of God should be no more, "wo be unto the children of men." (V. 24-25). In these circumstances, mankind would be under the same condemnation as Moroni's Nephite brethren, who suffered the wrath of God because of their wholesale wickedness. Those who die without having enjoyed the gifts of the Spirit, who have not allowed Christ into their lives, who are past feeling, "die in their sins, and they cannot be saved in the kingdom of God." (V. 26).

Moroni promised: "The time speedily cometh that ye shall know that I lie not, for ye shall see me at the bar of God; and the Lord God will say unto you: Did I not declare my words unto you, which were written by this man, like as one crying from the dead, yea, even as one speaking out of the dust?" (V. 27, see v. 34, 2 Nephi 3:20 & 26:16, & Isaiah 29:4).

Those who have entered the fold of God and participated in the ordinances of the Priesthood are under a special obligation to obey the counsel of the Lord's servants as it has been recorded in The Book of Mormon. For "these words are not of men nor of man, but of me; wherefore, you shall testify they are of me and not of man. For it is my voice which speaketh them unto you; for they are given by my Spirit unto you, and by my power you can read them one to another; and save it were by my power you could not have them." (D&C 18:34-35).

The mission statement of Moroni and of all of the prophets who preceded him, even that of Jesus Christ Himself, is summarized in these verses: "Come unto Christ, and lay hold upon every good gift, and touch not the evil gift, nor the unclean thing. Yea, come unto Christ, and be perfected in him, and deny yourselves of all ungodliness." (V. 30 & 32). If we do this, "and love God with all (our) might, mind and strength, then is his grace sufficient." (V. 32). Grace is an attribute of His perfection that is possessed by God consisting of His love, mercy, and the power by which we may grow in spiritual stature. Thus, we may enjoy not only what He has, but also what He is. By preceding this verse with those that describe the various gifts of the Spirit, Moroni was able to bear witness of God's concern for us, and demonstrate how we may "grow in grace" as we enjoy in greater abundance the gifts of the Spirit. (See Commentary Reference to 2 Nephi 25:24).

As we do so, we will become more and more like our Heavenly Father. We will be able to follow the counsel of the Savior, Who commanded: "I would that ye should be perfect, even as I, or your Father who is in heaven is perfect." (3 Nephi 12:48, see Matthew 5:48). God is not jealous of His perfection, rather, He glories in the possibility that His children who obey Him and endure to the end in righteousness will become like Him. (See Moses 1:39). "If ye by the grace of God are perfect in Christ, and deny not his power, then are ye sanctified in Christ by the grace of God, through the shedding of the blood of Christ, which is in the covenant of the Father unto the remission of your sins, that ye become holy, without spot." (V. 33). It would be difficult to put more succinctly, yet more powerfully, the essence of the Gospel of Jesus Christ, than in this verse. All that Moroni had written builds to this climax. If we open our hearts to the Gospel of Jesus Christ, we can become holy, without spot, as was the Savior. "Holy," after all, is one of the name-titles of God Himself. (See Mark 1:24, Acts 3:14, 1 Nephi 22:21, 1 Peter 1:19, & Hebrews 9:14)

Finally, Moroni bid a fond farewell to an audience that would not read his words until long after his death and following his resurrection to glory. Of that reward he was confident, for he wrote: "I soon go to rest in the paradise of God, until my spirit and body shall again reunite." (V. 34).

Perhaps with prophetic vision., he saw his future mission, that he would be "brought forth triumphant through the air." (V. 34). John the Beloved described him thus: "And I saw another angel fly in the midst of heaven, having the everlasting gospel to preach unto them that dwell on the earth, and to every nation, and kindred, and tongue, and people." (Revelation 14:6). Millions of members of The Church of Jesus Christ of Latter-day Saints and hundreds of millions of others recognize his statue that stands atop many of the temples that are scattered throughout the world. With trumpet pressed to his lips, he awaits the Second Coming of The Lord.

For faithful Latter-day Saints, meeting their Elder Brother Jesus Christ will be a wonderful reunion. Moroni has given his assurance that he will be there also, "to meet (us) before the pleasing bar of the great Jehovah, the Eternal Judge of both quick and dead. Amen." (V. 34).

Observations

The cataracts that
were created by the Lamanites'
concessions to sin clouded their vision,
as the records so abundantly reveal. Their
narrow perspective forced them into making
comfortless compromises, leaving the landscapes
of their lives as nothing but empty shells. When they
didn't take advantage of the therapy of repentance, the
prognosis remained poor for eyes that had lost the
ability to see clearly, and that could no longer
make the distinctions between good and
evil, and could no longer adjust to
differentiate light from
darkness.

Sometimes all too quickly, and at other times agonizingly slowly, apostate Nephites who had sold their souls to the Devil for a mess of pottage were dragged down to a hell on earth that was of their own construction. Their bad habits were the result of repetitively impulsive behaviors that, in a rising tide of wickedness, continually eroded away at the foundations of free will. They were fettered by the chains of their compulsions. Too late, they realized that unlimited freedom leads to tyranny.

For wicked Lamanites (and frequently back-sliding Nephites!) repentance was always waiting in the wings, ready to be liberally applied as a balm to repair bruised egos, bitter feelings, and battered birthrights.

Lehi
taught that
the exercise of free
will in an atmosphere
of opposition propels us
onward toward immortality
and eternal life, as long as we
rely on ordinances, covenants,
and the Atonement of Christ
to remove the sand of sin
from our gears.

We
are slow to
mischief when
we undertake the
opportunity to study
The Book of Mormon,
to look beyond telestial
temptations and temporal
trivia; and if we possess the
will to adjust our perspective
so the Atonement may become
a powerful motivator for good
as it removes the stain of sin
from the tapestry that is the
tableau of our lives in the
telestial winter of our
lone and dreary
world.

In our
day, we are
witnessing how
electronic media
can interfere with
our relationship with
the Holy Ghost, Whose
influence is vital to the
execution of the celestial
doctrine of the Atonement
that is powerfully taught
in the pages of The Book
of Mormon.

The Atonement of Christ
could have saved the Lamanites
from their natural state of carnality,
sensuality, and devilish inclinations. It
activates the Law of Mercy, which mitigates for
those who conform to its requirements the effects
of the first Law, that demands Justice. It could have
lifted them to a state of holiness, spirituality, angelic
innocence, and happiness. It might have also prepared
them to feel comfortable in their homes on earth and
ultimately in their heavenly home, where they
would find themselves in the presence of
angels softly singing celestial
lullabies that express
only love.

God
always knows
what is best, and
He had confidence
in the divine potential
of the Nephites to develop
His nature. He commanded
them to repent, to be baptized,
and to generate perfect faith. All
of these realistic goals were within
the reach of Lehi's posterity, and they
became the guiding principles of all
those who hoped to one day gain
readmittance to His
Kingdom.

Following
the Lord's post-mortal
ministry in the Americas, the
principles of the gospel intuitively
motivated the Nephites to embrace noble
characteristics (see 4 Nephi 1:2-3) that
prompted them to shrink from sin,
and even to think of it
as repulsive.

Ultimately, the Atonement was the only weapon in the Nephites' arsenal that they needed in order to vanquish Satan. Their knowledge of gospel principles re-enthroned the Savior, in their hearts, as the God of this earth.

Nephite prophets had to repeatedly emphasize to their people that the baubles of Babylon are a bribery; they are the brazen opposites of the incorruptible riches of eternity.

The insolvency of Satan's seductions cannot be mitigated by a third-party bailout by worldly governments, whose self-serving interests are so predictable. The only effective remedy every time that Book of Mormon peoples yielded to his nepotism was to repent. (See Helaman 6:21-30).

Agency and opposition are always before us, and repentance becomes as a sacred sentinel. It beckoned both Lamanites and Nephites to enter in at heaven's gate, to discover the Rest of God.

The Devil
consistently gave
the wrong directions
to Laman and Lemuel.
"Don't listen!" we felt like
shouting. He persistently
encouraged them to follow
his detour from the strait
and narrow way, that led
through telestial traffic,
conceptual cul-de-sacs,
religious roundabouts
and doctrinal dead
ends, from which,
escape was only
possible thru
repentance.

To appreciate
how thoughtfully the
divine principle of repentance
has been conceived, we need to go
back to that inventive period when
matter was organized, the elements
were brought into harmony out of
chaos, and a beautiful Garden
was created eastward in
Eden. (See 2 Nephi
2:19-25).

Repentance
guided both the Nephites
and the Lamanites thru the
growing pains and the mental,
emotional, physical, and spiritual
instability that are related to early
childhood development. How they
responded to the principle largely
determined their success or their
failure as responsible adults
who had the opportunity to
contribute to the welfare
of their societies.

When Adam
and Eve transgressed
God's law in the Garden of
Eden, it was not because they were
weak. It was because they were strong.
Our first parents were spiritual giants.
They were mighty oaks; the Lamanites
were but acorns; Gods in embryo,
to be sure, but in many cases,
only acorns … just like
the rest of us.

When the Nephites
were at their very best, and
they enthusiastically embraced
the doctrine of Christ, it made life
eternal, love immortal, and death
only a horizon and nothing
save the limit of their
sight.

No matter
how heavy the burden
may have been that both the
Lamanites and Nephites created
for themselves due to their neglect of
their spiritual well-being, Jesus Christ,
Who has always been the mediator of a
heavenly Weight-Watchers Program,
stood ready to lift them up at the
last day, and award them
the appropriate number
of points for good
behavior.

It was of no matter in the
long run that the Lamanites,
for all intents and purposes, had
become dead weight. The Savior had
the fortitude to carry their burdens for
them until they had been revitalized and
could once again walk and not be weary,
and resume their active participation in
the marathon of life without becoming
either light-headed or dragging
their feet.

Those who settle for the moral mediocrity of character crippling personality traits and who deny the blessing of guidance from the Holy Spirit thru The Book of Mormon, can never get enough of what they don't need, because no matter how much they think they may have, it will never satisfy them.

Because they did not notice their pitiable spiritual fitness, the Nephites often failed to exercise with repentance. That neglect fogged the mirrors on their souls when they stepped out of the shower, and so they never really appreciated that their expanding waistlines were the inevitable result of their indulgence in treats that had been saturated with sin.

Perhaps it will only be when we have hit rock-bottom, and we hear an awful noise ringing in our ears, as the whole earth groans under the ponderous weight of sin in the absence of its inhabitants' reliance upon the Atonement, that we will be ready to accept the Savior, as were the Nephites of old, round about the land of Bountiful. (See 3 Nephi Chapter 9).

Death is
God's stamp
on a golden ticket
that will reintroduce
us to the secret garden
of our primeval childhood,
and that will reacquaint us
with the wonders of eternity
that are lying in wait for
each of us, just beyond
the veil. (See 2 Nephi
9:10-20).

Our
Lord Jesus
Christ taught that
we must be perfect, for
otherwise, we cannot inherit
His Father's kingdom. (See 3
Nephi 12:48). His meaning may
have been that we must always strive
to be perfect in our repentance.

On the
one hand, The Book of
Mormon illustrates how we
are blessed to enjoy a sense of
permanency and strength thru
obedience, while on the other hand,
the baubles of Babylon are exposed as
nothing but briberies and cheap tricks.
They are the opposites of the Savior's
reassurances to the faithful that
they will inherit the riches
of eternity.

Our faith in
Jesus Christ compels us to
place our trust in a divine design,
rather than in devilish doctrines. (See
2 Nephi 9:13). In The Book of Mormon, we
are invited to believe, as did Hans Christian
Anderson, that each of our lives is a "fairy tale
waiting to be written by the finger of God",
and that heaven is a magical kingdom
where dreams come true and we
can all live happily ever
after.

The
unrepentant
wicked can conduct
their lives in opposition to
the incontrovertible laws of
heaven for only so long before
critical mass is reached. Then,
readjustment will be required
to bring the disobedient back
into a harmonious state of
balance with nature.
(See Alma 41:
10-11).

The
Gospel
sets us free to
be creative, and
it sets us creative to
become more free as it
unleashes the doctrine
of Christ to work its
magic.

The
Book of Mormon
asks that we ignore
our natural instincts
and place our trust in
the Savior of the world,
who will lead us to the
highlands of the
morning.

One of the more comforting
messages that speak to us out
of the dust, from the pages of
The Book of Mormon, is that
we can receive the strength
to endure the suffering
that is not of our own
doing, but that is
a part of life.

The Book
of Mormon ignites
our craving to be clean,
which finds expression
in the celestial sparks
that fuel the fire of
our yearning to
continually
repent.

The
Book of
Mormon helps
to bring us into
harmony with the
eternities. It shows us
how we may overcome the
world by liberating us from
internment to the inexorable
immutability of the laws that
govern both temporal and
eternal realms.

Our
progression
is hinged upon
the principles of the
Atonement, repentance,
and forgiveness, which just
happen to be the polar opposites
of condemnation, damnation, and
life without light. These opposites are
powerfully illustrated by numerous
examples in The Book of Mormon.
(See 2 Nephi 2:10-14).

If we
ignore the
celestial laws
that are the only
homing beacons that
are powerful enough to
penetrate swirling mists
of darkness in the telestial
world, we have tacitly chosen
an alternative course leading
to our destruction, as we run
aground on the rocky coasts
of faithlessness. The Book of
Mormon was written that we
might rely upon the merits
of Christ, our Savior and
our Redeemer through
the Atonement. He is
the sole Author of
our salvation, as
well as our
hope.

The Book of
Mormon illustrates
that those who refuse
to repent have less
will power than
won't power.

We see over
and over again in
The Book of Mormon
that those who refused to
repent were frequently past
feeling and were overtly and
covertly rebellious. They had
stiff-necks and were hard
hearted. They lacked the
sensitivity, pliability,
malleability, and
flexibility of the
meek and the
humble.

As
Benjamin
said (see Mosiah
2:25), those who
are enamored with
themselves can never
experience the mind
and soul expanding
epiphany that they
are less than the
dust of the
earth.

The Book of Mormon amply demonstrates that those who are prideful seek after signs. Because they are past feeling, they require a higher and higher intensity of stimulation to experience the same levels of terrestrial and theological gratification. What they have been given will never be enough for them.

In The Book of Mormon, we are repeatedly introduced to those who were faithful and long-suffering. When things seemed that they could be no worse, they were at their best, because then they were particularly sensitive to the comfort that comes thru the whisperings of the Spirit.

It is in The Book of Mormon
that we encounter those struggling
creatures we characterize as Saints, who
charitably forgave all those who had wronged
them, who patiently received both counsel and
chastisement, who meekly learned to be humble,
who quietly rendered service, and who, by
their good example, taught others to
go about performing acts of
quiet Christianity.

As we
prayerfully
study The Book of
Mormon, the fruits of
our labors will be revealed
in spectacular simplicity
and plainness. The walls of
opposition to our purposeful
investigations will crumble
and fall. In our struggles, the
Lord will comfort and succor
us with the bread of life. As we
journey through a harsh and
unforgiving environment in
mortality, seeking the Lord
while He may be found, an
oasis will spring up in
the desert, and living
water will slake
our thirst.

In a perfect
storm of faith, belief, and
knowledge, the light of Christ
switched on, and was observable as
a bright new star that had been touched
by the finger of God. It was as if He had
used hydrogen fuel to power the chain
reaction of a nuclear furnace in the
center of the cosmos, to warm all
of His creations. (See 3
Nephi 1:21).

The best examples from The Book of Mormon of a true Zion society fostered an atmosphere of cooperation, conciliation, and collaboration that encouraged the Nephites to share resources with each other in order to achieve solutions to their problems that would orient them, as a people, toward heaven. (See 4 Nephi 1:2-3 & 15-18).

Throughout
The Book of Mormon,
the proud stubbornly held
to their own opinions rather
than yielding their hearts to
heavenly direction. They were
quick to fill their own lamps
with oil, as they thought, but
were then penurious when
they were encouraged to
share their bounty
with others.

In The Book of Mormon, the unrepentant were prone to argument, abusing their authority by exercising unrighteous dominion, while the humble spoke softly, sought peaceful solutions, invited the Spirit to guide them in their interpersonal relationships, and acknowledged their love of God and man as the engine that powered their behavior.

Because
they persevered along
the arduous pathway leading
to repentance, the Spirit taught
the faithful Nephites how they might
engage in fashioning defensive weapons
within their armories of thought. With these
tools, the Holy Ghost showed them how to
construct heavenly fortifications of
love, joy, strength, and peace, even
as they repetitively dealt with
their rebellious brethren,
the Lamanites, on
a practical
level.

Repentant
Nephites nurtured
their relationship with
our Heavenly Father and
the Holy Ghost. They became
the fashioners of their fortunes,
even as they learned to rely on
reserves that were only found
in Jesus Christ, and that,
sometimes to their great
surprise, they realized
were greater than
themselves.

The righteous
Nephites were repeatedly
faced with occasions when
withdrawals had to be made from
their spiritual bank accounts. When
they relied on the Atonement, they put
the principle of repentance to its ultimate
test. They did not write checks that could
not be cashed. They knew that only after
regular deposits had been made over time,
could they count on the cornucopia of
comfort created by the cushion of
confidence that was a currency
flowing from conduct that
was consistent with the
core curriculum of
contrition.

When the repentant Nephites
were pure in heart, they experienced
intrinsic countermeasures to wicked
imaginations. They were motivated by
altruism, self-restraint, self-discipline,
self-denial, and self-sacrifice, enjoying
all of these blessings as they listened
with their hearts to the promptings
of the Spirit that came to them
as a gentle breeze.

The Nephites were slow
to mischief only when they were able
to look past their telestial temptations
and the temporal trivia that cluttered
their lives; when they possessed the
will to adjust their perspective
so that the achievement of
righteous goals became
their obsession.

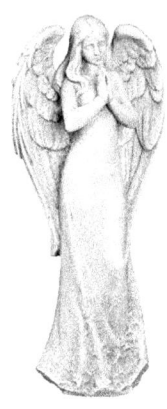

Each time the Nephites
ignored the influences of the
Light of Christ and the Holy Ghost
that nurtured their innate urge to abhor
mischief, but instead allowed themselves to
be habitually distracted by trifling concerns,
they sinned by omission and risked settling
for life in a marshland of mediocrity that
could quickly degenerate into the
quicksand of sin, from which
there would be no easy
escape.

It was
their honesty with
themselves that tested
the mettle of the Nephites'
convictions. In repentance,
they had placed their bets on
our Redeemer, but they'd have
no proof until they'd acted on
the basis of trust. Then, came
the confirmation of the reality
as feelings of self-confidence
grew and purposeful actions
replaced tentative overtures.
In effect, when they were
at their best, they let
go and let God.

Each and every day,
we choose to repent or not
to do so, hopefully making
an affirmative decision that
we pray might be reinforced
with the rebar of resolve as
we study The Book
of Mormon.

The Day
of Judgment
did not lie over some
distant horizon for the
Nephites, but was their present
reality. They thought, spoke, and
acted in accordance with the telestial,
terrestrial, and celestial laws that were
ever before them. Just as a barometer
is used to measure the direction in
which the weather is headed, their
capacity for repentance helped
them to be continually aware
of the direction they should
be going if they hoped to
regain the shelter of
their heavenly
home.

It was after they
had known hardship
that the Sons of Mosiah
developed empathy. They
overlooked the shortcomings
of the wicked Lamanites, and
they were quick to forgive them
their trespasses. As they learned
to avoid being judgmental while
exercising the acquired behavior
of benevolent blindness, they
were better able to help their
recalcitrant brethren to
reach their potential.
(See Alma
17:4).

Their acceptance
of the absolute necessity
of the principle of opposition
in all things (see 2 Nephi 2:11)
to be exercised within the operating
guidelines of The Plan of Salvation
never gave the Nephites a license to act
recklessly or to capitulate to the Dark
Side, and to somehow avoid being
accountable. The still knew the
difference between right and
wrong and they had the
capacity to make
good choices.

Yielding to the enticements of Satan always left the Nephites gasping for a breath of celestial air.

For
the Nephites,
repenting meant
forsaking the carnal
nature that was nothing
more than a shadowy after
image of Lucifer's rebellion
at the Council. (See 2
Nephi 24:12).

Over
and over, the
Nephites had to
rediscover that the
Atonement is the one
and only fire retardant
that can be dumped onto
the raging inferno of sin.
Everything else just seems
to feed the flames. As they
say, the highway to hell
is paved with good
intentions.

A puckish observation is that revenge is a
dish that is best served cold, when we are no longer
caught up in the heat of the moment, but think we can
afford to be crafty, cunning, and calculating as we plot our
pernicious payback. But that strategy is like swallowing
poison and hoping it will kill the other guy. The
Lamanites, with a few notable exceptions,
rarely seemed to have learned
this life-lesson.

At times,
overzealous evangelicals
seem to be overly-eager to take up a
sword of vengeance, as if it were somehow
their God-given right and responsibility to
pass judgment on unbelievers. In contrast to
those who use religion to legitimize vindictive
behavior, Latter-day Saints believe that the
Savior must surely have smiled upon the
simple expressions and acts of charity
of The Sons of Mosiah, that proved
to be incredibly more effective
in paving the way toward
a reconciliation with
the Lamanites.

As we are
carried along and
enveloped by the Spirit
during the course of our
scripture study, we feel the
influence of the Holy Ghost
as an all-consuming fire
in the bones.

As
we study The
Book of Mormon,
our spiritual bank
accounts overflow with
deposits that may later be
withdrawn as an annuity
of joy in the kingdom
of heaven.

Those who decline the offer
of the riches of eternity that have been
unfolded to their view by the prophets in
The Book of Mormon are doomed to
live their lives in scarcity of
their basic spiritual
needs.

Throughout
The Book of Mormon, we
are taught hard lessons about
the hidden costs of self indulgence,
and are cautioned about the inherent
dangers of indebting ourselves to
the usurious interest rate that is
unmercifully levied by
the Devil.

Those who
have made their Book
of Mormon study a life-
long habit wouldn't dream
of postponing enrollment in
a curriculum patterned after
heaven, nor would they defer
their Gospel-oriented studies
in favor of worldly pursuits
that ask for pitifully little
in terms of commitment
or effort, and that offer
very little in terms
of reward.

If mortality
could be visualized in
spatial dimensions, it would
take the shape of an hourglass,
with the strait gate represented by
a narrow midsection. After passing
through that constriction following
an exercise of faith and purposeful
repentance, stimulated by a study
of The Book of Mormon, amazing
vistas would open up to reveal
unparalleled opportunity
to our eyes.

If we
lack a Book of
Mormon perspective,
we can get caught in
conceptually confusing
cul-de-sacs that prevent us
from comprehending the real
purposes of life. We wander to
and fro, dazed, and disoriented,
and we risk becoming as flotsam
and jetsam, tossed about upon a
stormy sea, leaving our lives
with neither direction nor
meaning.

The
Book
of Mormon
shows us how to
successfully flex
our spiritual muscles
and exercise our moral
agency in a forum of free
will that self-confidently
engages opposition in a
vigorous tug of war.

The Book
of Mormon infuses
us with the high octane
fuel of faith, detonating
the fire of our fortitude as
it propels us onward toward
heaven where a convocation of
angels has gathered to form a
welcoming committee. They're
anticipating that we'll come
roaring in, full throttle, to
lay claim to our eternal
reward and to keep our
date with destiny.

The Book of Mormon rests on solid footings that are reinforced by the rebar of righteousness. Its foundation of truth, life, and light, is none other than the Stone of Israel.

We need to
be cautious as we
make our way along the
path that leads to repentance
and forgiveness, because if our
desire to be clean in the sight of
God is approached casually, we
are as vain imposters, as is
repetitively illustrated
by many examples
in The Book of
Mormon.

The
Book of
Mormon asks
that we don't write
checks that cannot be
cashed. More importantly,
so does our Redeemer. He has
limitless reserves in His heavenly
bank account, and has given us his
debit card's easily memorized 10 letter
PIN – <u>R e p e n t a n c e</u> – that can then
be applied to life, no matter what our
current circumstances might be,
rich or poor, bond or free,
prince or pauper.

The Book of Mormon teaches us that the children of men can be transformed by the grace of God into His sons and daughters.

We are accountable
for our own actions, which
will either destroy us or, with the help
of The Book of Mormon, lift us into the
embrace of angels. We cannot have it both
ways. If we sow sparingly, we shall reap
sparingly, but if we sow bountifully
we shall reap bountifully. (See
2 Corinthians 9:6).

Jeremiah, who was a contemporary of Lehi, counseled Israel: "Ask for the old paths, where is the good way, and walk therein, and ye shall find rest for your souls." (Jeremiah 6:16).

The Book of Mormon teaches us in all things to give thanks, for our Father has made promises to us "with a covenant that they shall be fulfilled, and all things wherewith (we) have been afflicted shall work together for our good." (D&C 98:3). For our own part, "the woods are lovely, dark, and deep. But we have promises to keep, and miles to go before we sleep." (Robert Frost).

The Book
of Mormon blesses
us with the faith to see
stepping stones and not
stumbling blocks. Thus,
even negative experiences
and crises of confidence
can be transformed into
opportunities that have
favorable outcomes
to be savored.

The
Book of
Mormon teaches
us to forget about
what is absent and
instead concentrate
on what is available.
It doesn't allow what
might be missing to
frightfully paralyze
us, or certainly not
to defeat us, for we
are the sons and
daughters of
God!

The prophets of The Book of Mormon concentrated on available resources, and then encouraged their people to harness them thru the power of the Savior's example. He showed them how they could mold their spiritual and temporal reserves into forces for positive, substantial, and significant change.

The power
of The Book of
Mormon is that it
draws upon positive
energy and channels
it into a force that will
expand the sphere of
influence of the
Savior.

The teachings of The Book of Mormon can be a catalyst that will release the power of heaven in our behalf.

1,449 of the verses in The Book of Mormon state a life preserving truth: "It came to pass." It did not come to stay! Life unfolds before our eyes, often in surprisingly delightful ways.

Actively relying
upon the promptings
of the Holy Ghost that we
feel when we read The Book
of Mormon can become a
powerful generator of
positive energy.

Paul's formula
for ridding ourselves of
excess baggage was forgetting
those things which are behind us,
and reaching unto those things which
are before us. (See Philippians 3:13). All
good things will come to those who wait
upon the Lord to receive their own
independent testimony of
The Book of Mormon.

When we find
that we have become
unwilling passengers on
the emotional roller coaster
that can accompany our initial
forays into The Book of Mormon,
we realize that it may driven, in part
"in consequence of evils and designs
which do and will exist in the hearts of
conspiring men in the last days."
(D&C 89:4).

In The
Book of Mormon,
we learn that we can't
fix everything all at once.
The next life will be required to
achieve our perfection. For the time
being, we content ourselves to learn by
precept upon precept; and line upon line;
here a little, and there a little. (See Isaiah
28:10). Thus, we are given "consolation
by holding forth that which is to
come, confirming our hope!"
(D&C 128:21).

Traveling the
road to a testimony
of The Book of Mormon
often takes time, and in the
short term, there may be reverses.
But over the long haul, as we move
to higher plateaus, God's Plan will be
there. In times of discouragement, we
remember the observation of James:
"We count them happy which
endure." (James 5:11).

Job encouraged
us to "forget (our)
misery, and remember it
as waters that pass away."
(Job 11:16). Our difficulties in
times past is water under the
bridge. If it does little else,
The Book of Mormon
teaches us to
endure.

The judicious use of the Hebraic phrase "and it came to pass" in The Book of Mormon is evidence that the record is what it says it is - a translation from reformed Egyptian with ties to the Hebrew language.

Throughout the
narrative of The Book of Mormon, we
read about the righteous Nephites, and at
times about the repentant Lamanites, who
were able to outlast and counteract negative
influences by doing everything they could
to remain positive. When they endured in
righteousness, they were saved from the
self-defeating behaviors that would
have otherwise eaten away at
their foundations.

In The Book of Mormon,
the Nephites and Lamanites who
enjoyed the fruits of faith and the
spirit of repentance maintained an
unshakeable conviction that they
were the sons and daughters of
God with promises to keep
and miles to go before
they slept.

In The Book of Mormon,
Abinadi personifies the wisdom,
and the promise, of the Savior that
"whosoever will save his life shall
lose it. But whosoever will lose
his life for my sake, the
same shall save it."
(Luke 9:24).

Nephi walked the walk, and talked the talk. He not only believed in Christ, but he also believed Christ, when the Savior gently reassured him that he was celestial material. (See Helaman 10:6).

A light has been provided
for us at the end of the tunnel, for
those whose minds have been "blinded
by the subtle craftiness of men." (D&C
123:12). We have The Book of Mormon,
"a light that shineth in a dark place,
until the day dawn, and the day
star arise in (our) hearts."
(2 Peter 1:19).

Our testimony
of The Book of Mormon
that lead us to conversion
is a celestial spark that God
has put into each of us; it is
an element of the Merciful
Plan of the Great Creator.
Its purpose is to save
our souls.

"Gather the people
together, men, and women,
and children, and the stranger that
is within thy gates, that they may hear,
and that they may learn, and fear the Lord
your God, and observe to do all the words
of this law" that is found between the
covers of The Book of Mormon.
(Deuteronomy 31:12).

Only if
we have incorporated
into our lives principles of
truth as found in The Book of
Mormon, will we find the tools we
need to recognize, address, reverse,
and eliminate imbalance as it exists
in our society. It is from the vantage
point of the word of God that we can
see things more clearly. It is as if
we have escaped our mortal clay
with its confining limitations
that distort our perspective
and negatively twist our
attention inward, to
worldliness.

Since
opposition exists,
even as there is a Plan,
so must there be its chaotic
worldly counterpart, that we
see as its contrary. In our day,
the grip of fear paralyzes many
of God's children. More than ever,
we need The Book of Mormon, and
the assurance of the Spirit that our
lives are moving in the direction of
our dreams, and that our Heavenly
Father has given us all the tools we
will need to hitch our wagons to
the stars that mark the
pathway to the
heavens.

The Plan of
God gives every
thread in the fabric of
our own faith a vitality,
vim, vigor, and vivacity that
is unique to our holy vestments.
Their steadfast colors come to life
in The Book of Mormon and will
never fade, except with neglect or
or unbelief. They will remain
impervious to every blemish,
save the stubborn stains
of our unresolved
sins.

The world
thinks it can change
us by manipulating us and
by employing external controls
over us, but it fails miserably. On
the other hand, The Book of Mormon
demonstrates how to change thru the
transformation of our inner vessels,
and succeeds brilliantly. It does this
by fine-tuning or by re-calibrating
our internal compass so that we will
always remain oriented toward the
moral discipline of faith. When we
have experienced that conversion,
our obedience will no longer be
inconvenient, but will be our
quest. We will unreservedly
manifest a desire to labor
in the traces, alongside
our Savior

The Spirit allows us to see beyond
the limited horizon of our sight, and to be
touched by a vision of the virtue of the word of
God. This empowers us to savor, with a sharply
discriminating taste, the revealed truths of
The Book of Mormon. As its principles
and doctrines nourish us with their
ordinances and covenants, we
can discern the distinctive
flavors of eternity.

It makes very little difference to our Father whether we are combating the influence of the Seven Deadly Sins, or the garden-variety of transgressions that we commit every day. The doctrine that is repeatedly taught in The Book of Mormon requires that we repent of our sins before we can be admitted into the church thru baptism by immersion.

The Book of Mormon clearly teaches that the Holy Ghost plays a significant role as a sacred witness of our honesty with God, as we repent with broken hearts. His unimpeachable witness is as a baptism of fire that puts the finishing touches on the Atonement of Jesus Christ. When Mercy intervenes to satisfy the demands of Justice and cancels the penalties that are associated with our sins, we are blessed to become holy and without spot, in a rite of purification. Though our "sins be as scarlet, they shall be as white as snow. Though they be red like crimson, they shall be as wool." (Isaiah 1:18).

The great Plan
of God takes the bad
in stride, and asks that
we become acquainted with
evil as well as with good, with
pain as well as with pleasure, and
with darkness as well as with light;
with error as well as with truth, and
with punishment for the infraction of
God's eternal laws, as well as with the
blessings that will follow our obedience.
Myriad examples from the pages of The
Book of Mormon give us opportunities
to learn life-lessons from these
character building
experiences.

The Book
of Mormon illustrates how
our Savior can be the Power Broker
Who purchases our sins with the legally
recognized currency of the Atonement.
His voluntary act of sacrifice is perfectly
balanced and attuned to accomplish the
task at hand, but it is augmented by
faith, repentance, baptism, the Gift
of the Holy Ghost, and finally,
by the Sacrament, which is an
ordinance that squarely
addresses the renewal
of our covenants
with God.

The
Book of Mormon
has the capability to
become the fundamental
element of a tapestry whose
intricate design will reveal itself
in all of its glory as an expression
of our faith. We will attain the full
stature of our spirits only when our
nature is finally in conformity
to the pattern of heaven. Our
perfect frames will burst
free of the shackles of
our mortal clay, as
vibrant coats of
many colors.

The
infinite Atonement
of our Savior Jesus Christ
is the codicil to the best fire
insurance policy that could ever
have been written, indemnifying us
against the possibility of being burned
as stubble at the last day. As long as
we pay our premiums, we will receive
our immortal bodies as benefits in
the resurrection, so that we might
dwell in celestial burnings and
yet avoid being consumed.
Such is the power of the
doctrine of The Book
of Mormon.

Faithful participants
in life's Three Act Play are
now and forever independent in
that stage of development to which
their decisions have led them. Poised
upon the edge of forever, they need little
incentive other than an understanding of
the doctrine of The Book of Mormon, to push
off into the unknown possibilities of existence,
where strange new worlds remain to be explored,
to seek out new life, and new civilizations, and
to boldly go where no-one has ever gone before
without the benefit of the star maps that have
been providentially provided by the
Spirit of God.

It is God's work and glory for all of His children, sooner or later, to make their way to Christ by way of the Atonement, for it is the central feature of The Plan that has been explained in The Book of Mormon. It will be just as it was during the rule of King Josiah, who "went up into the house of the Lord, and all the men of Judah and all the inhabitants of Jerusalem with him, and the priests, and the prophets, and all the people, both small and great. And (they) made a covenant before the Lord, to walk after the Lord, and to keep his commandments and his testimonies and his statutes with all their heart and all their soul, (and) to perform the words of the covenant. And all the people stood to the covenant." (2 Kings 23:2-3).

When
the Spirit
focuses our attention
on The Book of Mormon,
we will have discovered the
unlimited energy source of the
cosmos. We will "discard the poor
lenses of our bodies, and peer thru
the telescope of truth into the infinite
reaches of immortality." (Helen Keller).
On the other hand, if we fail to nurture
our faith in the Great and Eternal Plan
of Redemption, if our engines stall for
lack of power, we may find ourselves
caught up in a flat spin from which
there may be no recovery.

Those
without faith
see things as they
are, and wonder "Why?"
The focused faithful dream
things that never were, and ask
"Why not?" They employ the guiding
principles of The Book of Mormon to work
thru their problems, rather than trying
to side-step around them on their own.
They make no small plans, for they
would surely lack the power
to stir their souls.

The sacrifice that
was made by the Savior
in the Garden of Gethsemane
reaches all the way across time,
and pushes us beyond our normal
capacity, by instilling within each
of us a quiet resolve to lengthen our
stride. Also, to avoid the fate of those
who only skeptically receive The Book
of Mormon, and to safeguard that our
faith will be animated by energy so
we will have no regrets as we move
along on our own personal Via
Dolorosa, we actuate the Light
of Christ and we invite the
Holy Ghost to dwell
with us.

We know
that weakness is a
part of the tapestry that
has been woven by God into
the fabric of our lives. We simply
turn to the inventory of thread that
He's provided in The Book of Mormon
that enables us to weave imaginative
new patterns that are reflections of
the celebration of our faith in our
Savior, as we participate in the
sewing classes that are at
the core of our mortal
curriculum.

As we
engage the teachings
of The Book of Mormon,
each one of us undertakes a
journey that leads to the feet of
the Savior and to His Atonement.
As we move along the Yellow Brick
Road thru the forest of faith toward
the Emerald City of Oz, we use the
brains we have been given to give
our voices courage, remembering
that the woods would be very
quiet if no birds sang but
those that sang best.

The Plan
teaches that
darkness cannot
abide the illumination
of faith. We will seize the
opportunity to be enveloped
in light, and learn to face the
sunshine of revelation that is of
God. The shadows may still exist,
but they will remain behind us. The
traveling companion of fear is despair,
but because of The Book of Mormon,
it will remain out of sight and
out of mind, where it can no
longer harm us.

Those who have been blessed
with the faith to understand where we came
from, why we are here, and where we are going,
regard The Book of Mormon, that answers these
questions, with an almost reverential awe.
The characterization of the Savior as
"the Word of God" takes on
a new meaning.

As we journey in faith through the harsh wasteland of Idumea, oases will spring up in the desert of life, to slake our thirst with living water. Our roots will find the foundation bedrock of The Book of Mormon, enabling it to securely anchor us to its principles and doctrine.

At the Waters
of Mormon, Alma
focused our ministering
efforts on our willingness to
mourn with those who mourn,
and to comfort those that stand
in need, and to be witnesses of
God, wherever we may be,
for as long as we
shall live.

If we do not
acknowledge the
stability of the divine
center of faith that is at
the heart of the Plan, and if
we do not then expend the energy
to cultivate its sense of permanency
by our obedience to the commandment
to search the scriptures, and particularly
the counsel of Isaiah (see 3 Nephi 23:1),
the elements of our lives must surely
fall apart and collapse into
disarray.

As Latter
day Saints,
we must rally
around The Book
of Mormon (see D&C
17:6), and become as
little children. As we do
so, we may be among the
first to realize how true
it is that "Father
knows best!"

The Book of Mormon can serve as a celestial bridge that elevates righteous Latter-day Saints over the variabilities of life, anchoring them to the kingdom of our God that lies peacefully out of reach of the turmoil and the confusion of the world.

As we
profess
our faith
in The Book
of Mormon, the
Lord encourages
us to move forward,
but not in the press of
a crowd that jostles for
position in the three-ring
circus of doctrinal dead
ends, conceptual cul de
sacs, and telestial
trivialities.

If we
ascend
the ladder
of faith, rung
by rung, we will
see lightnings and
mountains smoking,
and hear loud thunder
and the voice of trumpets
that speak in a language
that is inarticulate and
yet irrefutable. As the
Spirit speaks to us,
it will confirm the
truthfulness of
The Book of
Mormon.

As we faithfully carry out the work, and quietly face our responsibilities that relate to publishing peace and testifying of the truthfulness of The Book of Mormon, the righteousness of our efforts will be revealed to others in marvelous simplicity and in plainness. Walls of opposition to our progress will crumble and fall away. The Savior of Whom we witness will comfort us and will succor us with the bread of life.

When we feel an overpowering urge to push along the work with the aid of The Book of Mormon, we'll be blessed with a labor coach in the person of the Holy Ghost, providing us with just the right amount of encouragement we need to successfully deliver our testimony without being overbearing. We just need His small dose of spiritual pitosin.

The
Book of Mormon
inspires us to embrace
enduring characteristics
that are the personification
of the nurturing influence of
our Parents. We view others as
neighbors and not strangers.
We are less judgmental and
are more accepting of our
differences. We are less
suspicious and we are
more receptive to
new ideas.

The
testimony of
Jesus Christ is the
spirit of prophecy, and
every professor of faith is a
facilitator who helps to bring
others to the knowledge of The
Book of Mormon and to their
independent testimony of
its ability to bring them
closer to their divine
center.

As we hone our revelatory abilities, we build on experiences with the Holy Ghost that we have already had, that come to us as we patiently wait upon The Plan. These include our testimonies of Jesus Christ and of His Gospel, of the divine authenticity of The Book of Mormon, and of the inspired mission of Joseph Smith.

It must please our Heavenly
Father and to His Son Jesus Christ,
when our testimony meetings consist
of our discreet expressions that relate to the
guidance we've received from the Holy Ghost
that is beyond our natural understanding,
and that helps us as we face challenges, as
we make important decisions, and as
we go to the principles of The Book
of Mormon to grapple with
the greatest questions
relating to our
faith.

Professors of
faith are light bearers
who carry the torch of truth
as a beacon to guide those who
are having difficulty finding their
own way to The Book of Mormon. The
best and the brightest among them wear
heavy robes of responsibility, and operate
under the influence and direction of
God's priesthood.

The Plan encourages us to
hunger and thirst after righteousness,
and to be filled with the spirit of revelation
that comes through the Holy Ghost. We press
forward with dedication, feasting upon the
scriptures, and in particular, The Book
of Mormon. We receive both physical
and spiritual nourishment, as we
faithfully endure to the end,
with accountability to
our Savior and
our God.

No matter how
wide the net has been cast,
science can neither explain nor
dismiss the flickering shadows
of eternity that dance all around
us, while the familiar features of
mortality are illuminated by
The Book of Mormon, for
all of God's children
to see by the light
of their faith.

The
James
Webb Space
Telescope can
"see" 13.2 billion
light years into our
past, almost back to the
moment of creation, but it
cannot gaze into heaven for
five minutes. Only The Book of
Mormon can do that, with a little
help from the principles of the Plan
of Salvation, and then, only if we
have fallen under the mighty
influence of the Spirit
of God.

The Book
of Mormon
teaches us to be
more trusting and
to speak without guile;
to be more transparent and
less prejudicial; to have fewer
pretensions and be more genuine;
to be less prone to harsh judgment
and quicker to forgive others of
their supposed trespasses
against us.

The Book of Mormon
has been designed to help
us to overcome spiritual death by
showing us how we may come into God's
presence, as well as that of His Son, by way
of the Holy Ghost. His Spirit dazzles us with an
endless reserve of revelation. Its illumination reaches
to the furthest recesses of our minds, and the promised
blessings that are proffered by the combined capacity of
the intrinsic light that radiates from all three members
of the Godhead is beyond any description. Our binding
covenants bridge the gulf between the secular and the
divine that, in other circumstances, might exist for
us. No wonder that during the administration
of the most sacred ordinances of the gospel,
we address by name our Father, His
Son, and the Holy Ghost.

The Plan was
designed that we might
approach the altar of faith
at the feet of the Savior with
the questions that have been on
our minds. When we do so, we will
find ourselves poised at the edge of
forever. We will leap into a stream
of revelation, to be carried along
in a quickening current that is
nothing less than our personal
experience with God. It is by
the Spirit, and with the aid
of The Book of Mormon,
that we find the divine
guidance we need to
take our bearings
on eternity.

If we try to define heaven
and earth by subtraction, rather
than by addition, we are destined to
fail. The Book of Mormon is infinitely
richer and more satisfying than any
poor substitute a rational approach
might grudgingly concede could
exist. The revelation we receive
as we read that text is more
than we could ever hope to
know by relying only
upon the corruptible
lenses of our
bodies.

The Book of
Mormon gives each
of us the opportunity to
be repetitively re-vitalized,
as we are re-introduced to that
Magical Kingdom where our hopes
and our dreams really do come true,
and we all live happily ever after. When
we wish upon the star of Jesus, it makes
no difference who we are. Anything our
hearts desire will come to us. If we
put our hearts and our souls into
our dreams, no request will
be too extreme.

The Book of
Mormon charges the
air in the theater of life
as fire in the sky, with an
electricity that represents an
inevitable merger between the
universal encouragement of the
Light of Christ and the pointed
and providential guidance of
the Holy Ghost. Those who
are firm in their faith in
the script of The Plan
will find heaven, as
it knocks at their
door asking us
for a curtain
call.

The Book of Mormon blesses us with repetitive opportunities to have experiences when light and truth distil upon our souls. Just so, in the Sacred Grove, light "descended gradually," entering the quiet grove slowly enough that Joseph was able to gauge its approach until it finally reached him, and enveloped him within a dazzling brilliance. It was only then, that he "saw two Personages, whose brightness and glory (were beyond all) description," and who stood suspended in the air within the encircling light. (J.S.H. 1:17). We may not see Them, but when we are in the presence of those from the unseen world, we receive inspiration and revelation, and we can be certain that we are in holy precincts.

The Book
of Mormon
drives us to the
portal of baptism,
that our lives might
open up in an expansion
of eternal opportunities as
we obtain a remission of sins,
gain membership in the church,
and are personally sanctified by
the revelatory experiences that we
discover are embedded within our
evolving relationship with the
Holy Ghost. In a very real
sense, the Spirit of God
is with us.

In our day, technology of
every description gets in the way
of the revelation that we receive from
the Holy Ghost, that has always been
fundamental to embracing The Book of
Mormon as Another Testament of Jesus
Christ. When Odysseus returned home
to Ithaca after twenty years, no-one
recognized him, dressed as a beggar,
except for his dog, Argos. What did
Argos see that no one else could?
He was able to look past all the
"noise' and see into the heart
and soul of his beloved
Odysseus.

Those
who are ignorant
among us seem to be
forever attempting to drag
communication from the heavens
down to their own level so that it is
in harmony with their myopic view of
life. The world ridicules revelation and it
disparages its delivery. It scorns even the
most basic elements of the Plan including
The Book of Mormon. But these feeble
efforts ring hollow when compared
to the thunder, lightning, and
burning bush of Sinai.

One of the
terrible consequences
of the fascination of Babylon
with telestial titillation, and with
its fixation on the vain images of the
world, is its spiritual insensitivity to the
direction it would have received if it had
been even remotely interested in learning
about The Book of Mormon thru study and
also by faith; first thru familiarity with the
language of the Spirit, and secondly by
practiced fluency in the celestial tongue
that is spoken by Heavenly Father, by
His Son Jesus Christ, and by the
Holy Ghost.

The Book
of Mormon
introduces us
to the wonders of
a fertile matrix that
was carefully created
by our Father in Heaven
during His preparation of
the petri dish that has been
personalized to match our
individual circumstances,
in the learning lab
of life.

As we
rehearse in our
minds the expression
of our testimony of The
Book of Mormon, it is with
faith that we hear the music
of a celestial symphony that
has been scored for every
imaginable instrument.
We have the faith to
believe that our
voices will be
heard.

The faithful
have learned to keep their
faces oriented toward the light,
so that the shadows will always
remain behind them. Because of
the inherent luminosity of the
Plan and the warm glow that
emanates from the pages
of The Book of Mormon,
they may not even
be aware of the
darkness.

The gate
may be strait, and
the way is surely narrow,
but those who accept The Book
of Mormon as their guide will find
that it is within their ability to travel
a path of progression by threading the
eye of the needle and walking a fine
line past the seemingly unalterable,
unavoidable, and unstoppable
demands of disproportion
that seem to define
our world.

While
obedience to the tenets of
The Book of Mormon nurtures the
development of personality traits and
characteristics that are in concordance
with the symmetry of heaven, our sins
are harmful because they destroy our
capacity to nurture the equilibrium
that is a defining characteristic of
those who inherit eternal life. In
the nature of God's Plan, there
can be neither variableness,
nor even a shadow of
turning.

The
tenets of The
Book of Mormon are
the only homing beacons
that are powerful enough to
penetrate the swirling mists
of darkness in our terrestrial
world. If we discount them, we
have tacitly chosen a course
that can only lead us to our
destruction, doomed to run
aground in deteriorating
visibility on the rocky
coastlines of doubt
and crises of
faith.

We
who have
faith as we read
The Book of Mormon
fear no man. We are as
Bagheera, the powerfully
built black panther in "The
Jungle Book," who confided to
Mowgli the man-cub: "I had never
seen the jungle. They fed me behind
bars from an iron pan till one night I
felt that I was Bagheera the Panther, and
no man's plaything, and I broke the lock
with one blow of my paw, and came
away." (Rudyard Kipling).

The
Plan molds
us in mortality,
and establishes us
in eternity. We learn
to trudge along as we
rack up telestial miles, but
always in the anticipation of
heavenly smiles. We know that
the day will come when we will be
engaged as performers who have been
invited to attend a celestial symphony
that celebrates the power, might, majesty,
dominion, and glory of God.
(See Alma 12:15).

We never forget that
it was the restoration of truth,
exemplified in The Book of Mormon,
that was necessary to realign religious
practice with eternal principles. The Church of
Jesus Christ of Latter-day Saints exits today,
lest we be spoiled "through philosophy and
vain deceit, after the tradition of men,
after the rudiments of the world,
and not after Christ."
(Colossians 2:8).

As we
"listen" to Book
of Mormon prophets
who preach the gospel and
declare the truth, we feel that
"whoever speaks to us in the right
voice, him or her we shall follow as
the waters follow the moon. We do
so silently, and with fluid steps
anywhere around the globe."
(Walt Whitman).

Those who read and understand
the repeated exhortations in The Book
of Mormon are intuitively led to repent. It
is universally understood, it is immune to
conventional wisdom and cultural bias, and
it resists dogmatic clarification. It also
withstands the twisted influence of
the private interpretation of
the unenlightened.

The
Book of Mormon
reassures us to know
that although "the stars fade
away, and the sun himself grow
dim with age and nature sink in
years, we shall flourish in immortal
youth, unhurt amidst the war of
elements, the wreck of matter,
and the crash of worlds."
(Joseph Addison).

For
The Plan to
succeed, opposition
must exist as the basis
of a matrix of mayhem,
within which the fiery darts
of the adversary will trace an
incendiary trail of disorder. The
tendency toward turmoil lies in
wait to disrupt the poise of The
Plan, and to create confusion
in the minds of those who
are pressing forward, as
have so many thru The
Book of Mormon, to
realize the divine
center of their
faith.

Ever
since the
Fall, Satan
has enjoyed a
free pass to mingle
among the children of
men. This flushes him with
excitement, because he knows
how difficult it is for us to resist
our natural inclination to volatility.
Those who love to worship before golden
calves more than they love our Father in
Heaven and the holy scriptures, and in
particular The Book of Mormon, must
unavoidably demonstrate the aberrant
behavioral manifestations of their
misplaced adoration.

Adam and Eve fell that they and their posterity might know true happiness, and nurture the moral fiber that we recognize today as saving faith in both the ordinances of the gospel and the principles of The Plan of Salvation. Our Father in Heaven has introduced us to covenants, that we might employ our free will to consistently choose the harder right, and not the easier wrong. It is in The Book of Mormon that He has deposited both hidden treasures and the key to the happiness that has been prepared for His Saints.

The celestial
formula that defines
the equations of the divine
center of our faith lies within the
principles of The Plan of God that is
explained in The Book of Mormon. Its
permutations and combinations define
eternal laws with the intrinsic power to
push past conventional boundaries,
to modify our perceptions, and to
expand our control over our
experiences in the world
of every day.

The Book
of Mormon repeatedly
stresses the necessity of Jesus
Christ, the Savior of the world,
and it figuratively paints the
portrait of a turtle sitting on
top of a fence post. When we
repent, we know one thing
for certain. That turtle
had help getting
up there.

The Plan anticipated the
conditions wherein we are prompted
by the Light of Christ to make The Book
of Mormon a matter of serious inquiry. With
strategic nudges from the Holy Ghost, we are
guided to choose the harder right, as we make
the most of the cradle and crucible within
which we have been embedded, that is
a fiery cauldron of experience.

It will be difficult for those who've lived only a telestial existence to justify their behavior before God, in the face of the myriad signs and wonders that He has revealed as warnings and blessings. The Book of Mormon is only one of the "love letters" that have been built into His Plan, but that so many fail to read. But those who have witnessed any or the least of these, have seen God moving in His majesty and in His power. They loose the latchets of their shoes, as they kneel before burning bushes, amid the fire and smoke, and thunderings of Sinai.

When we
walk in the light of
life, we go out of our way
to grasp the principles of truth
that are embedded in The Book of
Mormon. We are filled with gratitude
to discover how the Lord Jesus Christ has
provided us with lavish accommodations
in the household of faith, has given us
a room with an unobstructed view of
heaven, and has made available the
services of a concierge Who
answers to the name of
the Holy Ghost.

If we are able to
generate saving faith in the
divine origins of The Book of
Mormon, and if we resolve to use
the power of The Plan of Salvation
to activate the spiritual energy that
is lying dormant within us, we will
surely profit by the administration
of the gifts of ministering angels
who regularly appear before us,
that are often disguised in
the bodily forms of our
friends and our
neighbors.

Author's Note

The Book of Mormon is a blueprint for our survival in The Last Days. It helps us to become the architects of our own fate and the masters of our destiny; to be as "children coming down like gentle rain through darkened skies, with glory trailing from our feet as we go, and endless promise in our eyes. We are strangers from a realm of light, who have forgotten all - the memory of our former life and the purpose of our call." But with the help of The Book of Mormon, we may learn why we're here, and who we really are. (Doug Stewart, "Saturday's Warrior," adapted).

The Book of Mormon allowed the Restoration to move forward and the Church to be organized. It gave us the gift of a fifth gospel (3 Nephi) that summarizes Christ's ministry in the New World. It fulfilled the prophecies of Isaiah and Ezekiel. (See Isaiah 29:14, & Ezekiel 37:16-17). It has empowered Church members to stand out prominently among their Christian neighbors, and it has endowed them with an element of singularity that distinguishes them from other Christian denominations, allowing the line in the sand separating the faithful from the world to be more clearly defined.

Because of The Book of Mormon, those who make their home in Idumea are differentiated from those who embrace the gospel. It gives its believers symmetry, balance, harmony, clarity, focus, and purpose. It illustrates stories of inspiration that touch them personally and individually, and it blesses them with truth in untarnished majesty that may be proclaimed without qualification or apology to the world. Those who read it unleash the unrestrained power of the Holy Ghost. Their lives are touched by invention, investigation, innovation, insight, intuition, and inspiration, whose catalyst is the Spirit.

Because of The Book of Mormon, we have another witness of Christ, and we learn to rely on Him not only as our protector but also as the generator of life itself. It provides a standard by which we may judge the Bible, and it describes a weapon that is more powerful than military might. Within its pages, the essential ordinance of baptism is re-defined, and the army of God is equipped with superior firepower as it teaches the nations with the word of God. Those who read it draw upon the life experiences of heroes from the past, and learn life-lessons from their own similar challenges.

Because of mentors in The Book of Mormon, we can better understand the saving principles and ordinances of the Gospel. With their profound spiritual insight, we discover who our Savior is, and we learn more about ourselves. With a correct understanding of the Fall, of repentance, and of the Atonement, we are no longer held hostage by guilt, but instead feel the sweet miracle of forgiveness. The Book of Mormon guides us to horns of sanctuary that are our refuge from a violent world, and it shows us how to be born again. It gives us the confidence to feel the tender mercies of God, experience His magnificent grace, find our way home, and obtain His Rest.

Without The Book of Mormon, the Church could not have been organized. So important is The Book of Mormon, that The Church of Jesus Christ of Latter-day Saints was only organized immediately following its publication. Fully ten years earlier, Joseph Smith had communed with The Father and The Son in the Sacred Grove. Three years later, he received several visits from the Angel Moroni. Between 1823 and 1830, he became personally acquainted with all of the important characters in The Book of Mormon and enjoyed additional visits from Moroni. Still, so important was The Book of Mormon to the Restoration of the Gospel, that the Church was not organized until it was hot off the press.

Without The Book of Mormon record, we would have no corroborating evidence that Christ fulfilled His promise to feed His other sheep. "Other sheep I have, which are not of this fold," He had said. "Them also I must bring, and they shall hear my voice; and there shall be one fold, and one shepherd." (John 10:16).

"And if ye shall believe in Christ ye will believe in these words, for they are the words of Christ, and he hath given them unto me; and they teach all men that they should do good. And if they are not the words of Christ, judge ye - for Christ will show unto you, with power and great glory, that they are his words, at the last day; and you and I shall stand face to face before his bar; and ye shall know that I have been commanded of him to write these things." (2 Nephi 33:10-11).

Without The Book of Mormon, prophecy would not have been fulfilled. The words of Christ are made known in The Book of Mormon, as well as in the Bible," and they have been "established in one." (1 Nephi 13:41). As Ezekiel wrote: "Take thee one stick, and write upon it, For Judah, and for the children of Israel his companions: then take another stick, and write upon it, For Joseph, the stick of Ephraim, and for all the house of Israel his companions. And join them one to another into one stick; and they shall become one in thine hand." (Ezekiel 37:16-17).

2,500 years before the visit by Moroni to Joseph Smith, Isaiah prophesied of the Lord's ministry: "I will proceed to do a marvellous work among this people, even a marvellous work and a wonder." (Isaiah 29:14). God did so with the translation, publication, and distribution of The Book of Mormon.

Without The Book of Mormon, Church members would stand out far less prominently as Christians. The great Book of Mormon prophet Benjamin exhorted: "I would that ye should take upon you the name of Christ, all you that have entered into the covenant with God that ye should be obedient unto the end of your lives. And it shall come to pass that whosoever doeth this shall be found at the right hand of God, for he shall know the name by which he is called; for he shall be called by the name of Christ." (Mosiah 5:8-10).

Without The Book of Mormon, the Church would lose much of its prominent singularity. "Take away the Book of Mormon and the revelations, and where is our religion? We have none." (Joseph Smith, Teachings, p. 71). The Book of Mormon sets Latter-day Saints apart as a peculiar people. To be peculiar in a biblical sense is to be "one's very own, exclusive, or special." (Bible Dictionary). Moroni told Joseph Smith: "Wherever the sound (of the Restoration) shall go it shall cause the ears of men to tingle, and wherever it shall be proclaimed, the pure in heart shall rejoice." ("Latter Day Saints' Messenger and Advocate", 2/ 1835, p. 79-80).

Without The Book of Mormon, Joshua's line in the sand would be far less clearly defined. Mormon observed "that after a people have been once enlightened by the Spirit of God, and have had great knowledge of things pertaining to righteousness, and then have fallen away into sin and transgression, they become more hardened, and thus their state becomes worse than though they had never known these things." (Alma 24:30).

Joseph Fielding Smith, Jr. cautioned the Saints: "When you joined the Church you enlisted to serve God. When you did that, you left the neutral ground, and you can never get back on to it. Should you forsake the Master you enlisted to serve, it will be by the instigation of the evil one, and you will follow his dictation and be his servant." (C.E.S. Manual, p. 258).

Without The Book of Mormon, we would have fewer negative examples of those who embrace darkness rather than the Gospel. Mormon said of those who did not belong to the Church, that they "did indulge themselves in sorceries, and in idolatry or idleness, and in babblings, and in envyings and strife, wearing costly apparel, being lifted up in the pride of their own eyes; persecuting, lying, thieving, robbing, committing whoredoms, and murdering, and all manner of wickedness." (Alma 1:32).

Without The Book of Mormon, we would have less symmetry, balance, harmony, clarity, focus, and purpose in our lives. President Ezra Taft Benson told the Saints that a Church member who does not study The Book of Mormon, "is placing their soul in jeopardy and neglecting that which could give spiritual and intellectual unity to their whole life". (C.R., 4/1975).

Without The Book of Mormon, we would have fewer stories of inspiration that touch us personally and individually. From within its pages, we can almost hear Moroni's voice: "Behold, I speak unto you as if ye were present, and yet ye are not. But behold, Jesus Christ hath shown you unto me, and I know your doing." (Mormon 8:35).

Without The Book of Mormon, there would be less truth in the world. The Book of Mormon "was written to be believed. Its one and only merit is truth. Without that merit, it is all that nonbelievers say it is. With it, it is all that believers say it is." (Hugh Nibley. "Of All Things," p. 93). Although it is the rule, as Washington Irving observed, that "history fades into fable; fact becomes clouded with doubt and controversy; the inscription moulders from the tablet; the statue falls from the pedestal," and that "columns, arches, pyramids are but heaps of sand, and their epitaphs, nothing but characters written in the dust," yet The Book of Mormon stands as a shining example of the divine model.

Without The Book of Mormon, we would miss, terribly, its witness of truth. The Book of Mormon "illumines reality, vitalizes memory, provides guidance in daily life, and brings us tidings of antiquity." It is "the evidence of time, the light of truth, the life of memory, the directress of life, the herald of antiquity, committed to immortality." (Cicero, "De Oratore," ii, 36). On its pages, "the centuries roll back to the ancient age of gold." (Horace, "Odes," IV, ii, 39).

Without The Book of Mormon, we would lack a sure witness of Jesus Christ. "For behold, (The Book of Mormon) is written for the intent that ye may believe (the Bible); and if ye believe (the Bible) ye will believe (The Book of Mormon) also; and if ye believe (The Book of Mormon) ye will know concerning your fathers, and also the marvelous works which were wrought by the power of God among them." (Mormon 7:9).

Without The Book of Mormon, we would have fewer opportunities to learn how to rely on the Savior. "No one can lift themselves to celestial glory. Our growth depends on the light of Christ, guidance of the Holy Ghost, and the power of the priesthood that is given us by God and his Son. The religion of Jesus Christ is not just a philosophy of life; it is the generator of life. If you go it alone, you cannot succeed. If you receive His power, you will increase and make it. There is no other way." (Sunday School Course Manual).

Without The Book of Mormon, we would lose an excellent standard by which to judge the Bible and other scriptures. For example, we would not have the Lord's teachings to the Nephites that are similar to His Sermon on The Mount, and we would lack the powerful recitations of Isaiah and of Malachi that are reiterated in its pages. In fact, "The Book of Mormon is the keystone of our religion and the most correct book ever written, and (we) can draw nearer to God by abiding by its precepts than any other book." (Joseph Smith)

Without The Book of Mormon, to what other body of scripture would we turn to emphasize the powerful premise that the pen is mightier than the sword? President Benson urged us to recommit ourselves to a study of The Book of Mormon. "If you do so," he promised, "you will find, as Alma did, that 'the word (has) a great tendency to lead the people to do that which is just - yea, it (has) more powerful effect upon the minds of the people than the sword, or anything else which (has) happened to them.' (Alma 31:5)." (C.R., 4/1986).

Without The Book of Mormon, where would we go to learn so clearly that one must have authority to administer the ordinances of the Gospel? Alma and his sons "preached the word, and the truth, according to the spirit of prophecy and revelation; and they preached after the holy order of God by which they were called." (Alma 43:2). If all churches were equal, then the true Church would not exist anywhere. If, in education, any program were the equal of any other, then receiving any degree would be based upon an indiscriminate course of study that would qualify the recipient in all fields of study. But this is contrary to the order of God.

Without The Book of Mormon there would be confusion regarding the ordinance of baptism. "The first fruits of repentance is baptism; and baptism cometh by faith unto the fulfilling the commandments; and the fulfilling the commandments bringeth remission of sins; and the remission of sins bringeth meekness, and lowliness of heart; and because of meekness and lowliness of heart cometh the visitation of the Holy Ghost, which Comforter filleth with hope and perfect love, which love endureth by diligence unto prayer, until the end shall come, when all the saints shall dwell with God." (Moroni 8:25-26).

Without The Book of Mormon, the soldiers in the army of Christ could not so easily preach, teach, expound, and exhort, as they bear witness of Christ. Mormon explained that The Sons of Mosiah "had given themselves to much prayer, and fasting; therefore, they had the spirit of prophecy, and the spirit of revelation, and when they taught, they taught with the power and authority of God." (Alma 17:3). "God help all honest men," said Marion G. Romney, "to be born again and come to be of sound understanding and to know the word of God and maintain the spirit thereof by study, fasting, prayer, and work, that we may be blessed with His power and authority!" (C.R., 10/1941).

Without The Book of Mormon, we might well lack the confidence to proclaim the Gospel. Through Isaiah, the Lord said: "Then shall ye, who are a remnant of the house of Jacob, go forth among (the nations); and ye shall be in the midst of them who shall be many; and ye shall be among them as a lion among the beasts of the forest, and as a young lion among the flocks of sheep, who, if he goeth through both treadeth down and teareth in pieces, and none can deliver." (3 Nephi 20:16).

Armed with The Book of Mormon, the mighty missionary army of the Lord's Church is "clear as the moon, and fair as the sun, and terrible as an army with banners." (D&C 5:14). "The nations of the earth shall tremble because of her, and shall fear because of her terrible ones." (D&C 64:43). "And it shall be said among the wicked: Let us not go up to battle against Zion, for the inhabitants of Zion are terrible; wherefore we cannot stand." (D&C 45:70). "Fear may seize upon them, and they shall stand afar off and tremble. And all nations shall be afraid because of the terror of the Lord, and the power of his might." (D&C 45:74-75).

Without The Book of Mormon, we would know nothing of the life experiences of so many others of God's children, who are so much like ourselves. "Behold, this is a choice land, and whatsoever nation shall possess it shall be free from bondage, and from captivity, and from all other nations under heaven if they will but serve the God of the land, who is Jesus Christ." (Ether 2:12). Without The Book of Mormon, it would be more difficult to understand that "happiness is the object and design of our existence, and will be the end thereof, if we follow the path that leads to it, and this consists of faith, virtue, uprightness, and keeping all the commandments of God." (Joseph Smith).

Without The Book of Mormon, to whom would we turn for mentors such as Captain Moroni? "Yea, verily, verily I say unto you, if all men had been, and were, and ever would be, like unto Moroni, behold, the very powers of hell would have been shaken forever; yea, the devil would never have power over the hearts of the children of men." (Alma 48:17). We would never have known men like Nephi, Jacob, Benjamin, Alma, The Sons of Mosiah, Abinadi, Helaman, and Samuel The Lamanite. We would miss the anticipation of striking hands with them when we meet at the pleasing bar of Christ. (See Jacob 6:13, 2 Nephi 33:15, & Moroni 10:27).

Without The Book of Mormon, there would be a conspicuously empty space on the bookshelf of time, instead of a prominently displayed chronicle written especially for our age. Hugh Nibley observed: "It is an exciting thing to discover that the man Lehi was a real historical character ... but it is far more important and significant to find oneself in this Twentieth Century standing as it were in his very shoes." ("The World and The Prophets," p. 196).

Without The Book of Mormon, we would less effectively cope with the mysteries of God, which are the saving principles and ordinances of the Gospel, received by the faithful through personal revelation. They are sacred. It is given unto many to know these mysteries, "nevertheless they are laid under a strict command that they shall not impart only according to the portion of his word which he doth grant unto the children of men, according to the need and diligence which they give unto him." (Alma 12:9). In other words, by judiciously exercising their knowledge of gospel principles that are explained in The Book of Mormon, the faithful can benefit from spiritual insight while at the same time guarding pearls that might otherwise be cast before swine, or trampled underfoot. (Matthew 7:6).

King Benjamin's discourse in The Book of Mosiah is a classic example of a General Conference type of address wherein the saving principles were unfolded to the membership of the Church. When we read his words, faithfully recorded verbatim by the prophet-historian Mormon, it is clear that he was concerned that his people might trifle with the words that he should speak. He recognized the serious nature of his topic, and wanted them to hearken to him, or pay strict attention, and to open their ears to listen carefully, and their hearts to feel the Spirit of his message, and their minds to understand. (Mosiah 2:9). This episode is one of many in The Book of Mormon that illustrate how the mysteries of God may be unfolded to our view. We have the testimony of Christ Himself that The Book of Mormon contains a comprehensive body of doctrine, "even the fullness of (His) everlasting gospel." (D&C 27:5).

Armed with The Book of Mormon, the Lord told Joseph Smith and Sydney Rigdon: "The time has verily come (December 1, 1831) that it is necessary and expedient in me that you should open your mouths in proclaiming my gospel, the things of the kingdom, expounding the mysteries thereof out of the scriptures according to that portion of the Spirit and power which shall be given unto you." (D&C 71:1). Joseph described his subsequent experience in these words: "Our minds being now enlightened, we began to have the scriptures laid open to our understandings, and the true meaning and intention of their more mysterious passages revealed unto us in a manner which we never could attain to previously, nor ever before had thought of." (J.S.H. 1:74).

To the faithful, the Lord promised: "I will reveal all mysteries, yea, all the hidden mysteries of my kingdom from days of old, and for ages to come." (D&C 76:7). Nevertheless, there were certain points of doctrine that were not yet clear. To his son, Alma declared: "Now these mysteries are not yet fully made known unto me; therefore, I shall forbear." (Alma 37:11). He felt that it was always better to keep one's opinion to oneself, rather than to speculate without the foundation of fact or specific revelation. Sometimes it is better to remain silent and be thought a fool, rather than to speak and remove all doubt.

Without The Book of Mormon, we would know far less about the purpose of life. "And now, I would commend you to seek this Jesus of whom the prophets and apostles have written, that the grace of God the Father, and also the Lord Jesus Christ, and the Holy Ghost, which beareth record of them, may be and abide in you forever." (Moroni, in Ether 12:41). Because of this book, we know that "Adam fell that men might be, and men are, that they might have joy," (2 Nephi 2:25), that "wickedness never was happiness," (Alma 41:10), and that we must hold "fast to the rod of iron". (1 Nephi 8:30). We are counseled: "Watch yourselves, and your thoughts, and your words, and your deeds". (Mosiah 4:30). But we also know: "By the power of the Holy Ghost, (we) may know the truth of all things," (Moroni 10:5), and that "when (we) are in the service of (our) fellow beings, (we) are only in the service of (our) God." (Mosiah 2:17).

Without The Book of Mormon, personal accountability would receive far less emphasis. It teaches that we "are free according to the flesh, and all things are given (to us) which are expedient unto men. And (we) are free to choose liberty and eternal life, through the great Mediator of all men, or to choose captivity and death, according to the captivity and power of the devil." (2 Nephi 2:27)

Without the unequivocal teachings in The Book of Mormon that are related to the Atonement of Jesus Christ, guilt might hold our future hostage. "Do ye suppose that ye shall dwell with (Heavenly Father) under a consciousness of your guilt?" asked Moroni. "Do ye suppose that ye could be happy to dwell with that holy Being, when your souls are racked with a consciousness of guilt that ye have ever abused his laws?" (Mormon 9:3).

Without The Book of Mormon, the tender mercies of the Savior, and the sweet miracle of forgiveness might be less lovingly treated. (See 1 Nephi 1:20, 8:8, & Ether 6:12). Fortified by Mormon's discourse on faith, hope, and charity, The Book of Mormon reports that "as oft as (the disciples of Christ) repented and sought forgiveness, with real intent, they were forgiven." (Moroni 6:8)

Without The Book of Mormon, we might be less likely to find peace in a violent world. Its gift is the peace of the Savior of the world, "not the peace of ease, of luxury, idleness, absence of turmoil, and strife, but the peace born of the righteous life, the peace that lifts the soul, that day by day brings us closer to the home of Eternal Peace, the dwelling place of our Father." (J. Reuben Clark, Jr.)

Without The Book of Mormon, we might not clearly understand that we have been born again. Those who enter into the Covenant "are born of him." (Mosiah 5:7). "All mankind ... must be born again, yea, born of God, changed from their carnal and fallen state, to a state of righteousness, being redeemed of God, becoming his sons and daughters." (Mosiah 27:25). A "Born Again Christian" is one who is in a covenant relationship with the Lord, and since only members of Christ's true Church can accomplish that by revelation and through the authority of the priesthood, if follows that the only real Born Again Christians are those who have a testimony of the divine authenticity of The Book of Mormon and follow its revelatory teachings that lead to faith, repentance, baptism, and the receipt of the Holy Ghost.

Without The Book of Mormon, we might not recognize the signs that confirm we have been born again. "And now behold, I ask of you, my brethren of the church, have ye spiritually been born of God? Have ye received his image in your countenances? Have ye experienced this mighty change in your hearts?" (Alma 5:14).

Without The Book of Mormon, finding our way home would be much more difficult. "Think of stepping on shore and finding it heaven. Of taking hold of a hand and finding it God's hand. Of breathing a new air and finding it celestial air. Of feeling invigorated and finding it immortality. Of passing from storm and tempest to the unbroken calm of God's Rest. Of waking up, and finding it Home." (Anonymous).

Without following the teachings and admonitions that are found within the pages of The Book of Mormon, we could not attain God's Rest. "We live in a day and in a world full of doubts and confusion, where people do not know what to believe, where tensions are high, where the pace is frantic and progress in terms of righteousness is not a popular goal. Violence and crudity are everyday patterns all around us. What a blessing it is to know there is a haven, a place of rest from the turmoil of the world. The prophets and the Savior have called upon us to enter into the rest of the Lord, where life has purpose and direction, and where priesthood power is possible." ("Gospel Doctrine Manual," p. 79)

Without The Book of Mormon, we might never know the truth of all things. (See Moroni 10:5). "He that will not harden his heart," taught Alma, "to him is given the greater portion of the word, until it is given unto him to know the mysteries of God, until he know them in full." (Alma 12:10).

The Book of Mormon contains a unique promise, found nowhere else in scripture. Moroni's formula is simple: "And when ye shall receive these things, I would exhort you that ye would ask God, the Eternal Father, in the name of Christ, if these things are not true; and if ye shall ask with a sincere heart, with real intent, having faith in Christ, he will manifest the truth of it unto you, by the power of the Holy Ghost. And by the power of the Holy Ghost ye may know the truth of all things." (Moroni 10:4-5).

Moroni firmly believed that it is the power of God that works miracles in our lives. He knew that the Light of Christ, sometimes called the Spirit of God or the Holy Spirit, and the Holy Ghost have been provided to nurture religious recognition leading to conversion. Therefore, he urged those who would read and study The Book of Mormon to "deny not the gifts of God, for they are many." (Moroni 10:8). All these gifts, he said, "are given by the manifestations of the Spirit of God unto men (and women), to profit them." (Moroni 10:8).

Without The Book of Mormon, there would be less joy in the world. Mormon said of those living after the ministry of the Savior among the Nephites: "Behold, there never was a happier time among the people of Nephi, since the days of Nephi, than in the days of Moroni." (Alma 50:23). Our day is also a wonderful time to be alive. A millennial era approaches. "How do you prepare for the Second Coming?" asked President Gordon B. Hinckley. "Well, you just do not worry about it. You just live the kind of life that, if the Second Coming were to happen tomorrow, you would be ready. Nobody knows what is going to happen. Our responsibility is to prepare ourselves, to live worthy of the association of the Savior, to deport ourselves in such a way that we would not be embarrassed if He were to come among us." ("Church News", 1/2/1999, p. 2).

Without The Book of Mormon, there would be less hope in the world. "Teenagers sometimes ask: "What's the use?" said Boyd K. Packer. "The world will soon be blown all apart and come to an end." That feeling comes from fear, not from faith. No one knows the hour or the day, but the end cannot come until all of the purposes of the Lord are fulfilled. Everything that I have learned from the revelations and from life convinces me that there is time and to spare for you to carefully prepare for a long life. One day you will cope with teenage children of your own. That will serve you right. Later, you will spoil your grandchildren, and they, in turn, will spoil theirs." (C.R., 4/89).

The scripture may yet be written that there never was a happier time among the children of men, than among those who had developed the habit of carefully and prayerfully studying The Book of Mormon, and using the principles taught therein, to guide them with safe passage through perilous times.

Those who live by faith
and embrace The Book of Mormon,
recognize that its teachings express a
crystal clear perspective, as a pattern
of heaven is traced out by the finger
of God, Who miraculously uses the
fabric of a telestial tapestry to
accomplish His work
and glory.

Addendum
A Sampling of Scriptures
(Helaman - Moroni)

"And so great was the prosperity
of the church, and so many the blessings
which were poured out upon the people, that even
the high priests and the teachers were themselves astonished
beyond measure. And it came to pass that the work of the Lord
did prosper unto the baptizing and uniting to the church of God,
many souls, yea, even tens of thousands. Thus, we may see that
the Lord is merciful unto all who will, in the sincerity of their
hearts, call upon his holy name. Yea, thus we see that the
gate of heaven is open unto all, even to those who will
believe on the name of Jesus Christ, who is the
Son of God. (Helaman 3:25-28).

"Pride ... began to enter ... into
the hearts of the people who professed
to belong to the church of God."
(Helaman 3:33).

"They did fast and pray oft, and did wax stronger and stronger in their humility, and firmer and firmer in the faith of Christ, unto the filling their souls with joy and consolation, yea, even to the purifying and the sanctification of their hearts, which sanctification cometh because of their yielding their hearts unto God." (Helaman 3:35).

"And now, my sons, remember,
remember that it is upon the rock of
our Redeemer, who is Christ, the Son of
God, that ye must build your foundation; that
when the devil shall send forth his mighty winds;
yea, his shafts in the whirlwind … it shall have no
power over you to drag you down … because
of the rock upon which ye are built, which
is a sure foundation, a foundation
whereon if men build, they
cannot fall." (Helaman
5:12).

"Behold,
the prophet Zenos, did
testify boldly; for the which
he was slain. And behold, also
Zenock, and also Ezias."
(Helaman 8:19-20).

"Ye know that I am an honest man, and that I am sent unto you from God."
(Helaman 9:36).

"Behold, thou art Nephi,
and I am God."
(Helaman 10:6).

"O how great is the nothingness of the children of men; yea, even they are less than the dust of the earth. For behold, the dust of the earth moveth hither and thither, to the dividing asunder, at the command of our great and everlasting God. Yea, behold, at his voice do the hills and the mountains tremble and quake. And by the power of his voice, they are broken up, and become smooth, yea, even like unto a valley." (Helaman 12:7-10).

"Your days of probation
are past; ye have procrastinated
the day of your salvation until it is
everlastingly too late, and your destruction
is made sure; yea, for ye have sought all the days
of your lives for that which ye could not obtain; and
ye have sought for happiness in doing iniquity, which
thing is contrary to the nature of that righteousness
which is in our great and Eternal Head."
(Helaman 13:38).

"The voice of the Lord came unto (Nephi), saying: Lift up your head and be of good cheer; for behold, the time is at hand, and on this night shall the sign be given, and on the morrow come I into the world, to show unto the world that I will fulfill all that which I have caused to be spoken by the mouth(s) of my holy prophets."
(3 Nephi 1:12-13).

"Return unto me,
and repent of your sins,
and be converted, that I may
heal you". (3 Nephi 9:33).

"And it
came to pass that thus did
the three days pass away. And it
was in the morning, and the darkness
dispersed from off the face of the land, and
the earth did cease to tremble, and the rocks did
cease to rend, and the dreadful groanings did
cease, and all the tumultuous noises did
pass away. And the earth did cleave
together again, that it stood."
(3 Nephi 10:9-10).

"More blessed are they who shall believe in your words because that ye shall testify that ye have seen me, and that ye know that I am. Yea, blessed are they who shall believe in your words, and come down into the depths of humility and be baptized, for they shall be visited with fire and with the Holy Ghost, and shall receive a remission of their sins."
(3 Nephi 12:2).

"Blessed are
all they who are persecuted
for my name's sake, for theirs
is the kingdom of heaven."
(3 Nephi 12:10).

"I would that
ye should be perfect
even as I, or your Father
who is in heaven, is perfect."
(3 Nephi 12:48).

"After
this manner
therefore, pray ye."
(3 Nephi 13:9).

"If ye forgive men their trespasses,
your heavenly Father will also forgive you.
But if ye forgive not men their trespasses, neither
will your father forgive your trespasses."
(3 Nephi 13:14-15).

"The light
of the body is the
eye; if, therefore, thine
eye be single, thy whole
body shall be full of light."
(3 Nephi 13:22).

"Thou hypocrite,
first cast the beam
out of thine own eye."
(3 Nephi 14:5).

"If ye then ... know how to give good gifts unto your children, how much more shall your Father who is in heaven give good things to them that ask him?" (3 Nephi 14:11).

"Many will say to me in that day: Lord, Lord, have we not prophesied in thy name, and in thy name have cast out devils, and in thy name done many wonderful works? And then will I profess unto them: I never knew you; depart from me." (3 Nephi 14:22-23).

"I am the law, and the light. Look unto me, and endure to the end, and ye shall live; for unto him that endureth to the end will I give eternal life."
(3 Nephi 15:9).

"And verily, verily, I say unto you that I have other sheep, which are not of this land, neither of the land of Jerusalem, neither in any parts of the land round about whither I have been to minister. For they of whom I speak are they who have not as yet heard my voice (nor) have I at any time manifested myself unto them. But I have received a commandment of the Father that I shall go unto them, and that they shall hear my voice, and shall be numbered among my sheep, that there may be one fold and one shepherd." (3 Nephi 16:1-3).

"Now I go unto the Father, and also to show myself unto the lost tribes of Israel, for they are not lost unto the Father, for he knoweth whither he hath taken them." (3 Nephi 17:4).

"No tongue can speak,
neither can there be written by
any man, neither can the hearts of
men conceive so great and marvelous
things as we both saw and heard Jesus
speak; and no one can conceive of the
joy which filled our souls at the
time we heard him pray for
us unto the Father."
(3 Nephi 17:17).

"They saw angels descending out of heaven as if it were in the midst of fire; and they came down and encircled those little ones about, and they were encircled about with fire; and the angels did minister unto them." (3 Nephi 17:24).

"In that day,
for my sake shall the
Father work a work, which
shall be a great and a marvelous
work among them; and there shall be
among them those who will not believe it,
although a man shall declare it unto them.
But behold, the life of my servant shall
be in my hand; therefore, they shall
not hurt him, although he shall
be marred because of them."
(3 Nephi 21:9-10).

"And now, behold, I say
unto you, that ye ought to search
these things. Yea, a commandment I
give unto you that ye search these things
diligently, for great are the words of Isaiah".
(3 Nephi 23:1).

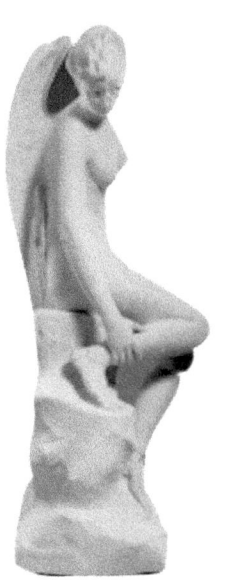

"Will a man rob God? Yet ye have
robbed me. But ye say: Wherein have
we robbed thee? In tithes and offerings. Ye
are cursed with a curse, for ye have robbed me,
even this whole nation. Bring ye all the tithes into
the storehouse, that there may be meat in my house;
and prove me now herewith, saith the Lord of Hosts,
if I will not open you the windows of heaven, and
pour you out a blessing that there shall not
be room enough to receive it."
(3 Nephi 24:8-10).

"There cannot be written in this book even a hundredth part of the things which Jesus did truly teach unto the people." (3 Nephi 26:3).

"Behold,
I know your thoughts."
(3 Nephi 28:6).

"How be it my church save it be called in my name? For if a church be called in Moses' name then it be Moses' church; or if it be called in the name of a man then it be the church of a man; but if it be called in my name, then it is my church, if it so be that they are built upon my gospel." (3 Nephi 27:8).

"This is the gospel which I have given unto you - that I came into the world to do the will of my Father, because my Father sent me. And my Father sent me that I might be lifted up upon the cross; and after that I had been lifted up upon the cross, that I might draw all men unto me ... And it shall come to pass, that whoso repenteth and is baptized in my name shall be filled.
(3 Nephi 27:13-20).

"Verily, I say unto
you, whatsoever things ye shall ask
the Father in my name shall be given unto
you. Therefore, ask, and ye shall receive; knock,
and it shall be opened unto you; for he that
asketh, receiveth; and unto him that
knocketh, it shall be opened."
(3 Nephi 27:28-29).

"And behold, the heavens were opened, and they were caught up into heaven, and saw and heard unspeakable things. And it was forbidden them that they should utter; neither was it given unto them power that they could utter the things which they saw and heard. And whether they were in the body or out of the body, they could not tell; for it did seem unto them like a transfiguration of them, that they were changed from this body of flesh into an immortal state, that they could behold the things of God." (3 Nephi 28:13-15).

"Ye need not imagine
in your hearts that the words
which have been spoken are vain,
for behold, the Lord will remember
his covenant which he hath made unto
his people of the house of Israel."
(3 Nephi 29:3).

"Wo unto him that shall deny the revelations of the Lord, and shall say that the Lord no longer worketh ... by prophecy, or by gifts, or by tongues, or by healings, or by the power of the Holy Ghost."
(3 Nephi 29:6).

"Neither were there Lamanites, nor any manner of -ites, but they were in one, the children of Christ, and heirs to the kingdom of God".
(4 Nephi 1:17).

"I, Mormon,
make a record of the
things which I have both
seen and heard, and call it
the Book of Mormon."
(Mormon 1:2).

"Behold, this my joy was in vain, for their sorrowing was not unto repentance, because of the goodness of God; but it was rather the sorrowing of the damned, because the Lord would not always suffer them to take happiness in sin. And they did not come unto Jesus with broken hearts and contrite spirits, but they did curse God and wish to die … and I saw that the day of grace was passed with them, both temporally and spiritually." (Mormon 2:13-15).

The Book of Mormon was preserved for our day because each of us must stand "to be judged of (our) works, whether they be good or evil." It helps us to "believe the gospel of Jesus Christ," and it serves as another witness to "the Jews, the covenant people of the Lord ... that Jesus, whom they slew, was the very Christ and the very God." It helps us to "repent and prepare to stand before the judgment-seat of Christ."
(Mormon 3:20-22).

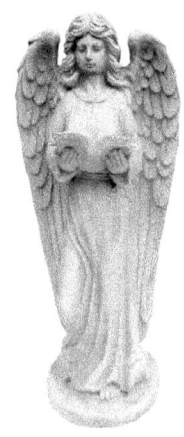

"It is by the wicked that the wicked are punished; for it is the wicked that stir up the hearts of the children of men unto bloodshed." (Mormon 4:5).

"I, Mormon, wrote an epistle unto the king of the Lamanites, and desired of him that he would grant unto us that we might gather together our people unto the land of Cumorah, by a hill which was called Cumorah, and there we could give them battle". (Mormon 6:2).

"I made this record out of
the plates of Nephi, and hid up
in the hill Cumorah all the records
which had been entrusted to me by
the hand of the Lord, save it were
these few plates which I gave
unto my son Moroni."
(Mormon 6:6).

"O that ye had repented before this great destruction had come upon you. But behold, ye are gone, and the Father, yea, the Eternal Father of heaven, knoweth your state; and he doeth with you according to his justice and mercy."
(Mormon 6:22).

The Book of Mormon was "written for the intent that ye may believe (the Bible); and if ye believe (the Bible), ye will believe (The Book of Mormon) also; and if ye believe (The Book of Mormon) ye will know concerning your fathers, and also the marvelous works which were wrought by the power of God among them." (Mormon 7:9).

"My father hath been slain in battle, and all my kinsfolk, and I have not friends nor whither to go; and how long the Lord will suffer that I may live, I know not."
(Mormon 8:5).

"Blessed be he that
shall bring this thing to light; for it
shall be brought out of darkness unto light,
according to the word of God; yea it shall be
brought out of the earth, and it shall shine
forth out of darkness, and come unto the
knowledge of the people; and it shall
be done by the power of God."
(Mormon 8:16).

"But behold, we know no fault, nevertheless God knoweth all things; therefore, he that condemneth, let him be aware, lest he shall be in danger of hell fire."
(Mormon 8:17).

"I speak unto you
as if ye were present, and yet
ye are not. But behold, Jesus Christ
hath shown you unto me, and I know
your doing." (Mormon 8:35).

"When
ye shall be brought
to see your nakedness
before God, and also the glory
of God, and the holiness of Jesus
Christ, it will kindle a flame
of unquenchable fire."
(Mormon 9:5).

"Turn ye unto the Lord;
cry mightily unto the Father
in the name of Jesus, that perhaps
ye may be found spotless, pure, fair,
and white, having been cleansed by the
blood of the Lamb, at that last and
great day." (Mormon 9:6).

"I speak unto you who deny
the revelations of God, and say
that they are done away, that there are
no revelations, nor prophecies, nor gifts,
nor healing, nor speaking with tongues,
and the interpretation of tongues; behold, I
say unto you, he that denieth these things
knoweth not the gospel of Christ; yea,
he has not read the scriptures; if so,
he does not understand them."
(Mormon 9:7-8).

"Do we not read that God is the same yesterday, today, and forever, and in him there is no variableness, neither shadow of changing?" (Mormon 9:9).

"Condemn me not
because of mine imperfection,
neither my father, because of his
imperfection, neither them who have
written before him; but rather give thanks
unto God that he hath made manifest unto
you our imperfections, that ye may learn
to be more wise than we have been."
(Mormon 9:31).

"Fools mock, but they shall mourn;
and my grace is sufficient for the meek,
that they shall take no advantage of your
weakness." (Ether 12:26).

"I will show unto the Gentiles their weakness, and I will show unto them that faith, hope, and charity bringeth (them) unto me – the fountain of all righteousness." (Ether 12:28).

"Ye shall call on the Father in my name, in mighty prayer; and after ye have done this, ye shall have power that to him upon whom ye shall lay your hands, ye shall give the Holy Ghost; and in my name shall ye give it, for thus do mine apostles."
(Moroni 2:2).

"The manner of
their elders and priests
administering the flesh and
blood of Christ unto the church;
and they administered it according
to the commandments of Christ;
wherefore we know the manner
to be true; and the elder or
priest did minister it."
(Moroni 4:1).

"The manner of administering the wine – Behold, they took the cup, and said: O God, the Eternal Father we ask thee, in the name of thy Son, Jesus Christ, to bless and sanctify this wine to the souls of all those who drink of it, that they may do it in remembrance of the blood of thy Son, which was shed for them; that they may witness unto thee, O God, the Eternal Father, that they do always remember him, that they may have His Spirit to be with them. Amen." (Moroni 5:1-2).

"That which is of God inviteth and enticeth to do good continually; wherefore, every thing which inviteth and enticeth to do good, and to love God, and serve him, is inspired of God." (Moroni 7:13).

"The Spirit of Christ is given to every man, that he may know good from evil; wherefore, I show unto you the way to judge; for every thing which inviteth to do good, and to persuade to believe in Christ, is sent forth by the power and gift of Christ; wherefore, ye may know with a perfect knowledge it is of God."
(Moroni 7:16).

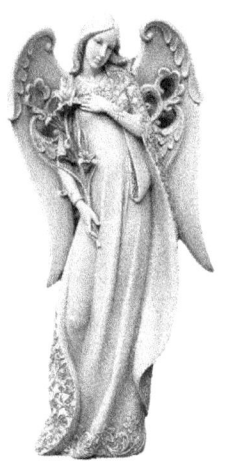

"Seeing that ye know the light
by which ye may judge, which is the
light of Christ, see that ye do not judge
wrongfully ... Search diligently in
the light of Christ that ye may
know good from evil."
(Moroni 7:18-19).

"If a man be
meek and lowly in heart,
and confess by the power of
the Holy Ghost that Jesus
is the Christ, he must
needs have charity."
(Moroni 7:44).

"Charity suffereth long, and is kind, and envieth not, and is not puffed up, seeketh not her own, is not easily provoked, thinketh no evil, and rejoiceth not in iniquity but rejoiceth in the truth, beareth all things, believeth all things, hopeth all things, endureth all things." (Moroni 7:45).

"Charity is the pure love of Christ, and endureth forever; and whoso is found possessed of it at the last day, it shall be well with him."
(Moroni 7:47).

"Pray unto the Father with all the energy of heart, that ye may be filled with this love, which he hath bestowed upon all who are true followers of his Son, Jesus Christ; that ye may become the sons of God; that when he shall appear we shall be like him, for we shall see him as he is." (Moroni 7:48).

"Behold, I am laboring
with them continually; and when
I speak the word of God with sharpness
they tremble and anger against me; and when
I use no sharpness they harden their hearts against
it; wherefore, I fear lest the Spirit of the Lord hath
ceased striving with them." (Moroni 9:4).

"I bid unto all, farewell. I soon go to rest in the paradise of God, until my spirit and body shall again reunite, and I am brought forth triumphant through the air to meet you before the pleasing bar of the great Jehovah, the Eterna Judge of both quick and dead. Amen."
(Moroni 10:34).

The
Holy Ghost
is our mentor and
our teacher. If we are
good students, have done
our homework, and have made
our study of The Book f Mormon
a priority in our busy lives, He will
recompense us with an illumination
of the principles of God's Plan that
will bathe our minds in a cascade
of insight, intuition, inspiration,
and revelation. He will give us
the answer key to the exam
that will follow shortly
on the heels of our
curriculum in
mortality.

"I told the brethren that the Book of Mormon was the most correct of any book on earth, and the keystone of our religion, and (we) would get nearer to God by abiding by its precepts, than by any other book."
(Joseph Smith).

Commentary and Compendium Index

Commentary Volume One
Born in The Wilderness

- 1 Nephi
- 2 Nephi
- Jacob
- Enos
- Jarom
- Omni
- Words of Mormon
- Observations
- Author's Note
- Addendum – A Sampling of Scriptures

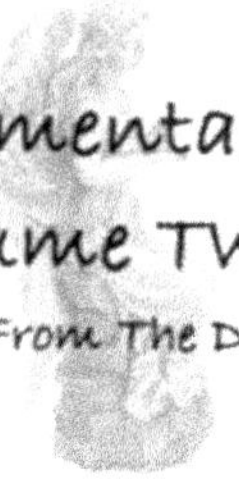

Commentary Volume Two
Voices From The Dust

- Mosiah
- Alma
- Observations
- Author's Note
- Addendum – A Sampling of Scriptures

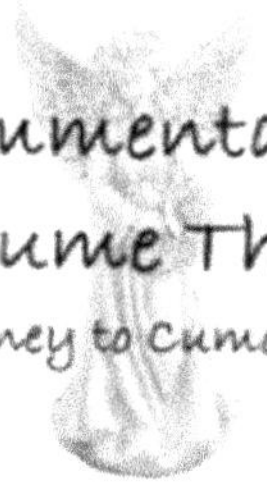

Commentary Volume Three
Journey to Cumorah

- Helaman
- 3 Nephi
- 4 Nephi
- Mormon
- Ether
- Moroni
- Observations
- Author's Note
- Addendum – A Sampling of Scriptures

Compendium
Volume One

- Questions Answered by The Book of Mormon
- Observations
- Familiar Scriptures

Compendium
Volume Two

- Questions Answered by The Book of Mormon
- Without The Book of Mormon
- Observations
- A Few of My Favorite Things
- Familiar Scriptures

Compendium
Volume Three

- Observations
- Essays That Relate to Teachings in The Book of Mormon

Compendium
Volume Four

- Observations
- Essays That Relate to Teachings in The Book of Mormon

Compendium
Volume Five

- Observations
- Essays That Relate to Teachings in The Book of Mormon

Compendium
Volume Six

- Observations
- Essays That Relate to Teachings in The Book of Mormon

Compendium
Volume Seven

- Hebrew Poetry in The Book of Mormon
- Synonymous Parallelism
- Antithetical Parallelism
- Synthetic Parallelism
- Climactic Parallelism
- Chiasmus
- List of Book of Mormon Scriptures That Illustrate Hebrew Poetry
- Observations
- Introduction to The Isaiah Chapters
- "And it came to pass" in The Book of Mormon
- "And thus we see" in The Book of Mormon
- "Behold" in The Book of Mormon

A Book of Mormon Commentary

Born in The Wilderness
Volume One
First Nephi thru Words of Mormon

Voices From the Dust
Volume Two
Mosiah thru Alma

Journey to Cumorah
Volume Three
Helaman thru Moroni

Compendium
Volumes One – Seven

www.ingramcontent.com/pod-product-compliance
Lightning Source LLC
Chambersburg PA
CBHW061400010526
44107CB00012B/1006